Daily Treasure

Avril Game

New Wine Press
P.O.Box 17
Chichester
PO20 6YB
England

ISBN 1 874367 85 X

Printed in England by Clays Ltd., St. Ives plc

DEDICATION

This book is dedicated to my dear Dad who has unknowingly, in so many ways, shown me glimpses of my wonderful Heavenly Father. Thank you, Dad.

Also to Phil, my husband, whose love and loyal support over more than thirty years is appreciated more than words can tell.

Andy, Steve & May Elin, Jonathan & Sam and Rebecca - you have brought such joy and encouragement to us as you live for Jesus. How thankful to God we are for each one of you and the great blessing you are to us.

Most of all I dedicate this 'Daily Treasure' to the glory of my wonderful Heavenly Father, who always has time for me even when I don't always have time for Him.

ACKNOWLEDGEMENTS

Special thanks to Rosaleen Coulson for the beautiful illustrations and for all the hard work that she, especially, along with her husband Paul and son Alex have put into 'Daily Treasure' with their technical expertise.

My thanks also go to Adriene Terrill who began painstakingly typing this book and spurred me into action to get it into print. Also to Jo Mason who along with Rosaleen and my daughter, Rebecca, did the proof reading.

Many others have helped to birth this book with their love, support, encouragement and prayers, especially my husband Phil with all his wisdom. I am deeply indebted to everyone.

Thank you.

1st January

DAY AT A TIME

My Child,

Learn to live a day at a time. If you try to add the worries and pressures into today's timetable you will find it so difficult to cope. Each day will bring surprises, new pleasures and problems to solve and decisions to be made. Learn to be content with the "now" - the day you are living, whatever it may bring.

If you look too far ahead into the future it may allow fear to creep into your heart. I am the God of today - the Great I Am. I will give you the grace and strength that you need for today. As your days so shall your strength be. Don't overload your days so that you are overwhelmed. Know My peace as you live each day and be aware of My presence to help you through each day. Each day is a gift from Me!

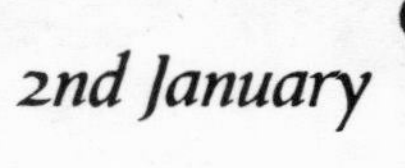

2nd January

RESOLUTIONS

My Child,

It is so easy to make resolutions and even be determined in your heart to keep them, yet so easily they are broken. It is one thing to decide and be determined but quite another to keep up that dedication day by day.

In your own strength you are but weak and do not have the power to overcome, however well-intentioned you may be. If you really want to keep all those resolutions you make then you need the power of My Holy Spirit. For with My power flowing through you, you will be able to do those things which today are a struggle and a chore and difficult for you. As you resolve to allow Me to fill you with My Spirit's power, you will discover how easy it is to keep your word and do those things that you really desire to do. Let Me help you to keep the resolutions you have made.

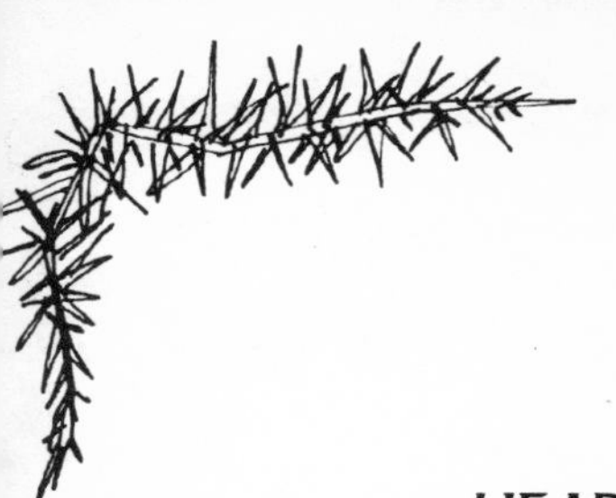

3rd January

HEART OF COMPASSION

My Child,

As you look at My people through My eyes you will discover My heart of compassion for the oppressed and down-trodden. It is so easy to look at people in a judgmental way without understanding. If you look beyond the people's behaviour and see what is in their heart, see their pain and suffering, you will find a depth of compassion that you didn't know was possible to experience.

If you listen with a heart of compassion, your own heart will be touched and you will long to bring My healing and wholeness into people's lives. You will minister My love, My words, My healing in the power of My Holy Spirit bringing My wholeness.

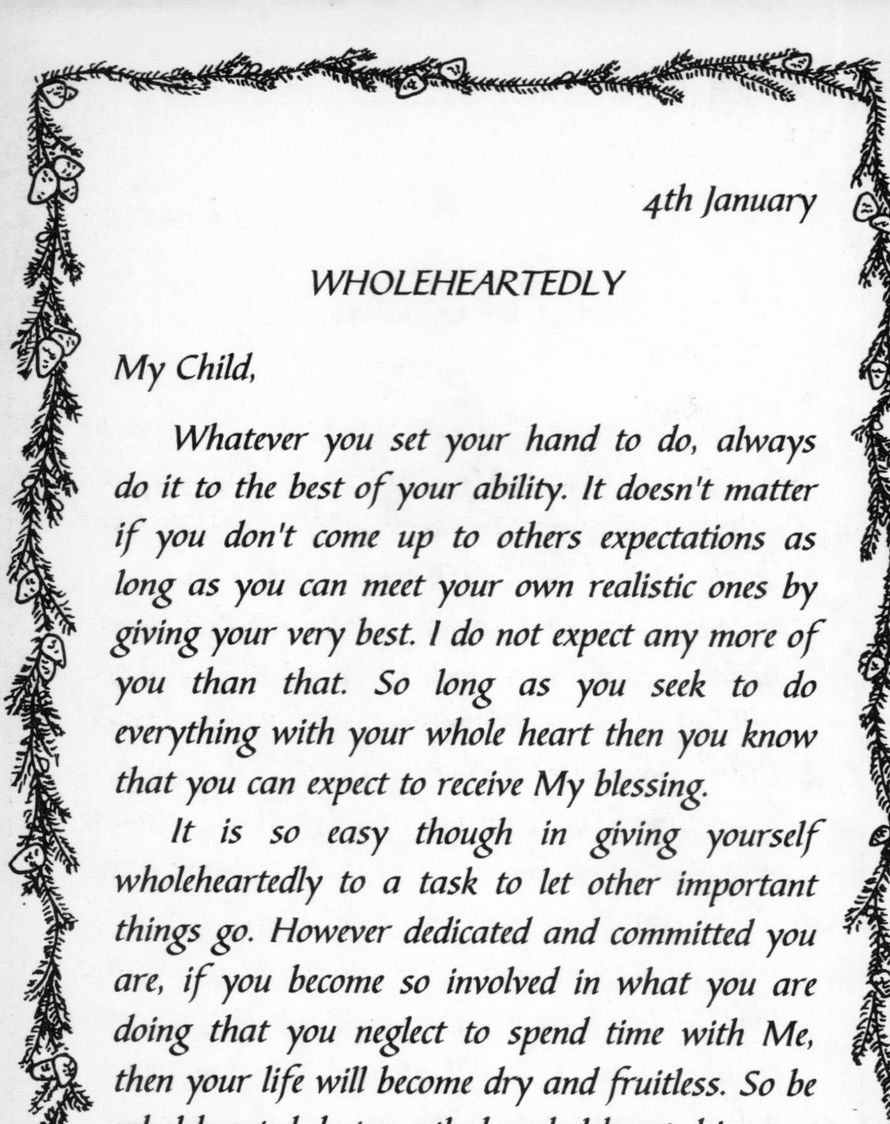

4th January

WHOLEHEARTEDLY

My Child,

Whatever you set your hand to do, always do it to the best of your ability. It doesn't matter if you don't come up to others expectations as long as you can meet your own realistic ones by giving your very best. I do not expect any more of you than that. So long as you seek to do everything with your whole heart then you know that you can expect to receive My blessing.

It is so easy though in giving yourself wholeheartedly to a task to let other important things go. However dedicated and committed you are, if you become so involved in what you are doing that you neglect to spend time with Me, then your life will become dry and fruitless. So be wholehearted, but mostly be wholehearted in your desire to put Me first and then do whatever I tell you wholeheartedly.

5th January

A ROSE

My Child,

If you look at a rose not only will you be astounded by it's beauty but also by it's fragrance. Yet every rose has thorns because of the delicacy of the flower.

Lives are like that too - sometimes they are so fragile that they have to be handled with care. They need to be protected from all that would seek to damage or destroy.

So it is that I watch over your life and the lives of those you love - seeing the beauty and recognising the fragrance, whilst acknowledging the need of protection as the life is nurtured and allowed to blossom. Such is the beauty in your life that I long to create, so that all who touch and draw near will see a reflection of Me!

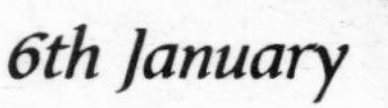

6th January

UNIQUE

My Child,

You are unique. There is no one like you, nor will there ever be. To me you are precious and special and I love you just as you are.

If you compare yourself with others it will cause you to lose sight of your uniqueness. For if you begin to think that you are better than others it will cause pride to enter your heart. If you feel you are not as good as others it will cause you to become anxious and fearful as you try to improve yourself, causing you stress and pressure. Do not compare yourself or want to be like others. Be free to be yourself - be real. For I created you to be you and I am working in you to become the person that I want you to be.

My eye is upon you for you are the apple of My eye and I love all those things that make you uniquely you!

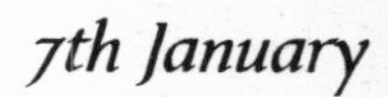

7th January

INTERCESSION

My Child,

As you long in your heart to be in a deeper place of intercession, know that I am drawing you into that place. It is so easy to come before Me with a shopping list, but I want you to be able to forget your own list so that you can still your heart to listen to Me and then discover My list. Then I will show you how to pray for those things which are on My heart and your heart will be thrilled as you discover more of the power and pre-eminence of prayer.

As you lay down your own burdens so you will find it easier to pick up Mine. You will discover a new dimension in prayer that will thrill your heart, and Mine too!

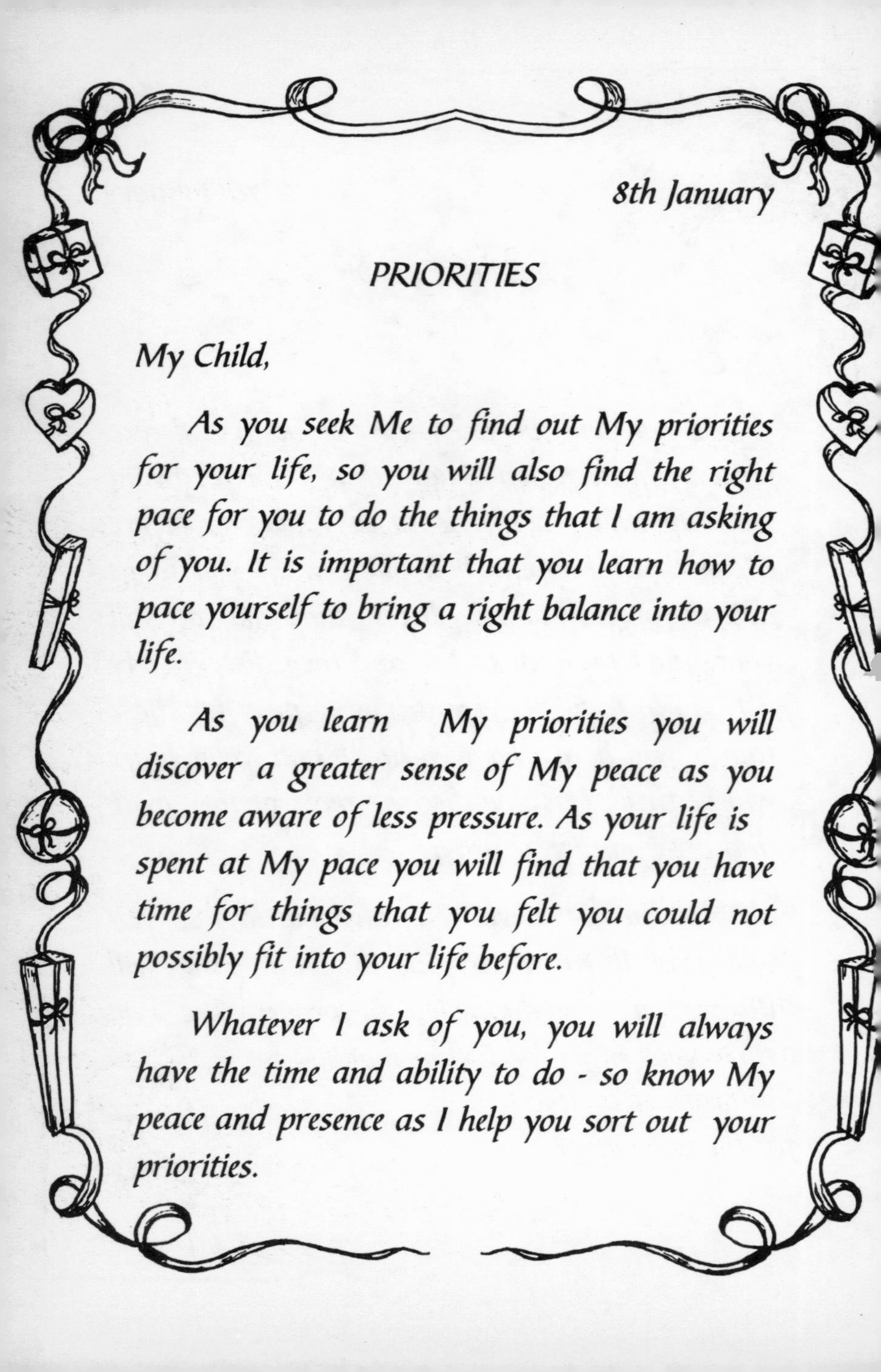

8th January

PRIORITIES

My Child,

As you seek Me to find out My priorities for your life, so you will also find the right pace for you to do the things that I am asking of you. It is important that you learn how to pace yourself to bring a right balance into your life.

As you learn My priorities you will discover a greater sense of My peace as you become aware of less pressure. As your life is spent at My pace you will find that you have time for things that you felt you could not possibly fit into your life before.

Whatever I ask of you, you will always have the time and ability to do - so know My peace and presence as I help you sort out your priorities.

9th January

GOOD SHEPHERD

My Child,

I am the Good Shepherd who gave His life for the sheep. Yet not all My sheep are safely gathered into the fold. Will you go out into the world, find My sheep and bring them in, even though it may be stormy and very inconvenient?

I will show you which ones will come into the fold. Some will refuse to come - do not try to force them but go and find the ones who are seeking the Shepherd so that you can guide them to Me.

My heart aches for the sheep that are out in the world and need to be gathered up in My arms. My heart of love wants to encompass them with those of My sheep who are safe and secure in the fold. Will you share My heart of compassion for the lost sheep?

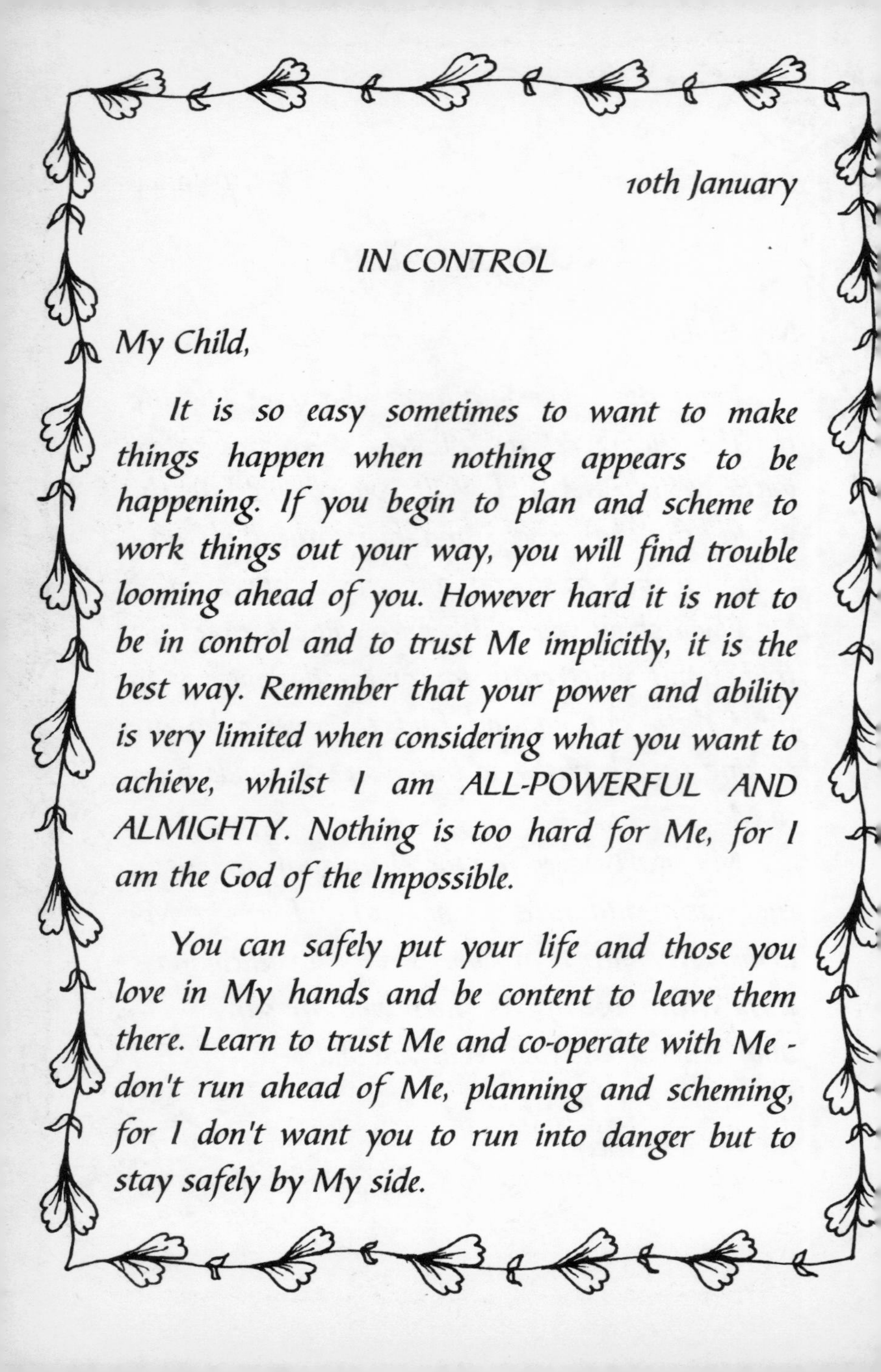

10th January

IN CONTROL

My Child,

It is so easy sometimes to want to make things happen when nothing appears to be happening. If you begin to plan and scheme to work things out your way, you will find trouble looming ahead of you. However hard it is not to be in control and to trust Me implicitly, it is the best way. Remember that your power and ability is very limited when considering what you want to achieve, whilst I am ALL-POWERFUL AND ALMIGHTY. Nothing is too hard for Me, for I am the God of the Impossible.

You can safely put your life and those you love in My hands and be content to leave them there. Learn to trust Me and co-operate with Me - don't run ahead of Me, planning and scheming, for I don't want you to run into danger but to stay safely by My side.

11th January

CONSCIENCE

My Child,

Each time you deliberately ignore your conscience you are hardening your heart. As you walk with Me and allow Me to speak to you, I will show you the difference between right and wrong. If you continually ignore your conscience then you will find it more difficult to hear My voice, until you cannot hear Me at all.

Be sure to act upon those pricks of your conscience to keep it clear. Always be ready to obey the still, small voice of conscience that will bring peace and harmony into your life.

Allow Me to sharpen your conscience where it has become a little dulled. Put your life under the microscope of My Holy Spirit to keep your conscience sharp and clear. This will put your feet on the path to holiness and becoming more like Me!

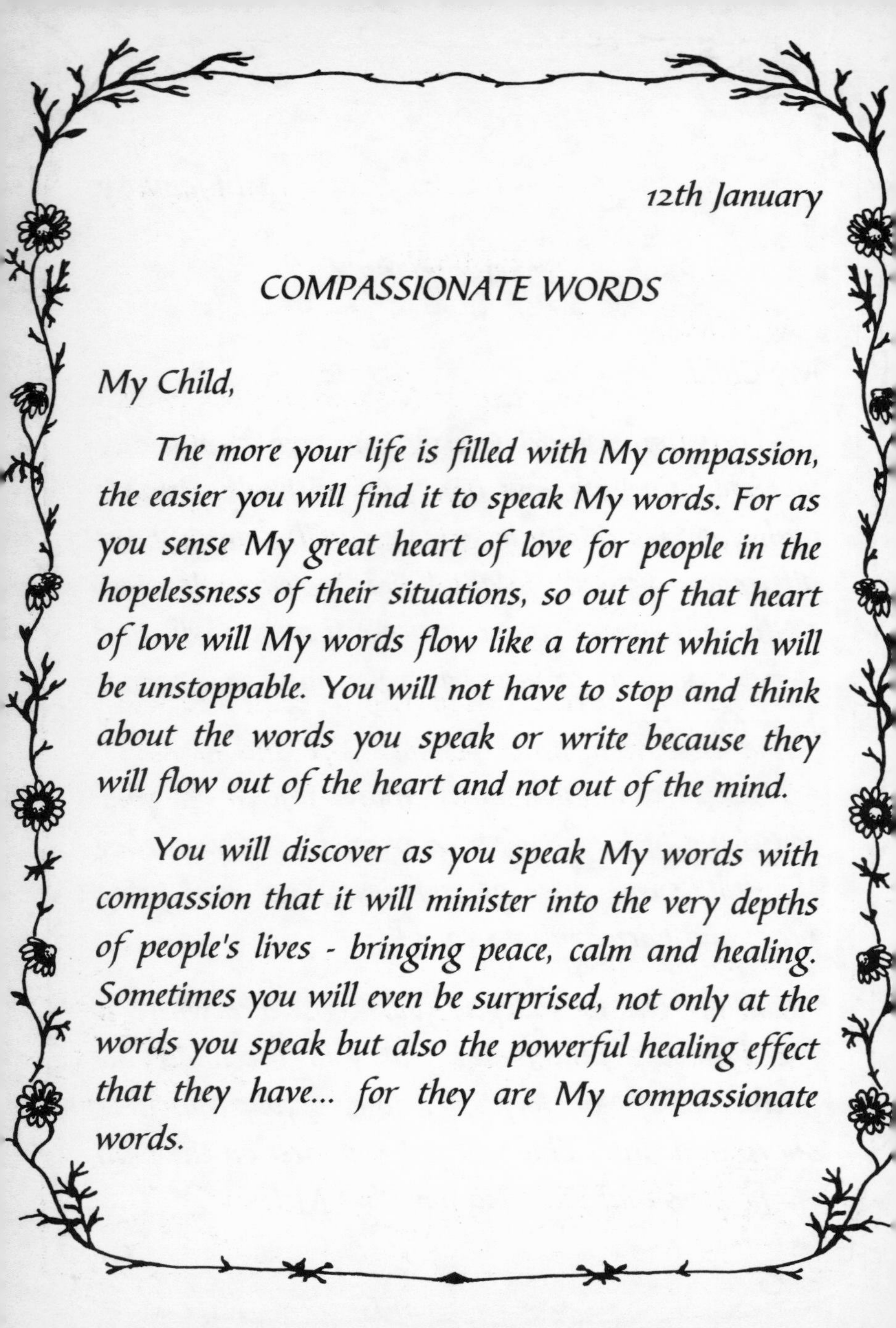

12th January

COMPASSIONATE WORDS

My Child,

The more your life is filled with My compassion, the easier you will find it to speak My words. For as you sense My great heart of love for people in the hopelessness of their situations, so out of that heart of love will My words flow like a torrent which will be unstoppable. You will not have to stop and think about the words you speak or write because they will flow out of the heart and not out of the mind.

You will discover as you speak My words with compassion that it will minister into the very depths of people's lives - bringing peace, calm and healing. Sometimes you will even be surprised, not only at the words you speak but also the powerful healing effect that they have... for they are My compassionate words.

13th January

SUBMISSION

My Child,

Each time you come to Me and ask Me what you should do and obey Me, you are learning to submit, for in submission you are handing over control. It is this resignation to another authority that is so difficult, even when the authority is the best that it can be.

As you surrender your will to Mine you will find that your heart becomes soft and humble. The struggle that may occur to bring you to the point of surrender will cause much anxiety - in surrender and submission you will find peace.

As you submit your life to Me there will be a new delight to do My will and a new joy in doing it.

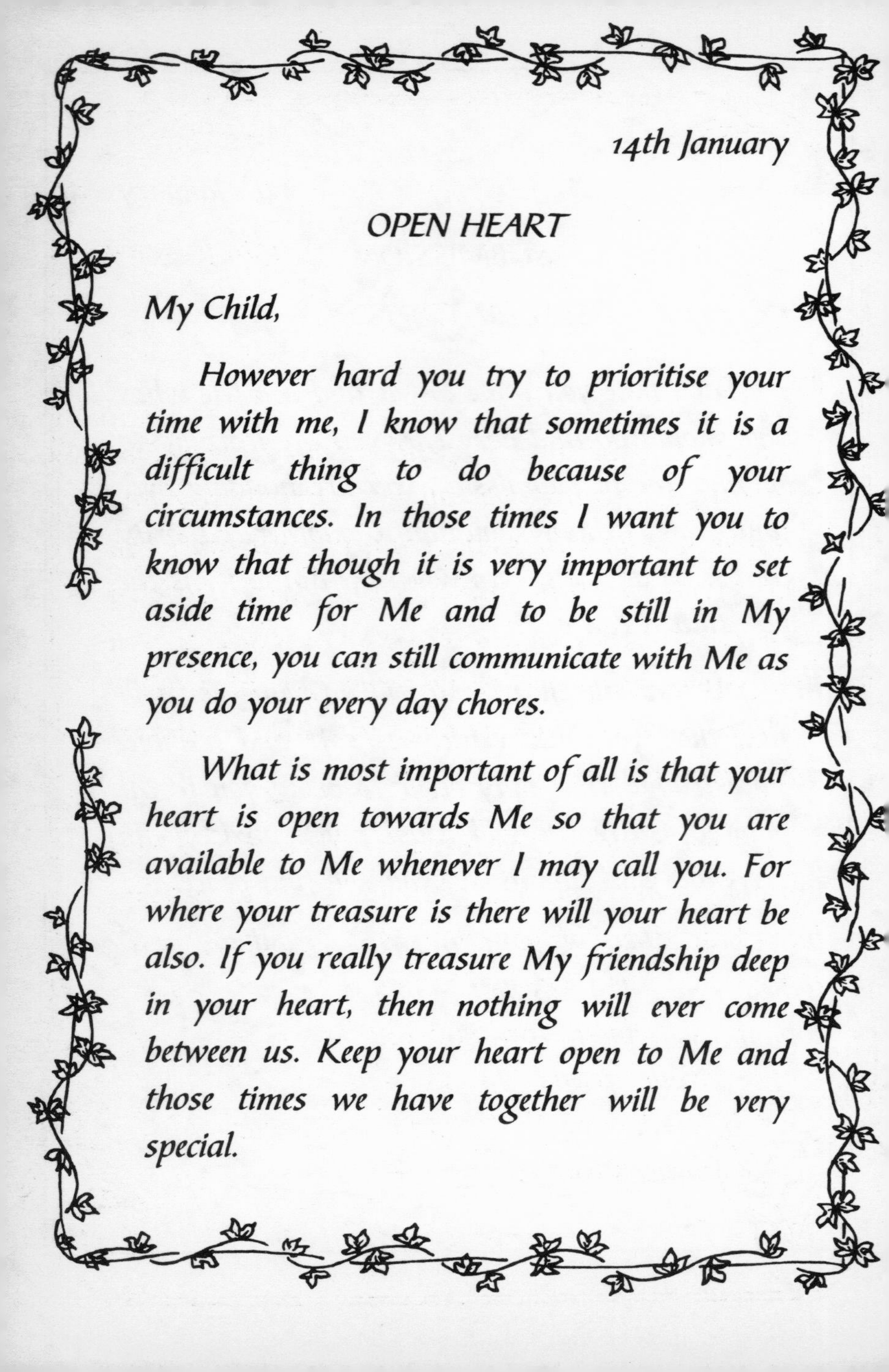

14th January

OPEN HEART

My Child,

However hard you try to prioritise your time with me, I know that sometimes it is a difficult thing to do because of your circumstances. In those times I want you to know that though it is very important to set aside time for Me and to be still in My presence, you can still communicate with Me as you do your every day chores.

What is most important of all is that your heart is open towards Me so that you are available to Me whenever I may call you. For where your treasure is there will your heart be also. If you really treasure My friendship deep in your heart, then nothing will ever come between us. Keep your heart open to Me and those times we have together will be very special.

15th January

SPECIAL FRIEND

My Child,

I want to be a very special friend to you; One who listens attentively to all you have to say and will love you just the same, whatever you share. All your secrets are safe with Me for I never betray a trust or break a confidence. I am available to you twenty-four hours a day whenever you need Me. I will never reject you or turn you away however needy you may be.

As you share with Me, like friend to friend, so I am able to help you and pour My love and wisdom into those areas of your life which need My gentle touch.

Oh how I love you and yearn for your friendship so that we can walk together and enjoy each other's company.

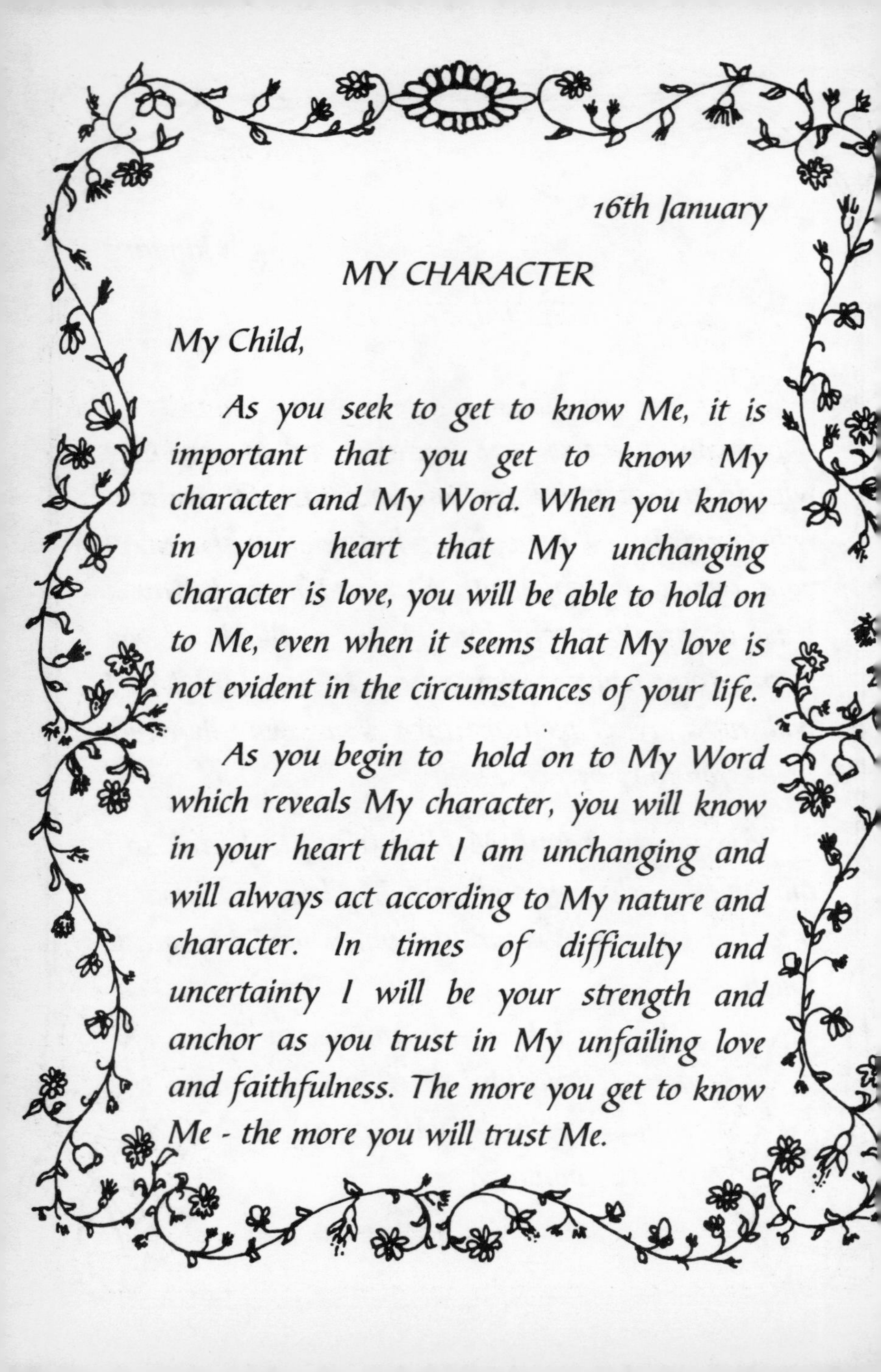

16th January

MY CHARACTER

My Child,

As you seek to get to know Me, it is important that you get to know My character and My Word. When you know in your heart that My unchanging character is love, you will be able to hold on to Me, even when it seems that My love is not evident in the circumstances of your life.

As you begin to hold on to My Word which reveals My character, you will know in your heart that I am unchanging and will always act according to My nature and character. In times of difficulty and uncertainty I will be your strength and anchor as you trust in My unfailing love and faithfulness. The more you get to know Me - the more you will trust Me.

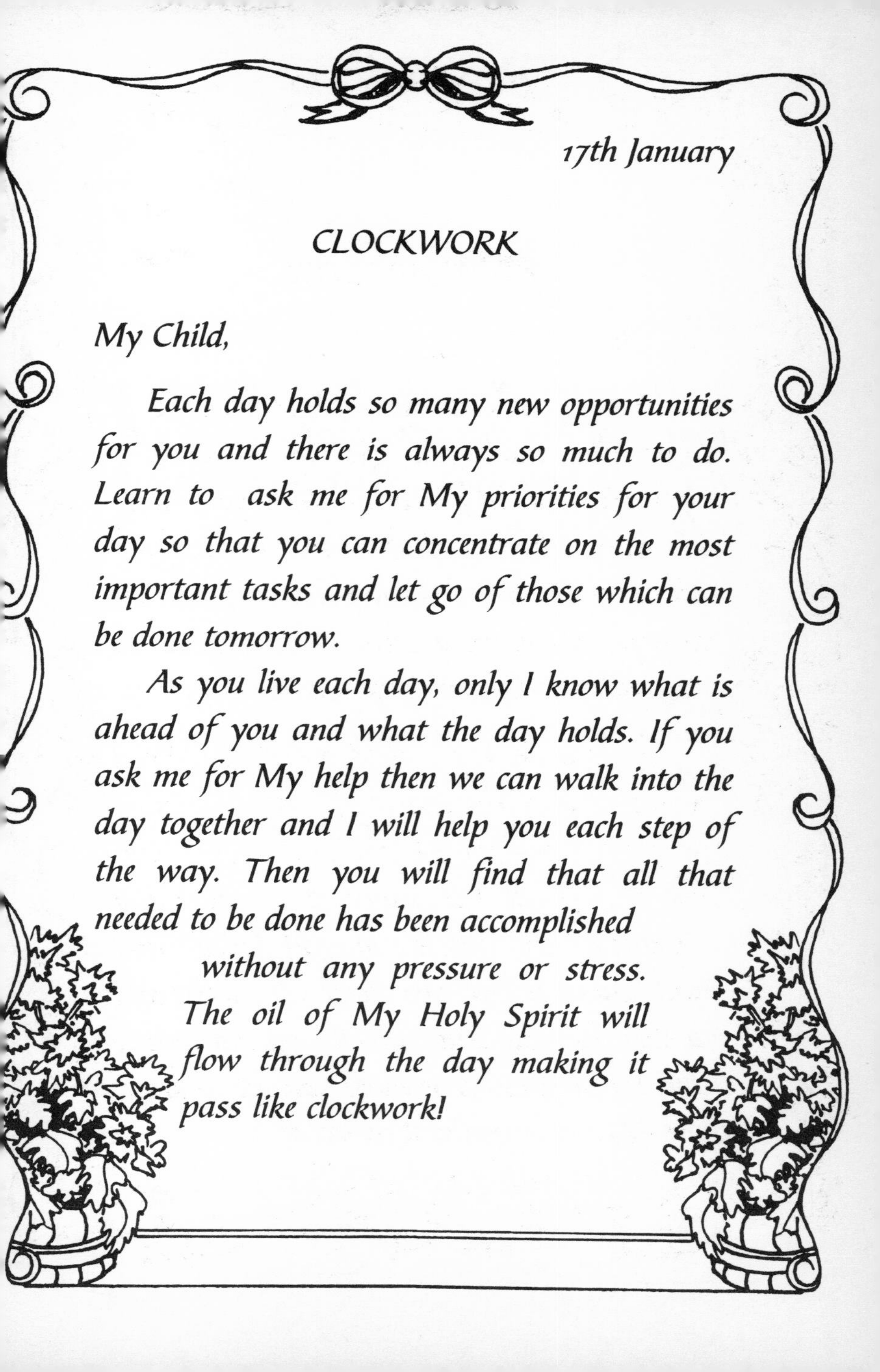

17th January

CLOCKWORK

My Child,

Each day holds so many new opportunities for you and there is always so much to do. Learn to ask me for My priorities for your day so that you can concentrate on the most important tasks and let go of those which can be done tomorrow.

As you live each day, only I know what is ahead of you and what the day holds. If you ask me for My help then we can walk into the day together and I will help you each step of the way. Then you will find that all that needed to be done has been accomplished without any pressure or stress. The oil of My Holy Spirit will flow through the day making it pass like clockwork!

18th January

HOLD ONTO ME

My Child,

The more you get to know Me and understand My character, the more you will be able to trust Me when you need to hold onto Me in faith.

If you can believe that I act only according to My character, then you will believe that all I do is pure, holy and true. Even though your circumstances may be making you doubt your faith, yet if you can trust Me, you will see Me working all things together for your good and My glory.

However difficult life may be for you, hold onto Me and believe My word - for I cannot go against My word and will always act out of a Father's loving heart towards you. As you get to know Me and experience more of My love, you will see I act with your best interests at heart.

19th January

FAITH EXERCISED

My Child,

Just as you need to exercise muscles to strengthen them and encourage them to grow, so it is with faith. If you ask for more faith then it will not be given you in a large dose - like taking medicine to remedy a situation. Rather you will be put in situations where you can exercise faith so that it will grow. The more your faith is exercised, the greater faith and ability you will have to trust Me in dire and difficult circumstances.

Are you prepared to exercise the faith you have, however small that faith may be? It may only be as small as a grain of mustard seed but it has much potential to grow. If you want more faith be prepared to exercise what faith you have.

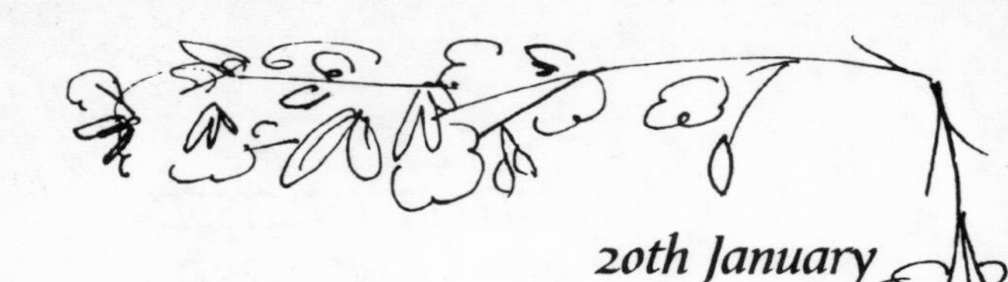

20th January

BEST FOR YOU

My Child,

If you are prepared to be patient and wait for My timing without trying to do it your way, then your patience will be rewarded. If you are prepared to lay down your own desires and ambitions and seek Me for My plans for you, then your selflessness will be rewarded. There is great joy for those who desire My ways and are prepared for Me to open up the way ahead of them.

Sometimes the waiting can cause much restlessness and that is when you need to know that I am working out all My plans and purposes for you in love. It is my delight to bring joy to you and give you surprises - then you will know I hear your cries and answer in the way that is best for you.

21st January

OPEN YOUR EYES

My Child,

Don't close your eyes to the needy around you because you feel repelled by the awfulness of what you see. If you bury your head in the sand and pretend not to notice, your ears will be deaf to the cry of the hurting. You cannot live in this world cocooned from all the danger and evil - rather you must learn how to show forth My light and love into a needy world.

My grace is sufficient for you in all those moments when you feel repulsed and you would rather not know. As you receive My grace, so you will feel My heart of compassion and weep My tears. I need those who will bring comfort and bind up the broken-hearted, setting the captives free. Are you prepared to do this for Me? Open your eyes and I will lead you to those who need My healing and love.

22nd January

HEALING TOUCH

My Child,

I know those things that you would naturally shrink back from because of the realisation of the task, but I want you to know that I am with you. My heart yearns for the damaged, unlovely ones who have been exploited and rejected. Oh how I long to gather them to Myself and let them feel the warmth of My love.

As you receive My heart of love and compassion, so you will find a longing in your heart to reach out to those who are untouchable. Of yourself you are not able but with My love flowing through you, you will discover more love in your heart than you can contain.....

it will overflow to those needing My healing touch.

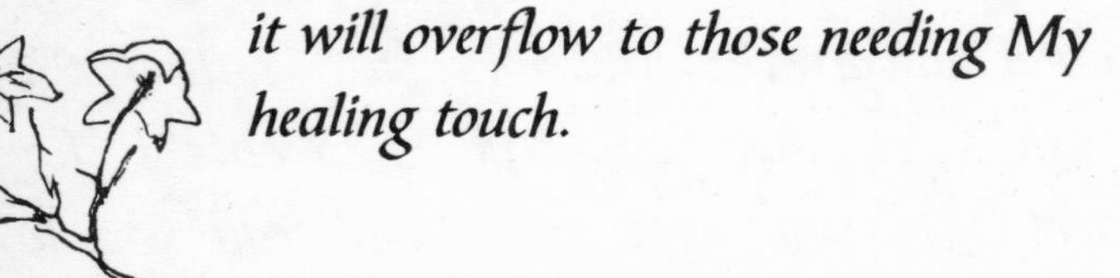

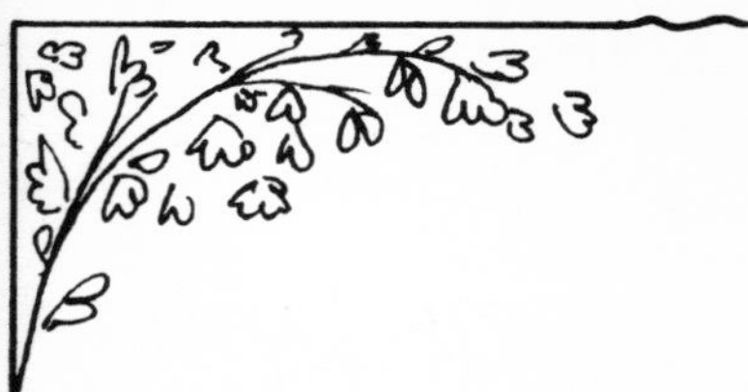

23rd January

EMPTY VESSEL

My Child,

As you come close to Me with an expectant heart, know that I will surely meet with you. As you long for that intimacy with Me and desire to be in My presence, know that this is also My desire for you. If you hunger and thirst after righteousness then you will be filled - your hunger and thirst will be completely satisfied. Not only will you be filled, but filled to overflowing so that others also will be fed.

Remember though, the emptier the vessel the more full they can become - the more of yourself that you empty, the more you can be filled by all the fullness of My Holy Spirit.

24th January

EBB AND FLOW

My Child,

Life is full of ebbs and flows like waves of the sea. When you sense that your life is ebbing it is time to consolidate all you have learnt of Me. It is a time to build on past experience and wait for My Holy Spirit to come again to bring about the flow that you are so longing to see. Because of the time of ebbing, when the flow comes it will be even more powerful than before.

So learn to be at peace whatever is happening in your life, for I will cause you to flow in My Spirit more and more.

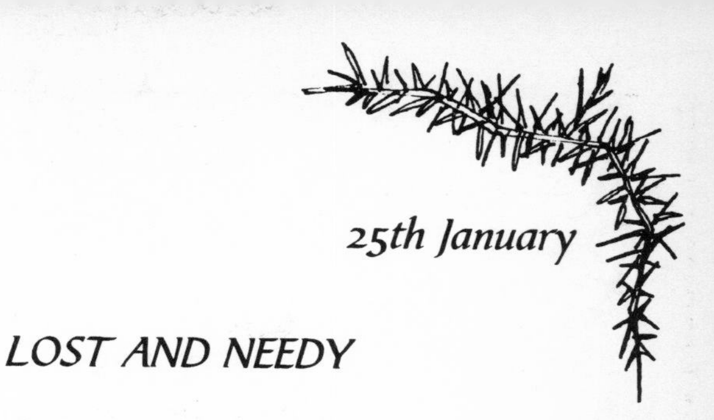

25th January

LOST AND NEEDY

My Child,

As you sense My heartache for the lost and needy, so you will be able to respond in obedience to all I ask of you. The depth of compassion will compel you to walk in places you would not chose to walk, but your feet will follow your heart.

My compassion for the lost and needy is too vast to measure. Just a tiny piece of My compassion would be enough to motivate you. As you surrender your life to Me and seek to do My will, you will be filled with My heart of love and compassion so that whatever you do will be in My strength and power and not your own. When My compassion is flowing through you it will reach the lost and needy.

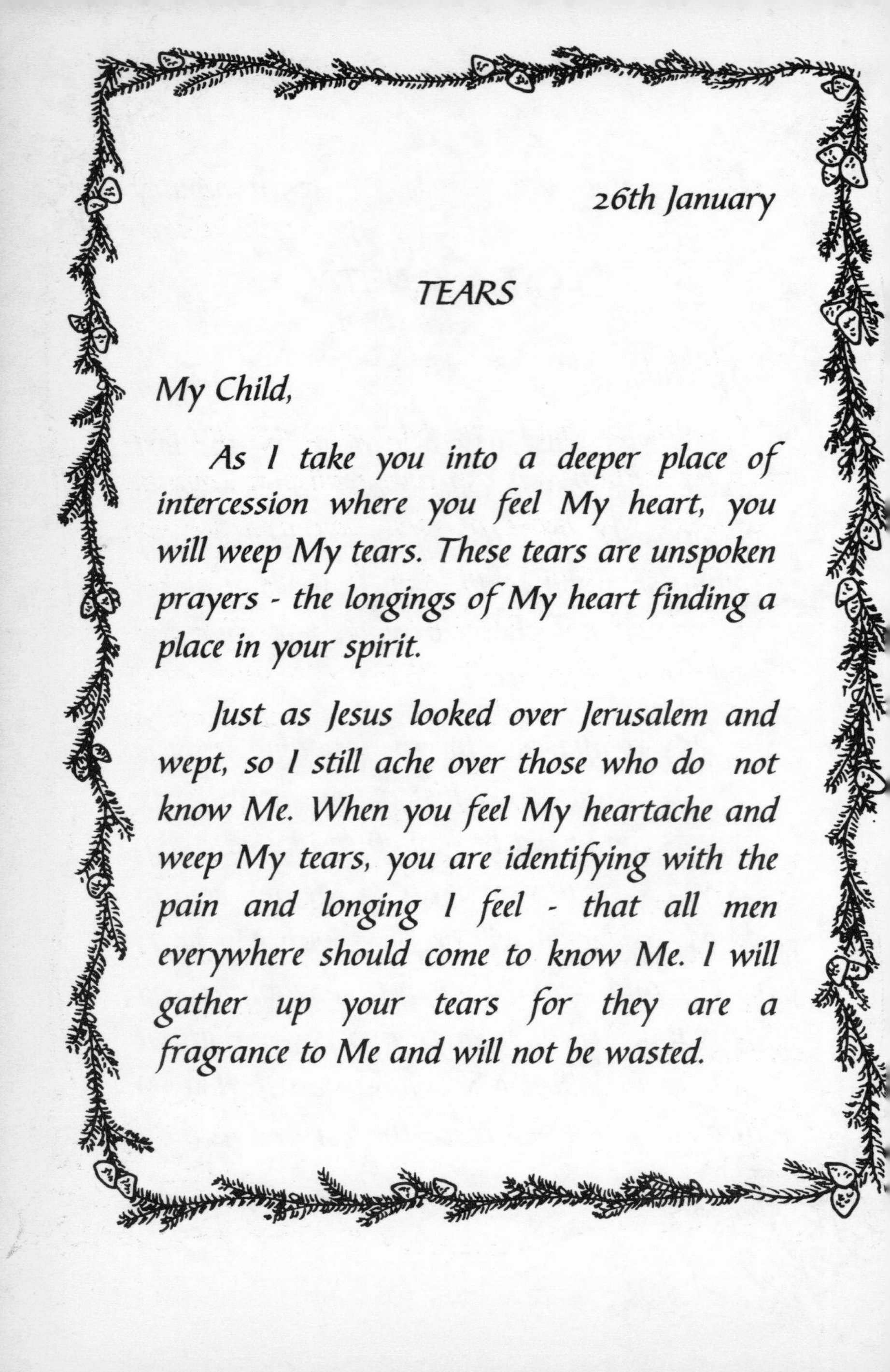

26th January

TEARS

My Child,

As I take you into a deeper place of intercession where you feel My heart, you will weep My tears. These tears are unspoken prayers - the longings of My heart finding a place in your spirit.

Just as Jesus looked over Jerusalem and wept, so I still ache over those who do not know Me. When you feel My heartache and weep My tears, you are identifying with the pain and longing I feel - that all men everywhere should come to know Me. I will gather up your tears for they are a fragrance to Me and will not be wasted.

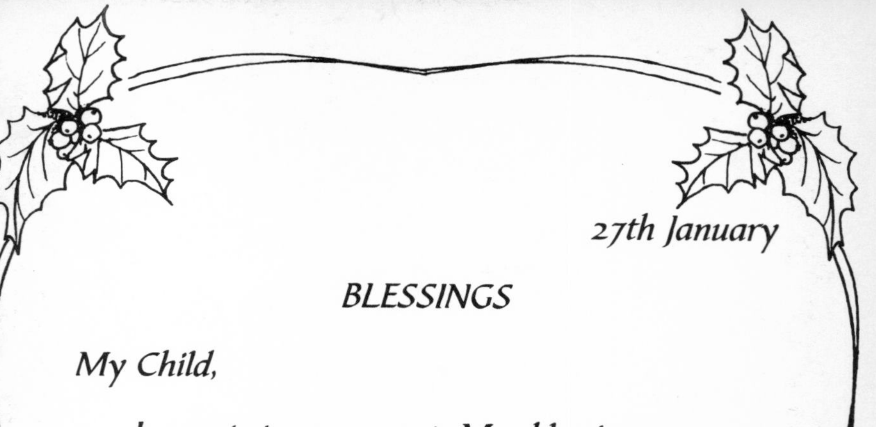

27th January

BLESSINGS

My Child,

I want to pour out My blessings on you much more than you can even realise or contain. It delights My heart to bless you and see you enjoying the fullness of My blessing. As you receive all the blessings that I long to give you, you will be filled with joy unspeakable and full of glory. This joy though is only a reflection of the joy in My heart as I bless you.

So enter into My blessings and know however greatly I bless you,there is always so much more that I want to give you and you can receive. Don't be satisfied with less than I want you to have and to enjoy, for My blessings are continual.

28th January

FIRE

My Child,

I want to set your heart on fire with a flame that will never go out. This fire will burn continually in you and as you speak My words it will be passed on to others. As you pass this fire on to others, so I will refuel you to keep you burning brightly for Me. It will never get low for I will always make sure that the coals of fire are burning brightly in your heart.

Others will long for this fire too and will come to you for warmth as they see how brightly it burns. Let Me set your heart aglow for Me and My kingdom.

29th January

ENFORCED REST

My Child,

Be still and know that I am God. I am in charge of all the situations and circumstances of your life. There are times when it is necessary to consolidate all you are learning and all I am doing. In those times of stillness, rest and quiet I am able to come and minister My peace into your heart to let all you are learning sink into you and become part of you.

Though you may not welcome the stillness or the enforced rest, it is a beneficial time for you so do not despise it.

As with food, you can only take in so much until it becomes part of you, so it is with all the spiritual food you receive. There is a time to eat and a time to rest and then comes the time to work when you are strong and able to. Now is a short time to be still before you are sent out into the vineyard to work and begin to gather the harvest in.

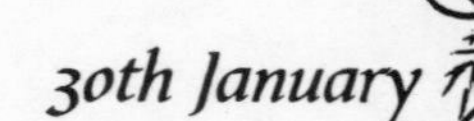

30th January

SEEK ME

My Child,

Don't let the pressures of all that you have to do overwhelm you. Know My peace and be still in My presence. Commit each day into My hands and I will guide you through it, helping you to sort out your priorities. As you are aware of My strength and power you will become more peaceful and feel more able to cope with the many tasks that have to be done. As we walk through each day together you will be surprised at what is accomplished and how easily everything falls into place.

Seek Me for My priorities for your life - yes for your daily living. Some tasks are essential but some can be left for another day.

If you seek Me first everything else will be added unto you.

31st January

LOVE DEFROSTS

My Child,

My love can thaw any ice-cold heart and cause it to defrost and feel the warmth. It is My love that can reach the deepest part of you and cause you to respond. No one is too far away to be reached by My love and by My Spirit's power at work, that love can be tangibly felt.

Allow My love to constantly defrost your own heart, for even if you think that your heart is already soft it can become even softer, more compassionate and pliable. Don't harden your heart, for it takes more of My love to soften it when it is hard. Let My love be poured on your heart to keep it pliable.

1st February

THE UNEXPECTED

My Child,

A sudden change in circumstances is always a difficult time to cope with. When the unplanned or unexpected happens, be sure that nothing takes Me by surprise. That is why you can rely on Me and depend on Me when it seems like things are out of your control. Be assured that I am in control and I am working everything out for your good, no matter how distasteful or unpleasant things appear to be.

Know that your security is in Me and that I am the Alpha and Omega who knows the end from the beginning. Do not let the unexpected cause your heart to panic or fear, but let it help you to know that you are secure in Me.

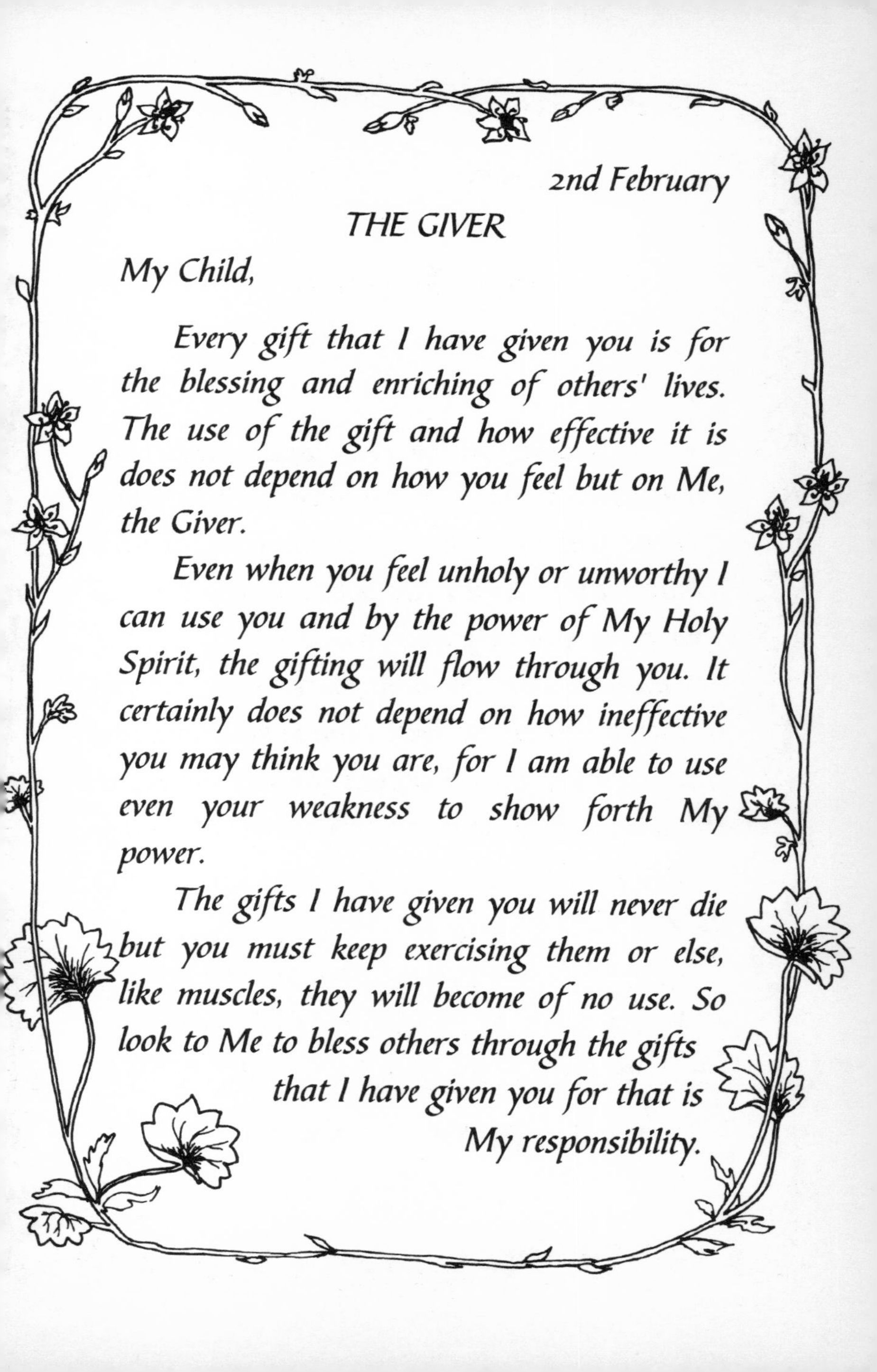

2nd February

THE GIVER

My Child,

Every gift that I have given you is for the blessing and enriching of others' lives. The use of the gift and how effective it is does not depend on how you feel but on Me, the Giver.

Even when you feel unholy or unworthy I can use you and by the power of My Holy Spirit, the gifting will flow through you. It certainly does not depend on how ineffective you may think you are, for I am able to use even your weakness to show forth My power.

The gifts I have given you will never die but you must keep exercising them or else, like muscles, they will become of no use. So look to Me to bless others through the gifts that I have given you for that is My responsibility.

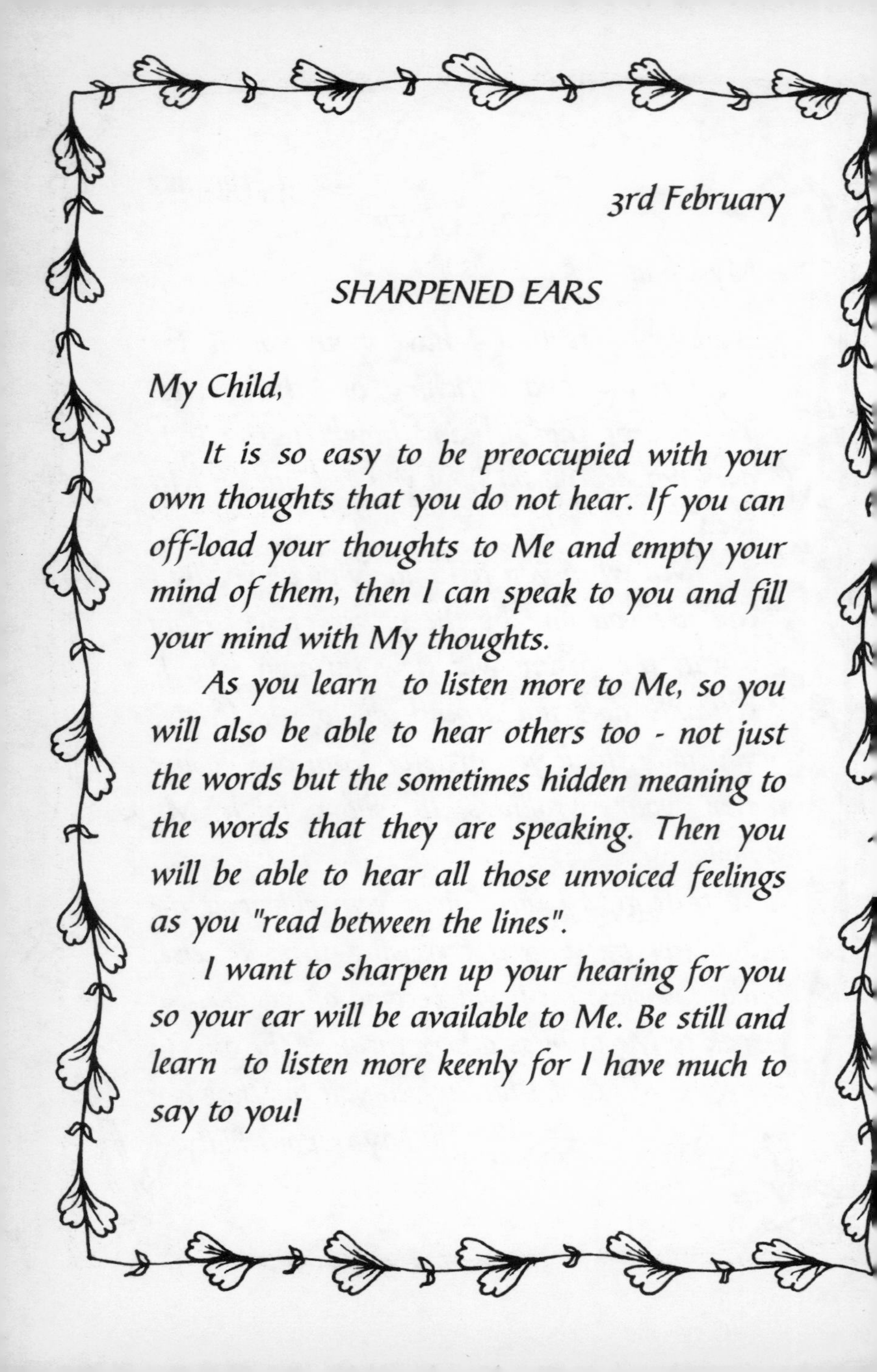

3rd February

SHARPENED EARS

My Child,

It is so easy to be preoccupied with your own thoughts that you do not hear. If you can off-load your thoughts to Me and empty your mind of them, then I can speak to you and fill your mind with My thoughts.

As you learn to listen more to Me, so you will also be able to hear others too - not just the words but the sometimes hidden meaning to the words that they are speaking. Then you will be able to hear all those unvoiced feelings as you "read between the lines".

I want to sharpen up your hearing for you so your ear will be available to Me. Be still and learn to listen more keenly for I have much to say to you!

4th February

SECURE

My Child,

The more you believe, receive and experience My love, the more secure you will be. Knowing that I will always love you, that My love is unconditional, will make you feel so safe because My love will never change. It is not dependent on who you are or what you do - it is dependent on My nature - which is LOVE.

You are special to Me, valued and chosen to be Mine, totally accepted and infinitely lovable because I created you. You will never have to fear My rejection for I cannot and will not reject you. You are secure in Me for your life is hid with Christ in God. Relax in the certain security and knowledge that you are in the palm of My hand, surrounded by My love.

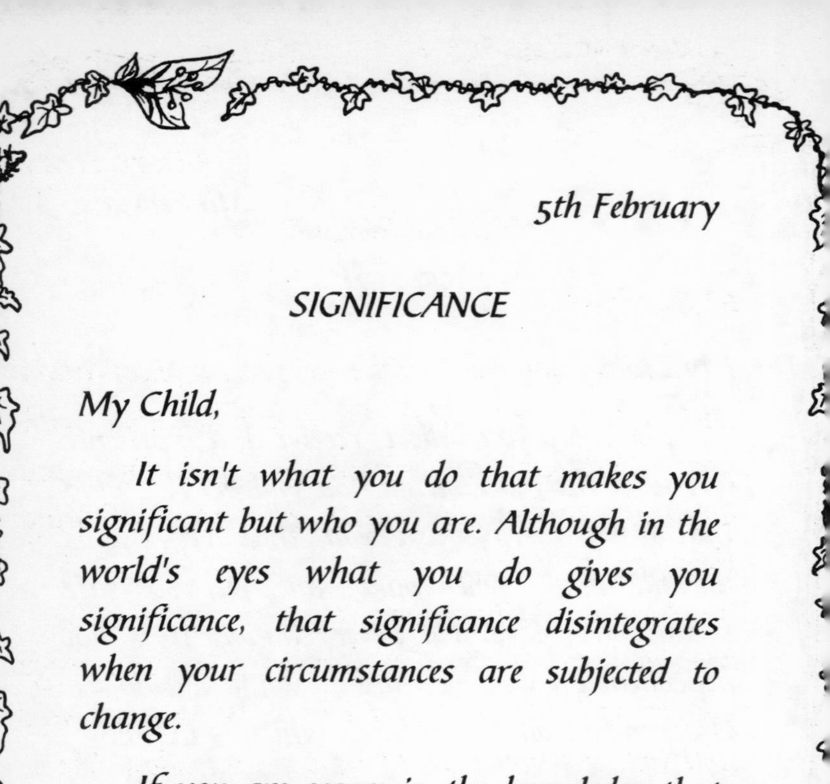

5th February

SIGNIFICANCE

My Child,

It isn't what you do that makes you significant but who you are. Although in the world's eyes what you do gives you significance, that significance disintegrates when your circumstances are subjected to change.

If you are secure in the knowledge that you are My child, then your significance will never change because you will always be who you are - My child. You have been adopted into My family and nothing will ever sever that close family tie. So you need never fear rejection, for you have been sealed by the Holy Spirit to be who you are - a child of the King.

6th February

COMMUNICATION

My Child,

Just as you need and long for communication with others, so I long for communication with you. Without communication, isolation and loneliness set in which lead to a sense of being forsaken.

Through My word I have and will communicate with you and this will encourage you to seek Me and find Me to know My ways and will. As you read My word and allow Me to speak to you, those channels of communication will be open. You know that My promises are true and you will not feel isolated, lonely or forsaken, for I have promised to be with you always. There are other ways too that I long to speak to you and share with you, for I am a God who longs to communicate. Be open to Me and all I have to say to you and we shall together enjoy communion which will strengthen our relationship.

7th February

SPEAK OUT

My Child,

It is not for you to weigh any words that I give you. That is for those who listen and receive. If you speak out that which I give then I will be with you and put My words in your mouth. It doesn't matter if you get it wrong as you will learn by experience. Be faithful to that which you believe I am giving you - don't be concerned about the effect the words will have on others for that will be My responsibility.

Learn more and more to listen to Me and I will share more and more with you. The words that I give you will build up and bless others and they will be encouraged. Then they will quickly be able to discern what is being said and will appropriate it to their lives.

Be bold and speak out for through your words others will be blessed.

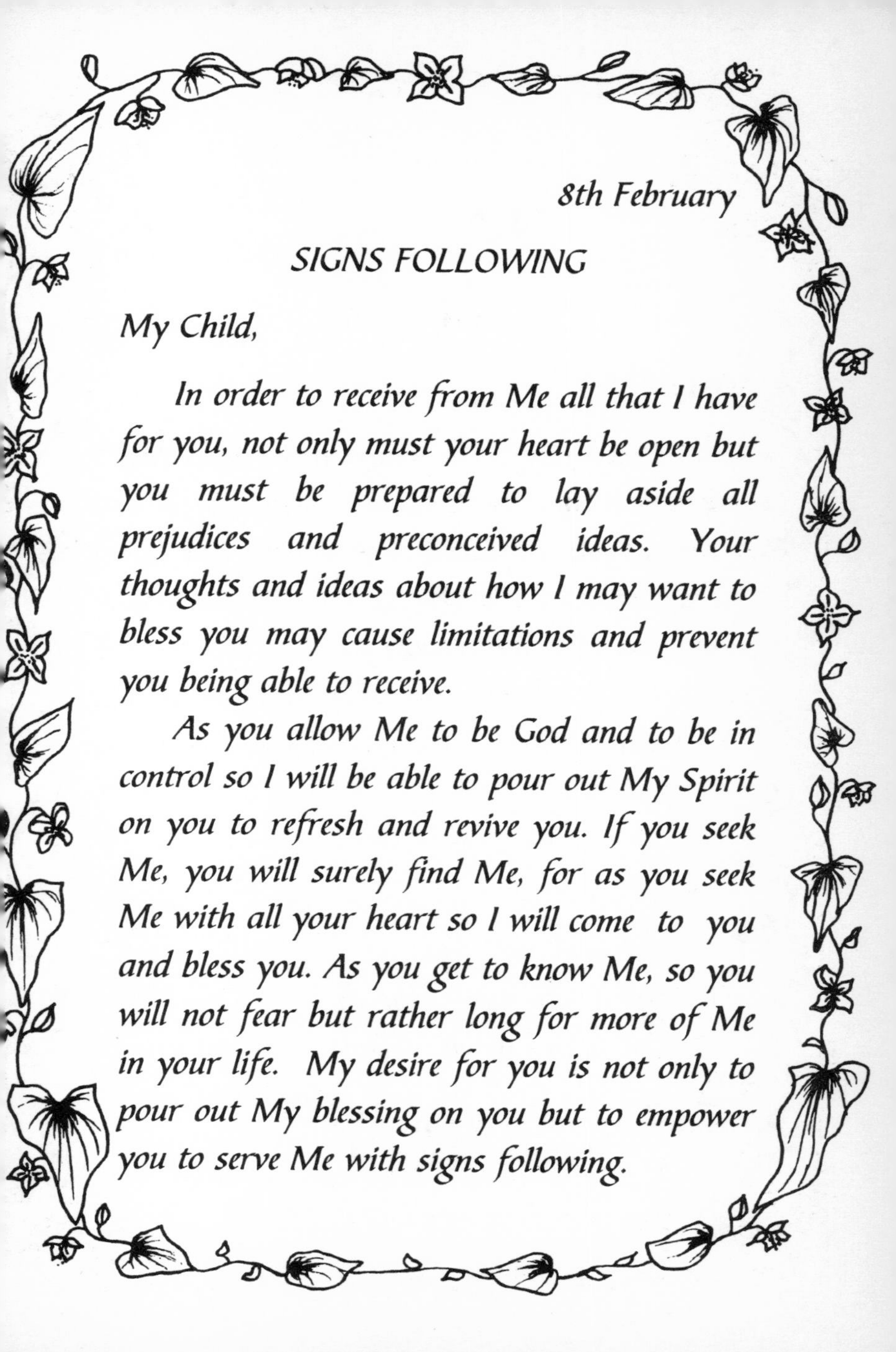

8th February

SIGNS FOLLOWING

My Child,

In order to receive from Me all that I have for you, not only must your heart be open but you must be prepared to lay aside all prejudices and preconceived ideas. Your thoughts and ideas about how I may want to bless you may cause limitations and prevent you being able to receive.

As you allow Me to be God and to be in control so I will be able to pour out My Spirit on you to refresh and revive you. If you seek Me, you will surely find Me, for as you seek Me with all your heart so I will come to you and bless you. As you get to know Me, so you will not fear but rather long for more of Me in your life. My desire for you is not only to pour out My blessing on you but to empower you to serve Me with signs following.

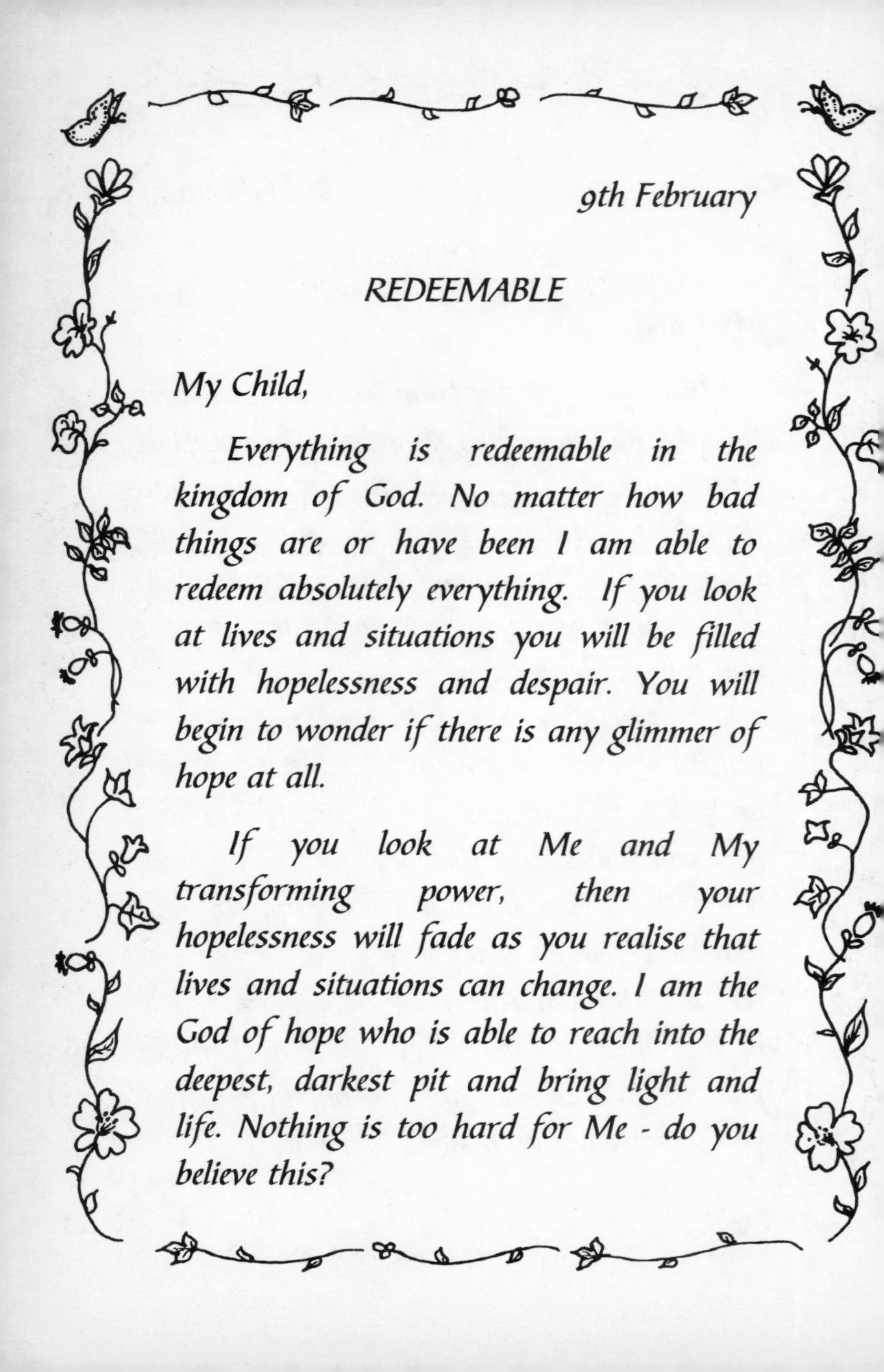

9th February

REDEEMABLE

My Child,

Everything is redeemable in the kingdom of God. No matter how bad things are or have been I am able to redeem absolutely everything. If you look at lives and situations you will be filled with hopelessness and despair. You will begin to wonder if there is any glimmer of hope at all.

If you look at Me and My transforming power, then your hopelessness will fade as you realise that lives and situations can change. I am the God of hope who is able to reach into the deepest, darkest pit and bring light and life. Nothing is too hard for Me - do you believe this?

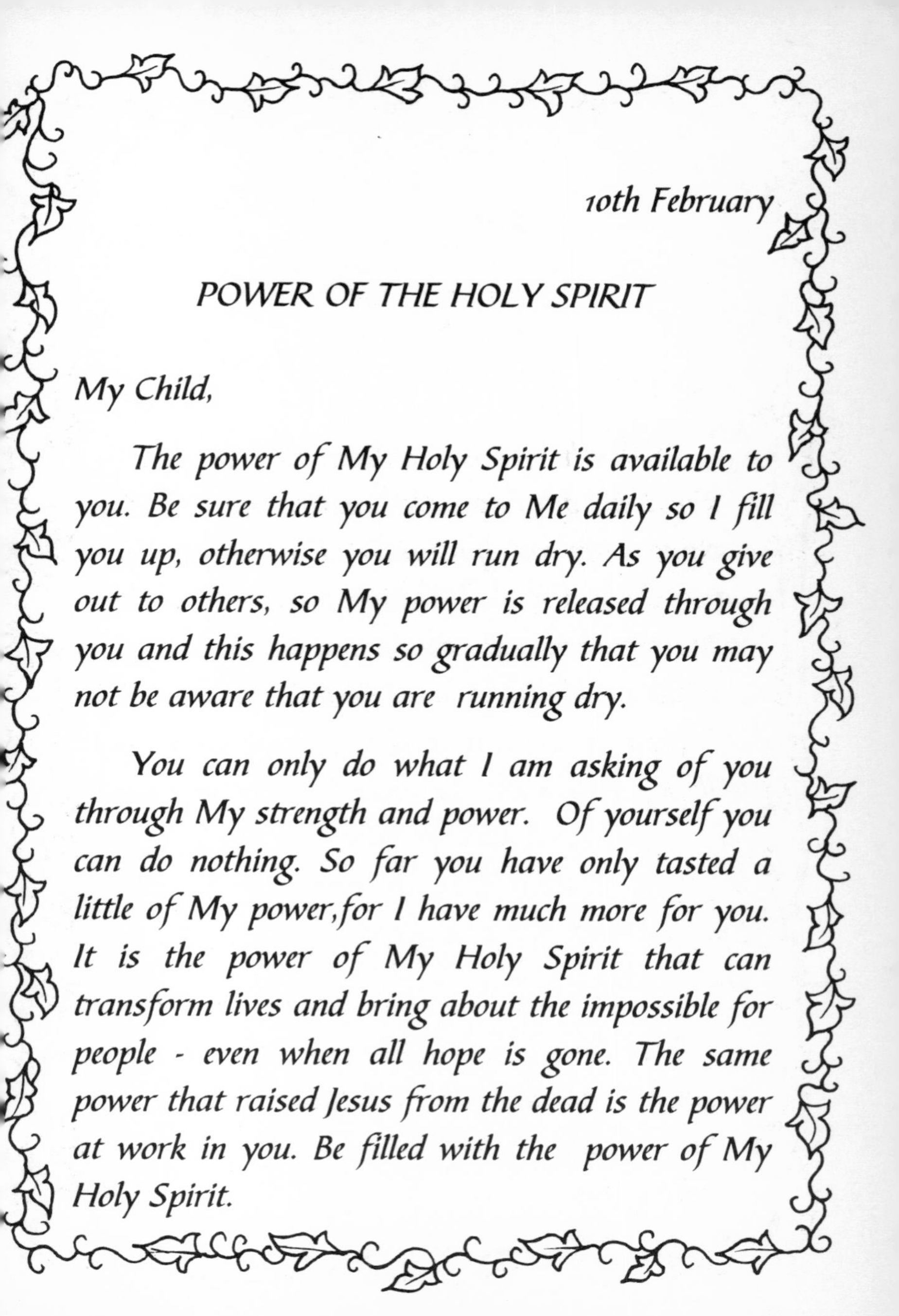

10th February

POWER OF THE HOLY SPIRIT

My Child,

The power of My Holy Spirit is available to you. Be sure that you come to Me daily so I fill you up, otherwise you will run dry. As you give out to others, so My power is released through you and this happens so gradually that you may not be aware that you are running dry.

You can only do what I am asking of you through My strength and power. Of yourself you can do nothing. So far you have only tasted a little of My power,for I have much more for you. It is the power of My Holy Spirit that can transform lives and bring about the impossible for people - even when all hope is gone. The same power that raised Jesus from the dead is the power at work in you. Be filled with the power of My Holy Spirit.

11th February

WORD OF LIFE

My Child,

My word to you is life and health. It is the food to keep you spiritually alive. As you feed on My word it will become part of you and will strengthen and sustain you through all the adversities of life. If you neglect to read My word you will starve and signs of that neglect will begin to show in your life. As you read My word, so it will be that the words I put into your heart will, by the power of My Holy Spirit, bring life and hope to others as you share them.

Take time to enjoy My word for in every page there will be something special for you.

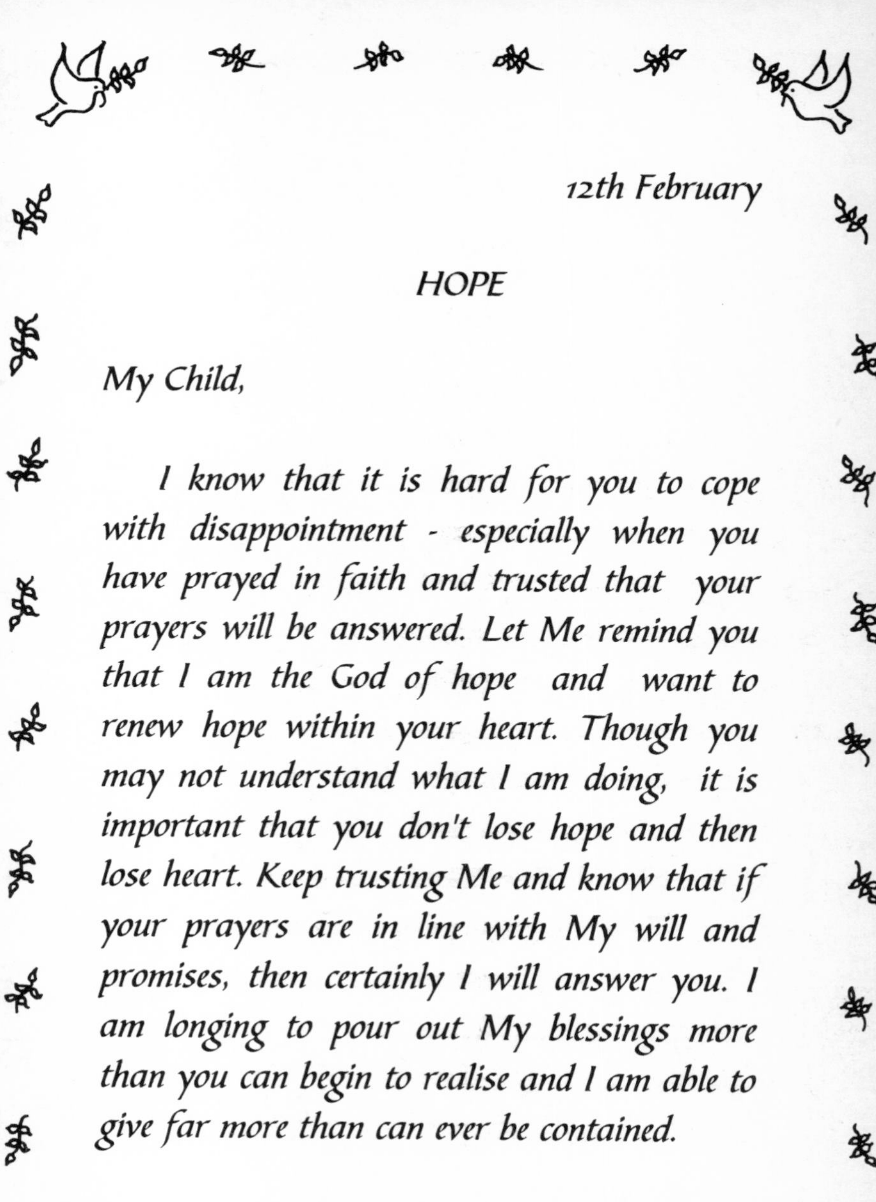

12th February

HOPE

My Child,

I know that it is hard for you to cope with disappointment - especially when you have prayed in faith and trusted that your prayers will be answered. Let Me remind you that I am the God of hope and want to renew hope within your heart. Though you may not understand what I am doing, it is important that you don't lose hope and then lose heart. Keep trusting Me and know that if your prayers are in line with My will and promises, then certainly I will answer you. I am longing to pour out My blessings more than you can begin to realise and I am able to give far more than can ever be contained.

13th February

MY GLORY

My Child,

As you spend time with Me you will become more like Me. The light and glory of My presence will fill and flood your life and shine out through you. It will be so natural for you, like breathing, that you will not even be aware of it.

Just like Moses, who spent many days in My presence, could not help reflecting My glory, so that same glory is available to all those who will seek Me and spend time with Me.

There is no substitute for spending time with Me and as you do so, discovering the beauty of My presence, so that beauty will shine through you.

14th February

ADAPTABLE

My Child,

Learn to be adaptable and don't be over-concerned if things don't happen in the way you had planned. Be prepared to submit your plans, ideas and desires to Me and allow Me to direct your ways. Everything that happens, even the unexpected can be turned into good. I am the God who can turn even curses into blessings.

Learn to know My peace and trust Me that I am in all the circumstances of your life. Don't expect Me to adapt to you, for I am the Potter you are the clay. Can the clay tell the Potter how to work and what to do? Surely that is the prerogative of the Potter. As you adapt to Me and My ways and plans so we can work together for your good and My glory.

15th February

GLORY

My Child,

As you come into My presence to worship Me, so you will get a glimpse of My glory as it comes in your midst. My presence and power will be experienced and you will realise afresh the awesomeness of seeing just a glimpse of My glory.

As you dwell in My presence, so you will become more like Me and long for more of Me to fill your life. I long to dwell in the midst of My people and to reveal Myself to them. Seek My face, dwell in My presence and see My glory.

16th February

FRESHNESS

My Child,

Each new day will bring a freshness to the relationship that you have with Me. You cannot live on yesterday's experience or on yesterday's food.

Hold a sense of expectancy in your heart that each day will produce a new and significant development in our relationship. The only way to keep any relationship alive is to enjoy the freshness of it daily. Yesterday's bread is always stale and harder to swallow and digest. Come to My Word each day expecting a specific word for that day and all the necessities of the day. My Word is like fresh bread and will satisfy all the needs and desires of your heart - don't settle for anything less.

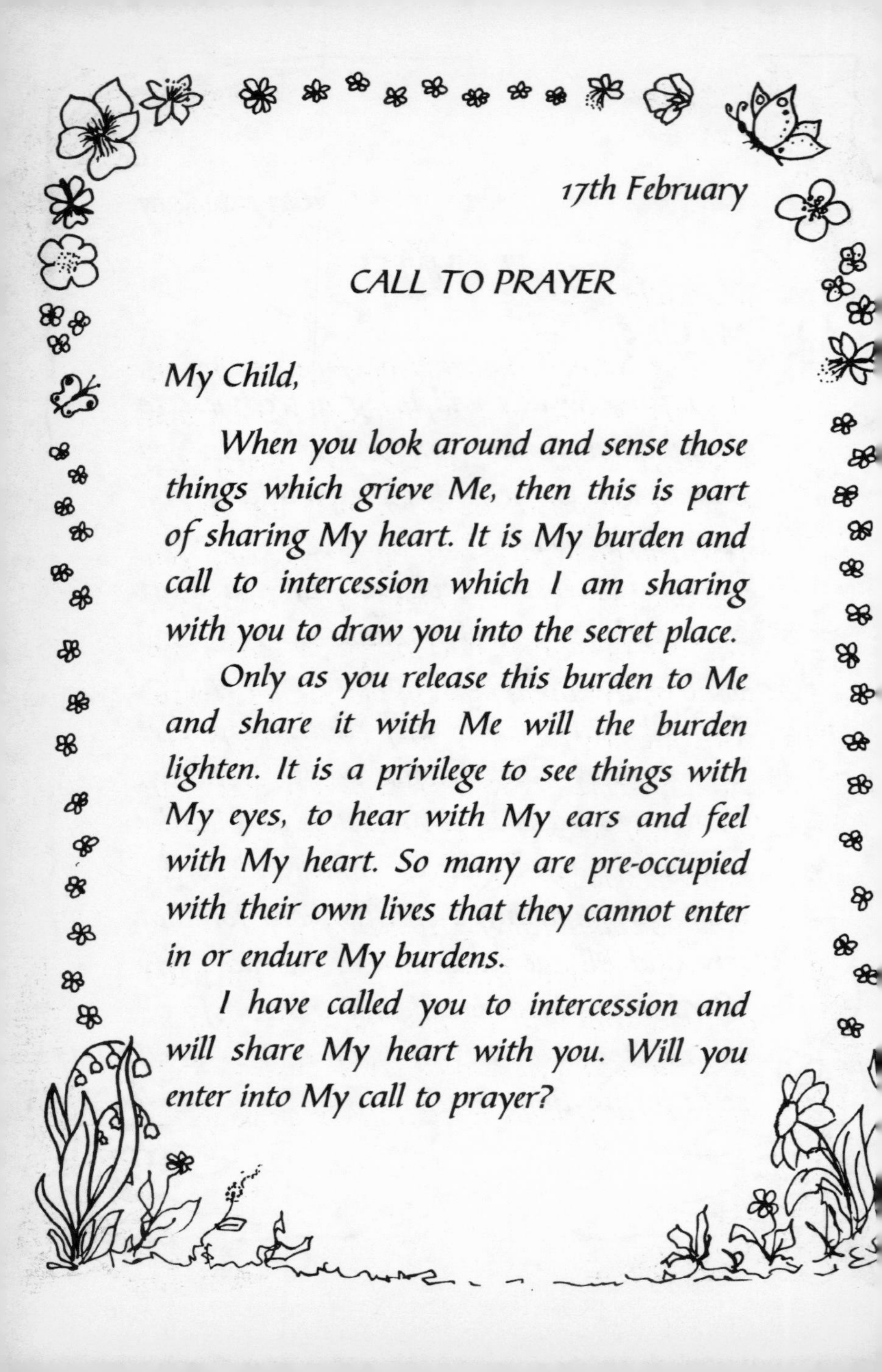

17th February

CALL TO PRAYER

My Child,

When you look around and sense those things which grieve Me, then this is part of sharing My heart. It is My burden and call to intercession which I am sharing with you to draw you into the secret place.

Only as you release this burden to Me and share it with Me will the burden lighten. It is a privilege to see things with My eyes, to hear with My ears and feel with My heart. So many are pre-occupied with their own lives that they cannot enter in or endure My burdens.

I have called you to intercession and will share My heart with you. Will you enter into My call to prayer?

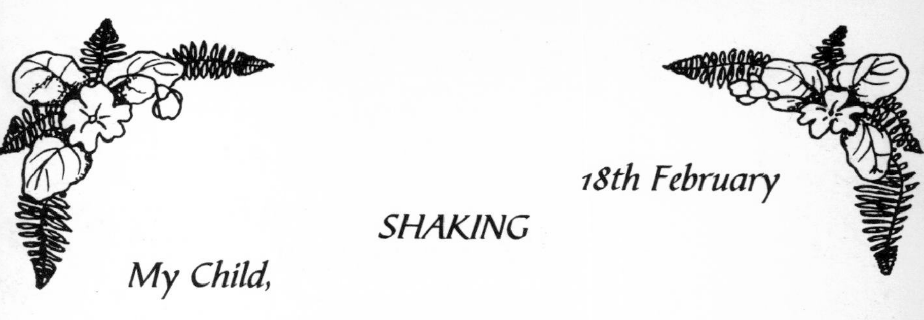

18th February

SHAKING

My Child,

The turmoil that you are in is a time of shaking. Whatever is of Me will remain and whatever is not of Me will fall away. You may be surprised at what will fall away. Yes I am doing a new thing for you and you must be prepared for change. Not change for the sake of change but change because I am doing a new thing and the old cannot remain with the new. Some change you will welcome and rejoice at - other change will take time to adjust to. As you trust Me for your security, so you will be able to cope with all the changes I am bringing about for you.

Keep close to My heart, for it is a place of peace and rest. I know the desire of your heart to seek Me - and I will honour that and you will find Me, even in the shaking.

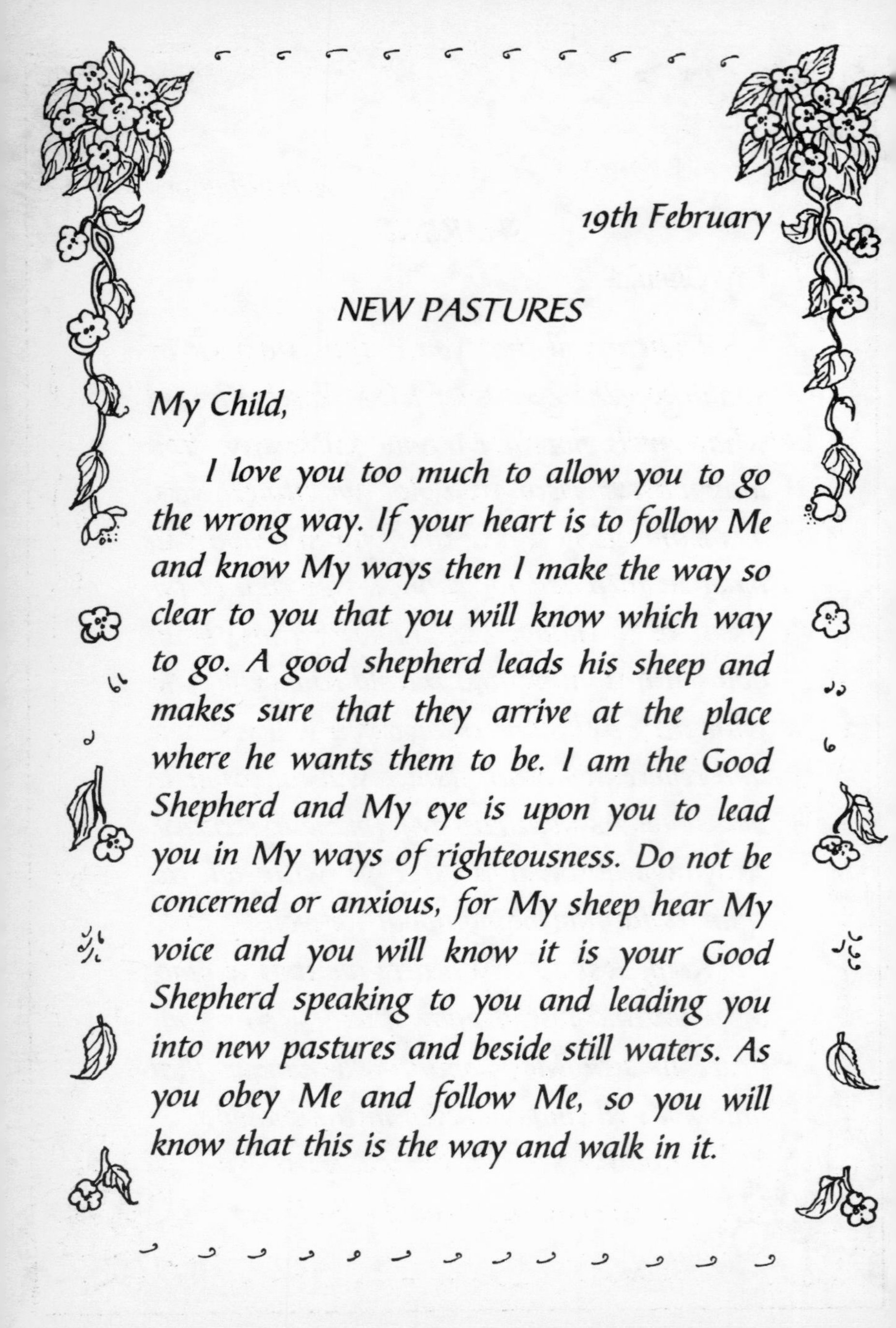

19th February

NEW PASTURES

My Child,

I love you too much to allow you to go the wrong way. If your heart is to follow Me and know My ways then I make the way so clear to you that you will know which way to go. A good shepherd leads his sheep and makes sure that they arrive at the place where he wants them to be. I am the Good Shepherd and My eye is upon you to lead you in My ways of righteousness. Do not be concerned or anxious, for My sheep hear My voice and you will know it is your Good Shepherd speaking to you and leading you into new pastures and beside still waters. As you obey Me and follow Me, so you will know that this is the way and walk in it.

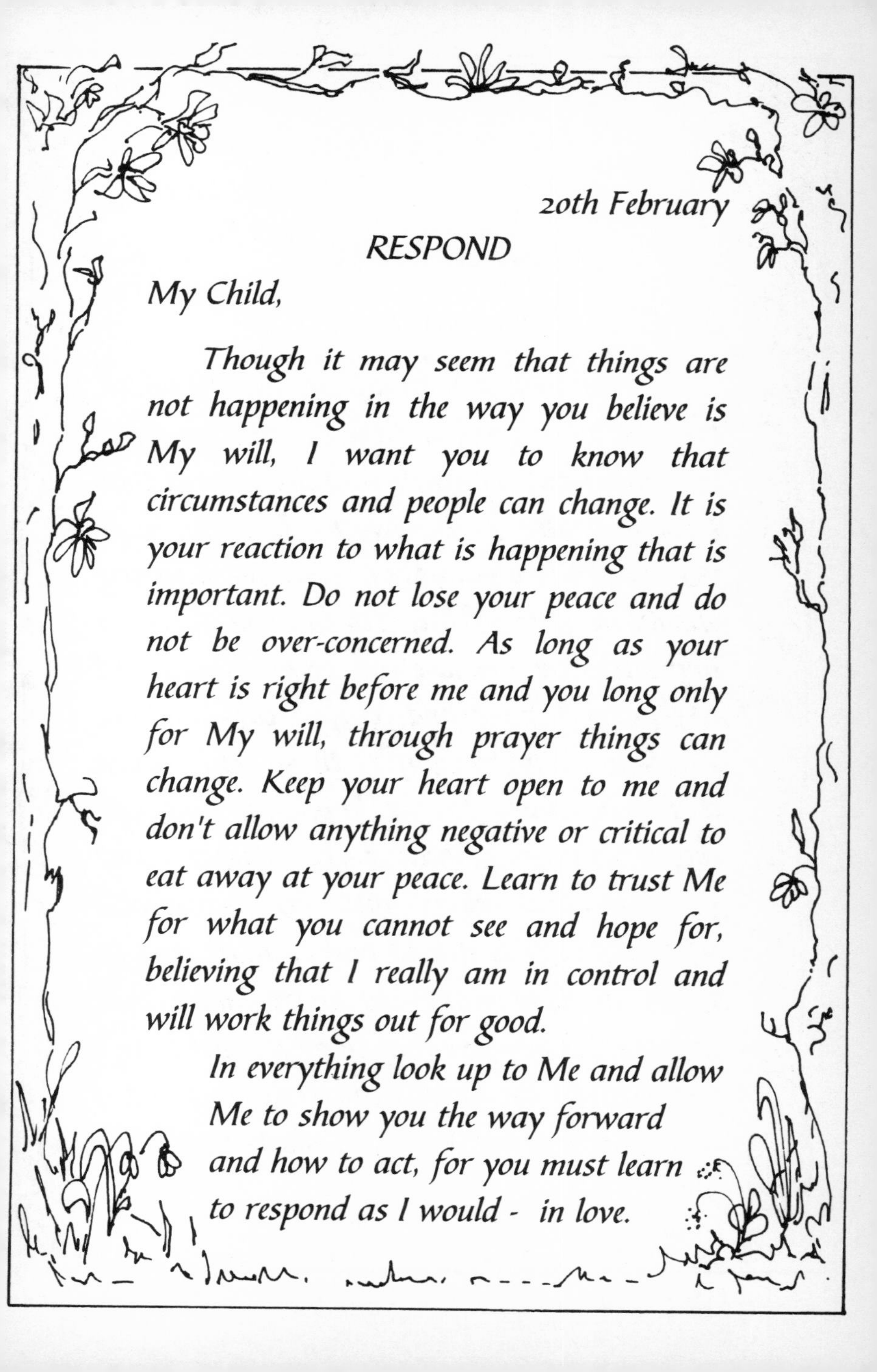

20th February

RESPOND

My Child,

Though it may seem that things are not happening in the way you believe is My will, I want you to know that circumstances and people can change. It is your reaction to what is happening that is important. Do not lose your peace and do not be over-concerned. As long as your heart is right before me and you long only for My will, through prayer things can change. Keep your heart open to me and don't allow anything negative or critical to eat away at your peace. Learn to trust Me for what you cannot see and hope for, believing that I really am in control and will work things out for good.

In everything look up to Me and allow Me to show you the way forward and how to act, for you must learn to respond as I would - in love.

21st February

SHOW MY LOVE

My Child,

As you look around and see the evil which has overtaken good and the devastating effect that this has on people's lives, be assured that I am in control of this world that I made. It was not in My plan that pain and suffering should be part of life. Yet through the pain and suffering My love can be ministered and My peace, healing and comfort can be given. Are you ready to comfort those that mourn and bring hope to the hopeless? This will mean sometimes having to change your priorities and plans and being available whenever there is a need and I call. It isn't so much speaking words as sharing love that counts. It is My love that comforts and brings peace, filling the heart with fresh hope and a will to carry on. Will you show forth My love?

22nd February

GOD OF HOPE

My Child,

I am the God of Hope. In Me can the real purpose of life be discovered. If you can only hope for the things of this life, then your hope is in vain. If your hope is for a better place and a better world to come, then your expectation will be realised. For in My house are many mansions and they are ready for all those who believe in Me. It is not possible for you to begin to imagine such a glorious place. But one day I will welcome you there. Your hope will be realised and there will be no more pain and suffering for I, Myself will wipe away every tear - this is your hope - hold fast to it for I am the God of Hope.

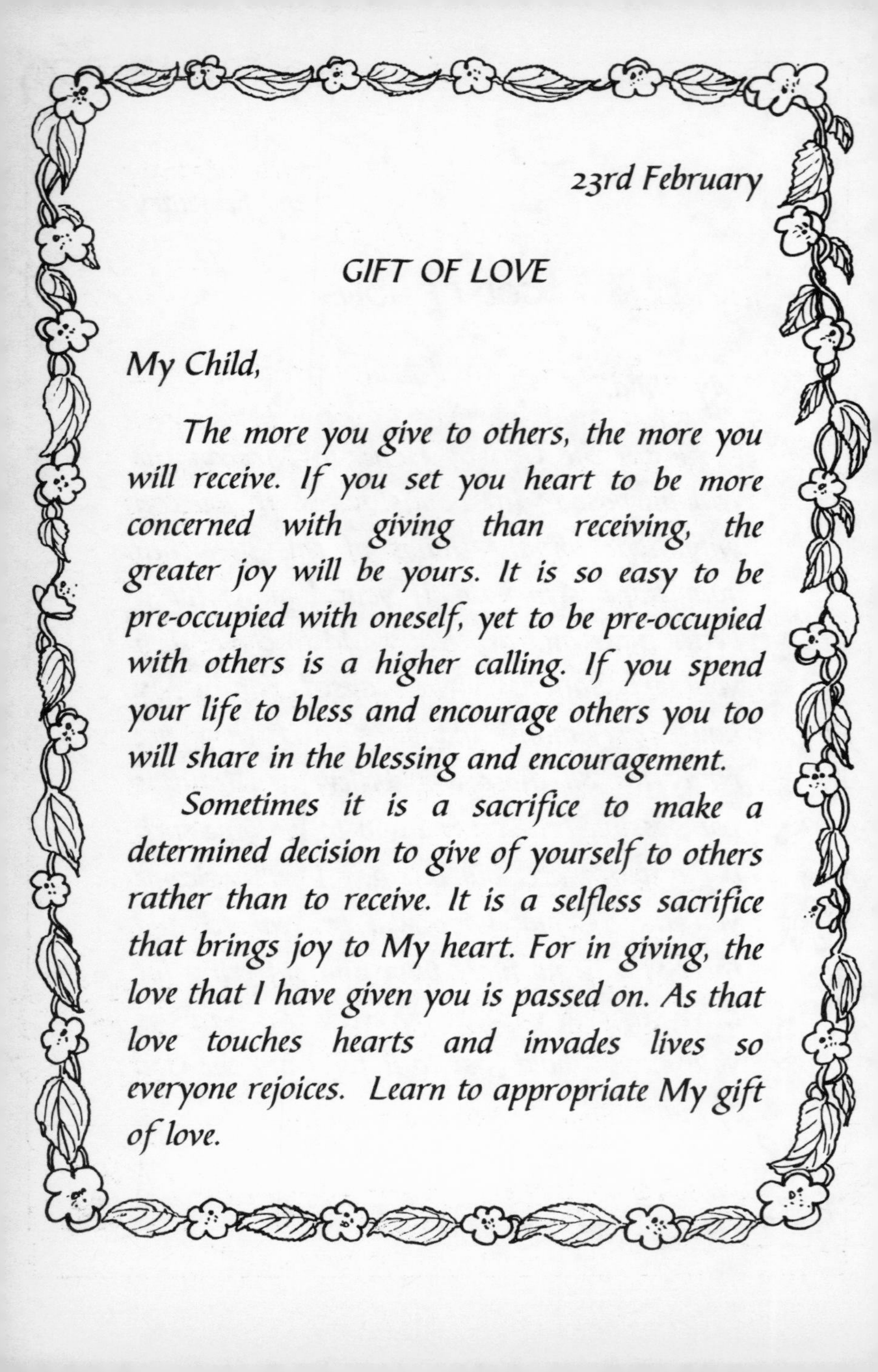

23rd February

GIFT OF LOVE

My Child,

The more you give to others, the more you will receive. If you set you heart to be more concerned with giving than receiving, the greater joy will be yours. It is so easy to be pre-occupied with oneself, yet to be pre-occupied with others is a higher calling. If you spend your life to bless and encourage others you too will share in the blessing and encouragement.

Sometimes it is a sacrifice to make a determined decision to give of yourself to others rather than to receive. It is a selfless sacrifice that brings joy to My heart. For in giving, the love that I have given you is passed on. As that love touches hearts and invades lives so everyone rejoices. Learn to appropriate My gift of love.

24th February

PARENTHOOD

My Child,

The birth of a child brings great joy - the birth of a child into My kingdom brings even greater joy, for all the angels of heaven rejoice. Through the joys of that parent-child relationship you can catch a glimpse of the relationship that I long to have with you.

As you enter into the joy of parenthood, so you will be able to understand more of My Father heart. As you delight in your children and are thrilled at the gifts they bring you, so you will sense something of My delight to receive all the offerings of your heart. However imperfect they may be, to Me they are beautiful, special and bring Me great joy.

Most of all to hear you say
'I love you'
touches My heart deeply.

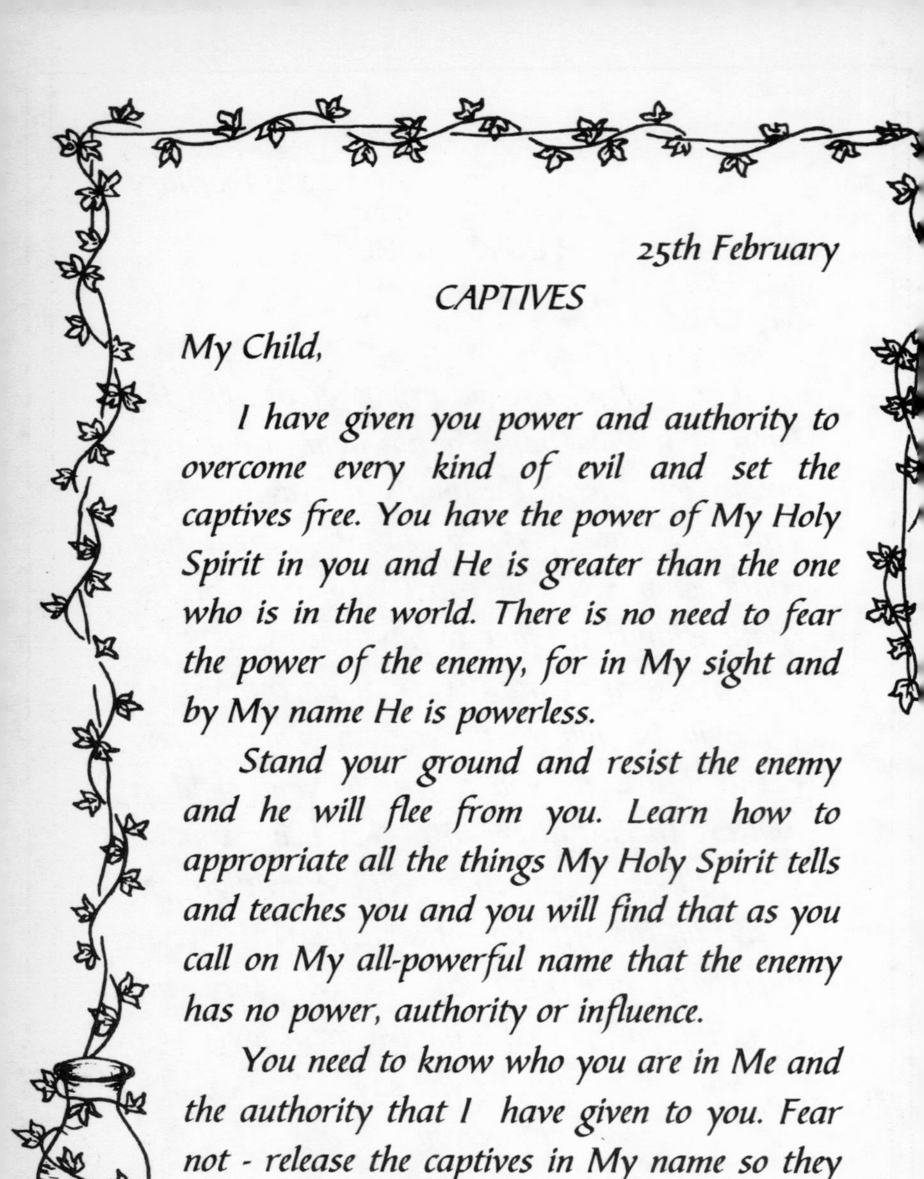

25th February

CAPTIVES

My Child,

I have given you power and authority to overcome every kind of evil and set the captives free. You have the power of My Holy Spirit in you and He is greater than the one who is in the world. There is no need to fear the power of the enemy, for in My sight and by My name He is powerless.

Stand your ground and resist the enemy and he will flee from you. Learn how to appropriate all the things My Holy Spirit tells and teaches you and you will find that as you call on My all-powerful name that the enemy has no power, authority or influence.

You need to know who you are in Me and the authority that I have given to you. Fear not - release the captives in My name so they can go and set others free.

26th February

LAUNCH OUT

My Child,

Don't be afraid to make a mistake, for that fear could stop you from being a blessing to someone. If you speak out what you think is right, even if it is wrong, I can so easily cover that for you. Sometimes you have to be prepared to take a risk, even to be misunderstood or misrepresented, but as you launch out so I will help you and teach you. As you become more concerned about obeying Me rather than what other people think of you, so you will become bolder and have more courage.

It is better that you speak out and make a mistake than not to speak out at all. It is not for you to judge the words that come to you, but to speak them out so that others may hear and respond.

27th February

FILLED AFRESH

My Child,

Each new day you need to be filled afresh with My Holy Spirit. It is so easy to run dry without realising it and then try to live out of that emptiness, which is foolishness.

When My Holy Spirit flows through you it will be like oil making things flow smoothly and freely. If you do not ask each day to be refilled you may not be aware of how dry you have become. As you give out to others, so you can be renewed and refreshed by My Spirit and topped up ready for the next assignment.

So do not neglect to come to Me and ask to be filled afresh for I am longing to pour out My Spirit on you. Then you will receive power to live for Me as you should and to be My witness.

Without Me you can do nothing for it is
not by might, nor power,
but by My Spirit.

28th February

OVERSTRETCHED

My Child,

Sometimes when there is so much to be done, it is so easy to take on more than you are able. At times like this you need to take stock of life and see how things can be different. However busy life is, it is important to seek Me for My priorities. If you continually take on too much then it will have an adverse affect on you.

It is so important that you learn to pace yourself so that you can do all that you know I have called you to do. Nothing else is important, only that which you know to be My will.

So know My peace and be free from all the pressure that says 'ought' to do this or that. For My desire for you is not to be overstretched but enabled to do My will and see the blessing that brings.

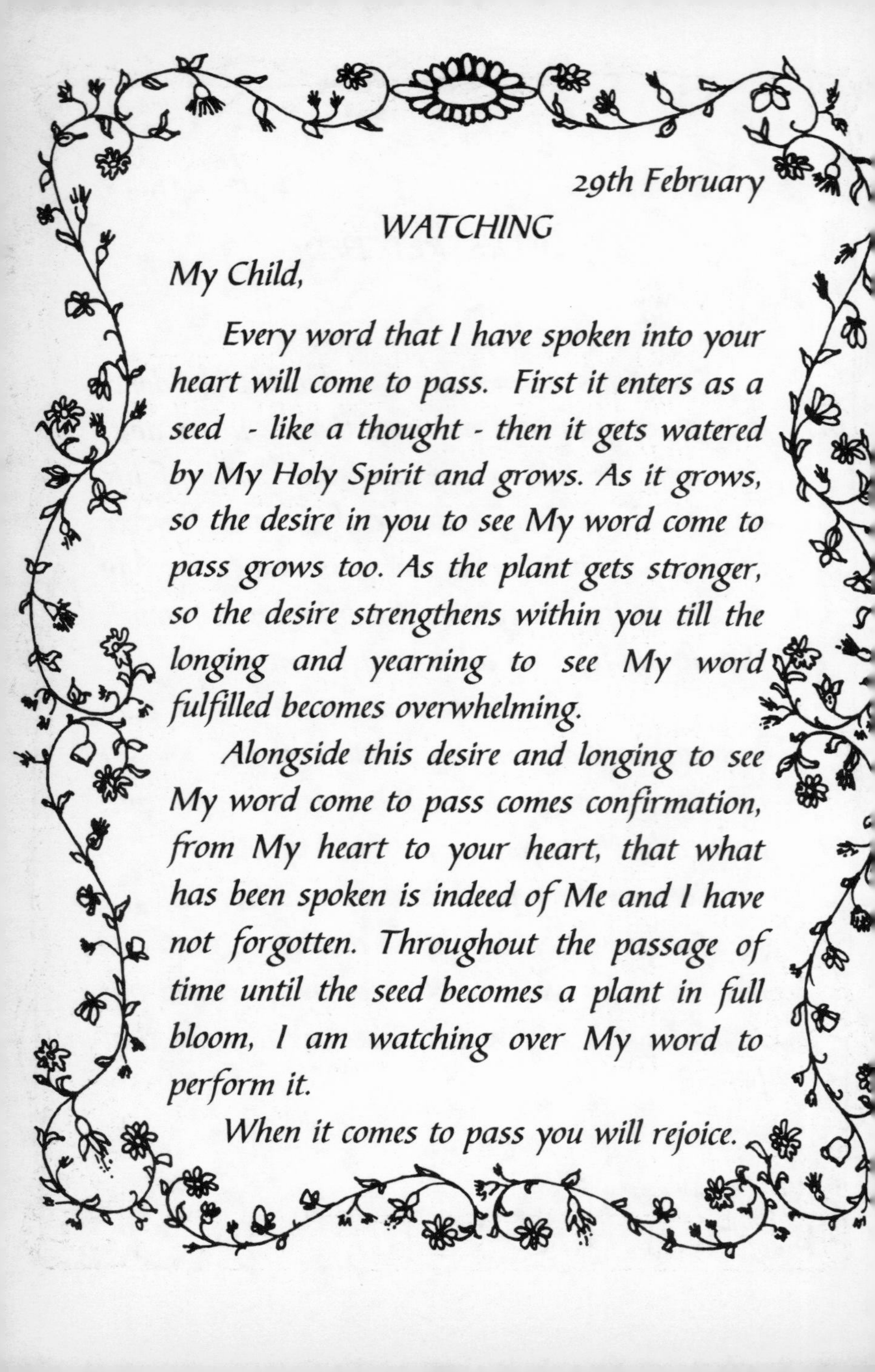

29th February

WATCHING

My Child,

Every word that I have spoken into your heart will come to pass. First it enters as a seed - like a thought - then it gets watered by My Holy Spirit and grows. As it grows, so the desire in you to see My word come to pass grows too. As the plant gets stronger, so the desire strengthens within you till the longing and yearning to see My word fulfilled becomes overwhelming.

Alongside this desire and longing to see My word come to pass comes confirmation, from My heart to your heart, that what has been spoken is indeed of Me and I have not forgotten. Throughout the passage of time until the seed becomes a plant in full bloom, I am watching over My word to perform it.

When it comes to pass you will rejoice.

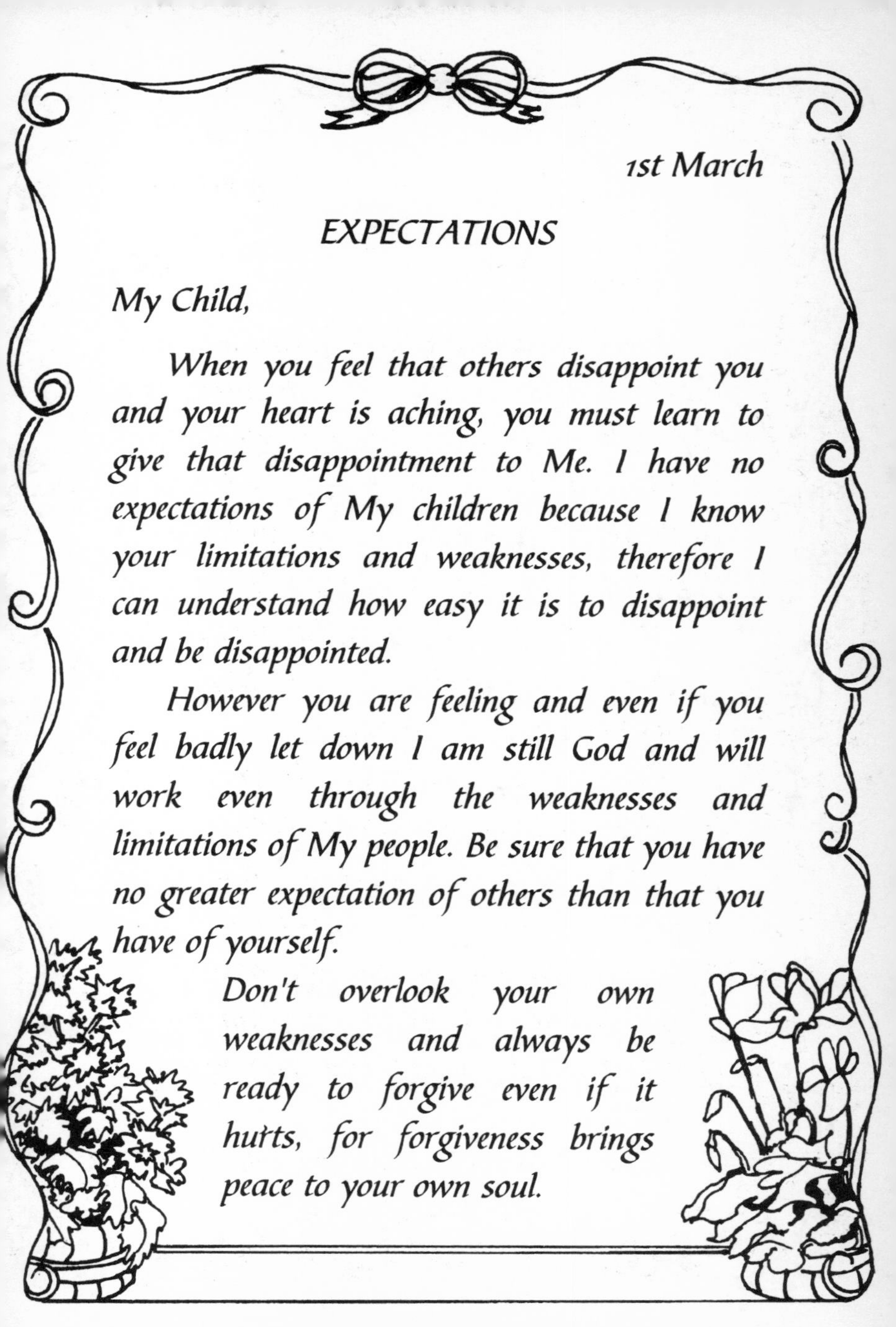

1st March

EXPECTATIONS

My Child,

When you feel that others disappoint you and your heart is aching, you must learn to give that disappointment to Me. I have no expectations of My children because I know your limitations and weaknesses, therefore I can understand how easy it is to disappoint and be disappointed.

However you are feeling and even if you feel badly let down I am still God and will work even through the weaknesses and limitations of My people. Be sure that you have no greater expectation of others than that you have of yourself.

Don't overlook your own weaknesses and always be ready to forgive even if it hurts, for forgiveness brings peace to your own soul.

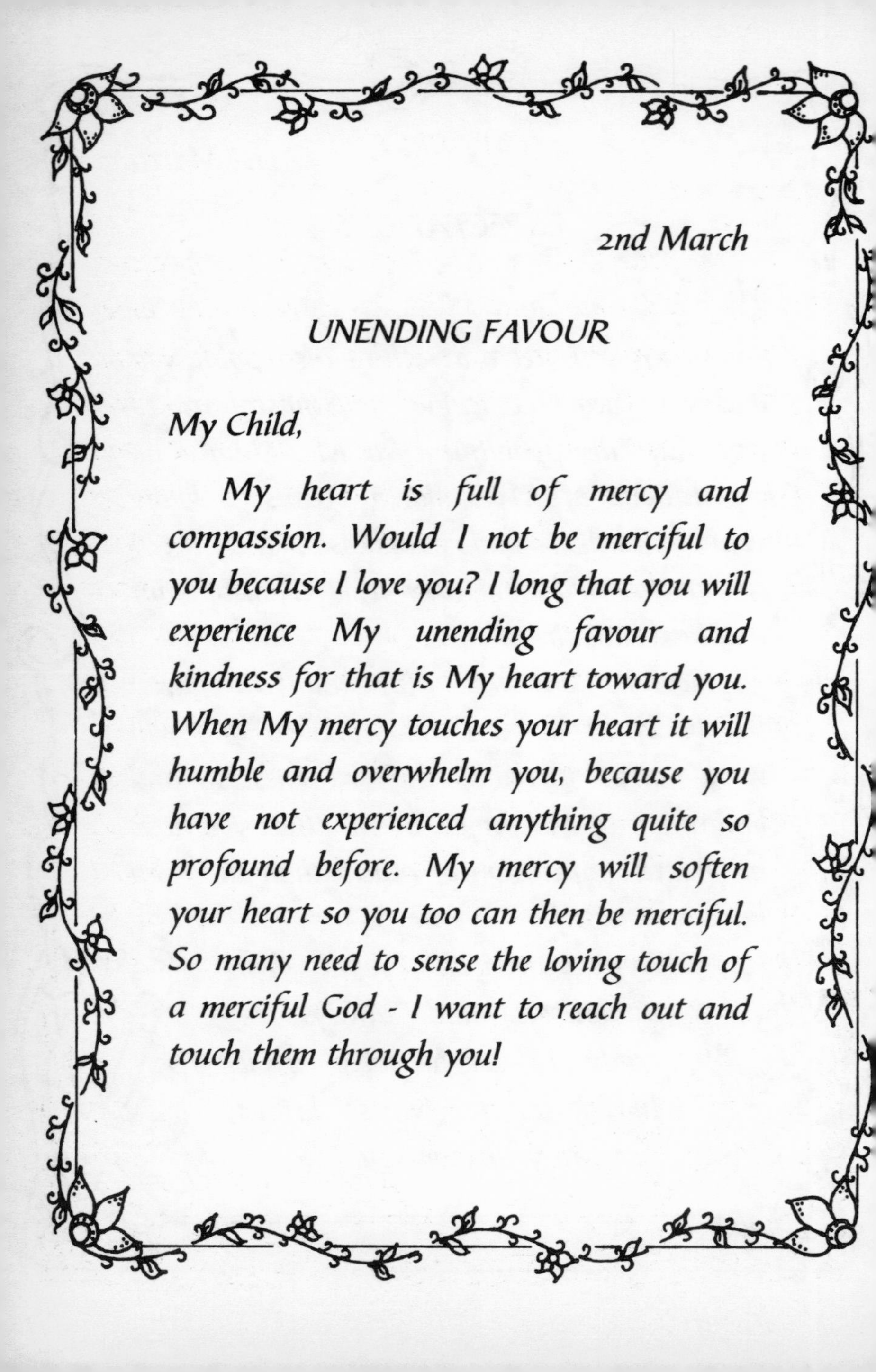

2nd March

UNENDING FAVOUR

My Child,

My heart is full of mercy and compassion. Would I not be merciful to you because I love you? I long that you will experience My unending favour and kindness for that is My heart toward you. When My mercy touches your heart it will humble and overwhelm you, because you have not experienced anything quite so profound before. My mercy will soften your heart so you too can then be merciful. So many need to sense the loving touch of a merciful God - I want to reach out and touch them through you!

3rd March

MY REST

My Child,

You need to know My rest. For in My presence is rest. It's that quiet place of peace in the inner depths of your being, even when the world around you is in turmoil. As you consciously seek My presence, you will discover more of that peace and rest. Nothing is more important for you than to discover My rest. For as you find that place of rest, so you will be able to act out of that place of peace and rest and not out of an anxious heart. As you learn what it means to 'be still' before Me you will be able to do much more in My supernatural power. The stillness and rest of My presence is the very source of power. As you are revived and refreshed, so you will not struggle and strive, for My Spirit will flow through you automatically and you will be amazed at how effortless life can really be. This is the secret of that place of rest in My presence.

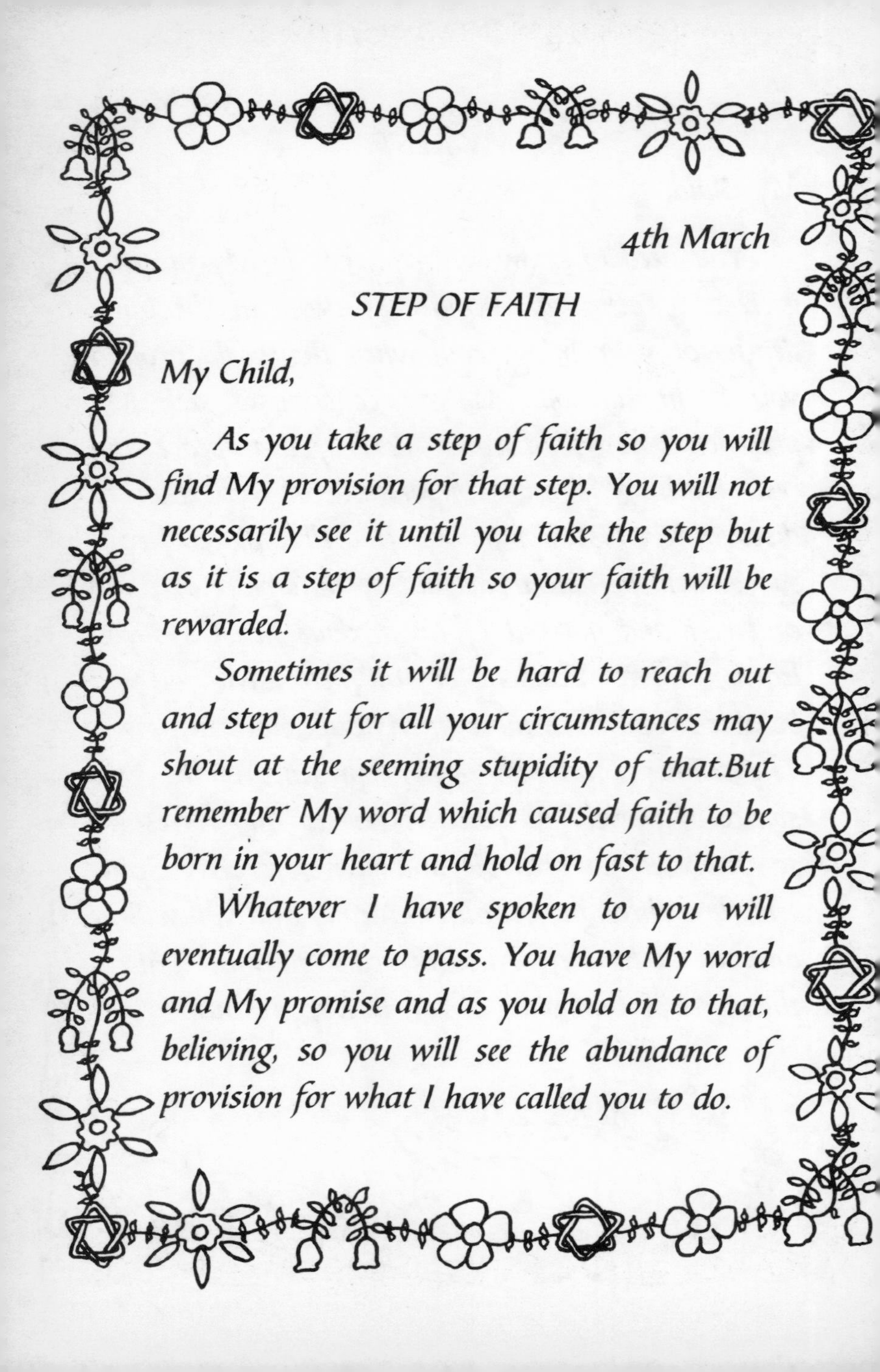

4th March

STEP OF FAITH

My Child,

As you take a step of faith so you will find My provision for that step. You will not necessarily see it until you take the step but as it is a step of faith so your faith will be rewarded.

Sometimes it will be hard to reach out and step out for all your circumstances may shout at the seeming stupidity of that.But remember My word which caused faith to be born in your heart and hold on fast to that.

Whatever I have spoken to you will eventually come to pass. You have My word and My promise and as you hold on to that, believing, so you will see the abundance of provision for what I have called you to do.

5th March

IDENTIFICATION

My Child,

Know My peace - all is well - despite your own circumstances you can know My peace. Do not let your heart be troubled for I see all those things that disquiet and disturb you. So often those very same things that you grieve over are causing Me pain too. You are just sharing My heart and entering into the realm of identifying with Me. Allow Me to take that yoke of pain from you and give you My peace - the peace of My presence. No burden is too big for Me.

Nothing is impossible and everything is redeemable in My Kingdom. Receive My peace - I am able to give My peace to you.

6th March

LEARN MY WAYS

My Child,

Everything that happens to you and every experience you pass through can be a learning process for you to learn more of My ways. It is an opportunity for you to act with integrity and to understand things that you haven't seen before. It also is an opportunity for you to learn to respond in love and not to react in an adverse way.

So when difficulties arise ask for My eyes to see that which is unseen and what you need to learn through that difficult situation. As you receive My insight so you will know My power to act according to My ways.

7th March

HOMECOMING

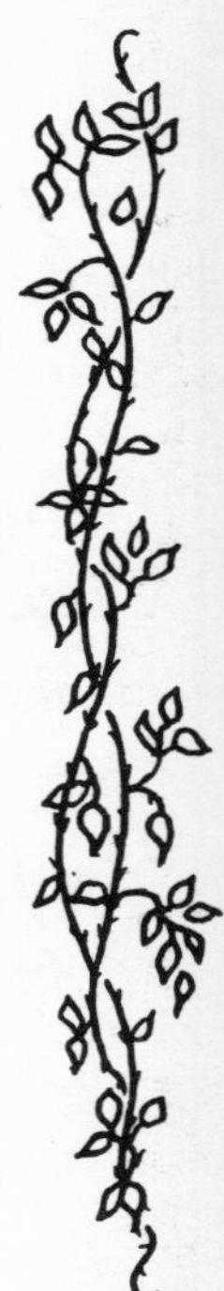

My Child,

Just as you thrill and rejoice at the homecoming of loved ones so the day will come when I rejoice at your homecoming. In that day there will be great joy and celebration for I will rejoice over you 'My Bride'.

As you plan and prepare to make everything ready for that day of joyful re-union, so I am preparing a place for you. In My Father's house are many mansions. You will be amazed and overawed at how beautiful it will be and the celebration will be the greatest celebration you have ever known.

This is your hope as you wait expectantly for that day when we shall meet face to face.

8th March

FRUIT

My Child,

When I speak a personal word to your heart it is like a seed which I have sown in you. Hold on to that word and do not doubt, for the enemy would seek to come and steal that seed so that it does not take root.

When I speak a personal word to your heart you will have that witness within that it is Me- for My sheep hear My voice. However, not everyone will have that witness so don't let that surprise you or shake your confidence that I have spoken. I will put those around you who do recognise My voice and they will be able to encourage you when you need that encouragement.

As My word comes to pass so all will see the fruit appear from the tiny seed.

9th March

CRISIS OF CONSCIENCE

My Child,

When you have a crisis of conscience and are in a dilemma remember that ultimately you are answerable to Me. Whilst you should be submissive to those in authority over you, there may be times when you are placed in such a position that you have to act according to your conscience and use your integrity. This will prove to be one of the most difficult things that you have to do.

Remember that if you keep your conscience clear you will easily be able to follow Me and submit to Me. You will know what you should do, even if it is a difficult decision. My peace in your heart will be the guide to let you know that you have done the right thing. If you aim to live to please Me, then I will help you through every crisis of conscience.

10th March

INTEGRITY

My Child,

If you walk in integrity and live only to please Me then you can trust Me to work out the consequences of your actions. If you honour Me then I will honour you and your righteousness will shine through.

So long as you make right and wise choices you can be sure that I will not only help you but will also protect you. If you are prepared to humble yourself, then others will humble themselves before you.

Sometimes it is not easy to follow Me and walk in integrity, living what you believe but as you do so you will discover the joy and peace of living for Me.

11th March

MEMORY RECALL

My Child,

Be aware of the prompting of My Holy Spirit to bring to your remembrance those things which may lie forgotten. Because I know you intimately I am able to speak straight into your heart and you will know it is Me reminding you of something. Everything in your memory is known to Me and I am able to bring about memory recall when necessary.

Those memories which lie hidden in the unconscious and are forgotten are able to be resurrected. I will be able to help you deal with the consequences of any memory which comes to light so that you will be blessed and encouraged by it.

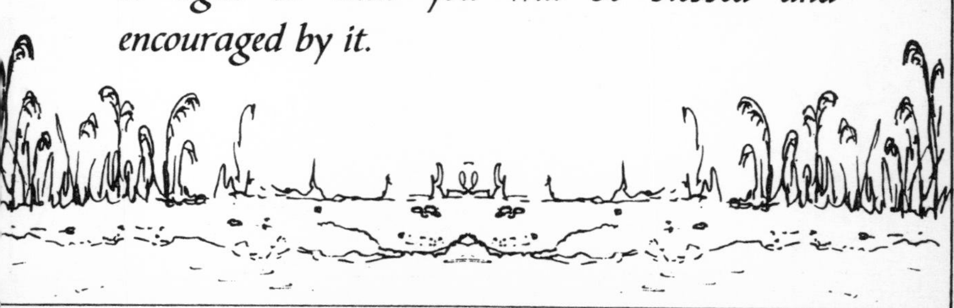

12th March

SURRENDER

My Child,

It is never easy to surrender as it involves the will and means dying to the flesh and all its desires. Remember Gethsemane! There it was necessary to submit to the Father and say 'Not My will but Yours be done'. Those words please the Father's heart more than any other words, for My will and ways are perfect. Surrender to My will brings peace and joy once the submission has taken place and the pain barrier crossed. That pain of dying to self brings joy unspeakable. It brings about resurrection life and a new way of living. Don't be afraid to surrender to My will for I will bring about much blessing for you if you submit and obey ME.

13th March

ETERNAL REWARD

My Child,

Living in a materialistic world as you do, it is so easy to be drawn into that way of life. It is a contented heart that can look and see what others have and not covet for themselves. Only as you find peace and contentment in Me will your heart be truly satisfied. Then you will not be tempted by the things of this world which will pass away and only last for a moment. Laying up treasure in heaven demands dying to this world's pleasure. If you can do this you will one day reap an eternal reward.

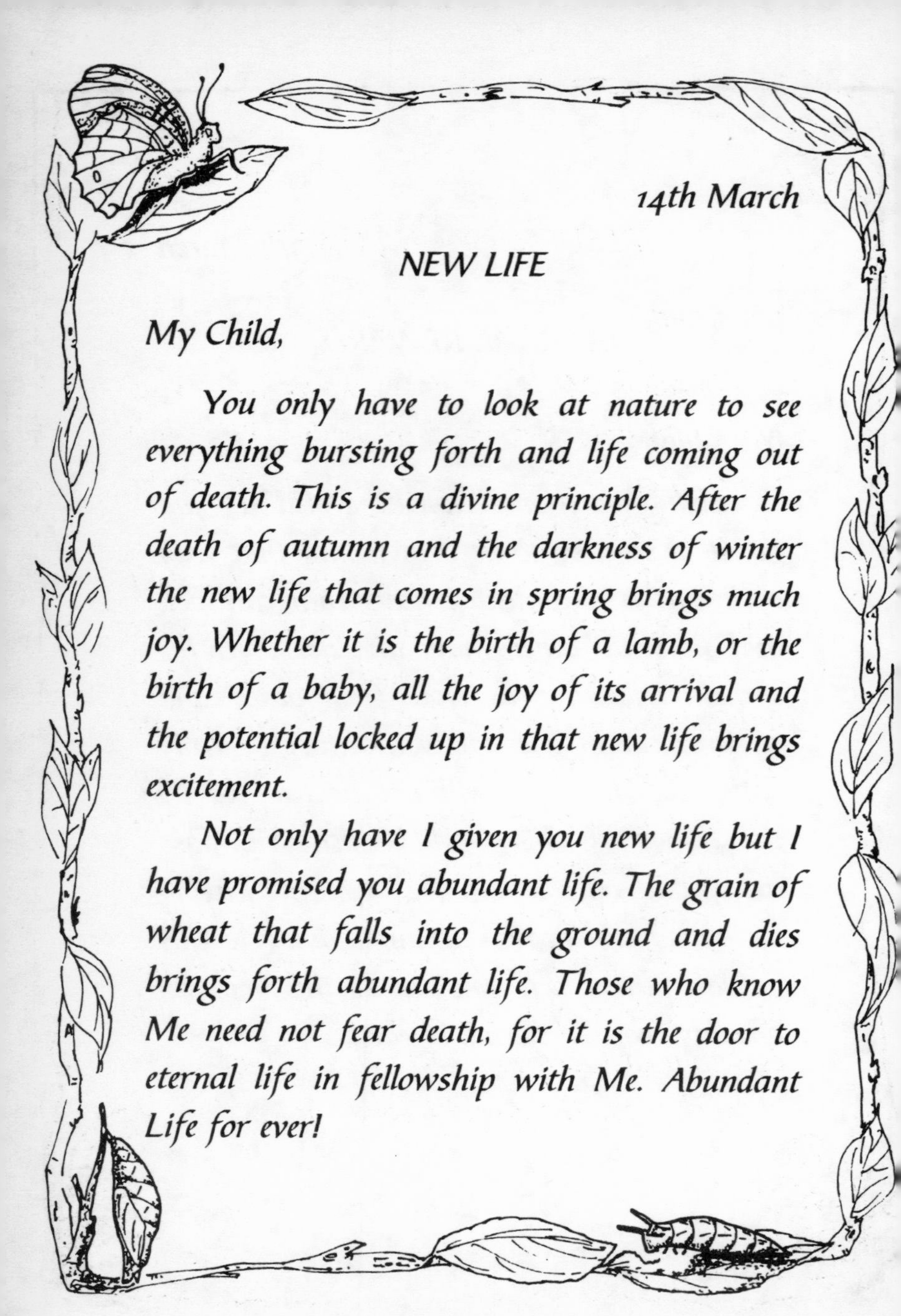

14th March

NEW LIFE

My Child,

You only have to look at nature to see everything bursting forth and life coming out of death. This is a divine principle. After the death of autumn and the darkness of winter the new life that comes in spring brings much joy. Whether it is the birth of a lamb, or the birth of a baby, all the joy of its arrival and the potential locked up in that new life brings excitement.

Not only have I given you new life but I have promised you abundant life. The grain of wheat that falls into the ground and dies brings forth abundant life. Those who know Me need not fear death, for it is the door to eternal life in fellowship with Me. Abundant Life for ever!

15th March

RESURRECTION POWER

My Child,

Through My resurrection power what was once a tragedy became a triumph. The same resurrection power is alive in you! It is the power of My Holy Spirit.

As My resurrection power flows through you so you will be able to triumph even over seeming tragedy. Things which look bleak and impossible will become possible by My power and strength. You will know that of yourself you can do nothing and are not able - but nothing is impossible for Me.

Because I have triumphed over sin, satan and death you too can know victory in your life. Whatever you encounter look at it with eyes that are open to see My resurrection power at work - it's the greatest power on earth.

16th March

HE IS RISEN

My Child,

It was the women who came early in the morning, weeping and grieving to minister to their Lord after His death. Their sorrow was turned to joy when the angels announced 'He is risen'.

So it is today, if you seek Me early, you will find Me. If you come to Me with heavy heart I can turn your sorrow into joy. Because I am alive today you too can come and talk with Me and commune with Me. As you long for fellowship with Me - I long to reveal Myself to you. As you long to get to know Me - I long to reveal My heart to you.

One day too you will see Me 'face to face' as the women at the tomb and you will be united with your Risen Lord for ever.

17th March

I HEAR

My Child,

I hear the cries and prayers of your heart. Every unspoken thought is heard by Me. Everything that you aspire to and want to do for My Kingdom I am aware of. I know how often and earnestly you have sought Me - even when it seems that there is no answer.

When you come to Me and pour out your heart to Me it delights My Father heart. I see, I know and I care. Yes, I long to answer your prayers in accordance with My will. I hear every word, every prayer, every cry.

Sometimes it seems that nothing is happening but at those times I am orchestrating My plans for your good. Just because you don't see the evidence doesn't mean I am not hearing you. It may take weeks or months or years but as your desires become My desires I will hear your prayers and give you the desires of your heart.

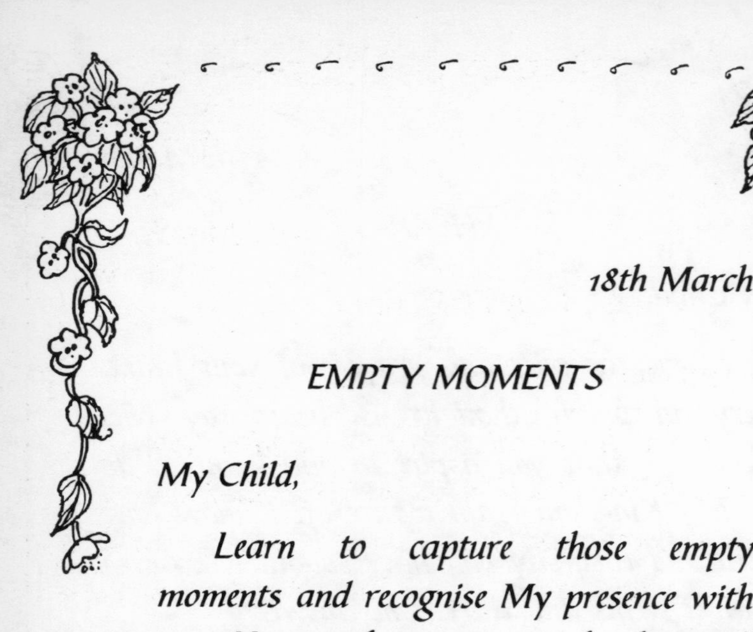

18th March

EMPTY MOMENTS

My Child,

Learn to capture those empty moments and recognise My presence with you. However busy you may be there will always be those times when your mind is not focused on anything in particular and you can then focus on Me. Being aware that I am with you will help you to find peace and direction in those busy moments. As you learn to practise My presence, so you will be able to cope with all the demands that each new day brings and not feel weary at the end of the day.

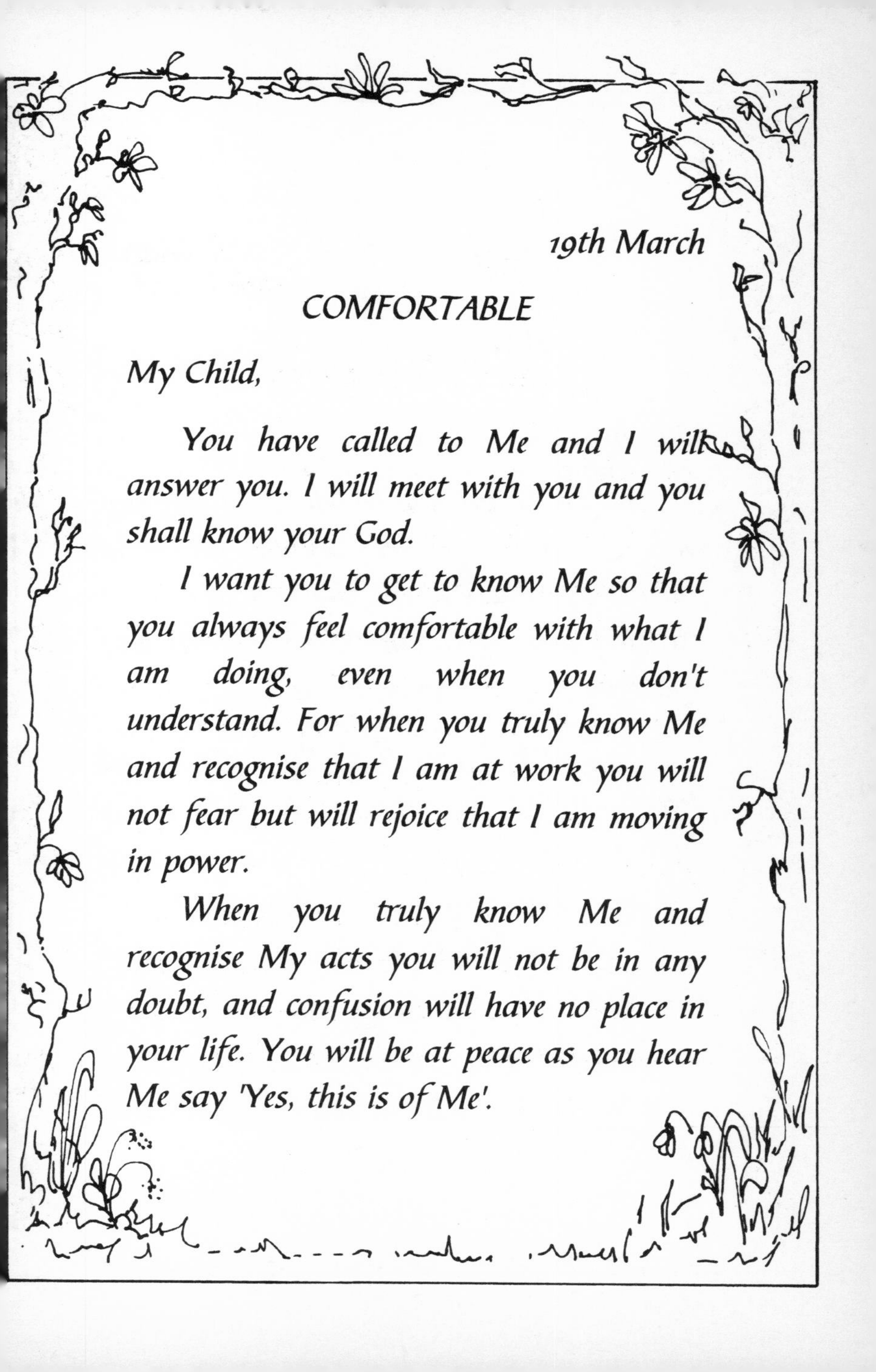

19th March

COMFORTABLE

My Child,

You have called to Me and I will answer you. I will meet with you and you shall know your God.

I want you to get to know Me so that you always feel comfortable with what I am doing, even when you don't understand. For when you truly know Me and recognise that I am at work you will not fear but will rejoice that I am moving in power.

When you truly know Me and recognise My acts you will not be in any doubt, and confusion will have no place in your life. You will be at peace as you hear Me say 'Yes, this is of Me'.

20th March

EVERLASTING LOVE

My Child,

You are so precious to Me and I love you with an everlasting love. My love will never fade away. There is nothing you can do to earn My love for I desire to shower My love upon you because My nature is love.

My love is higher than the heavens and deeper than the sea - unfathomable, inexhaustible and unending. It never changes and is not dependent on who you are or what you do but is always the same and always will be.

Overwhelming love, overflowing love from My Father heart to you - oh how I love you!

21st March

GENTLENESS

My Child,

Let your gentleness be shown to all. Gentleness is the fruit of the Holy Spirit in your life. When you speak and act with gentleness it will draw others to you for it is a rare quality and a very beautiful one.

Learn to respond in gentleness in all situations for this is the mark that My Holy Spirit dwells in you. It may not be a natural quality in your life but by My Holy Spirit's power it can be a supernatural one. As I deal gently with you in love so I want you to deal with others in the same way.

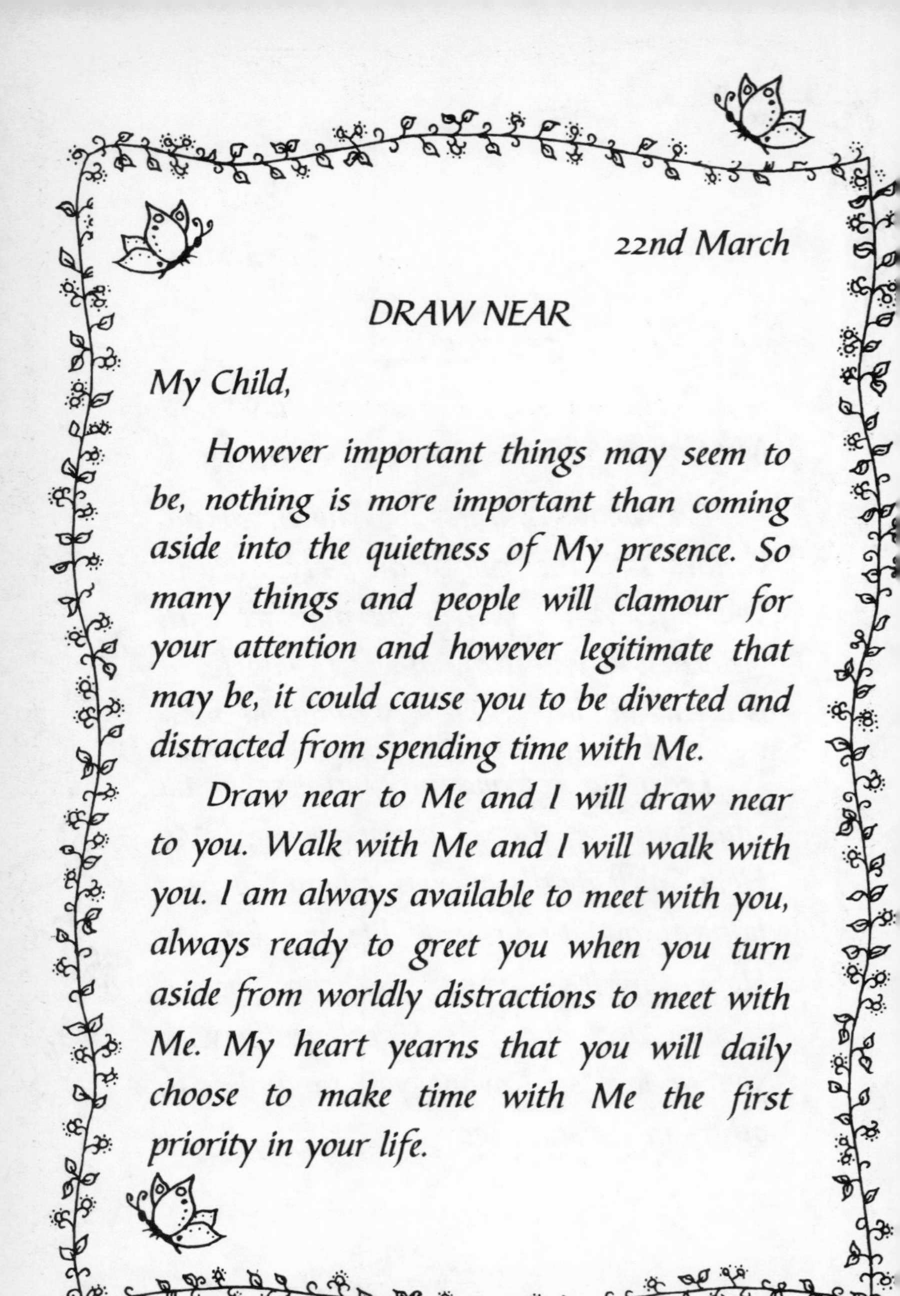

22nd March

DRAW NEAR

My Child,

However important things may seem to be, nothing is more important than coming aside into the quietness of My presence. So many things and people will clamour for your attention and however legitimate that may be, it could cause you to be diverted and distracted from spending time with Me.

Draw near to Me and I will draw near to you. Walk with Me and I will walk with you. I am always available to meet with you, always ready to greet you when you turn aside from worldly distractions to meet with Me. My heart yearns that you will daily choose to make time with Me the first priority in your life.

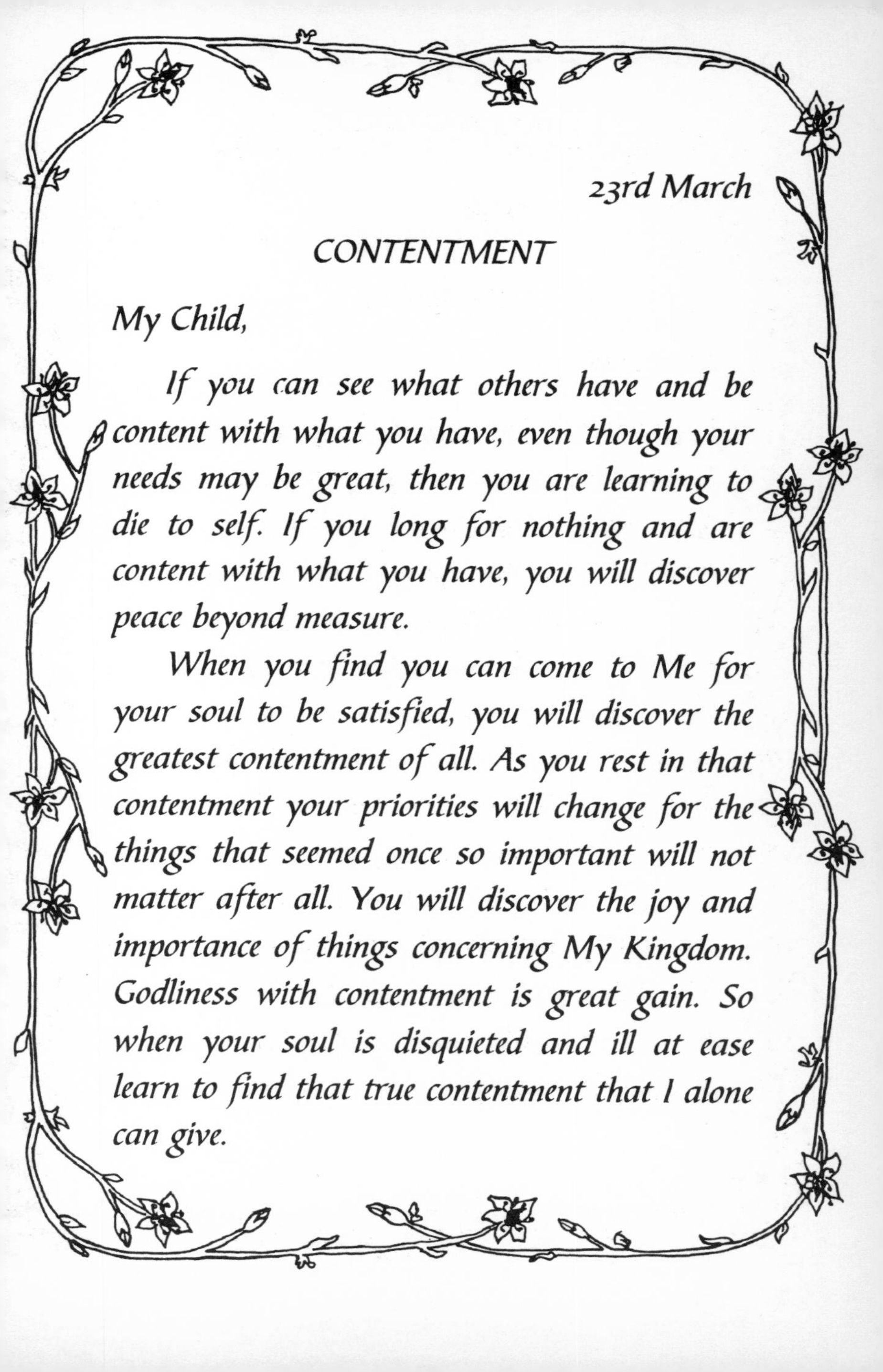

23rd March

CONTENTMENT

My Child,

If you can see what others have and be content with what you have, even though your needs may be great, then you are learning to die to self. If you long for nothing and are content with what you have, you will discover peace beyond measure.

When you find you can come to Me for your soul to be satisfied, you will discover the greatest contentment of all. As you rest in that contentment your priorities will change for the things that seemed once so important will not matter after all. You will discover the joy and importance of things concerning My Kingdom. Godliness with contentment is great gain. So when your soul is disquieted and ill at ease learn to find that true contentment that I alone can give.

24th March

'FATHER'

My Child,

I have chosen you to be My child. You have been adopted into My family. No longer are you a slave or even a servant for you have become My own dear precious child.

You have been bought with a price, even My Son's precious blood so that you could be adopted into My family. Now you possess an inheritance which is incorruptible, undefiled and which will never, ever fade away.

Since you have become My child you have all the rights and privileges of being an inheritor of the eternal Kingdom. Now you have access into My presence at any time, anywhere and the privilege not only to come into My presence but also to call Me 'Father'.

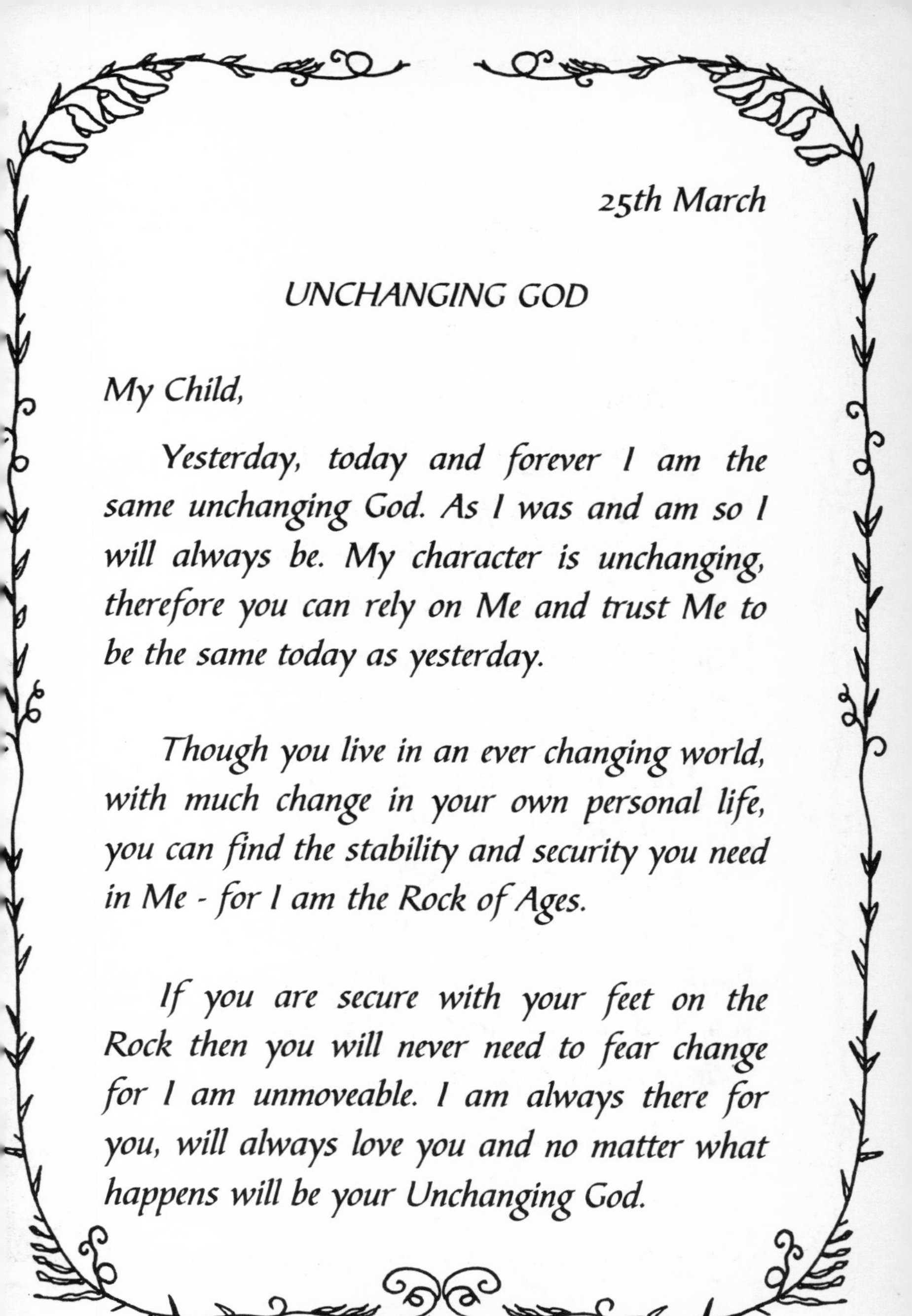

25th March

UNCHANGING GOD

My Child,

Yesterday, today and forever I am the same unchanging God. As I was and am so I will always be. My character is unchanging, therefore you can rely on Me and trust Me to be the same today as yesterday.

Though you live in an ever changing world, with much change in your own personal life, you can find the stability and security you need in Me - for I am the Rock of Ages.

If you are secure with your feet on the Rock then you will never need to fear change for I am unmoveable. I am always there for you, will always love you and no matter what happens will be your Unchanging God.

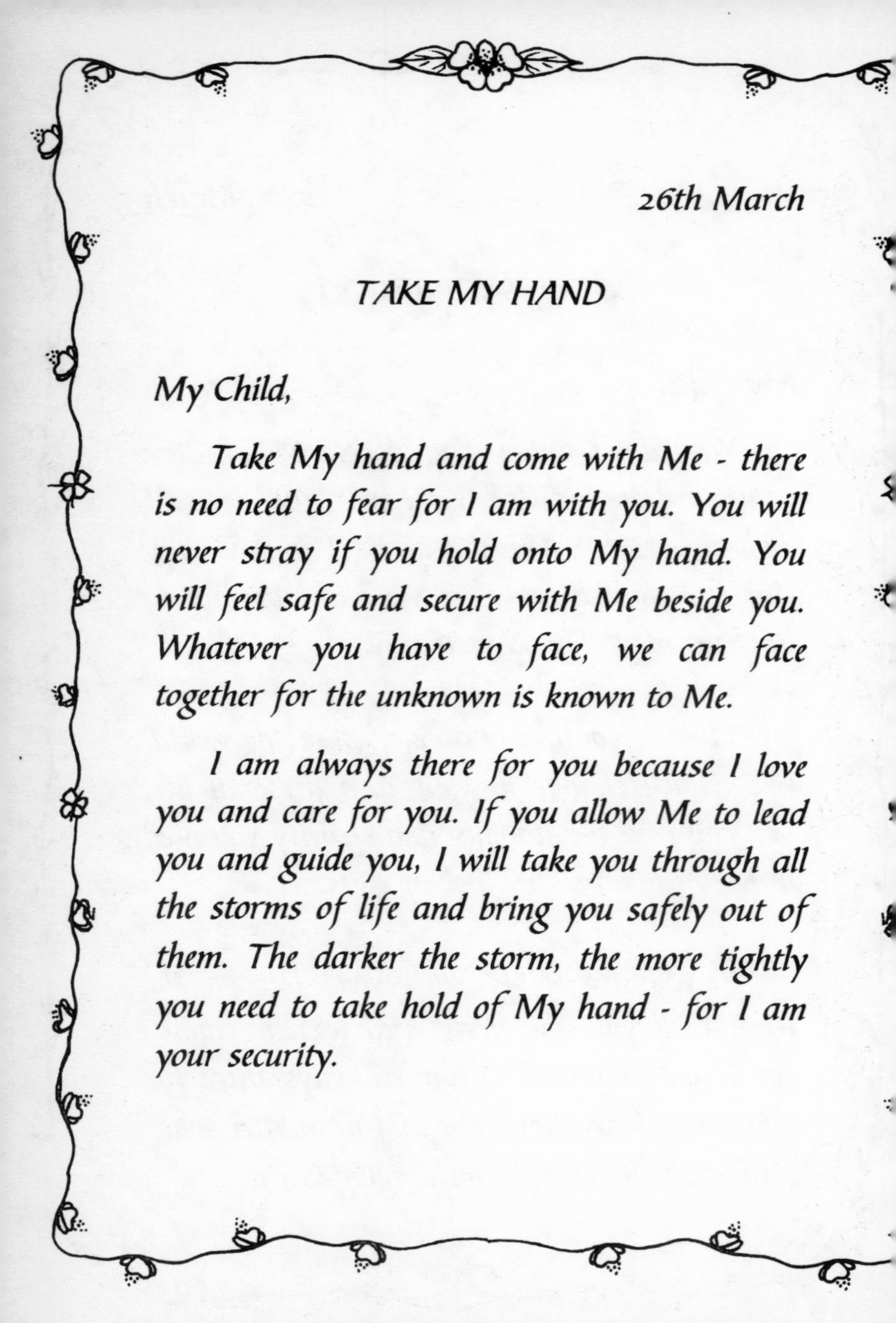

26th March

TAKE MY HAND

My Child,

Take My hand and come with Me - there is no need to fear for I am with you. You will never stray if you hold onto My hand. You will feel safe and secure with Me beside you. Whatever you have to face, we can face together for the unknown is known to Me.

I am always there for you because I love you and care for you. If you allow Me to lead you and guide you, I will take you through all the storms of life and bring you safely out of them. The darker the storm, the more tightly you need to take hold of My hand - for I am your security.

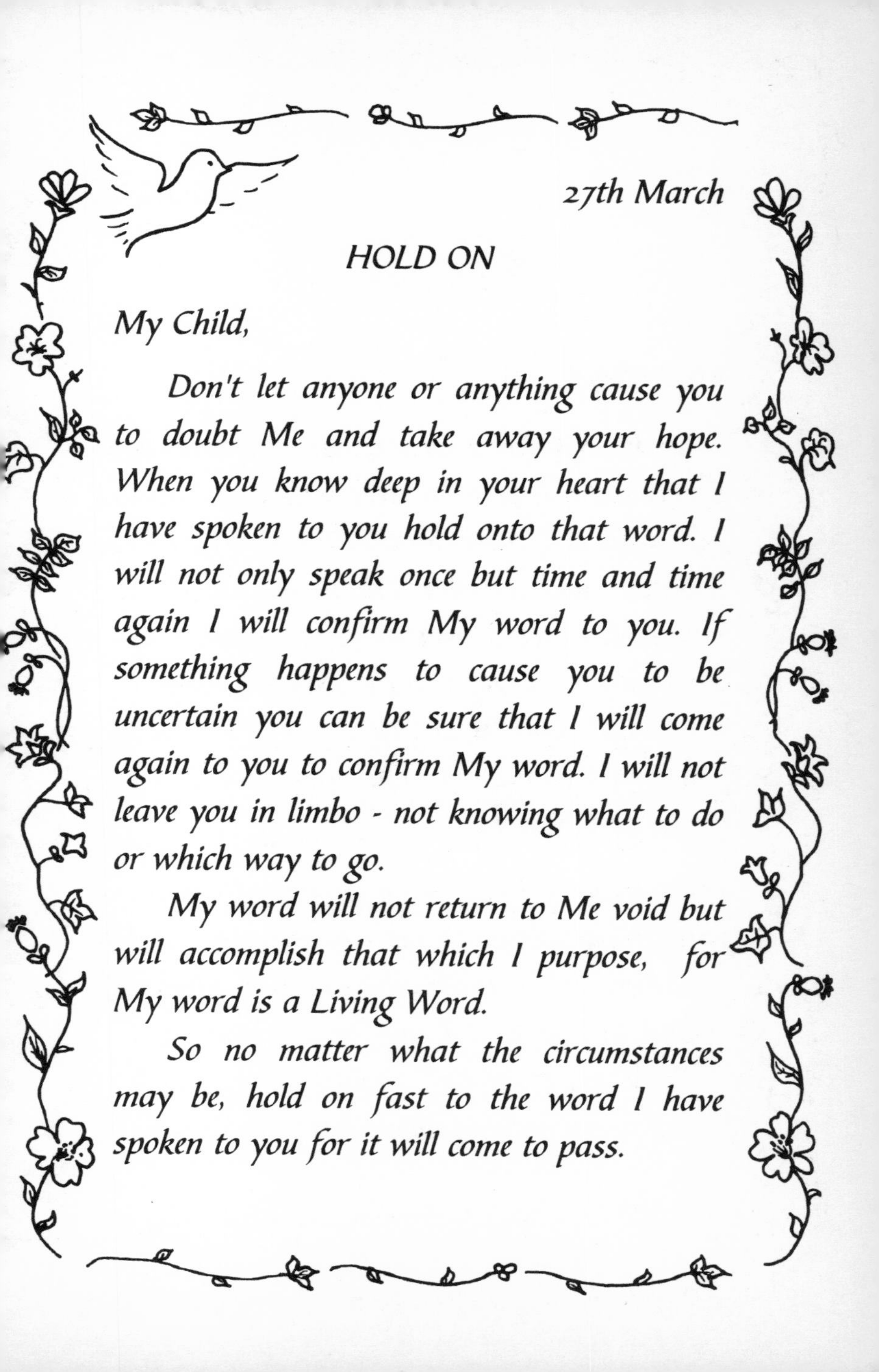

27th March

HOLD ON

My Child,

Don't let anyone or anything cause you to doubt Me and take away your hope. When you know deep in your heart that I have spoken to you hold onto that word. I will not only speak once but time and time again I will confirm My word to you. If something happens to cause you to be uncertain you can be sure that I will come again to you to confirm My word. I will not leave you in limbo - not knowing what to do or which way to go.

My word will not return to Me void but will accomplish that which I purpose, for My word is a Living Word.

So no matter what the circumstances may be, hold on fast to the word I have spoken to you for it will come to pass.

28th March

REVIVAL

My Child,

It is prayer that will usher in revival. For the longing in My heart is that revival will come to the nations. If My people will humble themselves, confess their sin and pray then I will hear from Heaven and heal their land. I am a merciful God who rejoices when men's hearts are humbled and softened so that I can do My work.

Revival must begin in you. It starts with examining your own heart and dealing with those things that hinder. Call to Me and I will answer you and show you great and mighty things which you know nothing about yet!

29th March

DISTANT

My Child,

When you feel at times that you are losing touch with Me or out of step with Me, just take time to examine your heart and see what is happening. I am always the same and never move away from you.

It may just be the busyness of life that causes you to feel distant. Search your heart to make sure that no sin has come between us. As you confess that sin, your peace and joy will once again be restored and you will once again experience the closeness you long for and have sorely missed.

However distant you may feel, or however much has come between us there is this hope and certainty - I am only a prayer away. As you call to Me and cry out to come close to Me once again so I will hear you. No longer will you be distant and far away but close to My heart.

30th March

COMING AGAIN

My Child,

Never lose sight of that hope within you that I am coming again. As I have promised so it will be. On that day every eye will see Me and every tongue confess that Jesus is Lord.

If you live with that expectancy in your heart, you will rejoice at My coming with great and exceeding joy. Your heart will thrill that the Bridegroom has come for His bride.

I am preparing a bride that is pure and holy - fit for the coming Bridegroom and King. Prepare your heart by walking in My ways and living in My truth for then you will be ready on that great and glorious day to meet Me face to face.

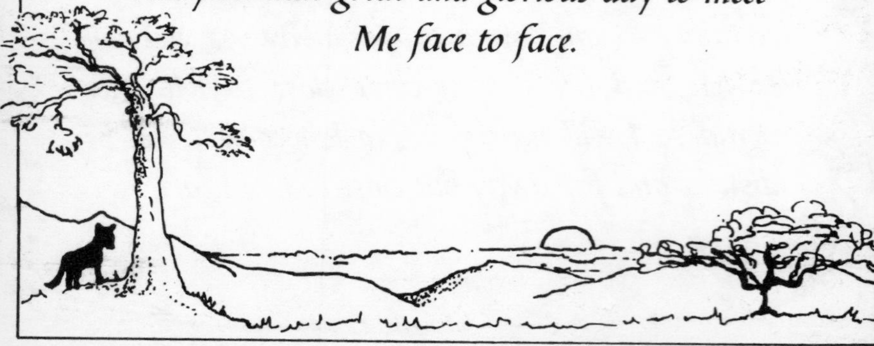

31st March

WORSHIP

My Child,

Take time to sit at My feet and worship Me for this is why you were created. Calm your heart and mind - be still in My presence so you can focus on Me and allow all other things to drop away.

As you begin to lift up your heart and voice to praise and worship Me, so you will enter into My presence and be aware that I am there, sharing precious, intimate moments with you. As you draw near to Me, so you will sense My closeness to you as you become aware of My Spirit's touch.

This is true worship of the heart -
acceptable to Me.

1st April

MY PLAN

My Child,

It is not because of what you do or who you are that I choose to use you. It's not because you are in any kind of position or authority that I give you gifts. How I work, what I do, how I use you is all dependent on Me for I am God.

I want to give to all My children whether they are struggling or coasting along. I want to bless them all - yes, I want to bless you so much - not because you deserve it but because My nature is to bless. Whether I choose you to bring about an outpouring of My Spirit is My sovereign choice alone.

So you do not have to struggle and strive for
My blessings, for I will bless you, not
because you are worthy of it but
because I love you. I will
use you because that is
My plan for you and
I delight to do so.

2nd April

MY POWER

My Child,

The enemy prowls around seeking whom he may devour but you can resist him. You do not have to yield to him and submit to his ways. As you stand against him in My name so you will find that because of Me and My greatness, he will flee.

Do not forget to use My word against the power of the enemy for My word is all-powerful and will cause him to flee from you.

You do not need to be afraid for greater is He that is in you than he that is in the world. By the Holy Spirit who lives in you the enemy can be overcome in your personal life and circumstances. Stand firm, stand your ground and be strong, for as you overcome all temptation and discover the joy of victory, you will know freedom from all guilt and condemnation and the greatness of My power.

3rd April

MY WORD

My Child,

As you take time each day to enjoy your food, do not neglect the spiritual food of My word. I want you to enjoy it even more than you do your daily food. It is important that you take time over your food so that you digest it properly - even more so over My word which is your daily bread.

If you neglect My word it will bring about starvation and poverty in your life. If you feed on My word it will be sustenance to your soul and you will be rich in the things that matter.

As you hunger for food so I am able to cause you to hunger for My word. Ask Me to create this hunger within you. Then you will find the direction, strength and encouragement that you need each day. My word is a lamp to your feet and a light to your path.

4th April

MISUNDERSTOOD

My Child,

I know how much it hurts when others misunderstand you. To be misunderstood is part of your calling to take up your cross and follow Me. I was misunderstood so I know how you feel and can enter into the pain. I will never, ever misunderstand you because I know you intimately.

If you can learn to face being misunderstood without it going deep into your soul then you can soon realise that it really doesn't matter what other people think of you. If you can be more concerned with what I think about you than what kind of impression you make on others, you will find a new freedom to be what I want you to be. It is so easy to misunderstand others so be sure that in your own heart you always give others the benefit of the doubt.

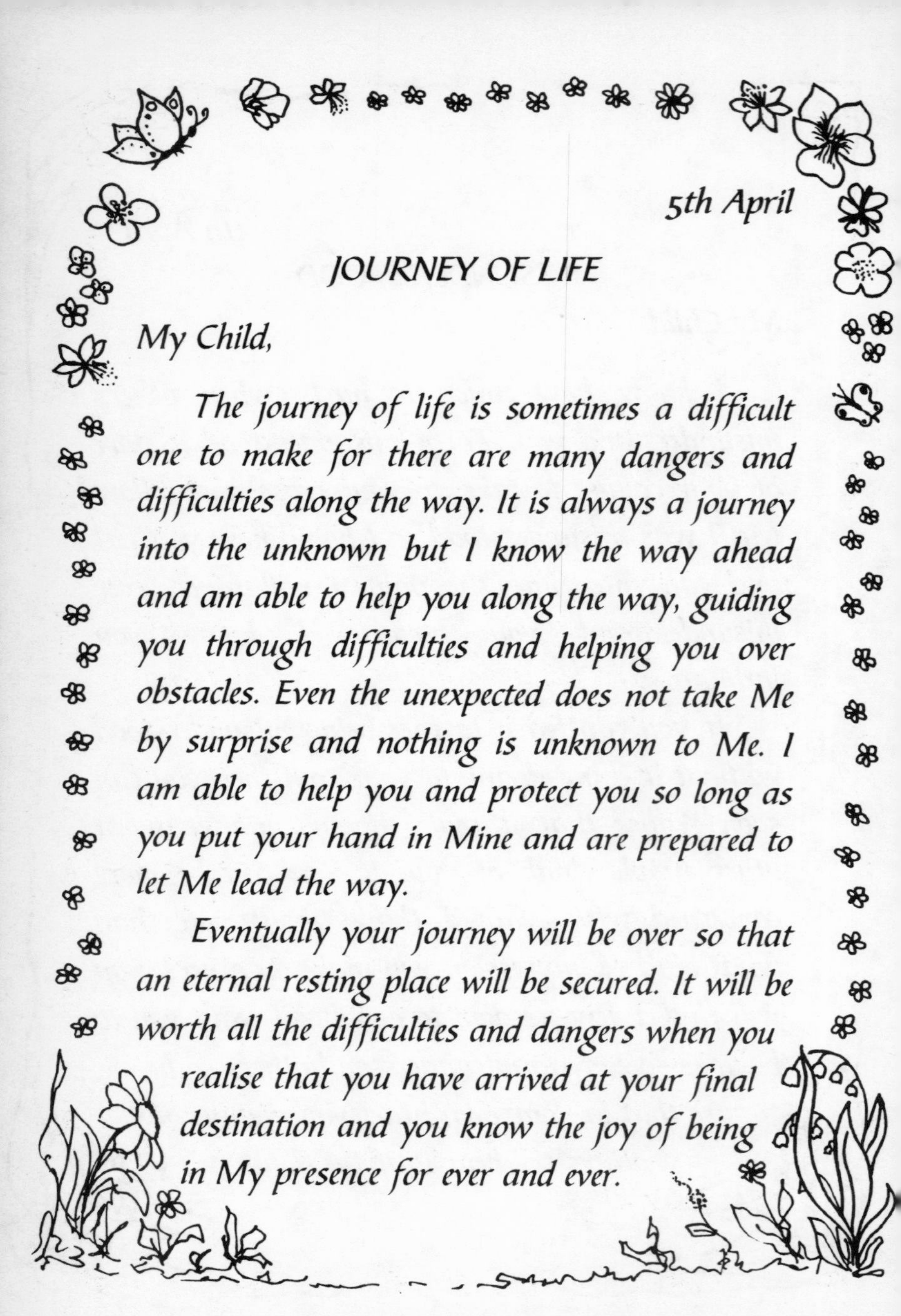

5th April

JOURNEY OF LIFE

My Child,

The journey of life is sometimes a difficult one to make for there are many dangers and difficulties along the way. It is always a journey into the unknown but I know the way ahead and am able to help you along the way, guiding you through difficulties and helping you over obstacles. Even the unexpected does not take Me by surprise and nothing is unknown to Me. I am able to help you and protect you so long as you put your hand in Mine and are prepared to let Me lead the way.

Eventually your journey will be over so that an eternal resting place will be secured. It will be worth all the difficulties and dangers when you realise that you have arrived at your final destination and you know the joy of being in My presence for ever and ever.

6th April

INNER PEACE

My Child,

In the midst of turmoil I am able to give you peace. That tranquillity of heart and mind is found only in Me whatever your circumstances are. Sometimes you can be in a place of peace and quiet where not a sound is heard - that is peace, but it is a peace that comes about because of outward circumstances. The peace that I give comes from Me direct to your heart. It is an inner peace despite all the outward circumstances. It is a peace that says all is well, you are safe and secure and gives you a sense of well-being, taking away all your fear and anxiety which would seek to undermine that peace.

My peace I give to you - it's a peace that passes understanding and is yours today if you receive it!

7th April

THE ANCHOR

My Child,

There is an anchor that is sure and steadfast - a hope which is your hope. It will never slip or break away, no matter how difficult the circumstances of life become. This will be to you a security and surety as you go through life - a stronghold even when you feel weak.

When you live in an ever-changing world as you do, an anchor that is solid and steady is like a rock. Indeed when an anchor is fastened to a rock it is unmoveable.

I am the rock and as your hope is fastened and secure on Me you will know that safety and certainty and security. As you have hope fixed on Me then you will be unmoveable in your faith.

Just be sure that your anchor is well secured for maximum security.

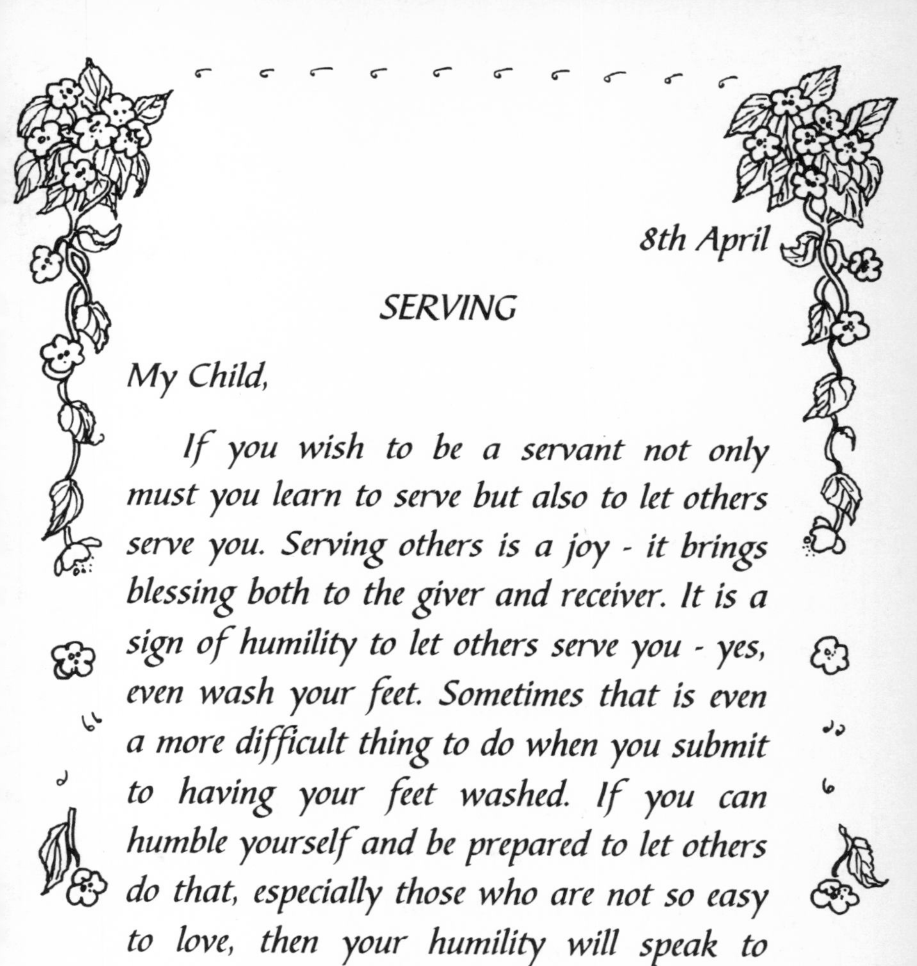

8th April

SERVING

My Child,

If you wish to be a servant not only must you learn to serve but also to let others serve you. Serving others is a joy - it brings blessing both to the giver and receiver. It is a sign of humility to let others serve you - yes, even wash your feet. Sometimes that is even a more difficult thing to do when you submit to having your feet washed. If you can humble yourself and be prepared to let others do that, especially those who are not so easy to love, then your humility will speak to others.

If you can learn to receive gracefully and let others serve you, then you will find that greater joy when your turn comes to serve others. It is a joy both to give and receive.

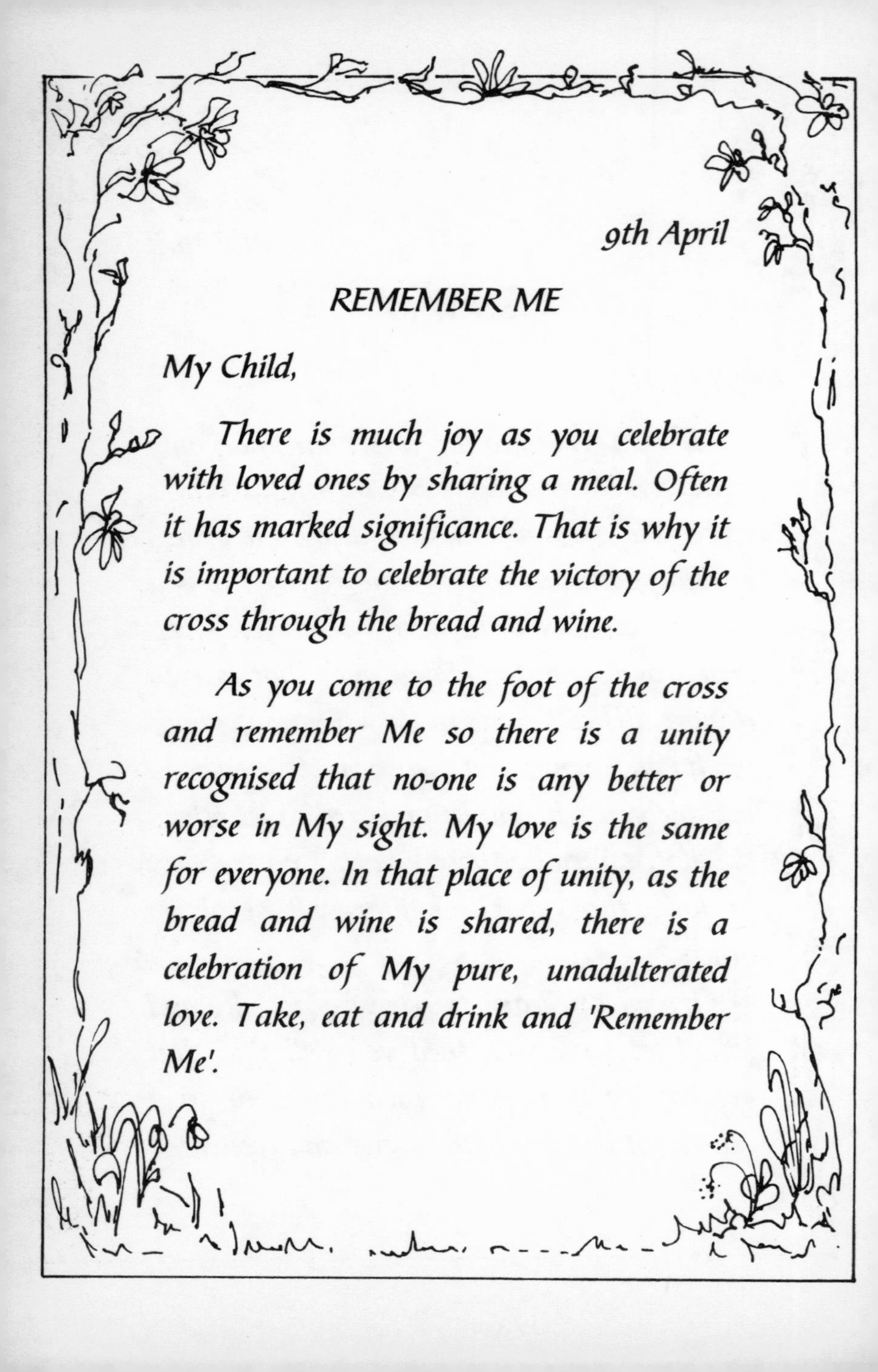

9th April

REMEMBER ME

My Child,

There is much joy as you celebrate with loved ones by sharing a meal. Often it has marked significance. That is why it is important to celebrate the victory of the cross through the bread and wine.

As you come to the foot of the cross and remember Me so there is a unity recognised that no-one is any better or worse in My sight. My love is the same for everyone. In that place of unity, as the bread and wine is shared, there is a celebration of My pure, unadulterated love. Take, eat and drink and 'Remember Me'.

10th April

HEART'S DESIRES

My Child,

I know your heart and your heart's desires and want you to know that nothing is hid from Me. I see those times when your heart is longing for Me and you feel such frustration deep inside, because you cannot meet with Me, for all the legitimate pressures on your time. I know that there are times when you long for that peace and space to be with Me and yet you are not able. I want you to know that it is Me who puts that desire in your heart to seek Me and long for Me, hungry and thirsty for communion with Me. I put that desire there because I long for you to come to Me. Follow your heart's desire and come...for I am waiting.

11th April

KEEP CLOSE

My Child,

Keep close to Me - don't wander off and be distracted by things which seem so tempting and inviting and yet are full of emptiness. No matter where you are, what you are doing, keep close to Me. Walk closely beside Me so we can enjoy each other's company and I can encourage you along the way. Keep close to My heart so that you can feel My heartbeat and know that all is well. As you keep close to Me, so I will share My heart with you - when you are distant that is not possible. Know that I am always with you every step of the way, every moment of the day - so keep close to Me.

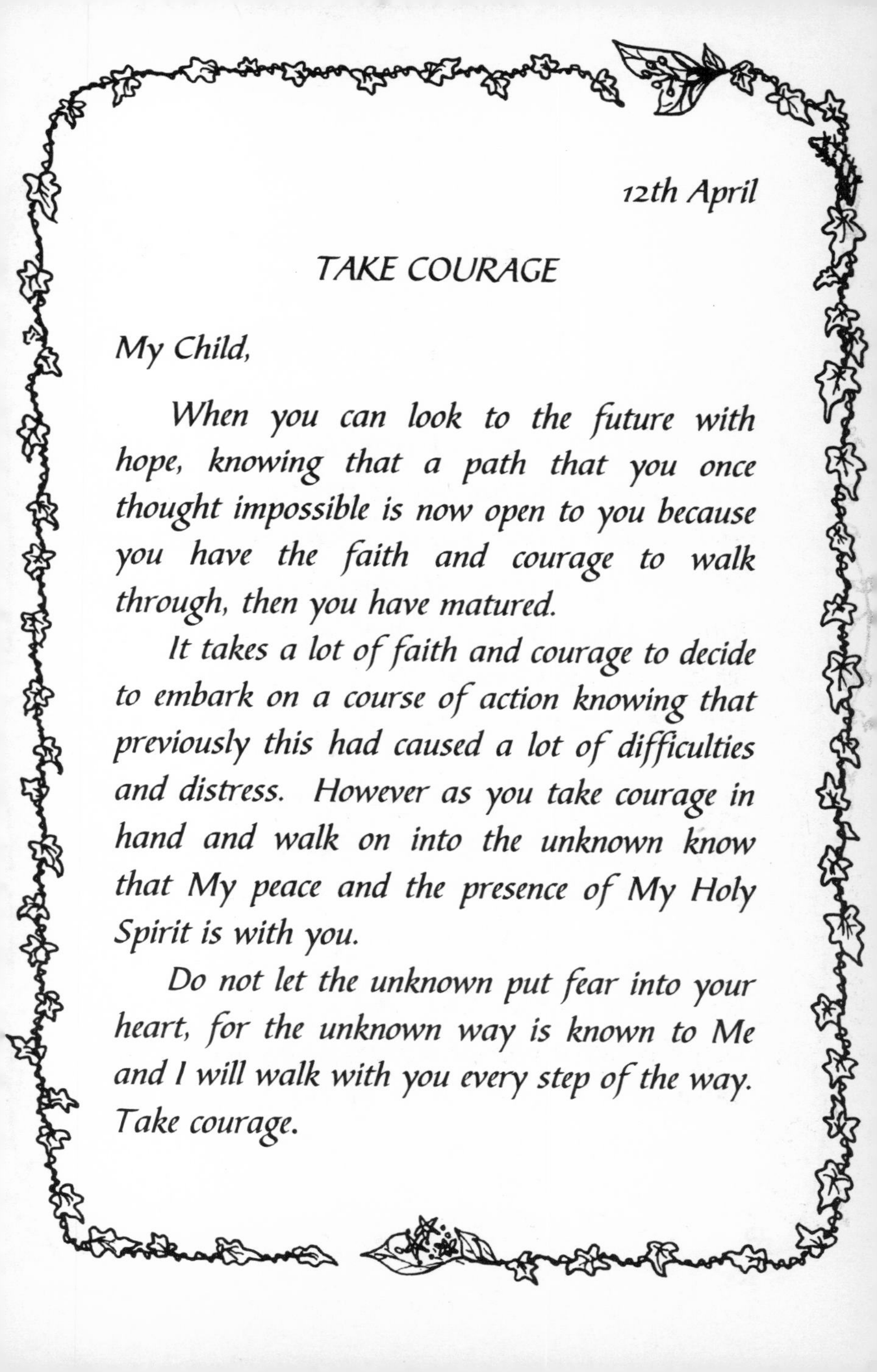

12th April

TAKE COURAGE

My Child,

When you can look to the future with hope, knowing that a path that you once thought impossible is now open to you because you have the faith and courage to walk through, then you have matured.

It takes a lot of faith and courage to decide to embark on a course of action knowing that previously this had caused a lot of difficulties and distress. However as you take courage in hand and walk on into the unknown know that My peace and the presence of My Holy Spirit is with you.

Do not let the unknown put fear into your heart, for the unknown way is known to Me and I will walk with you every step of the way. Take courage.

13th April

UNTO ME

My Child,

Today is a day of opportunity. I will give you many opportunities to serve others today. A kindly deed here and a caring word there are all part of serving. Sometimes just a listening ear to share a heavy load, a warm hug or embrace to say 'I care'.

Little things that are unnoticed by the world and yet very precious to Me are all part of serving. One of the simplest and most beautiful things that you can do is to smile. A smile brightens lives, including your own and is very contagious - try it and see!

Whatever you do or say, inasmuch as you have done it to the least of the brethren you have done it unto Me!

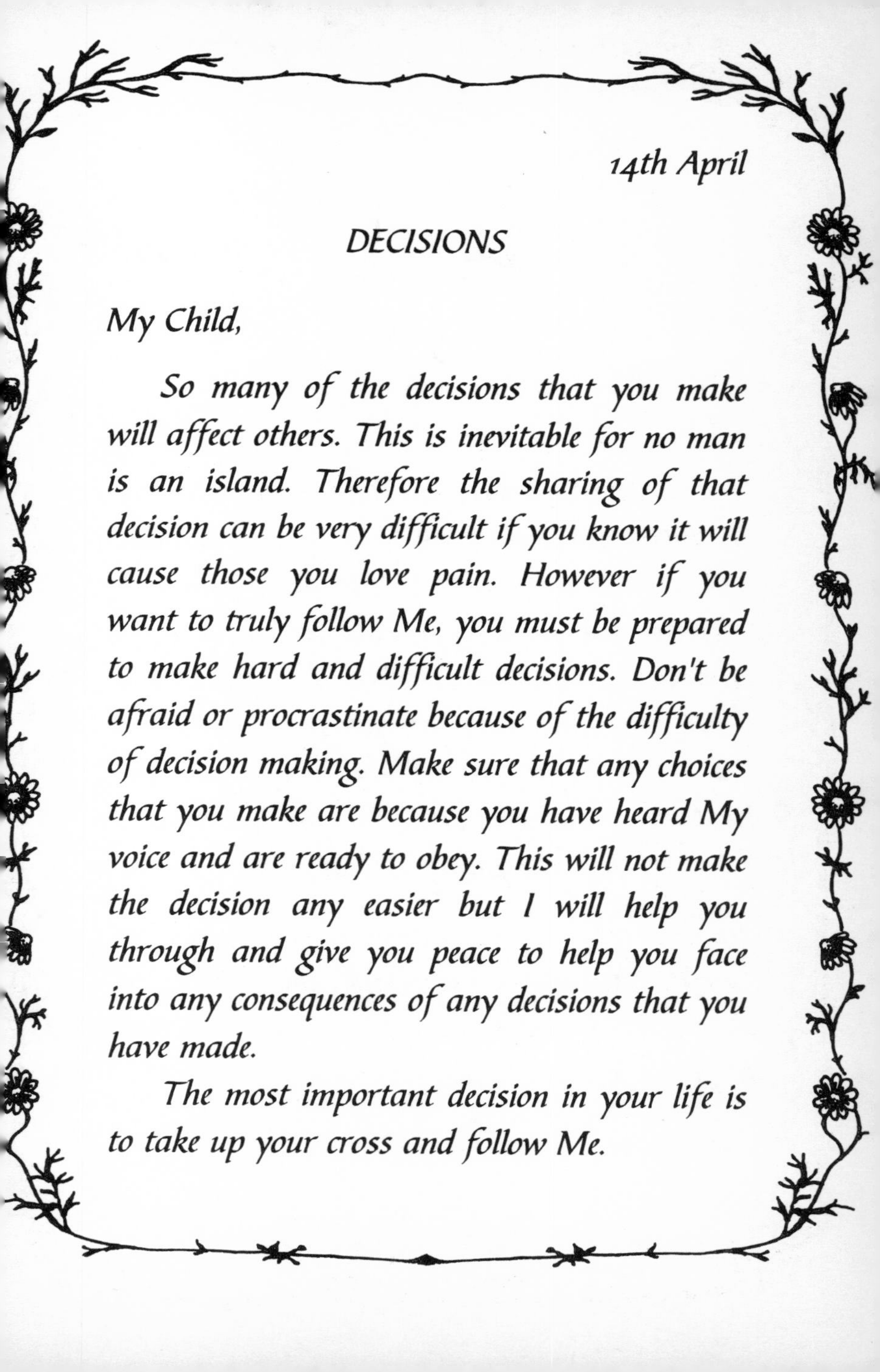

14th April

DECISIONS

My Child,

So many of the decisions that you make will affect others. This is inevitable for no man is an island. Therefore the sharing of that decision can be very difficult if you know it will cause those you love pain. However if you want to truly follow Me, you must be prepared to make hard and difficult decisions. Don't be afraid or procrastinate because of the difficulty of decision making. Make sure that any choices that you make are because you have heard My voice and are ready to obey. This will not make the decision any easier but I will help you through and give you peace to help you face into any consequences of any decisions that you have made.

The most important decision in your life is to take up your cross and follow Me.

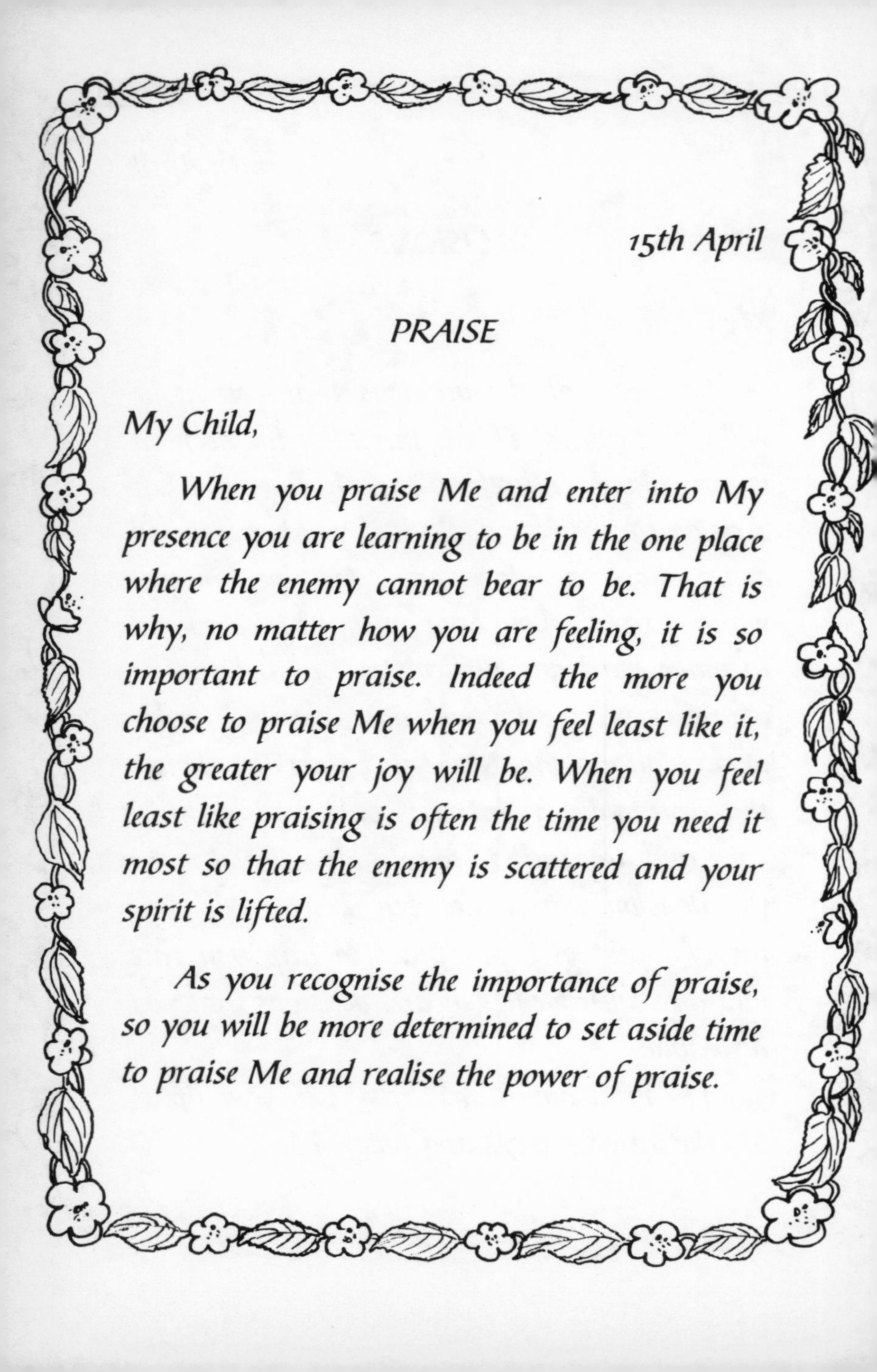

15th April

PRAISE

My Child,

When you praise Me and enter into My presence you are learning to be in the one place where the enemy cannot bear to be. That is why, no matter how you are feeling, it is so important to praise. Indeed the more you choose to praise Me when you feel least like it, the greater your joy will be. When you feel least like praising is often the time you need it most so that the enemy is scattered and your spirit is lifted.

As you recognise the importance of praise, so you will be more determined to set aside time to praise Me and realise the power of praise.

16th April

SEEDS OF RIGHTEOUSNESS

My Child,

If you neglect to read My word then, as in a neglected garden, the weeds will grow. The more neglected the garden, the stronger and more persistent the weeds will become, making it more difficult to remove them.

As you read My word you will sow seeds of righteousness in your life to keep the weeds at bay and yield a beautiful, fragrant harvest.

The effect of My word on your life will bring cleansing, purifying and renewing to your mind. It will establish you in My truth which will set you free.

Just a few minutes in My word each day will keep your life clean and refreshed, thus enabling you to live established and rooted in Me.

17th April

INDEPENDENT

My Child,

When you lose your way and call out to Me, I hear the cry of your heart and will restore you and put you back on the right path. The important thing is not for you to continue in that way but to recognise that you have lost your way and ask for My help.

So long as you are independent and think you can manage on your own, I cannot help you. But when you know you cannot find your way without Me I will swiftly come to your aid.

However 'lost' you may be feeling I am only a prayer away.

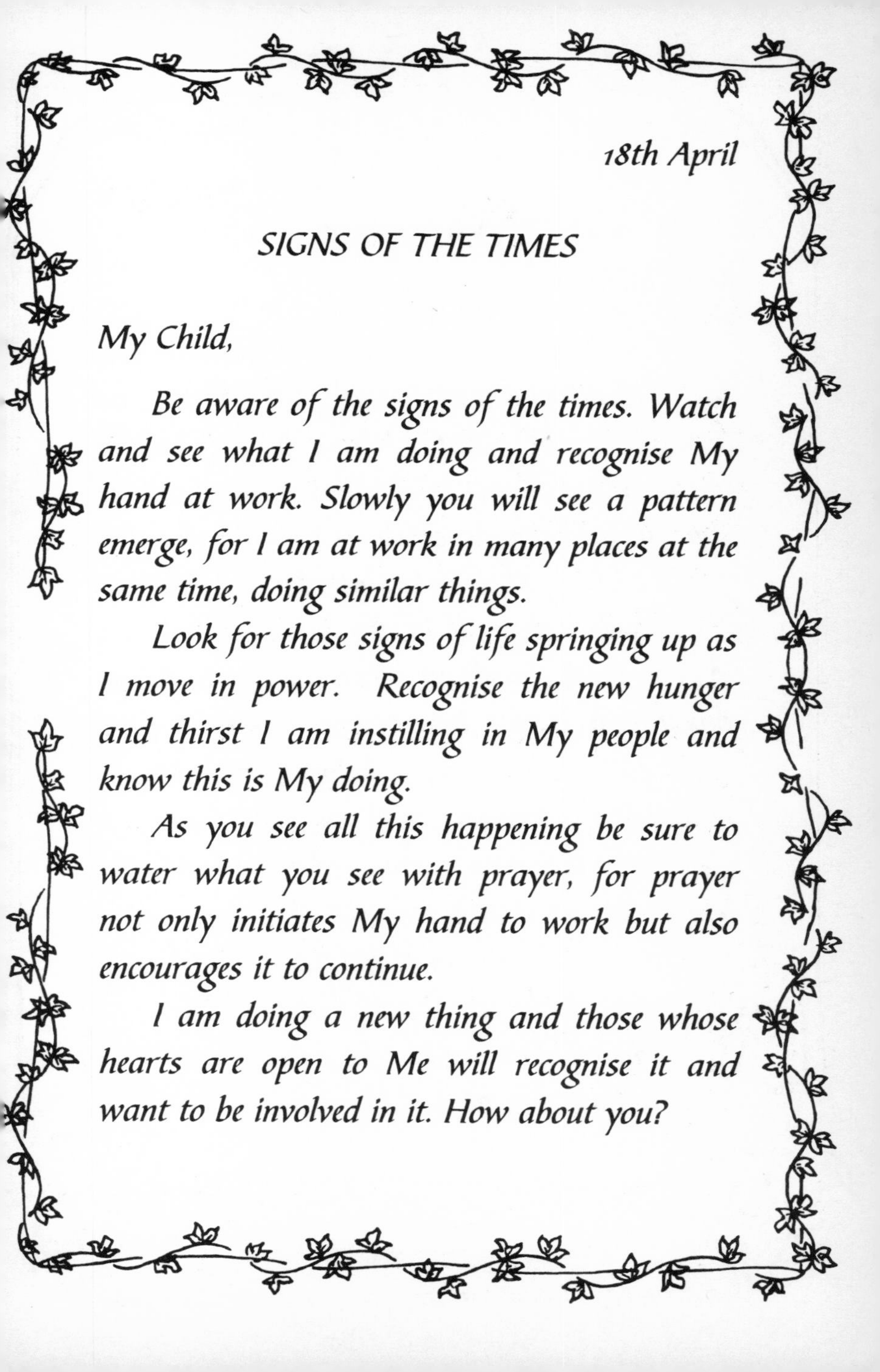

18th April

SIGNS OF THE TIMES

My Child,

Be aware of the signs of the times. Watch and see what I am doing and recognise My hand at work. Slowly you will see a pattern emerge, for I am at work in many places at the same time, doing similar things.

Look for those signs of life springing up as I move in power. Recognise the new hunger and thirst I am instilling in My people and know this is My doing.

As you see all this happening be sure to water what you see with prayer, for prayer not only initiates My hand to work but also encourages it to continue.

I am doing a new thing and those whose hearts are open to Me will recognise it and want to be involved in it. How about you?

19th April

EXPECTANT

My Child,

If you have no expectations because you fear disappointment you will have no anticipation of what I want to do. Whilst unreal expectations bring disappointments, if you can hold any expectations lightly before Me it will enable you to have faith for the future.

If you lose sight of the vision it will die. Where there is vision, there is hope. Much expectation is put into vision and this along with faith and prayer helps the vision to materialise. However, it is no good having a vision of your own - you need to seek Me for My vision so that I can put that expectation and faith into your heart for the future.

So look up and don't fear disappointment but be expectant of what I can do.

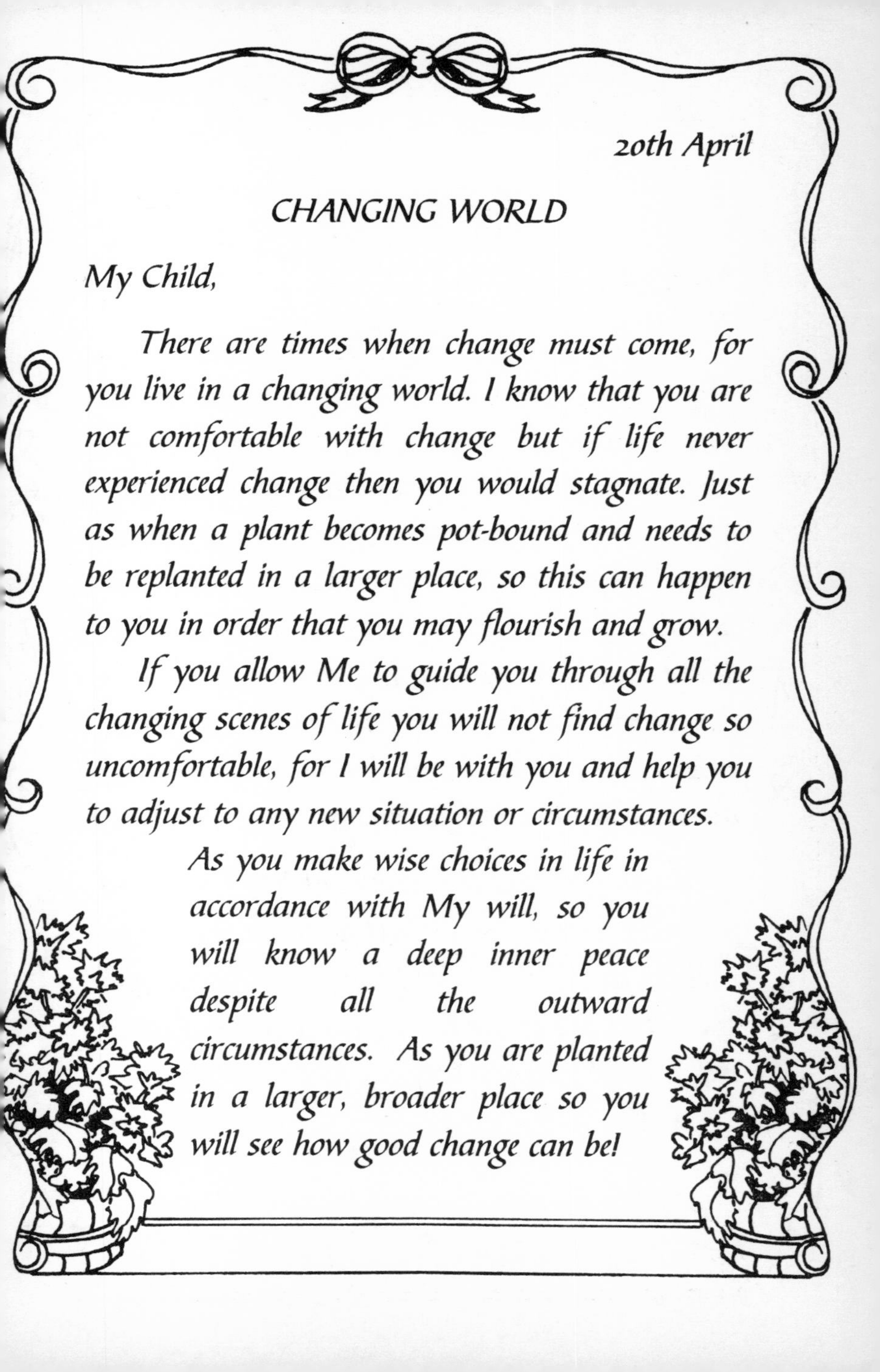

20th April

CHANGING WORLD

My Child,

There are times when change must come, for you live in a changing world. I know that you are not comfortable with change but if life never experienced change then you would stagnate. Just as when a plant becomes pot-bound and needs to be replanted in a larger place, so this can happen to you in order that you may flourish and grow.

If you allow Me to guide you through all the changing scenes of life you will not find change so uncomfortable, for I will be with you and help you to adjust to any new situation or circumstances.

As you make wise choices in life in accordance with My will, so you will know a deep inner peace despite all the outward circumstances. As you are planted in a larger, broader place so you will see how good change can be!

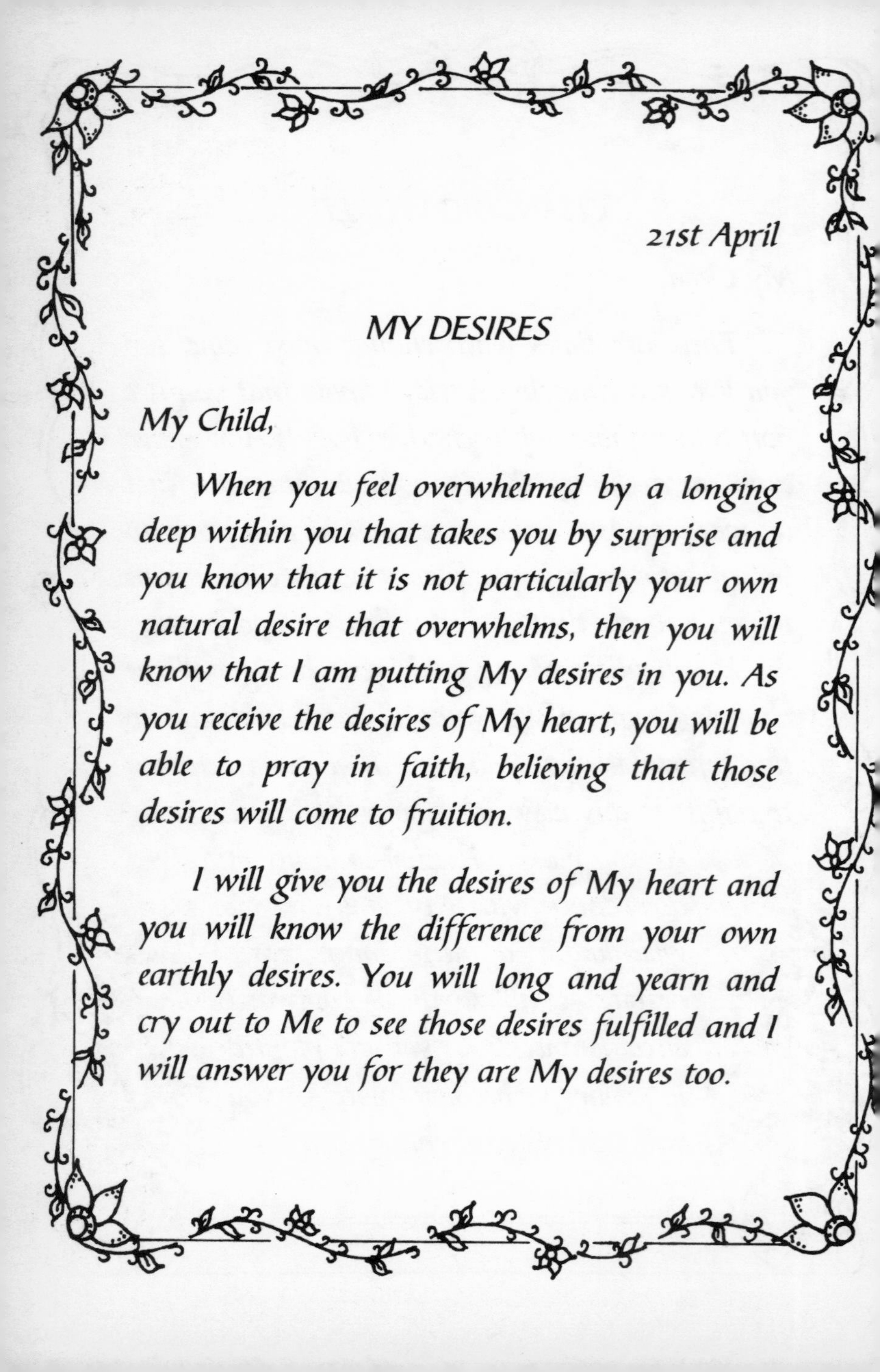

21st April

MY DESIRES

My Child,

When you feel overwhelmed by a longing deep within you that takes you by surprise and you know that it is not particularly your own natural desire that overwhelms, then you will know that I am putting My desires in you. As you receive the desires of My heart, you will be able to pray in faith, believing that those desires will come to fruition.

I will give you the desires of My heart and you will know the difference from your own earthly desires. You will long and yearn and cry out to Me to see those desires fulfilled and I will answer you for they are My desires too.

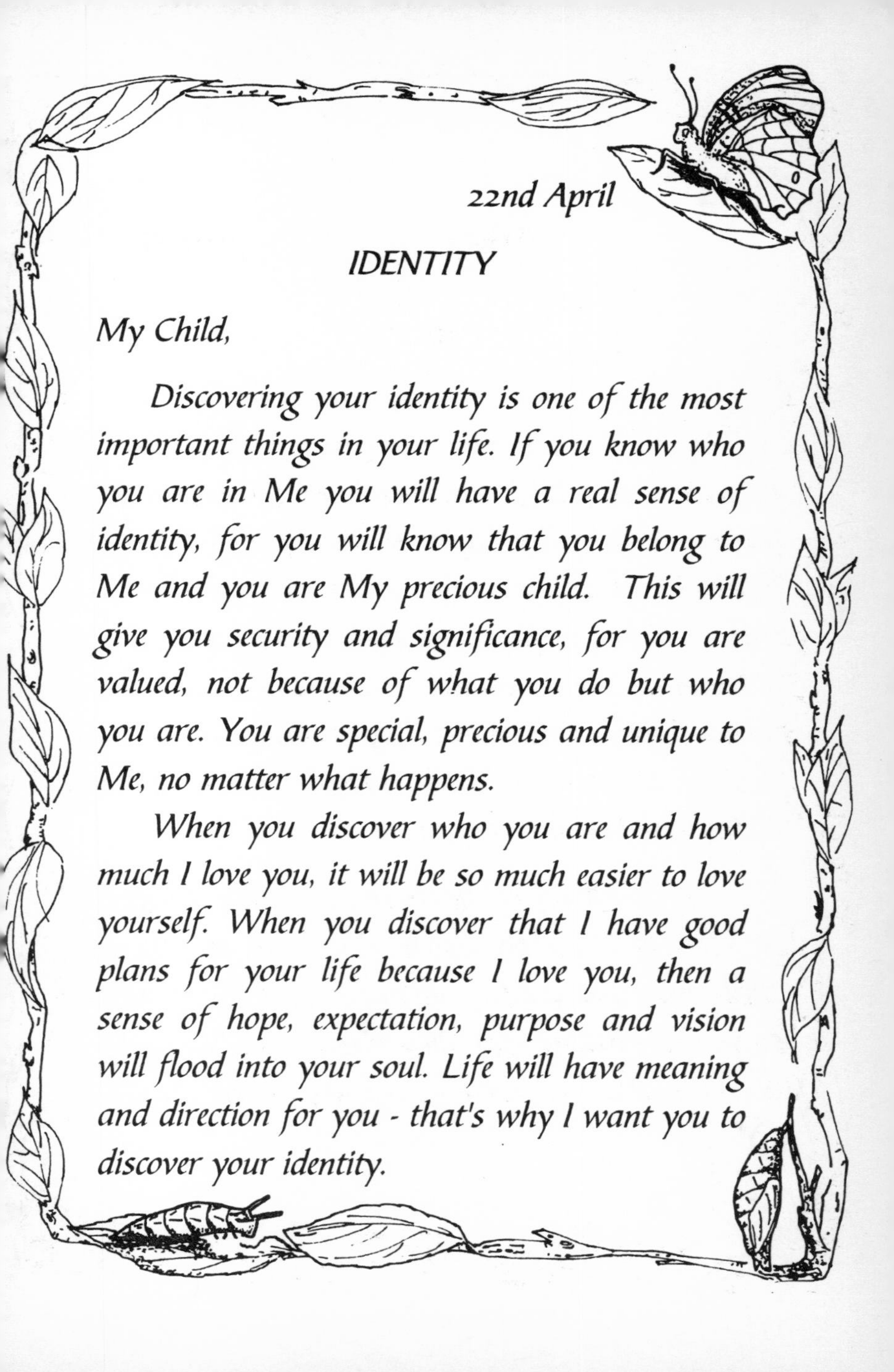

22nd April

IDENTITY

My Child,

Discovering your identity is one of the most important things in your life. If you know who you are in Me you will have a real sense of identity, for you will know that you belong to Me and you are My precious child. This will give you security and significance, for you are valued, not because of what you do but who you are. You are special, precious and unique to Me, no matter what happens.

When you discover who you are and how much I love you, it will be so much easier to love yourself. When you discover that I have good plans for your life because I love you, then a sense of hope, expectation, purpose and vision will flood into your soul. Life will have meaning and direction for you - that's why I want you to discover your identity.

23rd April

SOFT HEART

My Child,

Sometimes you can so easily put a shell of protection around your heart which causes it to harden. When this happens I use the difficult and hard things in your life to cause your heart to soften. Through the tears and trials I am able to give you a deeper compassion and a tenderness of heart as you come to Me. If you do not come to Me through these difficulties, it may be that your heart will get even harder.

Let Me have your heart so I can keep it soft and sensitive to My Holy Spirit. Allow Me to take that shell away and touch your heart with My gentleness so you can become more like Me.

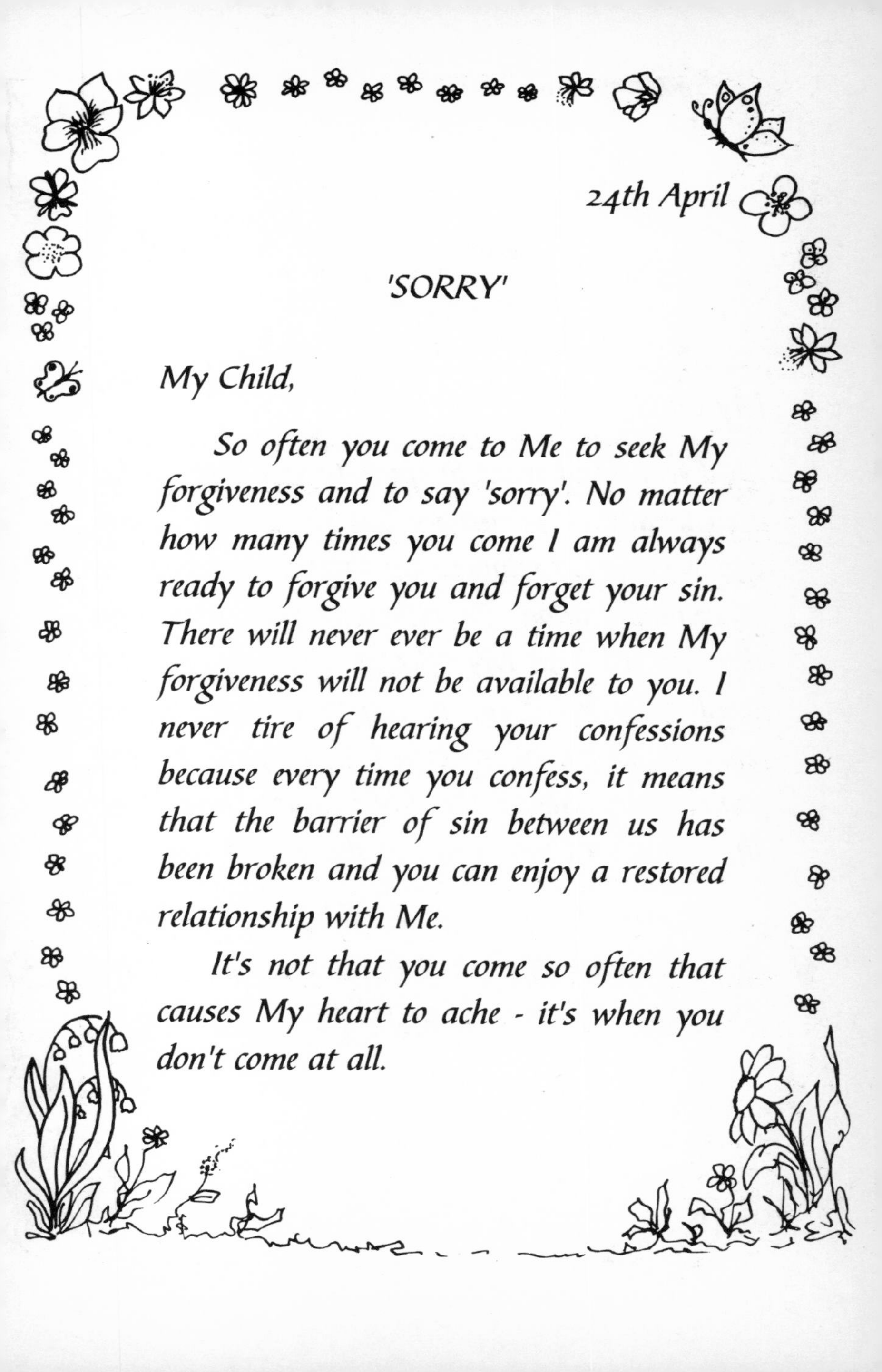

24th April

'SORRY'

My Child,

So often you come to Me to seek My forgiveness and to say 'sorry'. No matter how many times you come I am always ready to forgive you and forget your sin. There will never ever be a time when My forgiveness will not be available to you. I never tire of hearing your confessions because every time you confess, it means that the barrier of sin between us has been broken and you can enjoy a restored relationship with Me.

It's not that you come so often that causes My heart to ache - it's when you don't come at all.

25th April

EVERY DAY

My Child,

Every day I want to speak to you. Not rarely, occasionally or sometimes but every day. How can we enjoy a relationship together unless there is communication. Be expectant that each new day you will hear My voice. It may only be a still small voice but if you are expectant you will not miss it. Don't be surprised if I speak to you many times during the day because there is no limit to what I may want to share with you.

Hearing My voice and talking to Me should be a very natural part of the fellowship we enjoy together. So listen very carefully for My voice.

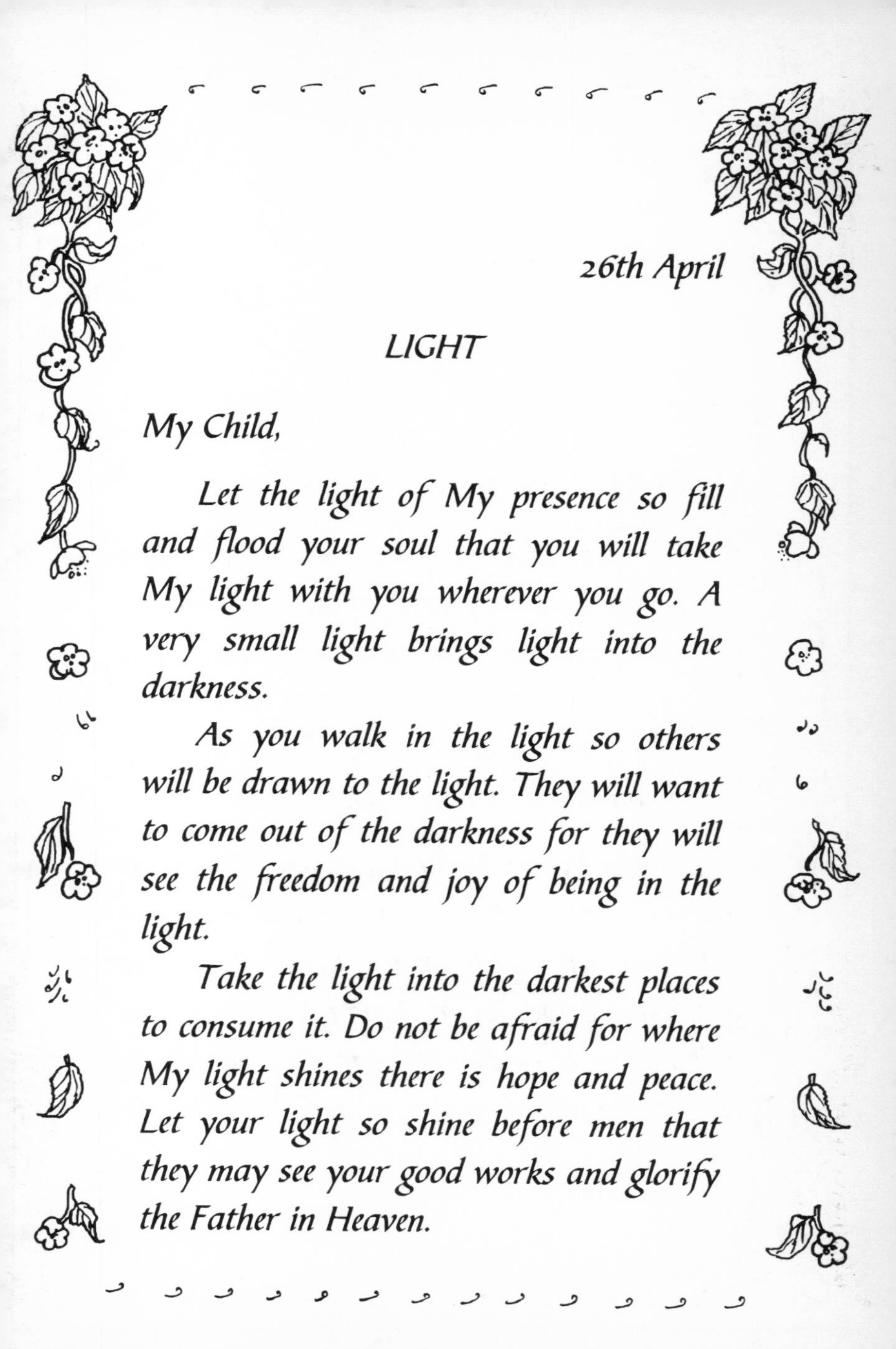

26th April

LIGHT

My Child,

Let the light of My presence so fill and flood your soul that you will take My light with you wherever you go. A very small light brings light into the darkness.

As you walk in the light so others will be drawn to the light. They will want to come out of the darkness for they will see the freedom and joy of being in the light.

Take the light into the darkest places to consume it. Do not be afraid for where My light shines there is hope and peace. Let your light so shine before men that they may see your good works and glorify the Father in Heaven.

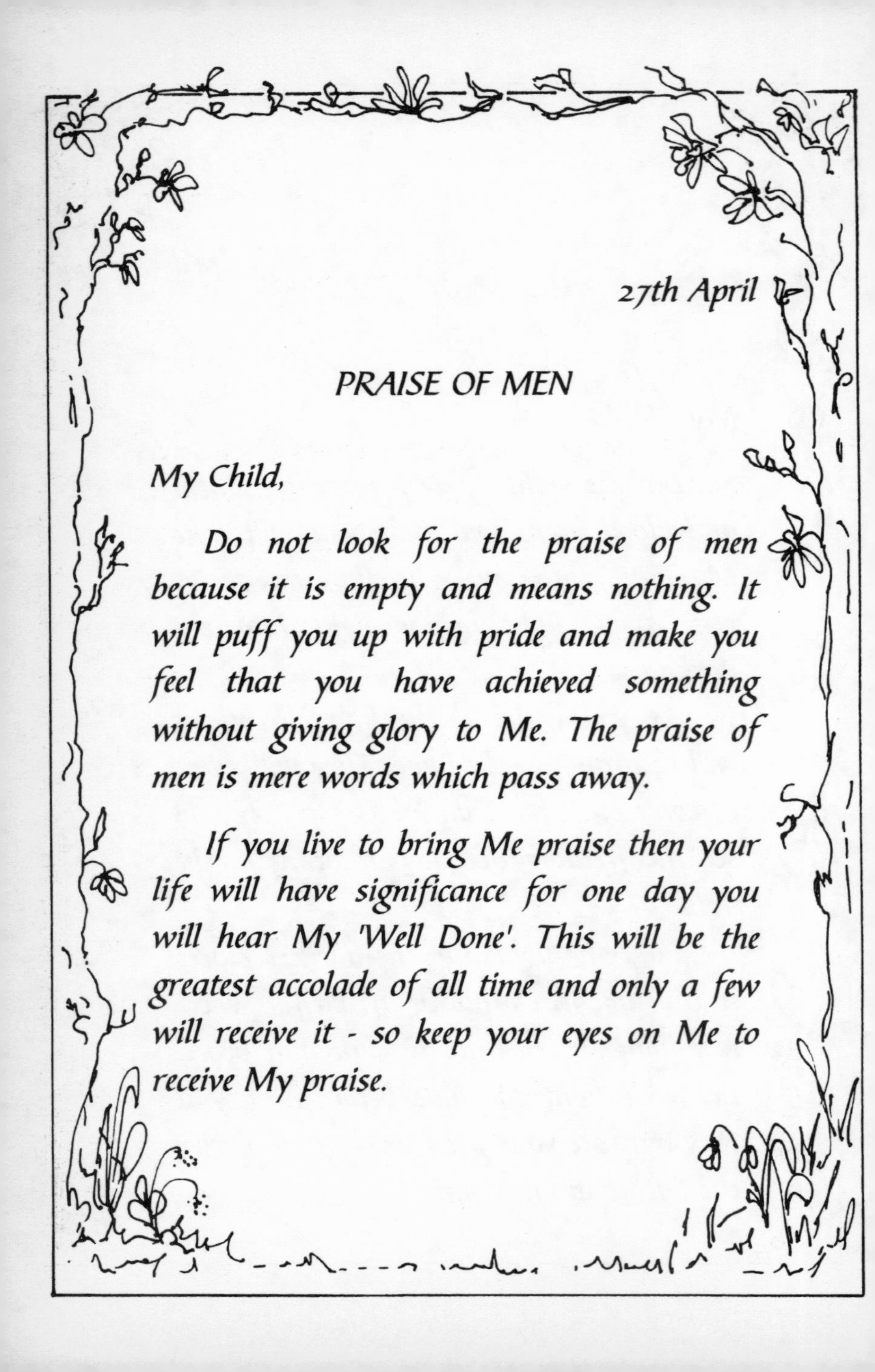

27th April

PRAISE OF MEN

My Child,

Do not look for the praise of men because it is empty and means nothing. It will puff you up with pride and make you feel that you have achieved something without giving glory to Me. The praise of men is mere words which pass away.

If you live to bring Me praise then your life will have significance for one day you will hear My 'Well Done'. This will be the greatest accolade of all time and only a few will receive it - so keep your eyes on Me to receive My praise.

28th April

ABUNDANT BLESSING

My Child,

The desire of My heart toward you is to abundantly bless you. I long for you to receive the abundance of all that I have for you. Do not limit Me by unbelief, for surely I will bless those whom I will bless. Do not think that I long to bless others, bypassing you. No one deserves My blessings, nor can they earn them but I long to pour out My blessing on you.

Have I not promised abundant life to all who believe? Am I not a God of abundance? If you can sense My Father heart of love towards you then you will know that you stand in the very place of My abundant blessing.

29th April

HEAVENLIES

My Child,

When you fly high in the sky in an aeroplane, although the scenery remains the same, the view is very different from that when you are on earth. From the heavenlies the spectrum becomes broader and it is easier to get a whole picture.

So it is that My perspective is totally different from yours and to understand My perspective you need to be seated in the heavenlies. When you look at things from an earthly perspective you only see part of the picture. Your view and perspective is very narrow and limited.

I want to take you into the heavenlies so you can see things from My point of view and enter into a new position of authority and understanding of who I am!

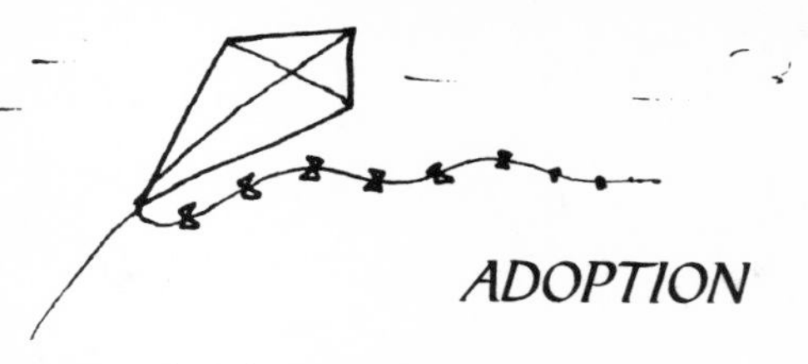

30th April

ADOPTION

My Child,

I have adopted you into My family so that knowing you were precious, chosen and loved you could reach out to others with My love. Unless you know what it is to be loved and receive love it is virtually impossible to pass that love on.

As you experience My love and that deep sense of well-being because I am your Father, so there are many who need also to experience My love. There are many who need to know what it is to 'belong' in My family and enter into all the joys of family life.

My family can be extended - there are no limits of number, race, creed, colour or even religion.

Adoption is open to all who would like it, so will you pass the news on!

1st May

POWER OF THE TONGUE

My Child,

Though the tongue is a little member of the body, it has great power. It can speak words of life or it can speak words of death.

Therefore think before you speak. Remember that out of the abundance of the heart, the mouth speaks. Always be ready to speak forth words of goodness and kindness filled with love. Do not underestimate the power of words to produce fruit - good or bad dependent on what you speak out.

Be careful to be known for your kind words only. You have the power to bless with your tongue so make sure that you speak out many blessings on others. As you discover the tremendous power of words, you can teach others so that they in turn will use their tongues to bless. Great are the blessings you can give to others through the power of the tongue.

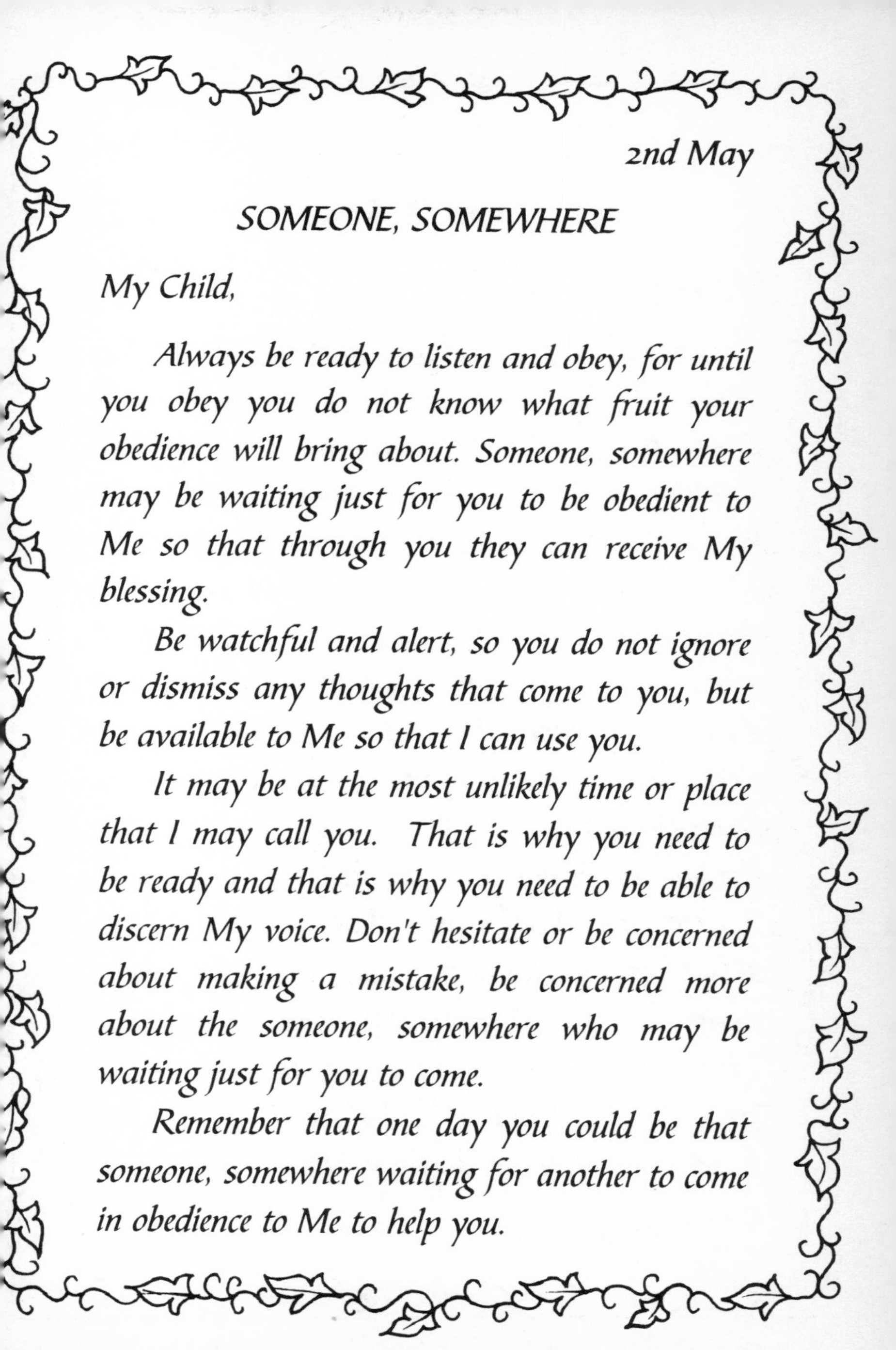

2nd May

SOMEONE, SOMEWHERE

My Child,

Always be ready to listen and obey, for until you obey you do not know what fruit your obedience will bring about. Someone, somewhere may be waiting just for you to be obedient to Me so that through you they can receive My blessing.

Be watchful and alert, so you do not ignore or dismiss any thoughts that come to you, but be available to Me so that I can use you.

It may be at the most unlikely time or place that I may call you. That is why you need to be ready and that is why you need to be able to discern My voice. Don't hesitate or be concerned about making a mistake, be concerned more about the someone, somewhere who may be waiting just for you to come.

Remember that one day you could be that someone, somewhere waiting for another to come in obedience to Me to help you.

3rd May

ALMIGHTY

My Child,

Never lose sight of the fact that I am the God of the Impossible. Throughout life you will come up against impossible circumstances and situations and you will not know what to do. It's at those times that you need to remember My power and My greatness. When you reach the end of your strength or the end of your wisdom then you can call unto Me. I may not do the impossible and change your circumstances or situation but I can give you the strength and wisdom to carry on. In that way the impossible has been achieved.

Do not lose faith that I can change situations too, for I am able to do far above and beyond what you may expect or imagine. There are no limitations or restrictions on Me for I am ALMIGHTY and there is nothing too hard for Me. If you really believe this it will change you!

4th May

PERFECT TIMING

My Child,

My timing is perfect. I am never late or too early but always on time. I know how hard it is to be patient and to wait for Me but when you are patient you will discover that all things work together for good to those who love Me. As you have patience and are prepared to wait for My timing and not rush ahead of Me, your patience will be rewarded.

I understand your frustrations at having to wait and know that living in an 'instant' society you long for instant answers. I am working out all My plans and purposes for good and My maximum glory. Then, at the right time, I will bring things that are nought into being. If you can trust Me to be on time - and I will be - though not necessarily when you like, expect or want, you will know My perfect timing.

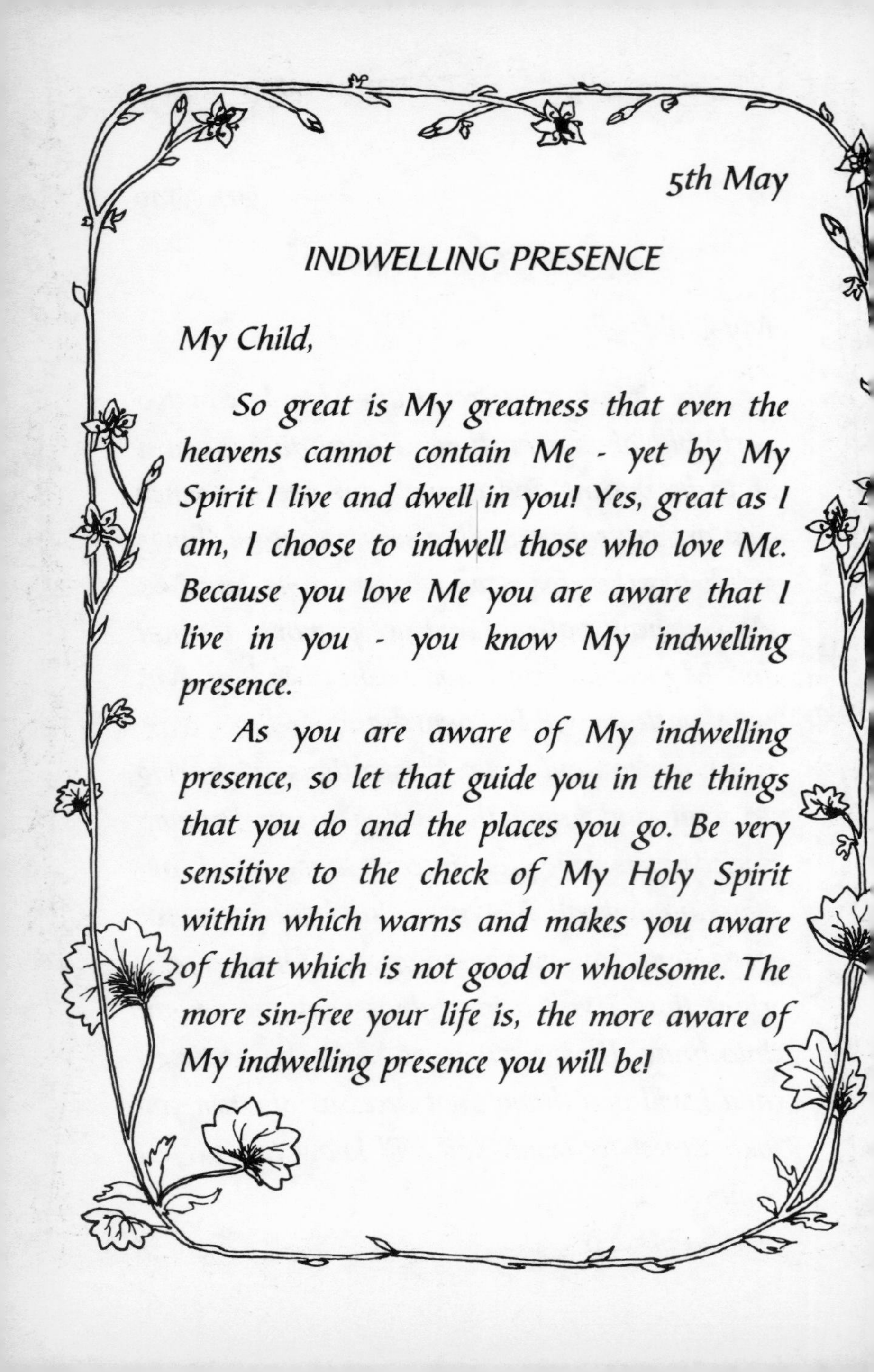

5th May

INDWELLING PRESENCE

My Child,

So great is My greatness that even the heavens cannot contain Me - yet by My Spirit I live and dwell in you! Yes, great as I am, I choose to indwell those who love Me. Because you love Me you are aware that I live in you - you know My indwelling presence.

As you are aware of My indwelling presence, so let that guide you in the things that you do and the places you go. Be very sensitive to the check of My Holy Spirit within which warns and makes you aware of that which is not good or wholesome. The more sin-free your life is, the more aware of My indwelling presence you will be!

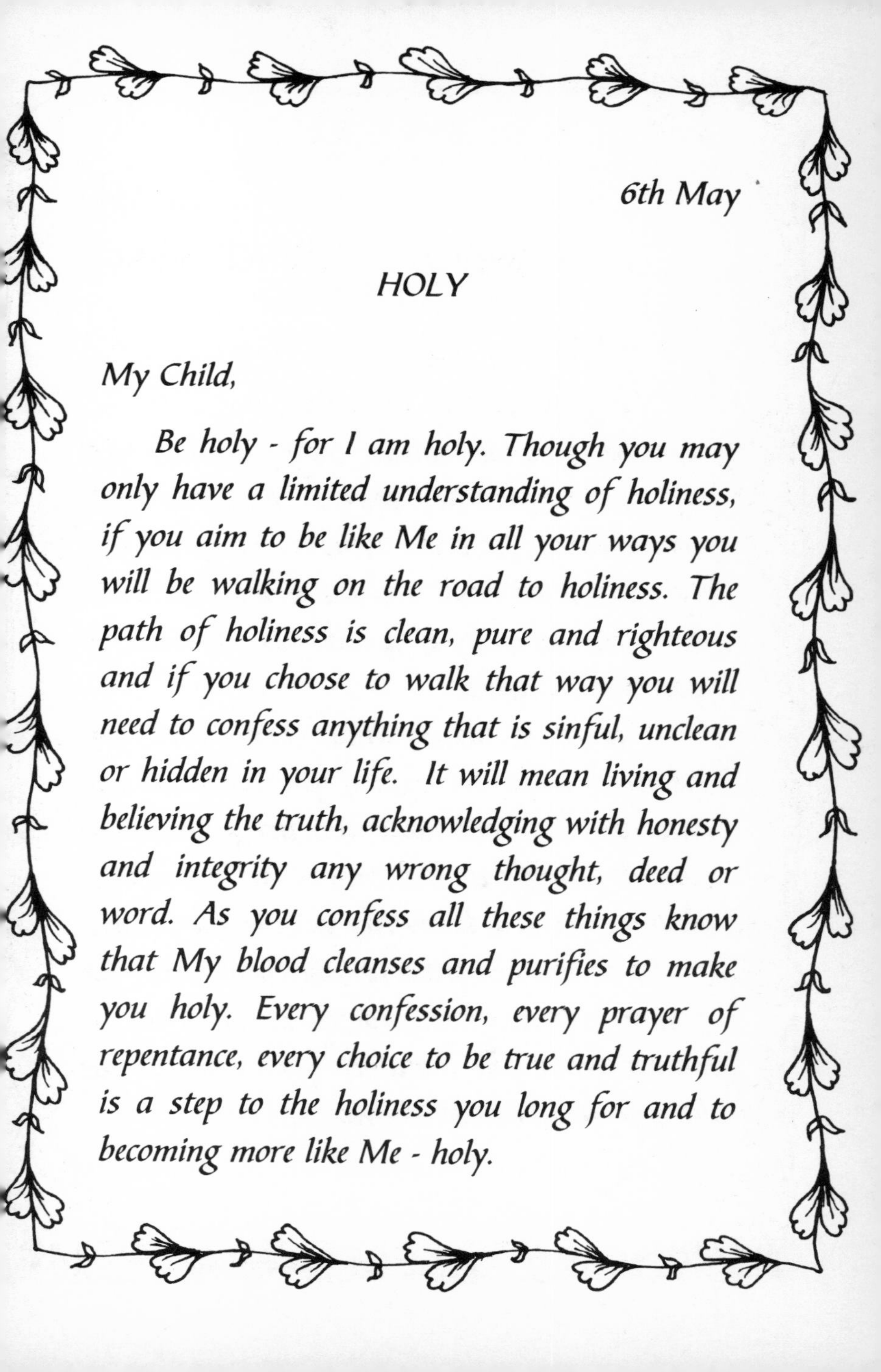

6th May

HOLY

My Child,

Be holy - for I am holy. Though you may only have a limited understanding of holiness, if you aim to be like Me in all your ways you will be walking on the road to holiness. The path of holiness is clean, pure and righteous and if you choose to walk that way you will need to confess anything that is sinful, unclean or hidden in your life. It will mean living and believing the truth, acknowledging with honesty and integrity any wrong thought, deed or word. As you confess all these things know that My blood cleanses and purifies to make you holy. Every confession, every prayer of repentance, every choice to be true and truthful is a step to the holiness you long for and to becoming more like Me - holy.

7th May

TEST THE WATERS

My Child,

When you are unsure as to whether you have really heard My voice or not, it is quite permissible to 'test the waters'. Only as you begin to act on what you think you heard will you know definitely if it really is My voice or your own thoughts.

If you never act on what you've heard, you will never know for sure if you discerned My voice correctly. The more you are prepared to commit yourself and discover that it was Me, the more you will know My voice in the future.

So do not be afraid to 'test the waters', for if your hope is firmly rooted in Me, then no matter what the outcome you will not be disappointed because My way is best for you!

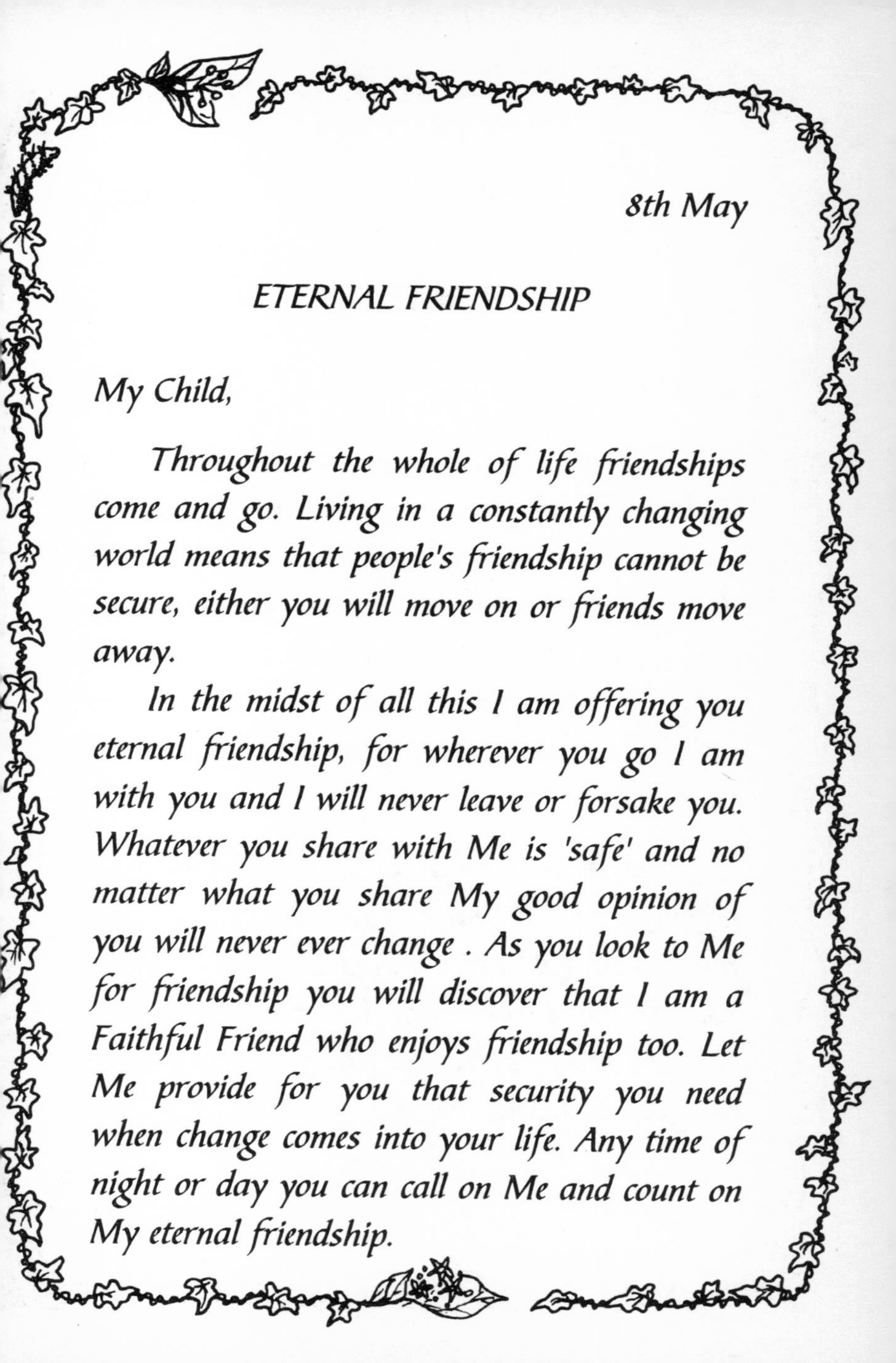

8th May

ETERNAL FRIENDSHIP

My Child,

Throughout the whole of life friendships come and go. Living in a constantly changing world means that people's friendship cannot be secure, either you will move on or friends move away.

In the midst of all this I am offering you eternal friendship, for wherever you go I am with you and I will never leave or forsake you. Whatever you share with Me is 'safe' and no matter what you share My good opinion of you will never ever change . As you look to Me for friendship you will discover that I am a Faithful Friend who enjoys friendship too. Let Me provide for you that security you need when change comes into your life. Any time of night or day you can call on Me and count on My eternal friendship.

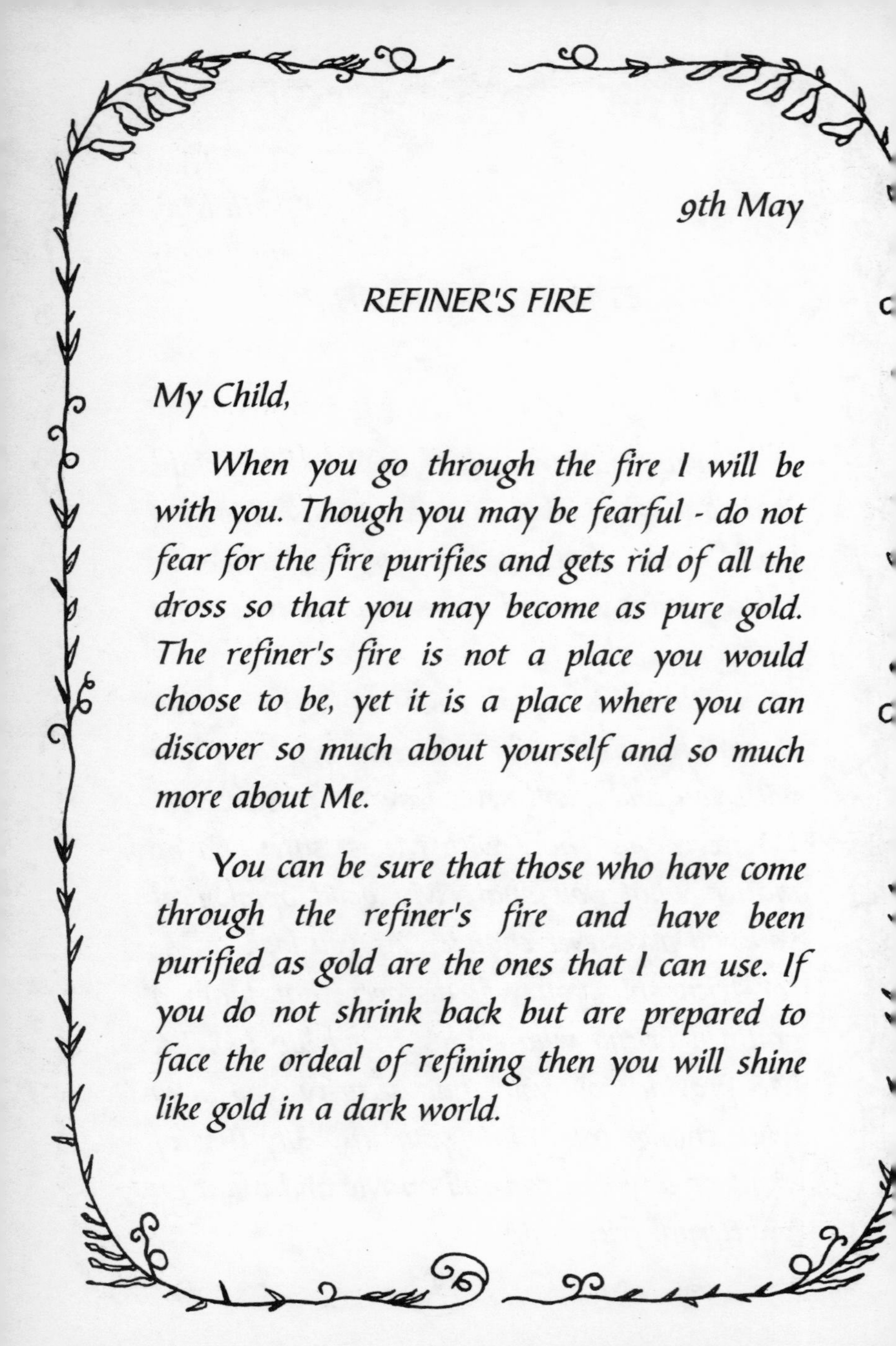

9th May

REFINER'S FIRE

My Child,

When you go through the fire I will be with you. Though you may be fearful - do not fear for the fire purifies and gets rid of all the dross so that you may become as pure gold. The refiner's fire is not a place you would choose to be, yet it is a place where you can discover so much about yourself and so much more about Me.

You can be sure that those who have come through the refiner's fire and have been purified as gold are the ones that I can use. If you do not shrink back but are prepared to face the ordeal of refining then you will shine like gold in a dark world.

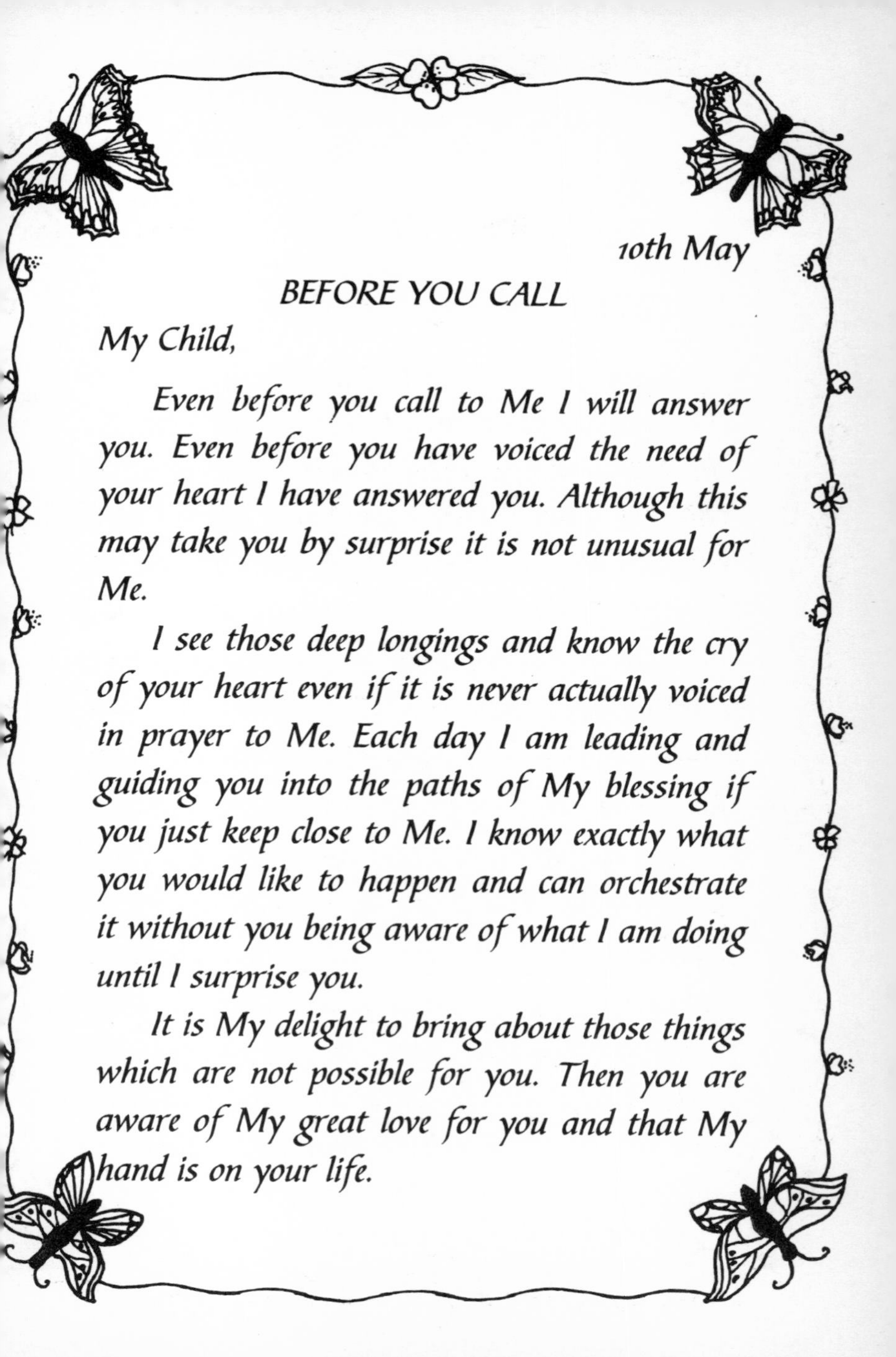

10th May

BEFORE YOU CALL

My Child,

Even before you call to Me I will answer you. Even before you have voiced the need of your heart I have answered you. Although this may take you by surprise it is not unusual for Me.

I see those deep longings and know the cry of your heart even if it is never actually voiced in prayer to Me. Each day I am leading and guiding you into the paths of My blessing if you just keep close to Me. I know exactly what you would like to happen and can orchestrate it without you being aware of what I am doing until I surprise you.

It is My delight to bring about those things which are not possible for you. Then you are aware of My great love for you and that My hand is on your life.

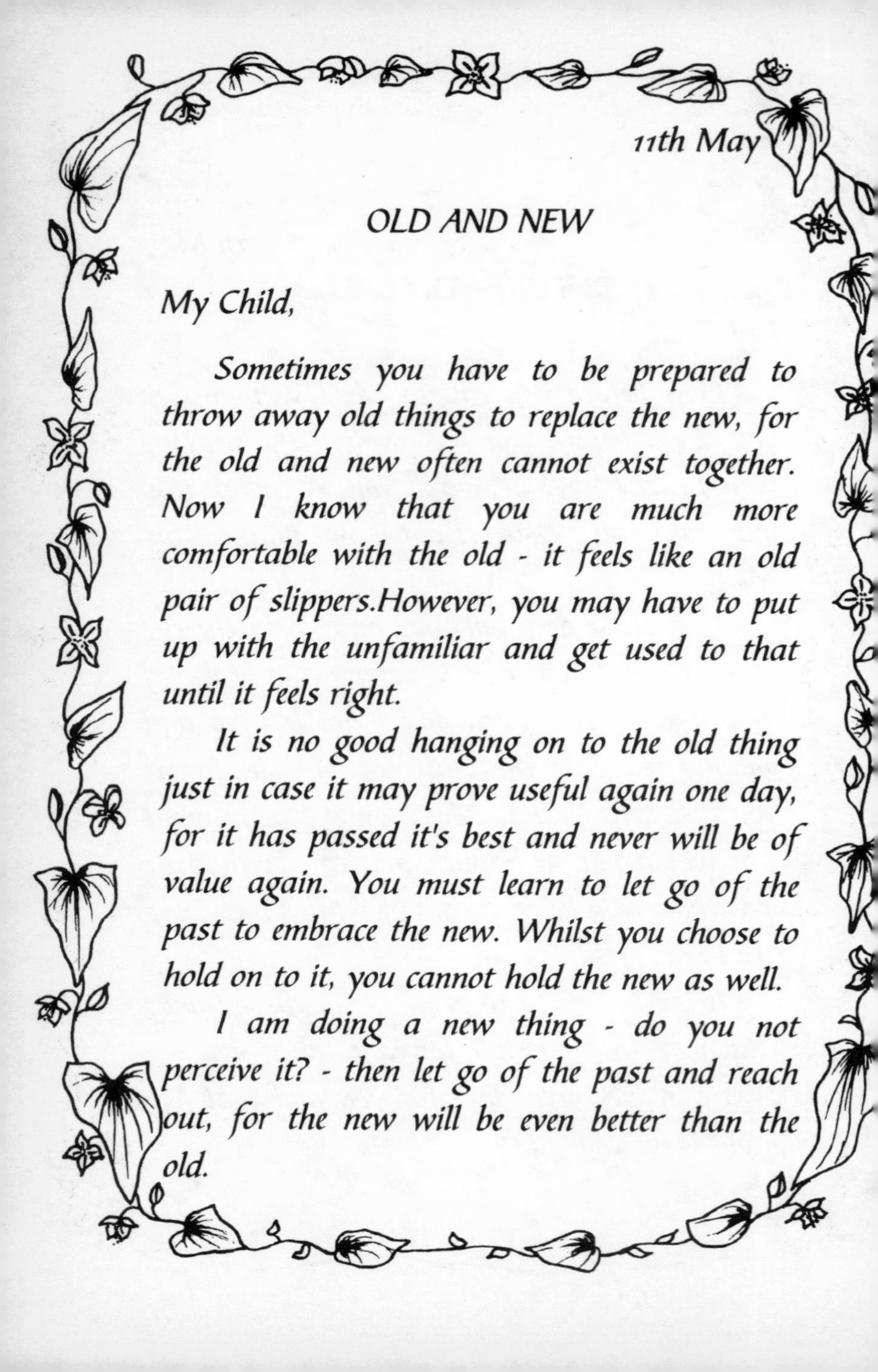

11th May

OLD AND NEW

My Child,

Sometimes you have to be prepared to throw away old things to replace the new, for the old and new often cannot exist together. Now I know that you are much more comfortable with the old - it feels like an old pair of slippers.However, you may have to put up with the unfamiliar and get used to that until it feels right.

It is no good hanging on to the old thing just in case it may prove useful again one day, for it has passed it's best and never will be of value again. You must learn to let go of the past to embrace the new. Whilst you choose to hold on to it, you cannot hold the new as well.

I am doing a new thing - do you not perceive it? - then let go of the past and reach out, for the new will be even better than the old.

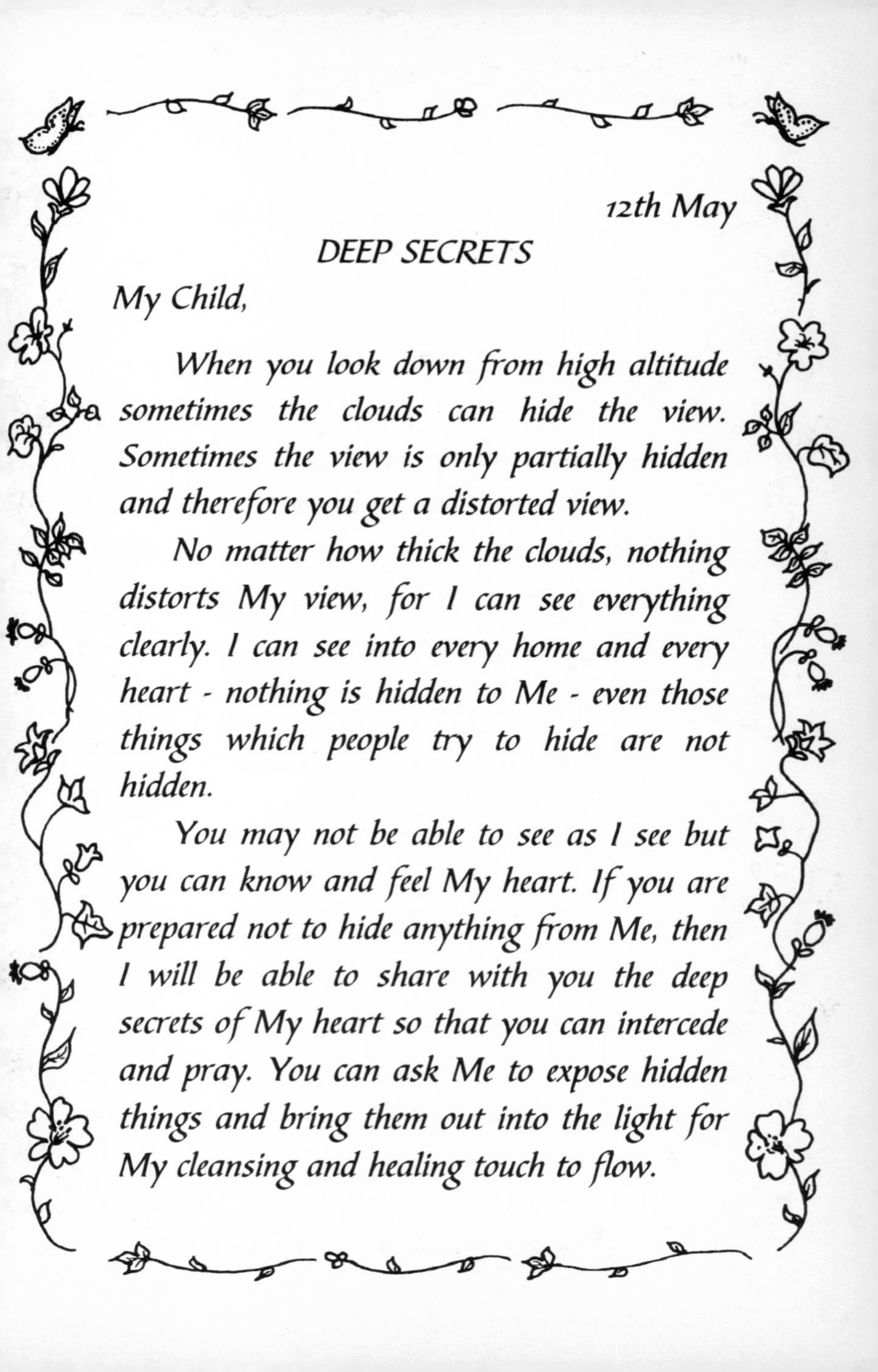

12th May

DEEP SECRETS

My Child,

When you look down from high altitude sometimes the clouds can hide the view. Sometimes the view is only partially hidden and therefore you get a distorted view.

No matter how thick the clouds, nothing distorts My view, for I can see everything clearly. I can see into every home and every heart - nothing is hidden to Me - even those things which people try to hide are not hidden.

You may not be able to see as I see but you can know and feel My heart. If you are prepared not to hide anything from Me, then I will be able to share with you the deep secrets of My heart so that you can intercede and pray. You can ask Me to expose hidden things and bring them out into the light for My cleansing and healing touch to flow.

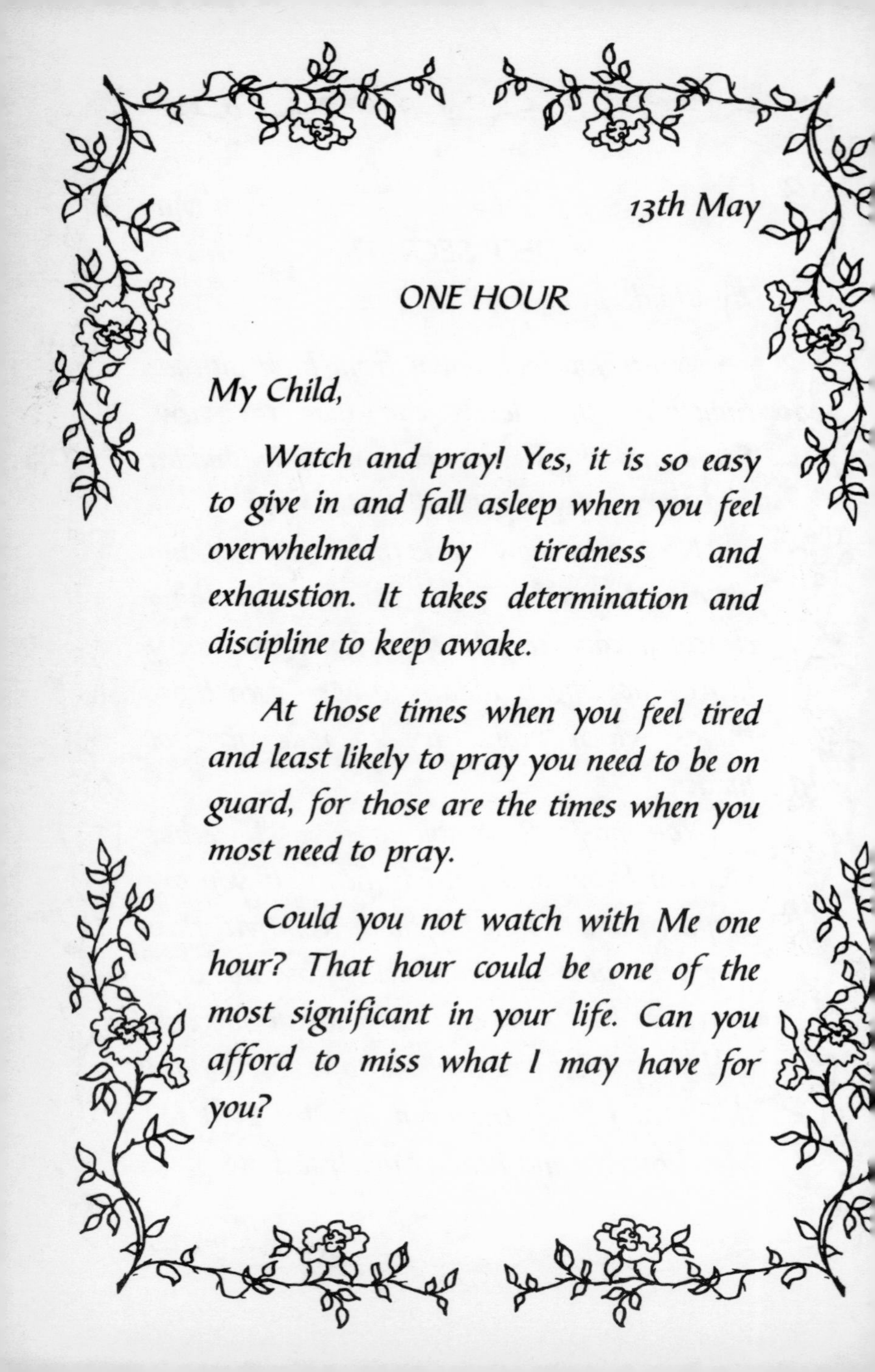

13th May

ONE HOUR

My Child,

Watch and pray! Yes, it is so easy to give in and fall asleep when you feel overwhelmed by tiredness and exhaustion. It takes determination and discipline to keep awake.

At those times when you feel tired and least likely to pray you need to be on guard, for those are the times when you most need to pray.

Could you not watch with Me one hour? That hour could be one of the most significant in your life. Can you afford to miss what I may have for you?

14th May

TIME WELL SPENT

My Child,

My Father heart rejoices and thrills when you come to Me, especially when I know that you have taken particular time and effort to be with Me. When you are prepared to lay everything else aside and come, when you have a deep longing inside to be with Me surely I will meet with you.

I know all the difficulties and distractions which hinder you from coming to Me. I know how determined you have to be to make time for Me. I understand that so often in your spirit you long to come but your flesh is weak. That is why when you overcome all these things to be with Me, My heart rejoices so. Whenever you come to spend time with Me know that it is time well spent, for it is one of the most important things that you can do.

15th May

HOPE WITHIN YOU

My Child,

Always be ready to give an account of the hope that is within you, for you never know when you may be asked to do so. When you are least prepared and in the most unlikely situations, you may be asked to share your faith. As you walk daily with Me experiencing the freshness of My presence, you will find that you have a wealth of experience to draw on and the power of My Holy Spirit to recall it. You will know that I am putting words in your mouth that you have not thought of yourself so you can be My witness to a lost, needy world.

16th May

BE DILIGENT

My Child,

Learn to be diligent in all that you do so that you are always able to give the best that you can. If you do things half-heartedly you will not have the satisfaction of a job well done.

Even if no-one else notices or pays any attention, everything you do is seen by Me. If you can live to please Me and not men by doing the most mundane things with all of your heart, you will receive My reward.

I do not expect you to do things perfectly, but if you are diligent and do your very best, you will receive the satisfaction that you did what you could - and that is all I ask of you!

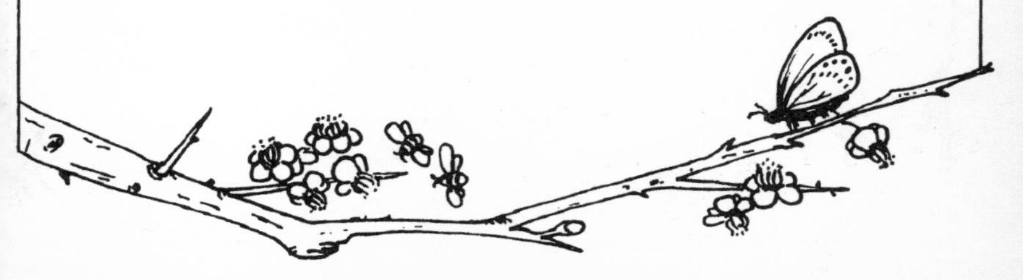

17th May

ENABLING

My Child,

I am with you to help you - yes, I will hold your right hand and sustain you for I am your God. No matter what you have to do, however big the task may appear to be, I will enable you to do it. If you look at all the difficulties before you begin, without allowing for My enabling, then you will surely be overwhelmed by the task before you have even begun. This allows anxiety to enter your heart and may cause you to be fearful.

If you seek My help, surely I will come to your aid. As you realise My greatness and power so the task will become smaller and together we can do it.

18th May

MY KINGDOM

My Child,

If you look at people and decide that they will not respond to the gospel, then not only are you judging them but also you are limiting My power to save to the uttermost.

You only look at the outside but I see deep into the heart and know those who will respond to My love. I will draw them to Myself so do not be hasty to judge who you think will respond, for you will have many surprises. Rather discover from Me those who are seeking Me and pray them into My Kingdom.

19th May

PLANS

My Child,

Are you prepared to lay aside all your plans for each day so that I can tell you about Mine? Are you willing to lay down all those things that you would like to do to enable you to spend time with Me and seek Me to know the things on My heart? So many people have plans that they are not prepared to forego - do you?

As you live in relationship with Me, more and more you will want to find out My plans and be available so that you can enter into them... that reveals how much you love Me and want to live for Me.

20th May

MY PRIORITIES

My Child,

It is so easy to procrastinate and put off today what you think you will be able to achieve tomorrow. Sometimes this may be legitimate for you. Be careful that it does not become a real pressure for you until you find that you cannot cope.

My yoke is easy and My burden light. It may be that you need to sort out your priorities to find My priorities for you. I will never put pressure on you - I want to make you aware of those warning signs before the pressure gets too much. If you learn to pace yourself and work at My pace you will discover a peace with no pressure or pain - only freedom to enjoy each day.

21st May

GENTLE RAIN

My Child,

When My Spirit comes it falls like gentle rain bringing freshness. It cleanses and revives as it touches your life. As the rain soaks into the soil and softens it, so My Spirit will soak your life and soften your heart. After the heat, the dryness and the parchedness of your soul, you will cry out and welcome the rain of the Holy Spirit.

The more rain that falls, the more drenched in My Spirit you will become. So the soil of your life will be ready for the new growth that will inevitably take place - welcome the rain of My Spirit.

22nd May

PRECIOUS PROMISES

My Child,

There will be seasons in your life when it appears that nothing is happening and your heart may begin to doubt promises that have been given to you. Remember Abraham who staggered not at the promises of God through unbelief and think of how long it was before he saw the fulfilment of those great and precious promises.

Hold on to the faith you have been given and do not allow the enemy to snatch it away. Keep your eyes focused on Me for I am greater than all the promises and will never break My word.

23rd May

RIGHT AND JUST

My Child,

I do not withhold things from you because I have a desire to harm you, for My heart is truly to bless you. However, there are times when you will be tested to see what's in your heart. Sometimes by withholding something from you that you earnestly desire I can see what's in your heart and if you have right attitudes. I only want the very best for you and am motivated by My great love for you so I will only do what is right and just.

24th May

BE ENCOURAGED

My Child,

Be encouraged! When you need that encouragement I will make sure that it comes to you, just at the right moment. Everyone needs encouragement and as you are encouraged so you can then encourage others.

Discouragement can be a real snare and a destroyer of faith - that's why it is so important to encourage. As your eyes are opened daily you will see those areas in everyday life where I am working to build you up and encourage you.

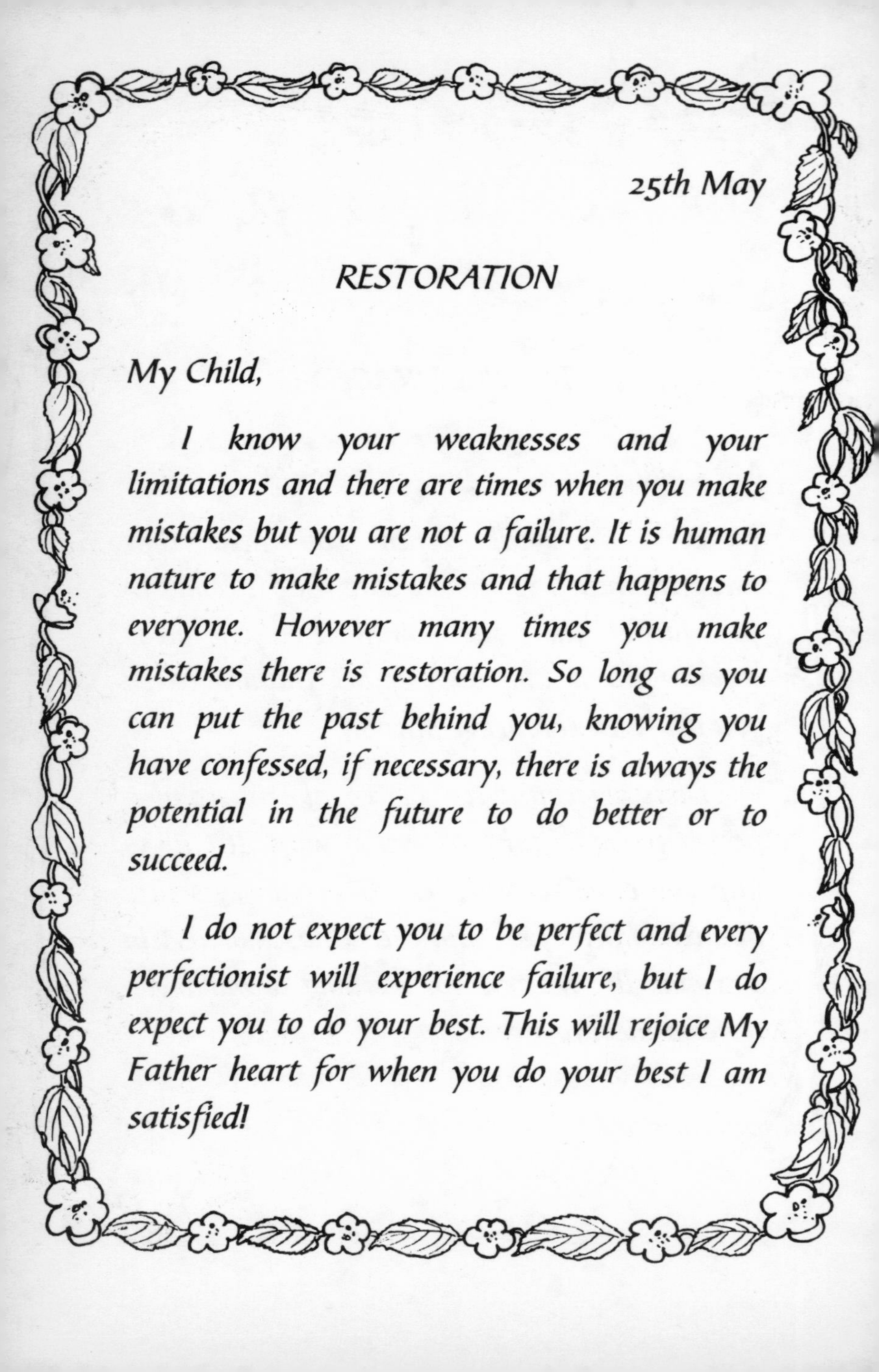

25th May

RESTORATION

My Child,

I know your weaknesses and your limitations and there are times when you make mistakes but you are not a failure. It is human nature to make mistakes and that happens to everyone. However many times you make mistakes there is restoration. So long as you can put the past behind you, knowing you have confessed, if necessary, there is always the potential in the future to do better or to succeed.

I do not expect you to be perfect and every perfectionist will experience failure, but I do expect you to do your best. This will rejoice My Father heart for when you do your best I am satisfied!

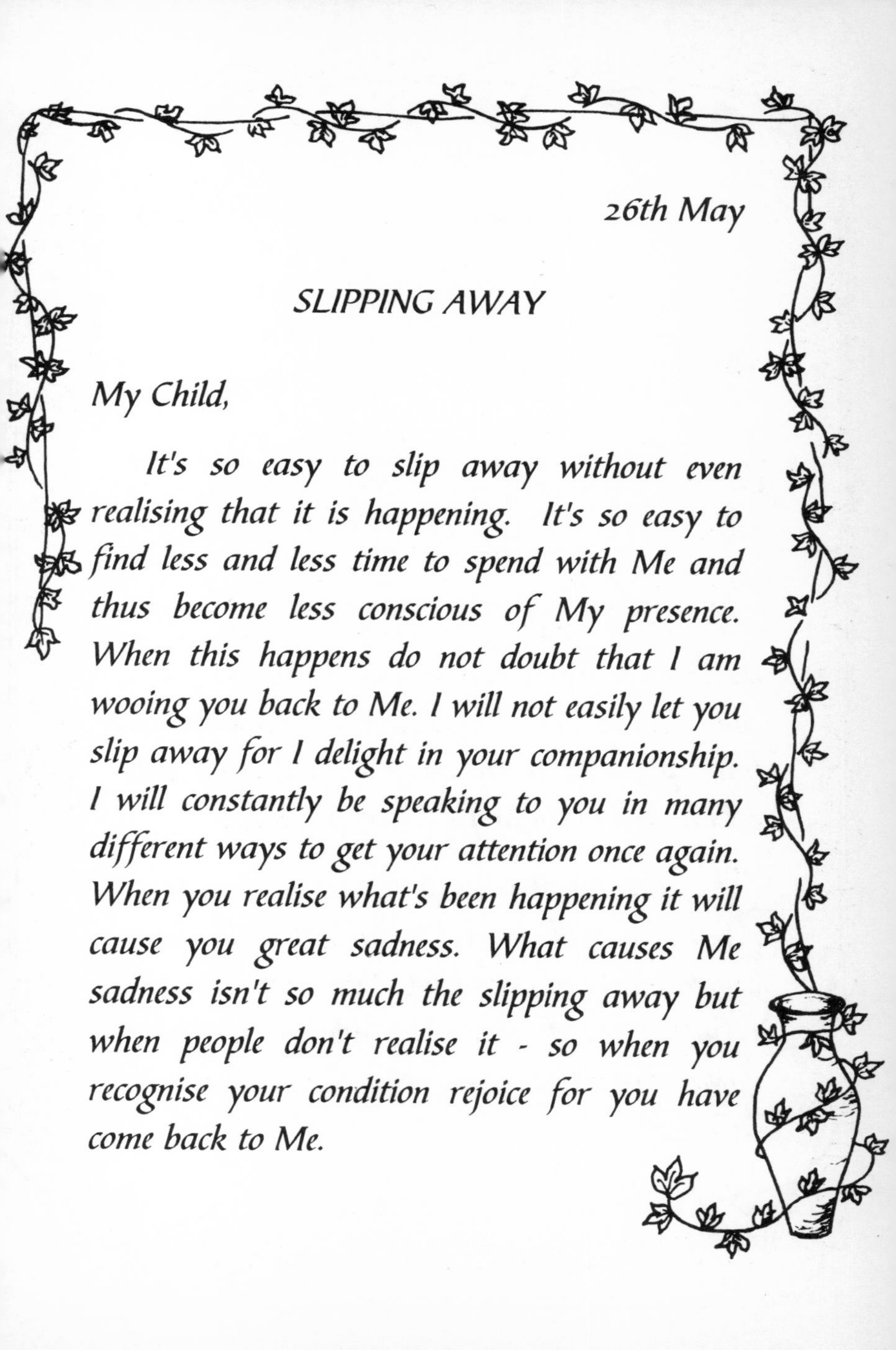

26th May

SLIPPING AWAY

My Child,

It's so easy to slip away without even realising that it is happening. It's so easy to find less and less time to spend with Me and thus become less conscious of My presence. When this happens do not doubt that I am wooing you back to Me. I will not easily let you slip away for I delight in your companionship. I will constantly be speaking to you in many different ways to get your attention once again. When you realise what's been happening it will cause you great sadness. What causes Me sadness isn't so much the slipping away but when people don't realise it - so when you recognise your condition rejoice for you have come back to Me.

27th May

PATIENCE

My Child,

Patience is something that does not come naturally. I know that you do not find it easy to wait. If only you could rest in the knowledge that My timing is perfect you would be at peace.

Resist the temptation to help things along for it is the way of fools and will land you in an awful lot of trouble.

If you can hang on in faith truly your patience will be rewarded. You will have great joy in knowing that you see the fulfilment of that for which you have waited so long.

28th May

WISE CHOICES

My Child,

Each new day brings with it so many different choices and decisions. Sometimes these choices will not be easy for you to make and will have serious consequences. The decisions that you make will show what's in your heart and if you are truly following Me or the way of the flesh. If your heart is right before Me and you have a desire to be obedient to Me, the choices that you decide upon are easier to enact.

If you ask for My help in all the decisions you make and choose to do My will, know that I will enable you to make wise choices.

29th May

PEACE OF MY PRESENCE

My Child,

Enjoy the peace of My presence and recognise that even when you are alone I am there with you. It is the fragrance of My presence that brings that calmness and quietness of heart, when you lay down your tools and sit at My feet.

No matter where you are that peace of My presence is always available to you. Be still - and in that stillness you will find Me.

The world longs for peace and even fights to obtain it, not knowing it can be found only in Me. You are blessed to have discovered the real meaning of peace, so hold on to it and value the peace of My presence.

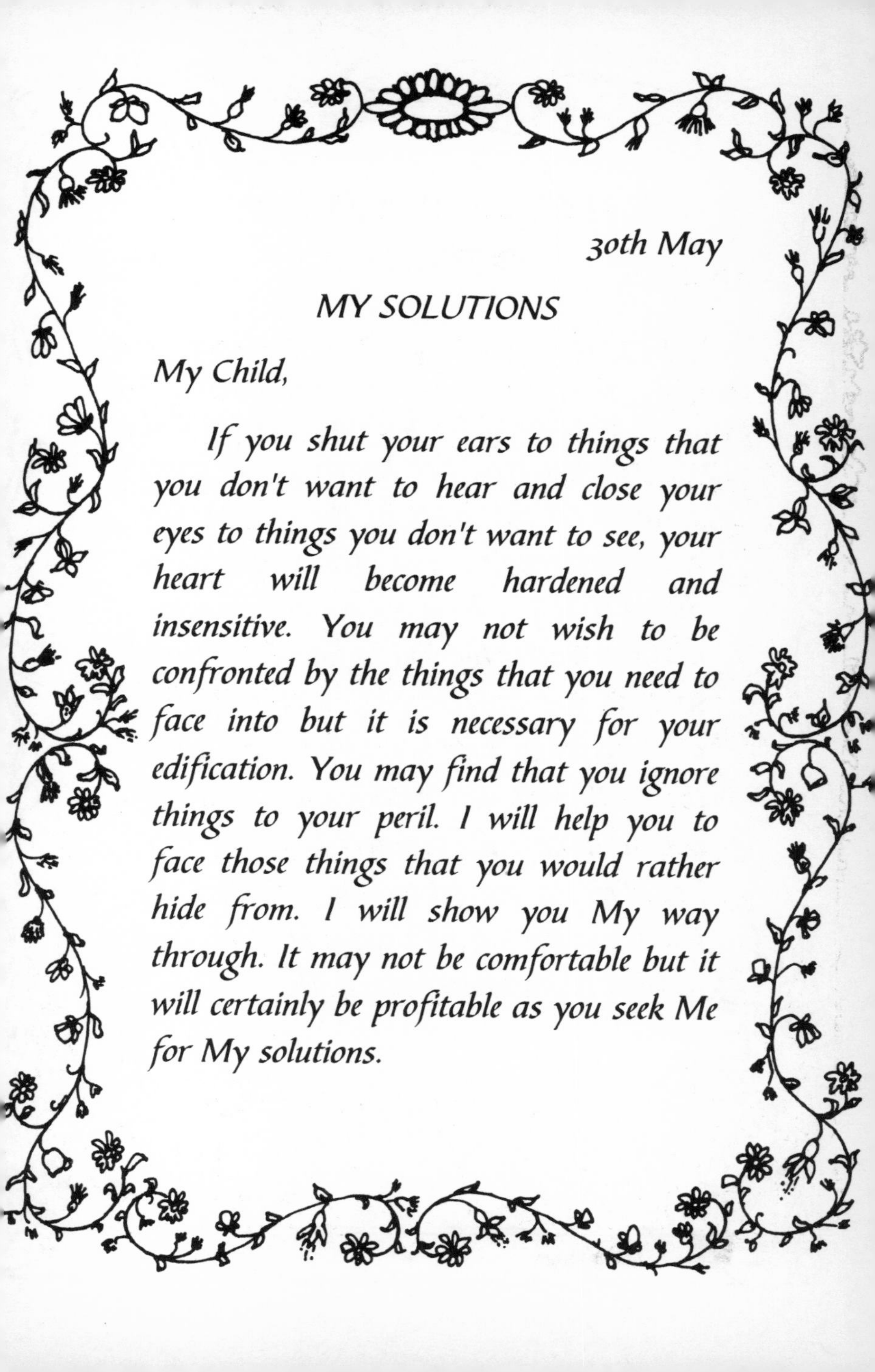

30th May

MY SOLUTIONS

My Child,

If you shut your ears to things that you don't want to hear and close your eyes to things you don't want to see, your heart will become hardened and insensitive. You may not wish to be confronted by the things that you need to face into but it is necessary for your edification. You may find that you ignore things to your peril. I will help you to face those things that you would rather hide from. I will show you My way through. It may not be comfortable but it will certainly be profitable as you seek Me for My solutions.

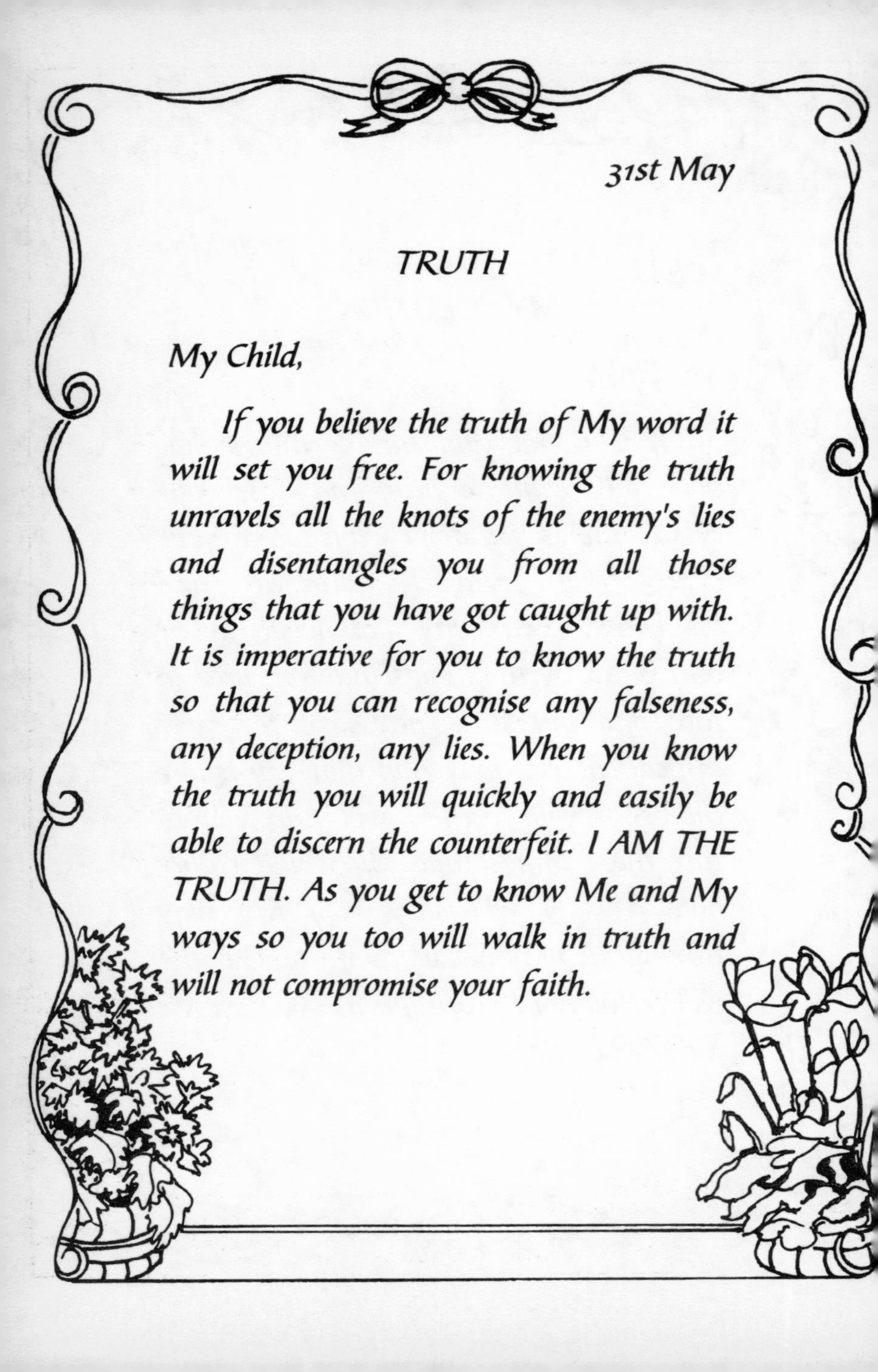

31st May

TRUTH

My Child,

If you believe the truth of My word it will set you free. For knowing the truth unravels all the knots of the enemy's lies and disentangles you from all those things that you have got caught up with. It is imperative for you to know the truth so that you can recognise any falseness, any deception, any lies. When you know the truth you will quickly and easily be able to discern the counterfeit. I AM THE TRUTH. As you get to know Me and My ways so you too will walk in truth and will not compromise your faith.

1st June

PRECIOUS

My Child,

You are so precious to Me. Yes, I know your faults and weaknesses and your limitations but you are still so precious. You may feel that you don't deserve anything and whilst you recognise that you have laid down all your rights, My heart's desire is toward you to bless you. I want to bless you because I choose to - I call you My child. Like any earthly Father who is good I will give you that which you need.

Look up into My face - you can call Me 'Abba' Father or 'Daddy'. So great is My love for you that I gave My Son so that you could be called My child. Even before you knew Me you were precious to Me and always will be!

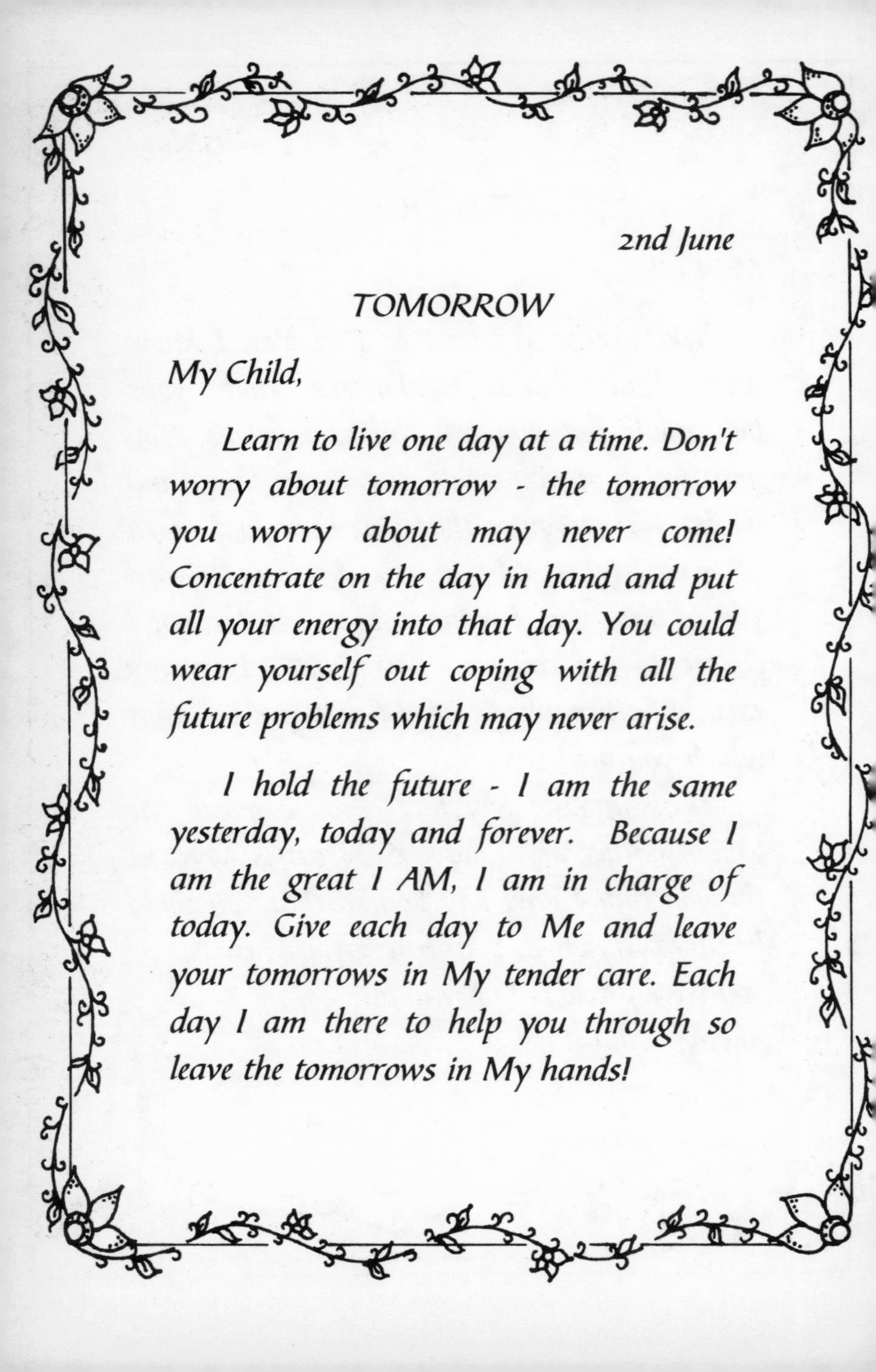

2nd June

TOMORROW

My Child,

Learn to live one day at a time. Don't worry about tomorrow - the tomorrow you worry about may never come! Concentrate on the day in hand and put all your energy into that day. You could wear yourself out coping with all the future problems which may never arise.

I hold the future - I am the same yesterday, today and forever. Because I am the great I AM, I am in charge of today. Give each day to Me and leave your tomorrows in My tender care. Each day I am there to help you through so leave the tomorrows in My hands!

3rd June

I AM COMING AGAIN

My Child,

I am coming again! Yes, the day of the Lord will come. If you could live every day in the certainty and expectancy of this would it change your life? No one knows when I am coming - but surely I will come. Therefore be on your guard. Be watchful, for it may be when you least expect it that out of the blue I will appear.

For you and those who love Me it will be a very welcome sight - at last the Bridegroom has come for His Bride.

So be ready, alert and watchful, for the signs of the times tell that My coming is nearer than you think.

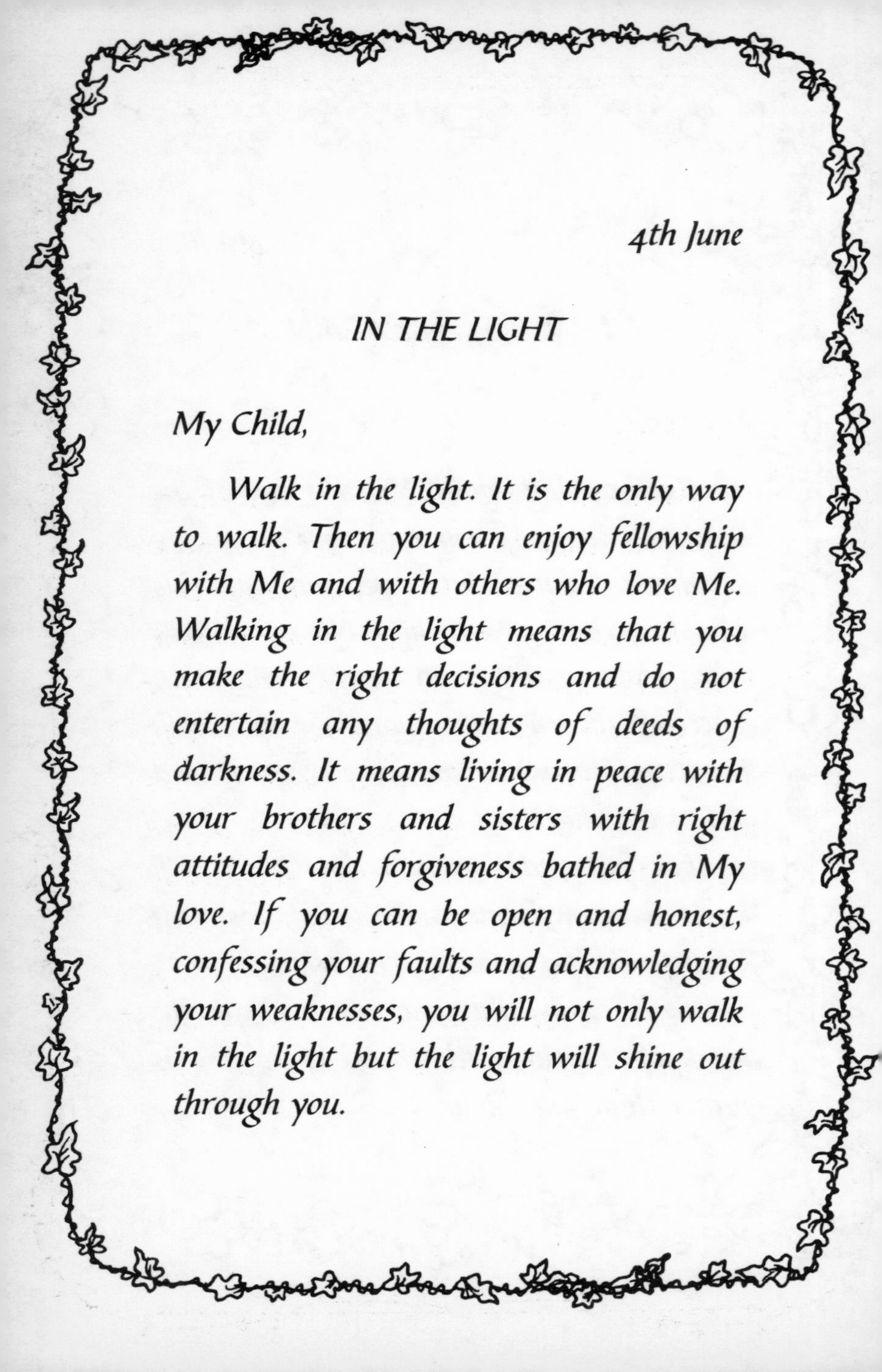

4th June

IN THE LIGHT

My Child,

Walk in the light. It is the only way to walk. Then you can enjoy fellowship with Me and with others who love Me. Walking in the light means that you make the right decisions and do not entertain any thoughts of deeds of darkness. It means living in peace with your brothers and sisters with right attitudes and forgiveness bathed in My love. If you can be open and honest, confessing your faults and acknowledging your weaknesses, you will not only walk in the light but the light will shine out through you.

5th June

BE AWARE

My Child,

Whilst you do not need to fear the enemy or be pre-occupied with him, you do need to recognise that you are in a battle even though you know that the victory is won. You cannot afford to be off guard, for that may give him an advantage that you don't want him to have. So be aware that he does have some power but greater power is in you than that which is in the world. You need to recognise his subtle ways so you can deal correctly with him. Do not treat him lightly, for he certainly needs to be resisted and denounced and put in his place - under your feet!

6th June

SINGLE-MINDED

My Child,

An athlete needs to be single- minded to succeed. The more disciplined and determined they are, the more the crowd applauds and cheers them on. However, if the same single-mindedness is given by you to following Me, the crowd will almost certainly not understand. You will almost certainly at some time be misunderstood and there will be those who will try to discourage you from serving Me wholeheartedly

You cannot expect the world to understand, but you can expect to suffer on My behalf. This is the way of the cross - it meant that I had to be single-minded in following My Father's will and now you can know the joy of being single-minded.

7th June

FREEDOM

My Child,

If you want to know freedom you must learn to live by My laws. It is the only way to peace and joy and complete freedom. If rules are not applied to a game chaos reigns and so it is with the 'game of life'.

If you can see My commands and laws as a blessing rather than a hindrance, then you will want to keep them. If you can live within those boundaries it will not inhibit you but give you the freedom to be yourself and enjoy the freedom I long to give you. This freedom is a peace of mind that knows no anxious thoughts or guilt or shame - freedom from all this is freedom indeed.

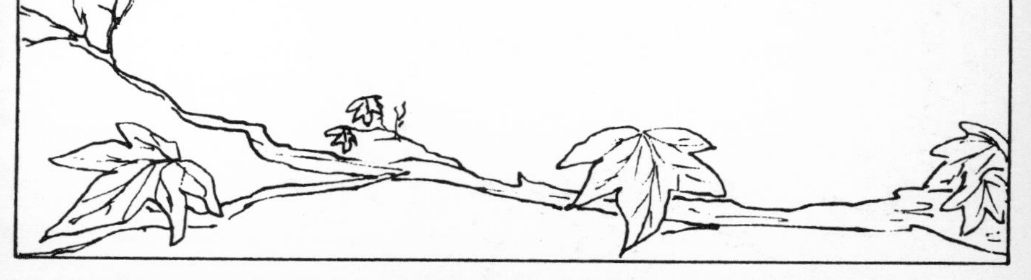

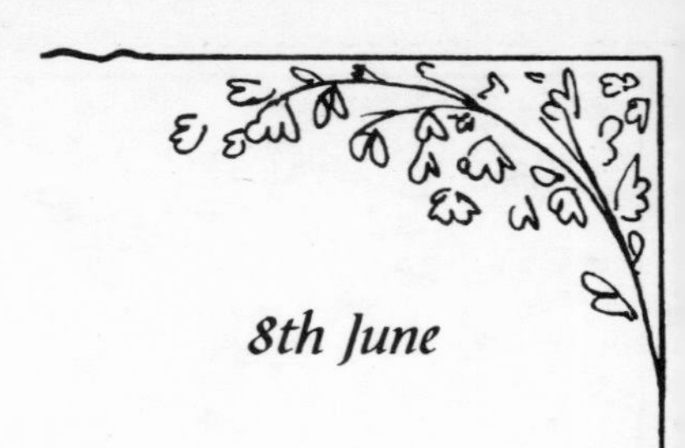

8th June

RAINBOW

My Child,

When you see a rainbow you are reminded of My faithfulness for I am a God who keeps My word and fulfils all My promises.

As it was in the days of Noah so today My promises remain the same. Whatever I have decreed in My word will eventually come to pass. You may have to wait in faith - indeed it could take much patience but your faith will be rewarded as you see My promises fulfilled. So when you see the rainbow in the sky, look up - for I will keep My promises.

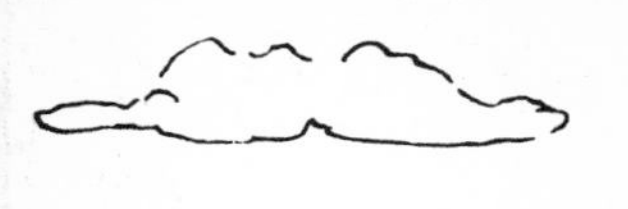

9th June

SO FAR AWAY

My Child,

You may feel that you have to walk very closely to hear Me and to be used by Me. It may be that you feel that you can be so far away that you wouldn't hear anyway. However far away from Me you may feel that you are, you are never outside of My voice range. Wherever you are, whatever you are doing, I can speak to you so that you can hear. Whether you choose to acknowledge My voice and respond is your choice. You can never ever step outside of My love for My love is in you and surrounds you. It is My love for you that motivates Me to keep calling you and it will be because of My love that you will respond.

10th June

FAVOUR

My Child,

You have favour with Me for I delight in you. Throughout all your life I will grant you favour for you are very special and precious to Me. You are the apple of My eye and My eye is constantly upon you to grant to you My favour. You need to be aware that I only plan good things for you because I love you. Whatever happens to you is always within the reach of My love and favour - yes, even the things you don't understand can show My favour.

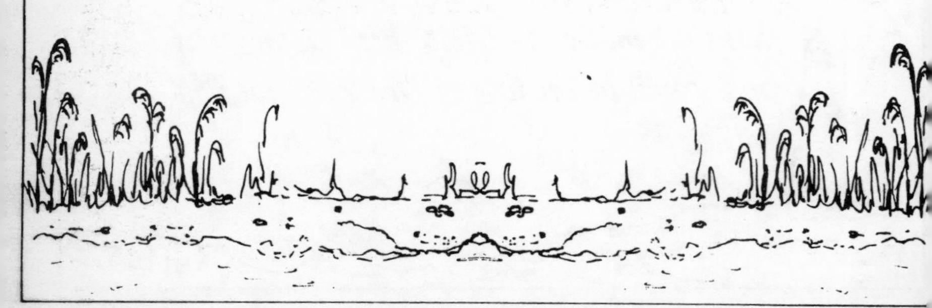

11th June

IN MY PRESENCE

My Child,

When you come into My presence to worship Me it is the highest and greatest thing that you can do. When your heart seeks to be in My presence above all else, you can have no greater desire or ambition. As you worship Me and desire to give to Me praise and honour so you will be drawn into My presence. When your desire to give to Me exceeds your desire to receive from Me, then you have truly discovered the pure joy that comes from worshipping Me alone.

12th June

PRAISE ME

My Child,

If you can praise Me when your heart is heavy then you will discover a joy unspeakable. As you focus on Me I will take you to a higher plain where you will see things from My perspective and enter into the glory of My world. It will lift your spirit and you will know that no matter how you feel I can restore to you the joy of your salvation.

Praise scatters the enemy and causes you to be reminded that I am so much bigger than you think I am.

13th June

PEACE AND JOY

My Child,

If your actions are right before Me but cause others to feel pain then you are not responsible for their pain. You must do what you believe to be right before Me and let the reactions of others not colour your own thinking. If you let the thoughts of others cloud your own decision making you are living to please them and not Me. Is this the way you really want to live?

However hard it may be to decide to follow Me it is the only way to peace and joy.

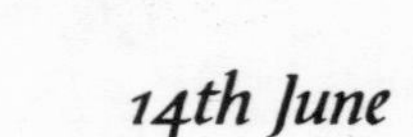

14th June

ENDURE FOR EVER

My Child,

It is not wrong to love beautiful things for I love beautiful things too. However, if you covet those things and even manipulate to get them, then that surely is wrong.

If you find that you love things of beauty and crave them even more than you do for Me, then that is what it means to love the world. All that is in the world will one day pass away but My word will not pass away but will endure for ever.

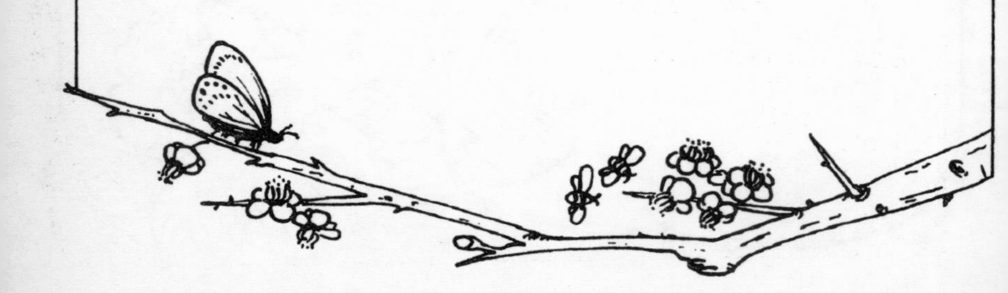

15th June

WAY OF THE CROWD

My Child,

Don't follow the crowd. Sheep always follow one another but make sure that you follow the shepherd. If you follow the Good Shepherd you will not be led astray for I will lead you to green pastures by quiet waters.

Remember that however great the majority is, they are not always right! It is not easy to swim against the tide but you will not be alone for I am with you.

My sheep hear My voice - I know them and they know Me. I love My sheep - indeed I gave My life for them. I will not lead you in the way of the crowd - I will lead you into new paths of righteousness.

16th June

POWER TO COPE

My Child,

There are so many things in this life that you will not be able to fathom out or understand. To try to do so leads to frustration and intolerance. There is no answer that could or would satisfy the many difficult circumstances and trying times.

If you can relinquish the right that you believe you have to understand, and lay it down at My feet, then I will give you the faith to trust Me and the power to cope with anything and everything. If you can believe that My hand is on your life for good, then you can lead a rewarding life in fellowship with Me.

17th June

LOOKING UP

My Child,

Oh My precious child, how I long for you to know My Father heart of love and provision. As an earthly child looks to their Father without fear or anxiety, so I want you to be always looking up to Me, trusting Me and putting your whole confidence in Me.

I will never fail you or let you down - no, never. I can meet your every need - whatever that need may be. If you really believe this your heart will be at peace. That's how I want you to be, at peace - knowing all is well because your Father knows and cares.

18th June

SHINE THROUGH YOU

My Child,

The more you humble yourself and walk in humility before Me, the more I can use you and lift you up. If you desire to see My name glorified more than your own name, then you will share My glory. If you seek the praise of men it will be futility and emptiness to you and mean nothing.

Learn to exalt and honour My name above everything else for in so doing you will lose sight of the focus which centres on you.

As you decrease and become humble in My sight, so I will increase in your life and My glory will shine through you.

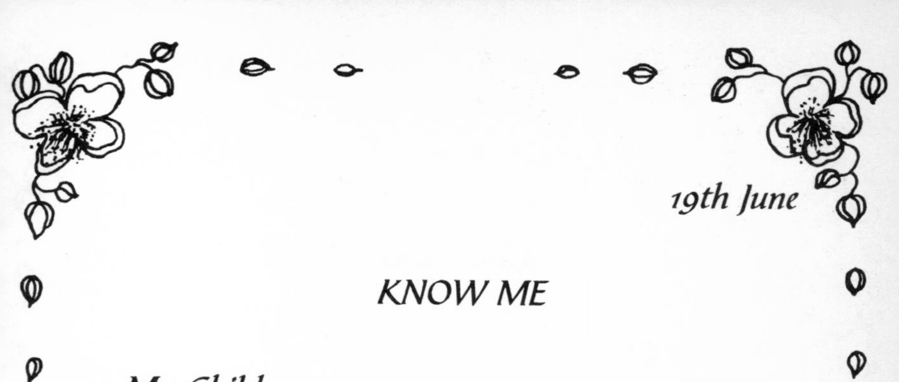

19th June

KNOW ME

My Child,

However hard you try and however much you want to understand Me that will never be possible, for if you understood Me you would be as I am - God. It is possible for you to learn of Me and get to know My ways, works and wisdom, even if it is only in a limited measure.

Though you may never be able to understand Me with your mind, it is possible to know Me with your spirit and this is most important of all. For knowing Me is life, health, joy, peace and wholeness. It is LIFE ABUNDANT to know Me.

20th June

IN THE HEAVENLIES

My Child,

Don't underestimate the power of prayer to move mountains, clear pathways and overcome obstacles. Prayer is a dynamic force which breaks down every barrier that opposes Me and allows My blessing to flow. It causes the impossible to become possible and that which is not, to come into being.

Every time you pray these dynamics are in operation - see what power is at your disposal through prayer. Cherish and guard those times of prayer, for at those times My blessing is being released - even when you can't see it, it is happening in the heavenlies.

21st June

STUMBLING-BLOCK

My Child,

Some of the things that happen to you I allow, to enable you to see more clearly into your heart.

You may think that you have no prejudices, until you see because of various situations that you are indeed prejudiced. Also you may not be aware of wrong attitudes until I put My finger on them.

I do not allow these things to come into your life to shame you, but to show you what a real stumbling-block they are. If you can deal with your prejudice and wrong attitudes, you will find a heart of love for the unlovely.

22nd June

LIFE ON EARTH

My Child,

The passing of a loved one is a solitary reminder of how short life on earth really is. Life on earth is very short compared to life in eternity which goes on for ever and ever and ever and ever...

Therefore live your life to make each day count. Live in an attitude of love and forgiveness towards your brothers and sisters, for life is too short for quarrels. Do not harbour bad feelings toward anyone - no, not for a moment, for it will cause you pain and misery. I want you to enjoy this life that I give you and live it to the full for My glory.

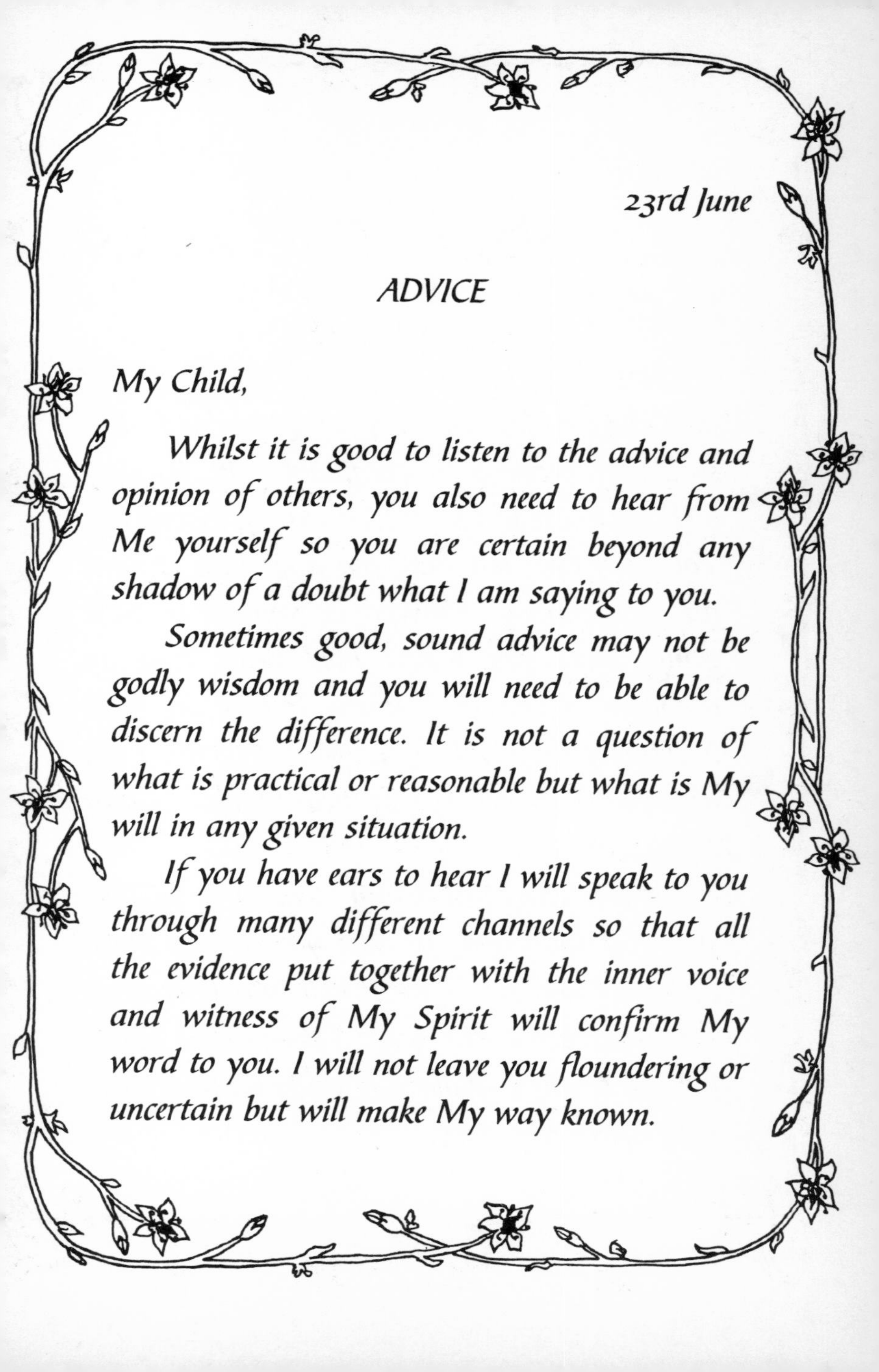

23rd June

ADVICE

My Child,

Whilst it is good to listen to the advice and opinion of others, you also need to hear from Me yourself so you are certain beyond any shadow of a doubt what I am saying to you.

Sometimes good, sound advice may not be godly wisdom and you will need to be able to discern the difference. It is not a question of what is practical or reasonable but what is My will in any given situation.

If you have ears to hear I will speak to you through many different channels so that all the evidence put together with the inner voice and witness of My Spirit will confirm My word to you. I will not leave you floundering or uncertain but will make My way known.

24th June

CHERISHED DREAM

My Child,

Sometimes when something you long for and cherish lies within your grasp and then suddenly becomes unobtainable, it is very difficult to die to that which was so longed for. You may even feel that you have been cheated and it is unjust. However as you die to those things that you would hold dear, even an ambition or cherished dream, if they are from Me surely they will be resurrected again. I am able to bring life out of death, hope out of hopelessness.

If this cherished dream is not My will for you and you die to it, then you will be much better off without it, for it will be a distraction and obstruction to you. Though the dying process to self is painful it yields much fruit in your life to My glory.

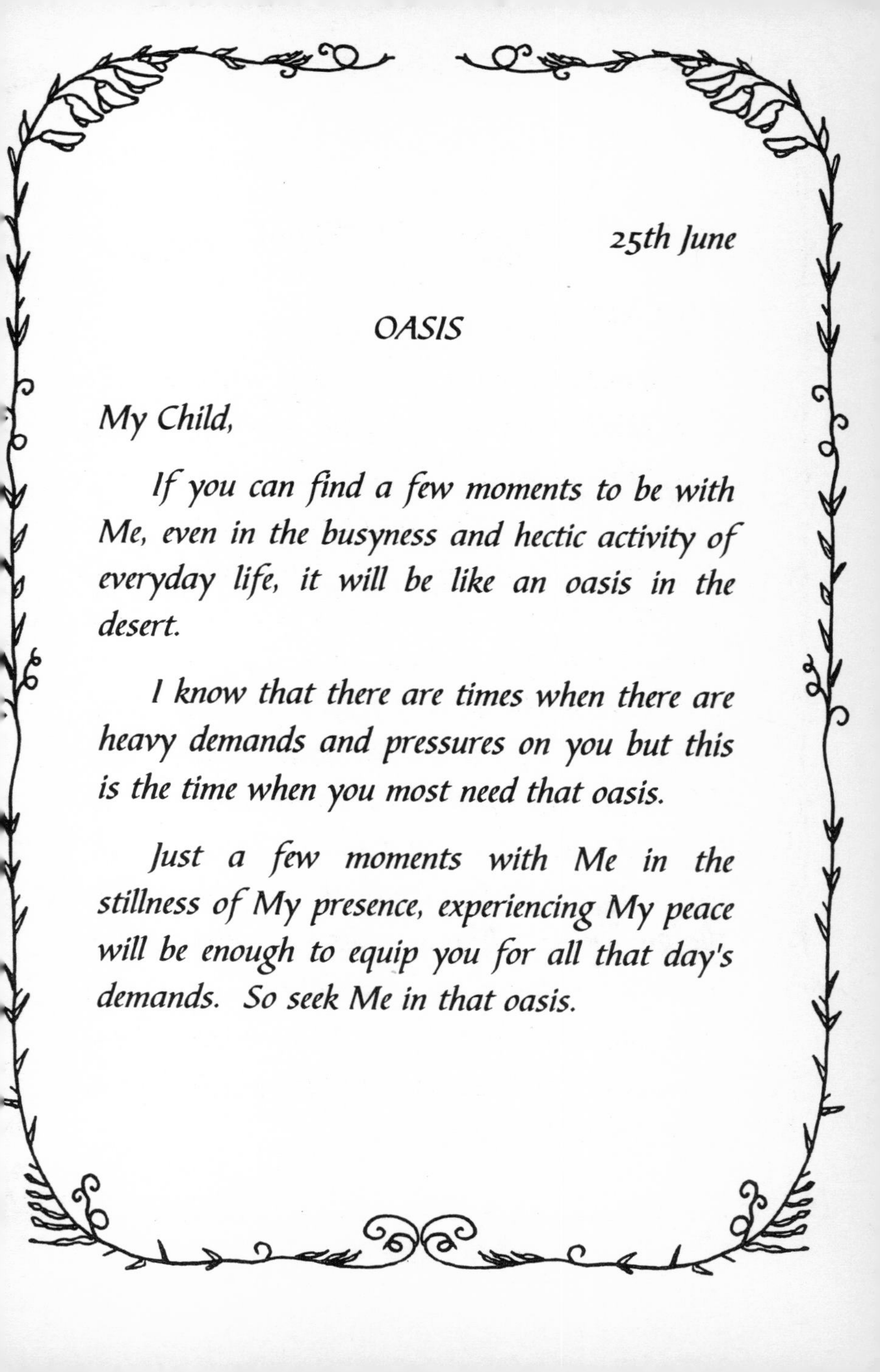

25th June

OASIS

My Child,

If you can find a few moments to be with Me, even in the busyness and hectic activity of everyday life, it will be like an oasis in the desert.

I know that there are times when there are heavy demands and pressures on you but this is the time when you most need that oasis.

Just a few moments with Me in the stillness of My presence, experiencing My peace will be enough to equip you for all that day's demands. So seek Me in that oasis.

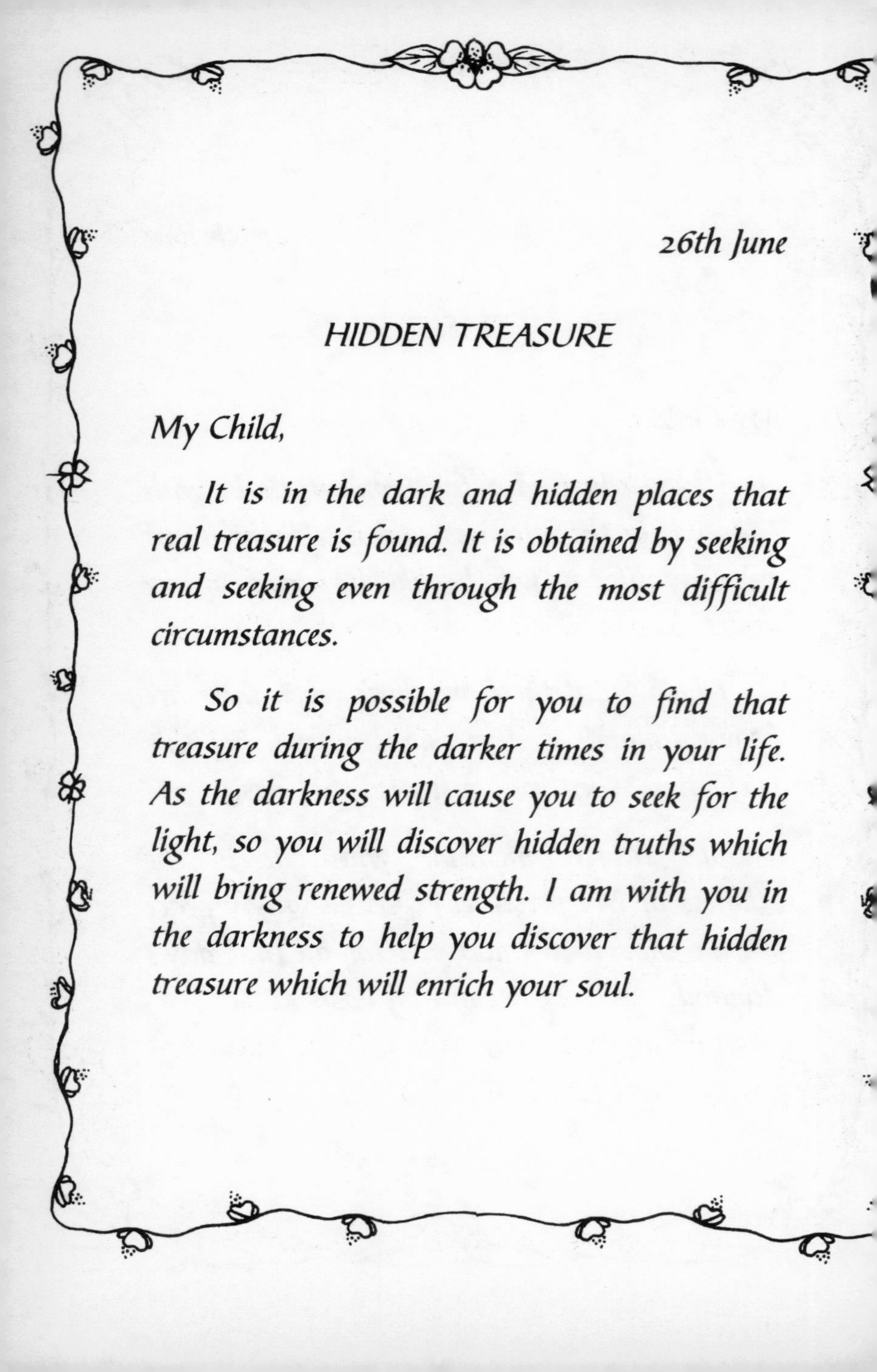

26th June

HIDDEN TREASURE

My Child,

It is in the dark and hidden places that real treasure is found. It is obtained by seeking and seeking even through the most difficult circumstances.

So it is possible for you to find that treasure during the darker times in your life. As the darkness will cause you to seek for the light, so you will discover hidden truths which will bring renewed strength. I am with you in the darkness to help you discover that hidden treasure which will enrich your soul.

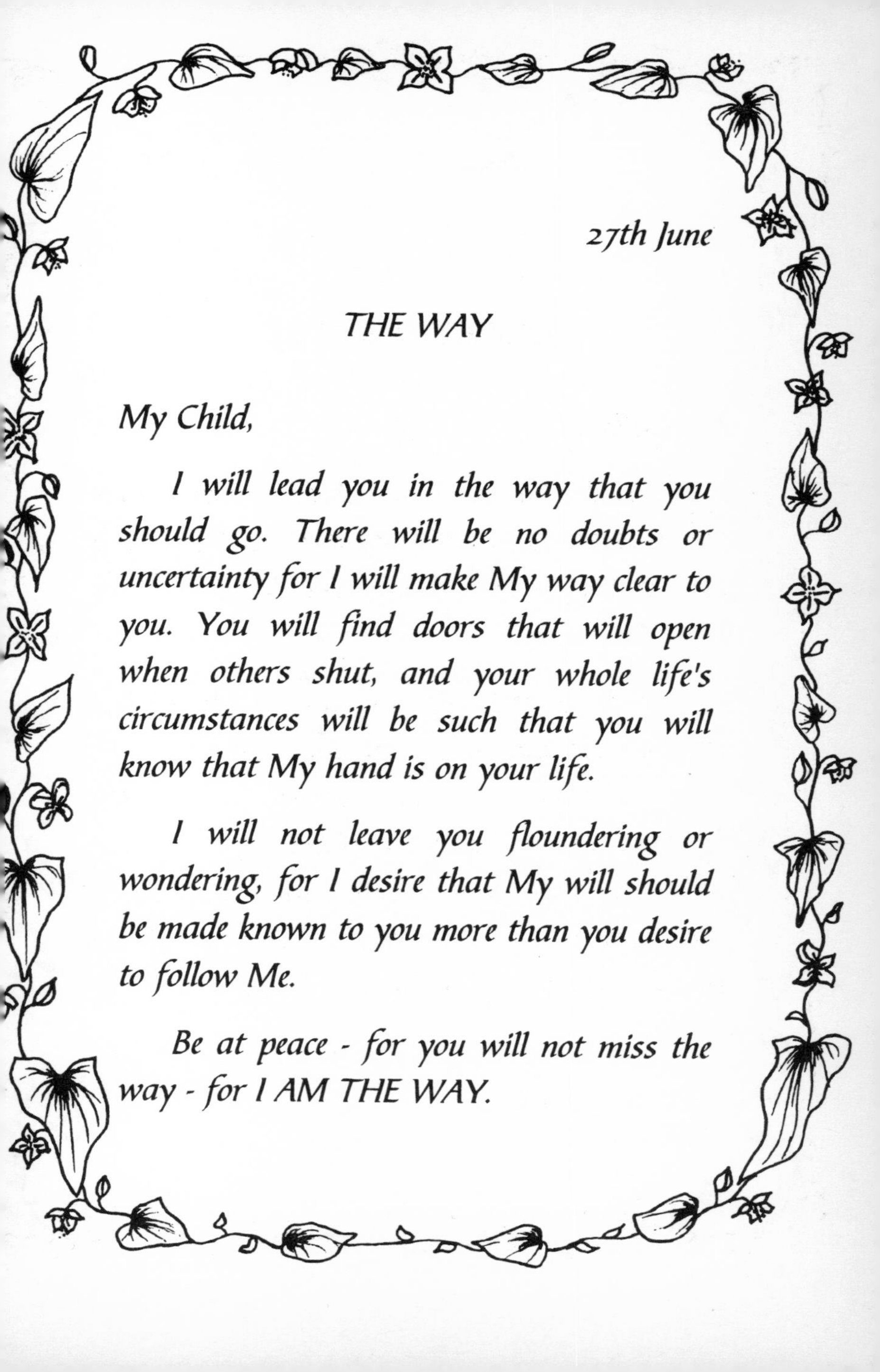

27th June

THE WAY

My Child,

I will lead you in the way that you should go. There will be no doubts or uncertainty for I will make My way clear to you. You will find doors that will open when others shut, and your whole life's circumstances will be such that you will know that My hand is on your life.

I will not leave you floundering or wondering, for I desire that My will should be made known to you more than you desire to follow Me.

Be at peace - for you will not miss the way - for I AM THE WAY.

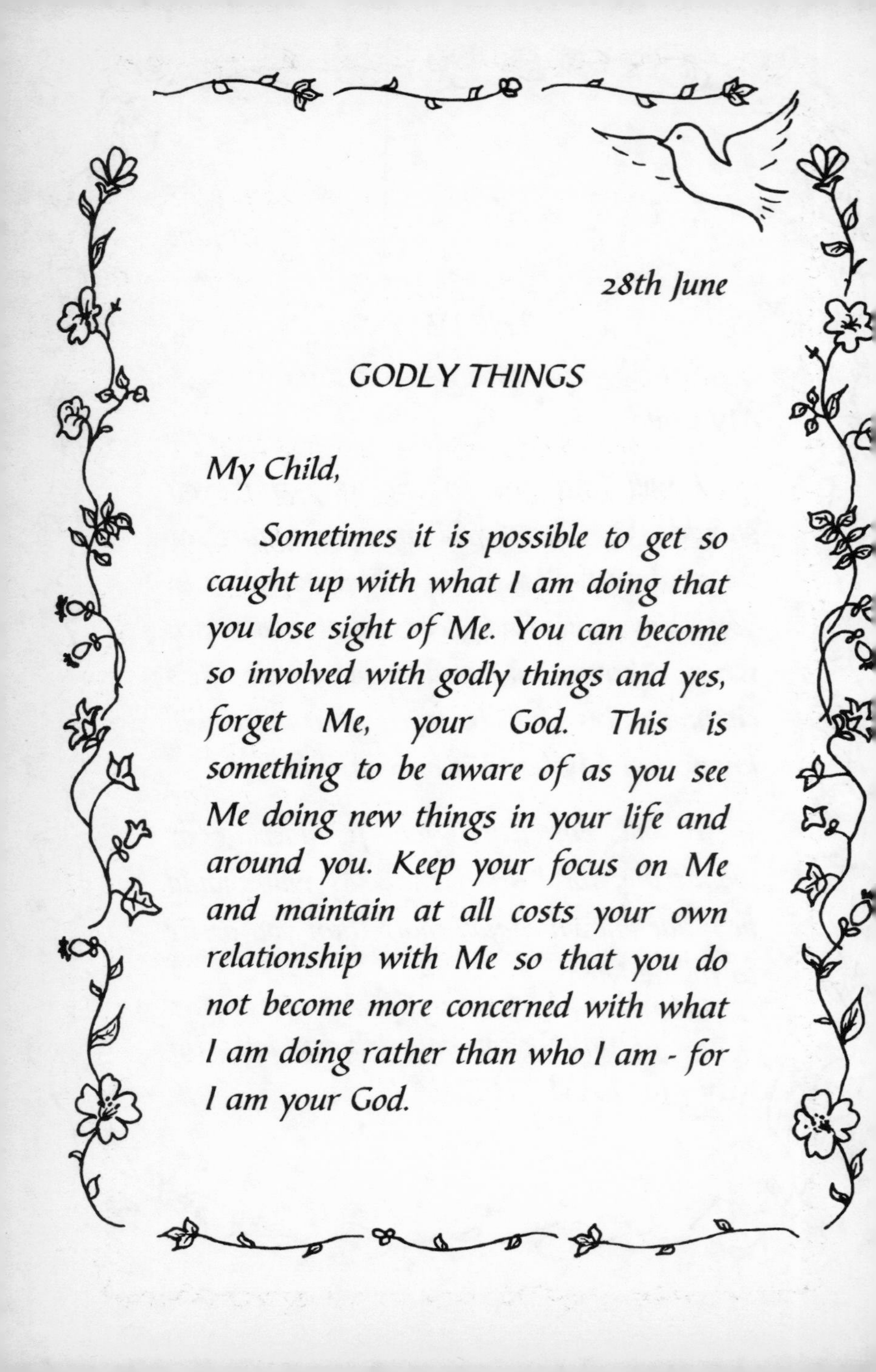

28th June

GODLY THINGS

My Child,

Sometimes it is possible to get so caught up with what I am doing that you lose sight of Me. You can become so involved with godly things and yes, forget Me, your God. This is something to be aware of as you see Me doing new things in your life and around you. Keep your focus on Me and maintain at all costs your own relationship with Me so that you do not become more concerned with what I am doing rather than who I am - for I am your God.

29th June

VALUABLE

My Child,

No one could ever love you like I do - I love you with a pure and perfect love. I count you as being so valuable and precious that I gave the very best I had to procure your salvation.

You are so special and precious and not only do I want you to know this but I want you to believe it because it is the truth.

You may not feel that special but to Me you are. My dearest child how I love you. Receive My love and believe the truths I have spoken to your heart which will set you free.

30th June

THE SHADOW

My Child,

If you abide close to My heart you will certainly experience the protection which is afforded to those who live under the shadow of the Almighty. If you choose to live in the distance there is no way that the shadow can reach you.

Only as you experience that closeness which comes from obedient living will you feel safe and secure under My shadow. You must learn to dwell in the secret place of the Most High so that you will never be outside of the shadow of the Almighty.

1st July

LOVE THE UNLOVED

My Child,

How easy it is to love those with whom you feel at one. This requires no compassion or caring for it comes naturally. Will you love the unloved and the unlovely for Me? If you do not befriend and care for them how will they ever know and experience My love.

It will take much effort on your part and you will need to see people with My eyes so that you can understand their hearts and what makes them 'tick'. This will not be easy but I will fill you with My love so it can flow from Me through you to all who need it.

2nd July

MY JOY

My Child,

I want you to experience My joy deep down in your heart. This is not to be confused with happiness which is linked to happenings. My joy is something which is not dependent on your circumstances or how you feel. It is readily available to all those who love Me for it is the fruit of the Holy Spirit dwelling within your heart and life. This joy springs from knowing that I have your well-being at heart and you are enjoying a close walk with Me daily. It does not fluctuate but is constant and available - to you!

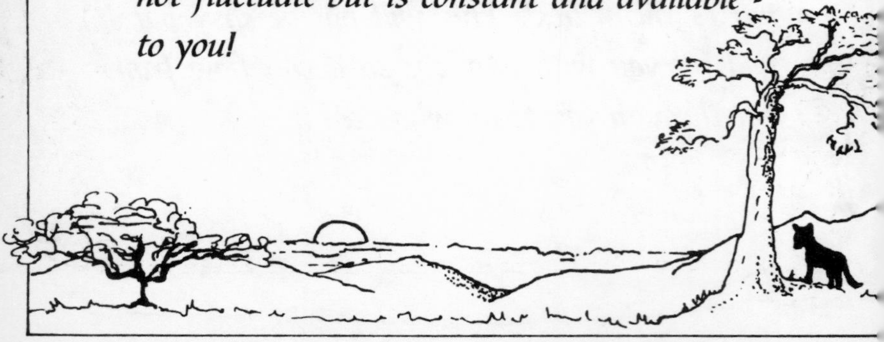

3rd July

POWER

My Child,

The promise of My Holy Spirit to you is that you shall receive power. Power to overcome sin and all the temptations of the enemy. Power to live a victorious Christian life because I overcame all the powers of darkness. When this power comes upon you, you will surely know it, for it will affect your life and transform you.

Instead of trying to live with the limitations of your own body, you will know My Holy Spirit flowing through you bringing the power that you need to live for Me.

4th July

SUFFICIENT GRACE

My Child,

Do not be concerned today with how you will face any suffering or persecution because it will cause your heart to fear and hinder you as you seek to follow Me.

I have promised to be with you always and to never leave you or fail you or forsake you. My grace is sufficient for you but you will not receive tomorrow's grace today. When you need that grace it will be there for all your tomorrows.

So many of My suffering children have discovered this and that is why they not only cope but praise Me in all circumstances.

Because I am with you and My grace is sufficient you will be able to experience My peace and joy in all your tomorrows.

5th July

A CAUTIOUS HEART

My Child,

A cautious heart can be an honourable thing provided that your heart is open to Me and can hear Me when I speak to you.

However much confirmation you need, I will give it to you, so that there is no need to doubt or fear what I am asking of you.

It is wise to be cautious so long as you do not hold back when you know in your heart what My will for you is.

Be ready to obey when I speak. When you have heard My voice give your cautious heart to Me and I will exchange it for an obedient one which will recognise that I am at work.

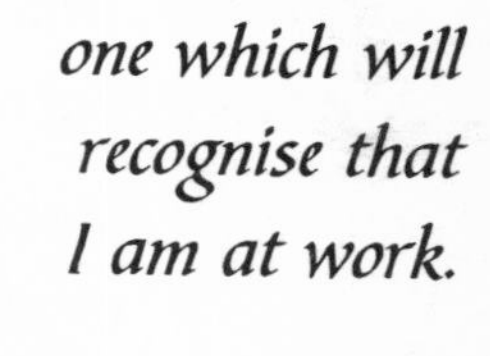

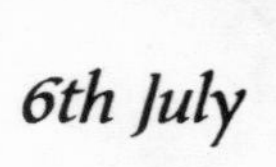

6th July

ON FIRE

My Child,

Sometimes when you feel that the flame is burning low in your heart, it may seem that it has been totally extinguished. Even though flames may die down, the embers are still hot and it only takes the gentle breeze of My Holy Spirit to fan those flames into being again. This can happen at any time as My Spirit desires. However, if you recognise that the flame in your heart is burning low and cry out to Me to light the fire again, surely I will answer you and set your heart on fire. Ask Me to send the wind of the Holy Spirit to activate the flame and you will once again experience My Holy Fire in your heart.

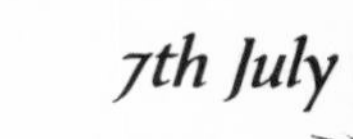

7th July

SETTLE FOR LESS

My Child,

Continue to steadfastly persevere in prayer. Do not give up, even when it appears that there is no answer. Continue to press in until you have the answer that you have been longing, crying and praying for. And even when you have part of the answer, which may not be completely what you have yearned for in prayer, press in even more to see the completed answer. For it is so easy to see prayer answered in part and settle for that. Do not settle for less than you have been interceding for - I am able to totally answer your prayers.

8th July

DEVOTED HEART

My Child,

Give Me the devotion of your heart for I am a jealous God and long for your devoted heart to be given to Me.

It is so easy to be devoted to people, hobbies, work, even church and yet somehow miss out on being devoted to Me. If in all your relationships and all the things that you do there is little devotion to Me, then you are missing out of the joy and satisfaction available to you.

A heart that is devoted to Me is full of joy and peace and can enjoy all aspects of life. Are you prepared to give Me the devotion of your heart?

9th July

SCENES OF LIFE

My Child,

Through all the changing scenes of life I am with you. Even though you may have rejected Me and at one time not wanted to know Me, still My hand has always been on your life. Because you are precious to Me My hand is upon you every day of your life and each moment of the day.

Life brings many changes - yet I change not. My loving care over your life is constant and unchanging. As I watched over your entrance into this world so I will continue to watch over you, for you are the apple of My eye.

10th July

SOULS WON

My Child,

Be bold and courageous - even in the face of opposition, for the power of My Holy Spirit will put My words in your mouth. If you desire to preach the gospel and to see souls saved, even if it be at personal cost to you, then I will give you the courage that you need to fulfil that desire.

Do not argue or give in to argument for that will not be convincing - instead let My Holy Spirit give wisdom and anointed words with boldness. It will not be by might or power but by My Spirit that souls are won into My kingdom.

11th July

MINE FOREVER

My Child,

I understand the pain that separation from loved ones bring, especially when that separation is permanent. I know how your heart aches and see those tears that no one else sees. Allow yourself the time to grieve for there is a time to weep when sorrow comes upon you and it is right and proper so to do.

Know in your heart that there is absolutely nothing in heaven or on earth that can separate you from Me or My love. You are Mine forever.

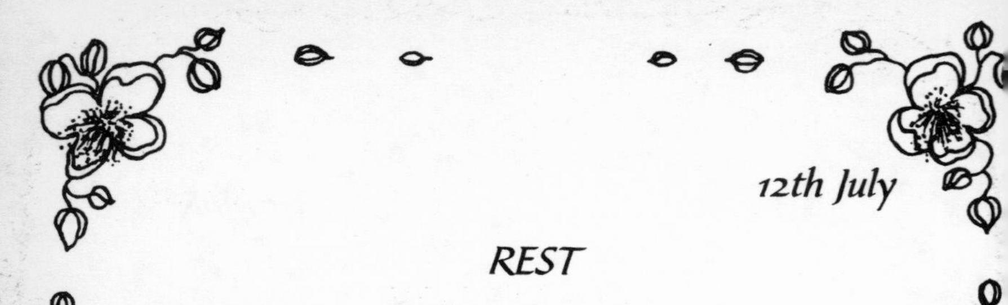

12th July

REST

My Child,

Come unto Me all you who are weary and heavy laden and I will give you rest. When you feel weary in body, mind and spirit you can know rest and refreshment as you come to Me.

Learn of Me for in those busy times on earth I found rest by going to the Father. There is no other place on earth that is such a sanctuary for you except to come to Me.

So many today long for rest yet though they may find rest for the body, the rest that they need for the mind and spirit eludes them.

Take My yoke upon you and learn of Me
for My yoke is easy and My burden light.

13th July

CORRECTION

My Child,

Do not take offence if others correct you, for it will ultimately lead to your good. Though it may offend you if others seek to correct you, especially if you sense a lack of love, it may be something that you need to hear.

With every word of correction spoken to you comes the need to discern the truth. As you share your heart with Me so I will reveal the truth to you. However, I will never, ever condemn you but will in love show you what you need to understand.

Whatever the truth of the situation make sure that your heart attitude is right before Me so you can walk in truth.

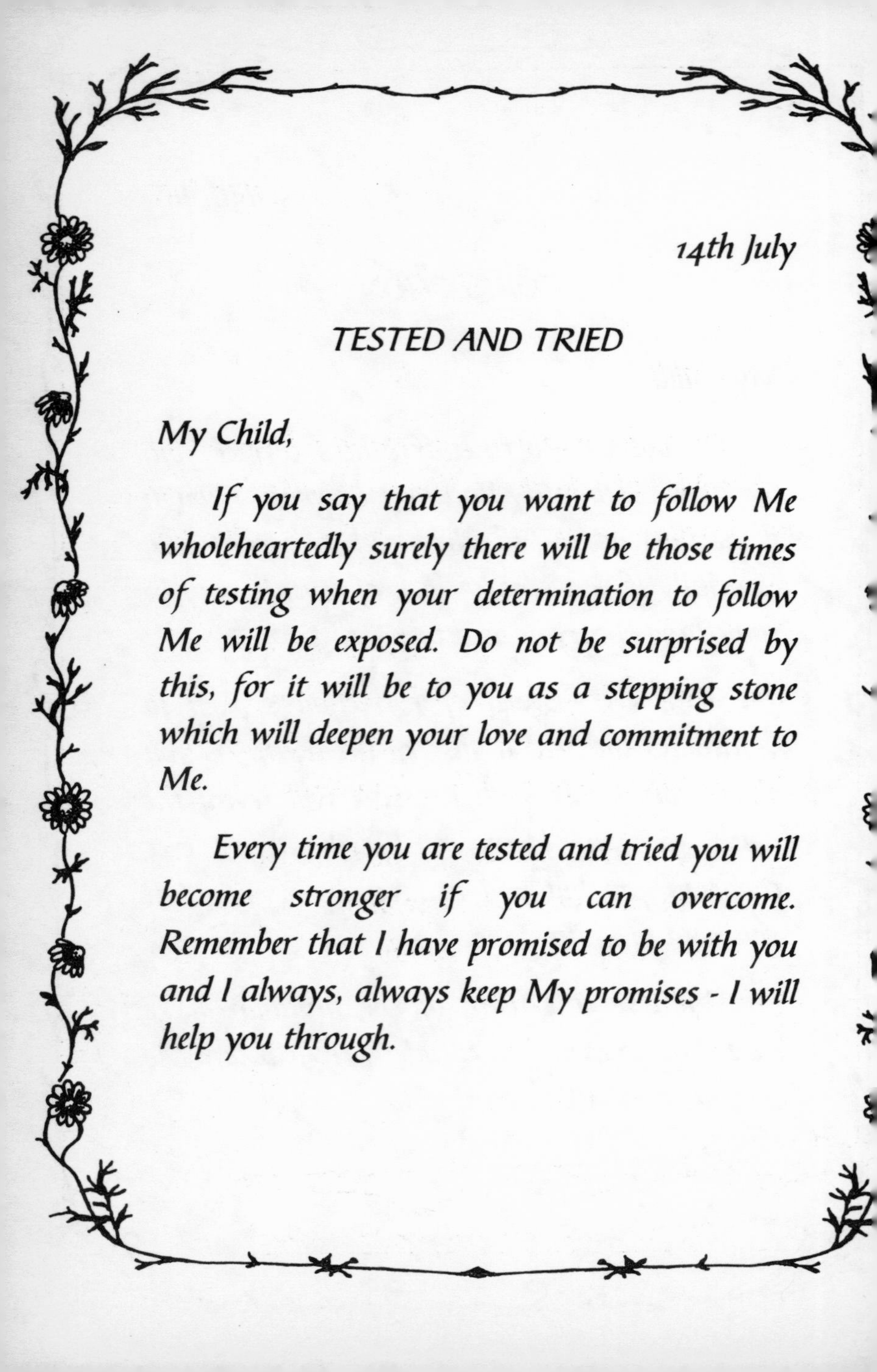

14th July

TESTED AND TRIED

My Child,

If you say that you want to follow Me wholeheartedly surely there will be those times of testing when your determination to follow Me will be exposed. Do not be surprised by this, for it will be to you as a stepping stone which will deepen your love and commitment to Me.

Every time you are tested and tried you will become stronger if you can overcome. Remember that I have promised to be with you and I always, always keep My promises - I will help you through.

15th July

A FRIEND

My Child,

There are many in this world who want to serve Me and do great things for Me but few who want to be a friend. Will you be My friend?

Will you be content just to be with Me, share with Me and enjoy My company with no strings attached? Will you trust Me and not betray Me, no matter what happens?

If you can be happy just to enjoy My friendship you will find that deep companionship of close friends which lasts into eternity.

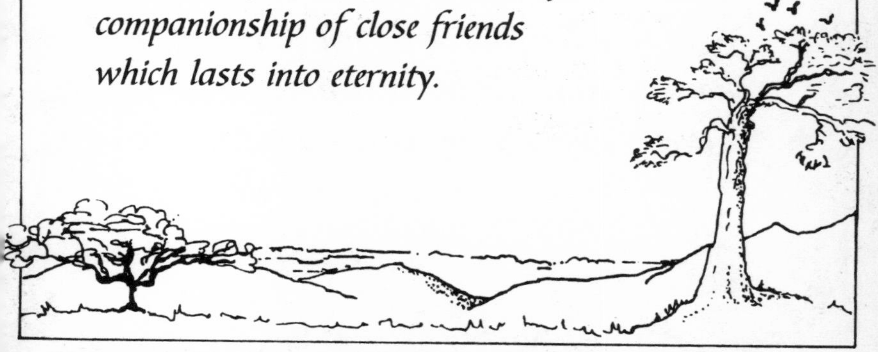

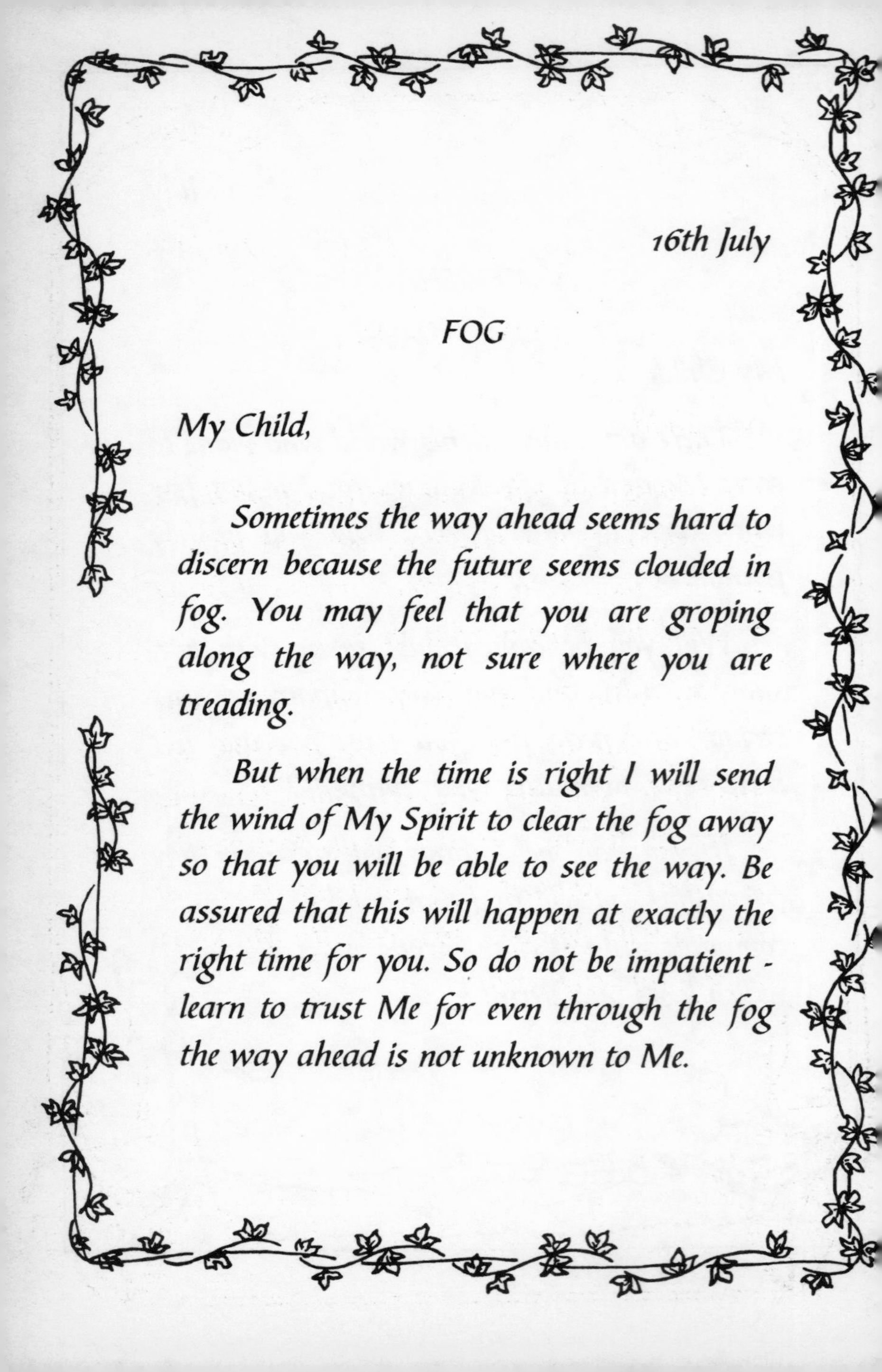

16th July

FOG

My Child,

Sometimes the way ahead seems hard to discern because the future seems clouded in fog. You may feel that you are groping along the way, not sure where you are treading.

But when the time is right I will send the wind of My Spirit to clear the fog away so that you will be able to see the way. Be assured that this will happen at exactly the right time for you. So do not be impatient - learn to trust Me for even through the fog the way ahead is not unknown to Me.

17th July

COMPASSION

My Child,

Unless you have that tenderness of heart you will not be concerned about the lost. It will not matter to you that many are being ushered into eternity without Me.

But with compassion in your heart you will cry out to Me for those who do not know Me. You will seek every opportunity to show forth My love and speak My words. Let Me fill you with My compassion so you can see with My eyes and feel with My heart to seek and save the lost.

18th July

ON LOAN

My Child,

Whatever you borrow is on loan to you and you have no right to hold on to it indefinitely. Though in your heart you decide you will return that which has been loaned, unless you actually do it, you are guilty of taking unlawful possession of another's property.

It is right for you to treat another's property with respect and not make it your own. Even if this is unintentional it is wrong and not the way that I want you to live.

I have called you to walk in integrity and want you to live in a way that honours Me. Therefore do not take possession of that which is not yours but restore it to the owner......then My blessing will flow.

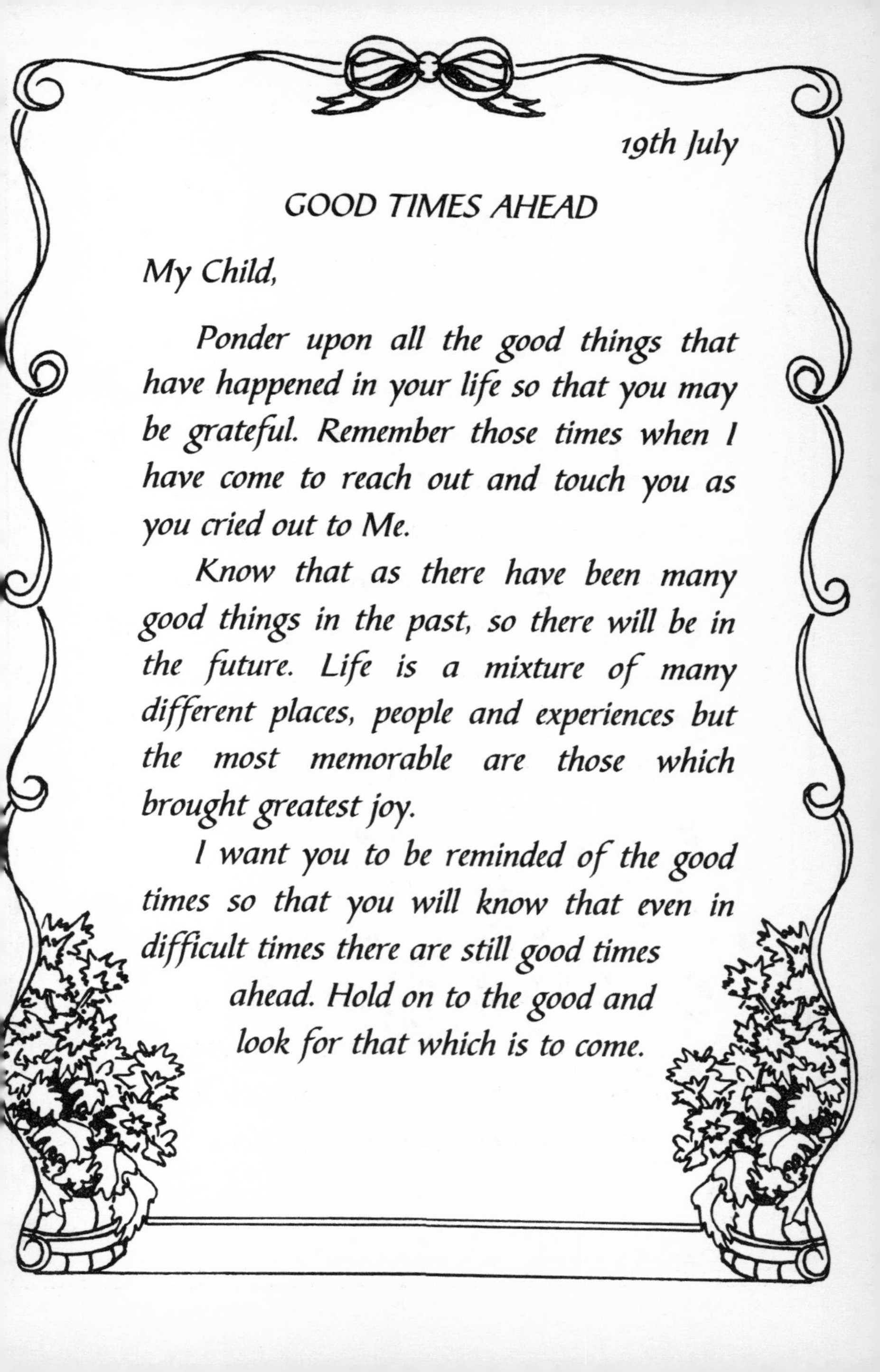

19th July

GOOD TIMES AHEAD

My Child,

Ponder upon all the good things that have happened in your life so that you may be grateful. Remember those times when I have come to reach out and touch you as you cried out to Me.

Know that as there have been many good things in the past, so there will be in the future. Life is a mixture of many different places, people and experiences but the most memorable are those which brought greatest joy.

I want you to be reminded of the good times so that you will know that even in difficult times there are still good times ahead. Hold on to the good and look for that which is to come.

20th July

FELLOWSHIP

My Child,

It is good for you to have fellowship with others for this will encourage you and build you up. As you fellowship together it will bring a sense of My presence and will enable you to share all the good things that I am doing in your lives. As you talk together of things concerning Me it will increase your hunger and thirst within to get to know Me better.

There is a power in unity and as you fellowship together in unity, you will see My power and presence manifest even when you do not expect it.
So do not be surprised that fellowshipping together brings great blessing.

21st July

HABITS

My Child,

Some habits are very good and help you to lead a disciplined life. Other habits may not be so good and are not necessarily helpful. If you can break free of old habits you will learn to walk in a new habit of righteousness.

Only as you begin to see that some habits are not helpful will you be able to renounce and repent of them where necessary. Afterwards I will fill you with My Spirit so that you will be able to walk in a new way by the power of My Holy Spirit. This will bring a new joy and freedom into your life.

22nd July

SAFE IN MY HANDS

My Child,

How much are you prepared to let Me take control of your life. If you give the control of your life to Me and hand it over to Me it will mean that you are no longer in control. This may cause your heart to fear until you remember that your life is much safer in My hands than in your own hands.

So long as you surrender your life to Me you never need to fear being out of control, for I will never ever hurt you or cause you harm. To be under My control is the safest place that you can be.

23rd July

TEARS FLOW

My Child,

As you look at the world around you there is so much injustice and evil that My heart aches. Because I have given the gift of free will, My hands are now tied - I cannot take that gift back even when I see the consequences of 'free will'.

The answer to the evil in this world lies in the cross. It was there that sin was overcome and the victory is Mine. I came to save a bleeding, dying world and to show that despite the evil, you can find hope and comfort when your tears flow.

24th July

INSPIRED WORDS

My Child,

When you walk closely with Me and allow My Holy Spirit to flow through you, constantly you will find that you are speaking inspired words which at the time seem no more than very pleasant words. In every day conversation you will be speaking out of your heart without realising the powerful effect that those words are having upon the listeners. This will also happen in your praying as your heart joins My heart and I put My words in your mouth. Do not be surprised that this happens to you and be aware that I am the God who takes the ordinary and makes it extraordinary.

25th July

DYNAMITE

My Child,

When you receive a specific word from Me, be sure to check out with Me who that word is for and the right time and way to give it. Words are very powerful and it is like having dynamite in your hands which has the power to destroy. However, used correctly dynamite can be great to pull down strongholds under controlled conditions.

Seek Me for wisdom and discernment to know how to handle all the words that you receive so that no one is damaged but all are edified and built up in their faith.

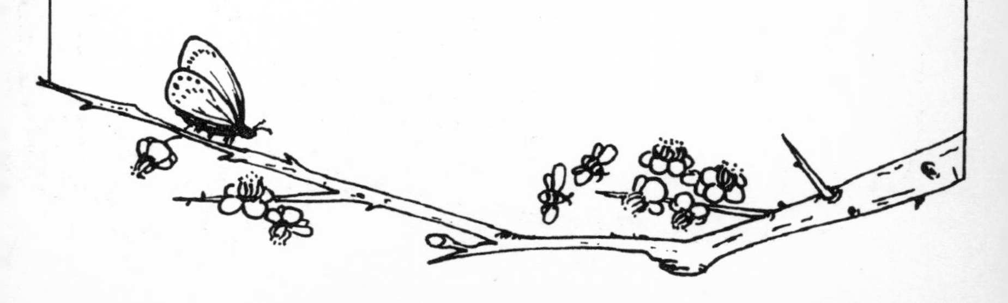

26th July

GREATER JOY

My Child,

If you give out of a heart of love and devotion to Me, then you will find that you are able to give more than you can afford because of the blessing that you will receive.

Whilst it is good to give because of the need of others, this will cause you only to give to meet the need which may not involve sacrificial giving.

Whatever you sow, you will accordingly reap - whether good or bad. This is a godly principle and will make you want to sow more. However, if you give out of a heart of love and devotion to Me you will find an even greater joy and reap a greater reward.

27th July

LIGHT OF SALVATION

My Child,

You cannot sit passively when you know that you have been called to 'Follow Me'. Rise up and take your stand in this world of increasing darkness. If you add your voice to all the other godly voices then the voice will get louder and people will hear.

Don't shut your ears and close your heart but turn away from evil unto Me for I am God. Be prepared to be a light in the darkness so that others will be able to experience the light of My salvation. A light cannot help shining, especially in the dark and having an influence in the dark. Shine out My light.

28th July

GREATEST FRIENDSHIP

My Child,

Learn to value the important things in life like peace, friendships and the beauty of the world in which you live. It is so easy to get caught up with the world's ways and ideologies that your priorities change.

Many of the things that are important in this life are free and cost you nothing, like the fragrance of a rose, the warmth of the sun and the peace of a quiet place away from all the hustle and bustle of life. If you can enjoy things like this and appreciate all that you have been given, you will find yourself rich indeed.... even more so if you have good friends, but remember the greatest friendship of all that you can have is with Me.

29th July

LOVE SPEAKS

My Child,

Throughout life your life will touch with those who have endured unspeakable pain and suffering. Their lives and behaviour will express the pain which is locked up on the inside. Even though you may find it difficult to cope, don't hide your face from them as this will cause them even more rejection.

Even if you don't know what to say just show them My love, for love speaks louder than words. Then they will not only feel your acceptance but Mine too and believe that there is hope.

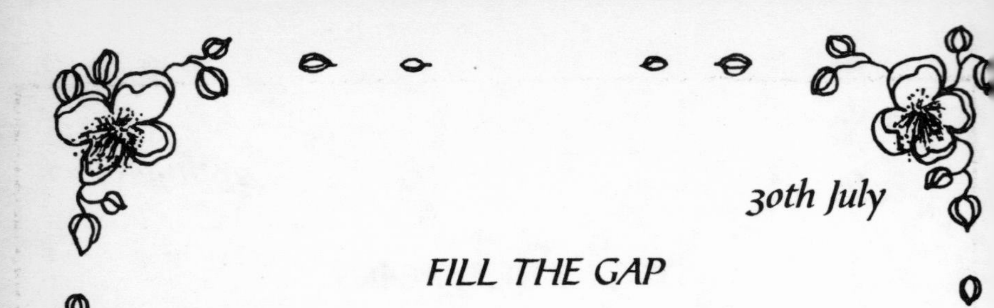

30th July

FILL THE GAP

My Child,

When someone you love goes out of your life and leaves a gap, be careful how you fill that void. Though you may feel sad and empty I want you to know that I can fill the gap.

Even those closest to you cannot always be near you - they have to live their own lives but I am ever present with you. I will never leave you.

You can be assured of My presence each and every day and no matter how big you feel the gap in your life may be - I am bigger than the gap.

31st July

HOLY GROUND

My Child,

If you really long to be drawn into a deeper place of intercession then come and take off your shoes for the ground is holy. Only those who experience and live in My holiness can be effective in the place of intercession.

Even if you do not feel worthy to enter the holy place of intercession, then you can still come because My precious blood avails for you today. There is plenty of room in this place of intercession - not many want to come . . . . yet the door is always open.

1st August

GROW IN GRACE

My Child,

If you stay in the place where I want you to be, even though you would rather be somewhere else, you will receive My blessing and approval.

However difficult you may find the situation and even if you would like to walk away from it, you can know My peace and strength to stay, until, at the right time, I release you into new things.

The more you would like to go, yet decide to stay, the more you will grow in grace. My timing is perfect and it is so important that you do not run ahead of Me because you could miss that special thing I have for you.

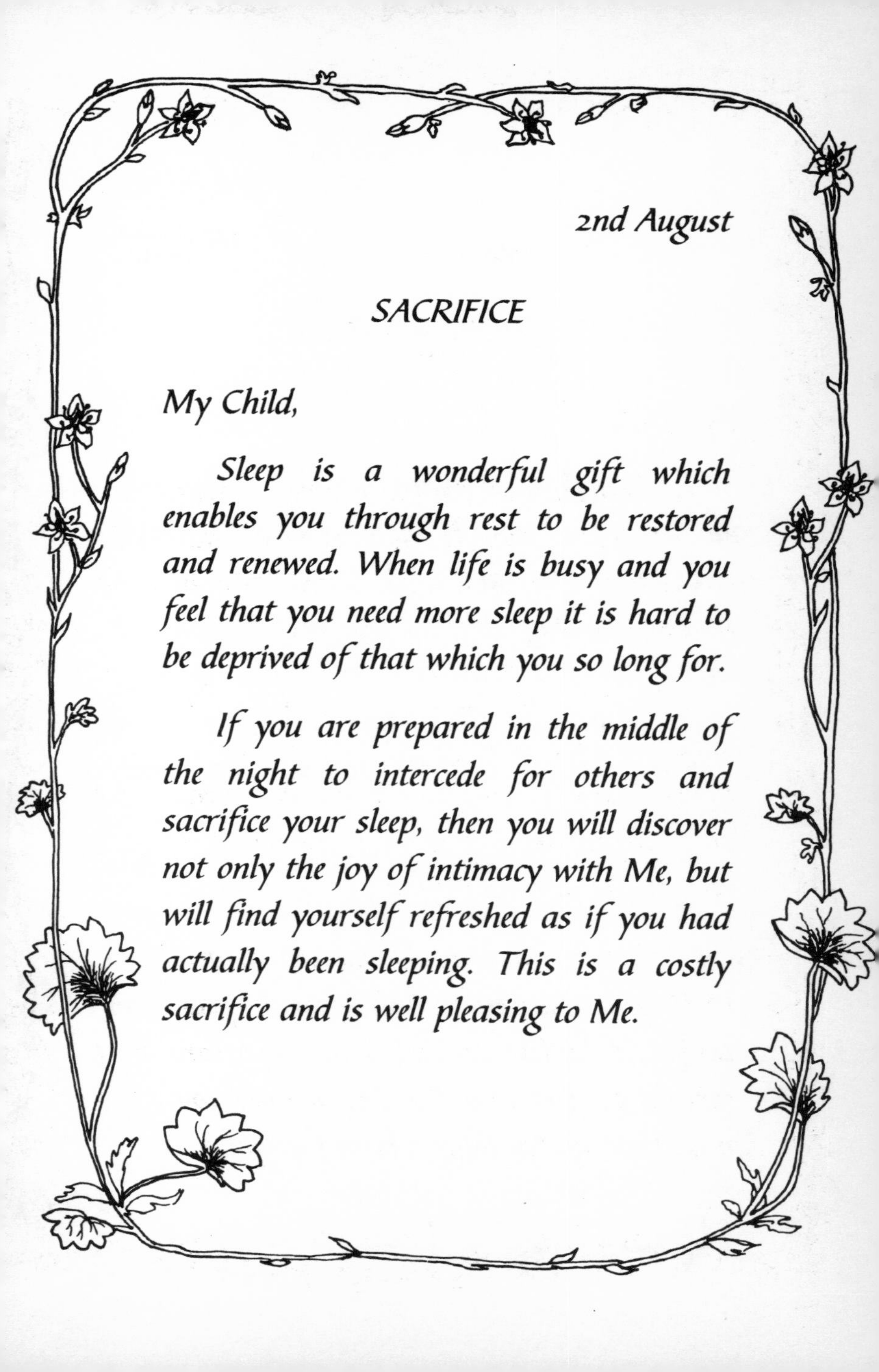

2nd August

SACRIFICE

My Child,

Sleep is a wonderful gift which enables you through rest to be restored and renewed. When life is busy and you feel that you need more sleep it is hard to be deprived of that which you so long for.

If you are prepared in the middle of the night to intercede for others and sacrifice your sleep, then you will discover not only the joy of intimacy with Me, but will find yourself refreshed as if you had actually been sleeping. This is a costly sacrifice and is well pleasing to Me.

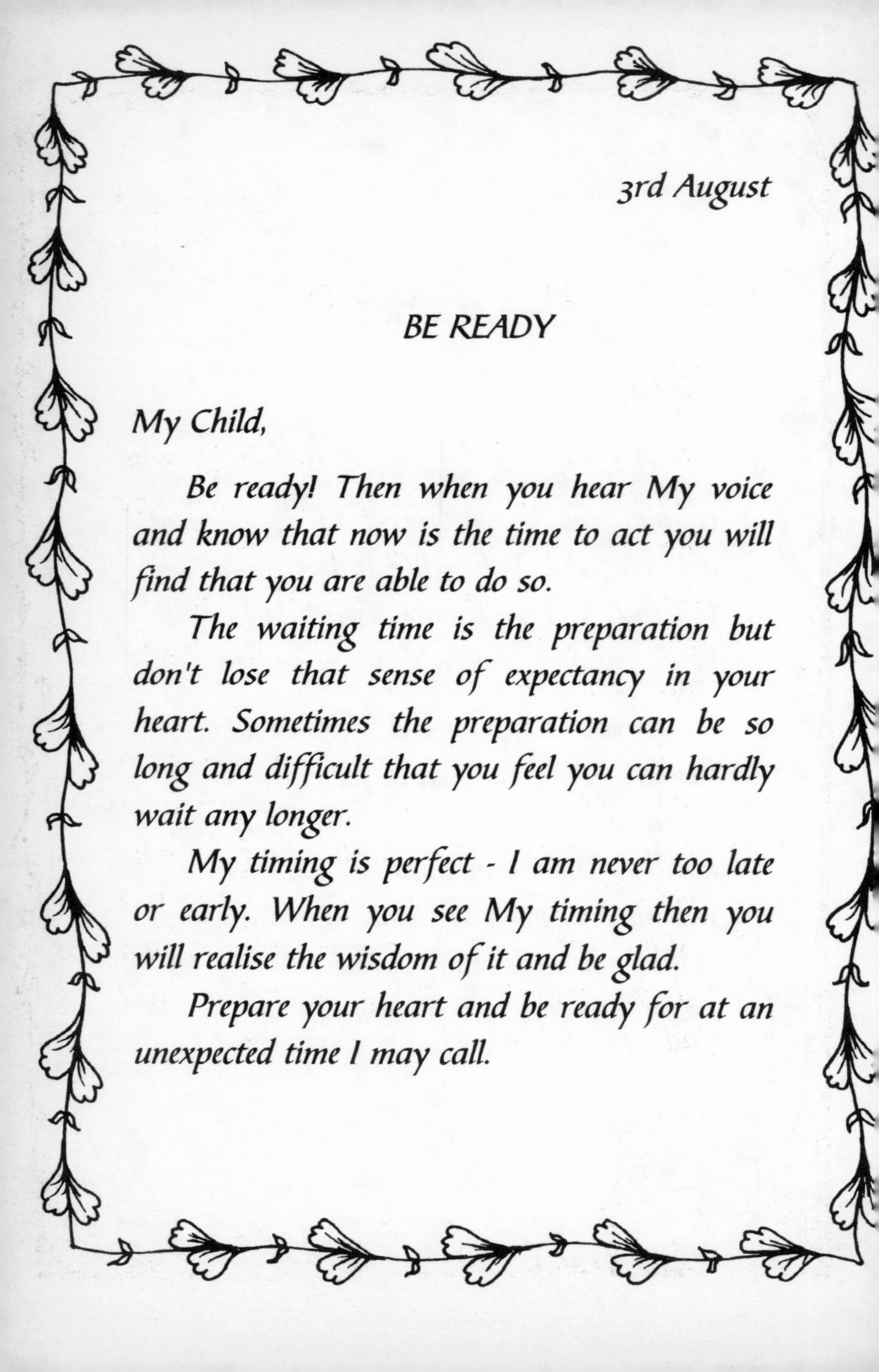

3rd August

BE READY

My Child,

Be ready! Then when you hear My voice and know that now is the time to act you will find that you are able to do so.

The waiting time is the preparation but don't lose that sense of expectancy in your heart. Sometimes the preparation can be so long and difficult that you feel you can hardly wait any longer.

My timing is perfect - I am never too late or early. When you see My timing then you will realise the wisdom of it and be glad.

Prepare your heart and be ready for at an unexpected time I may call.

4th August

MANY SURPRISES

My Child,

Do not look on the outside and judge who you think will respond to Me and enter My kingdom for there are many surprises in My kingdom. I can touch the hardest heart and break into the lives of those who you would consider most ungodly.

It is often the most unlikely person who responds and this can cause My children to doubt the integrity and faith of those who respond. However, if you walk close to Me I will show you those who will respond and though you may be surprised, your heart will be glad - for did I not indeed choose you!

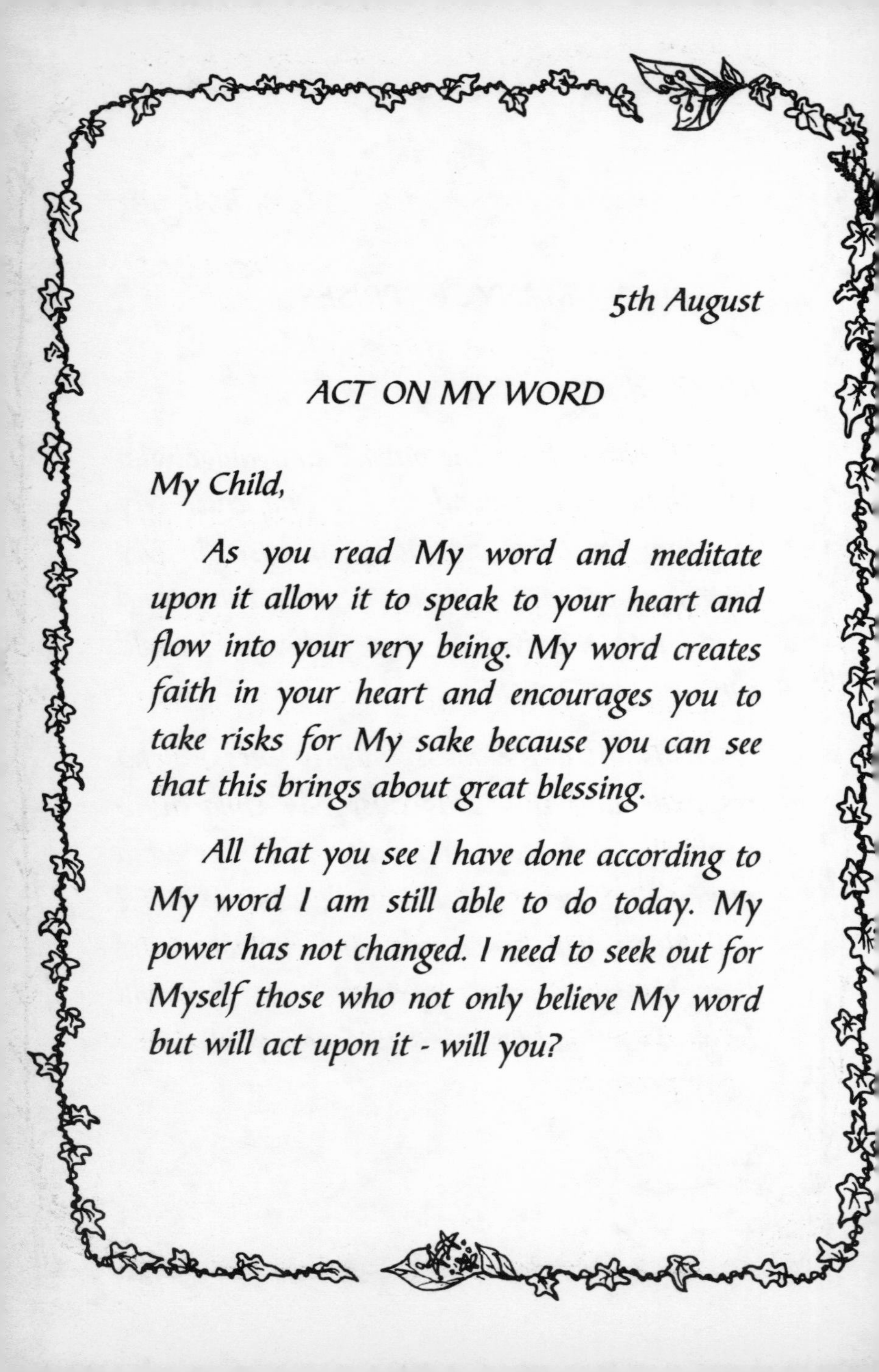

5th August

ACT ON MY WORD

My Child,

As you read My word and meditate upon it allow it to speak to your heart and flow into your very being. My word creates faith in your heart and encourages you to take risks for My sake because you can see that this brings about great blessing.

All that you see I have done according to My word I am still able to do today. My power has not changed. I need to seek out for Myself those who not only believe My word but will act upon it - will you?

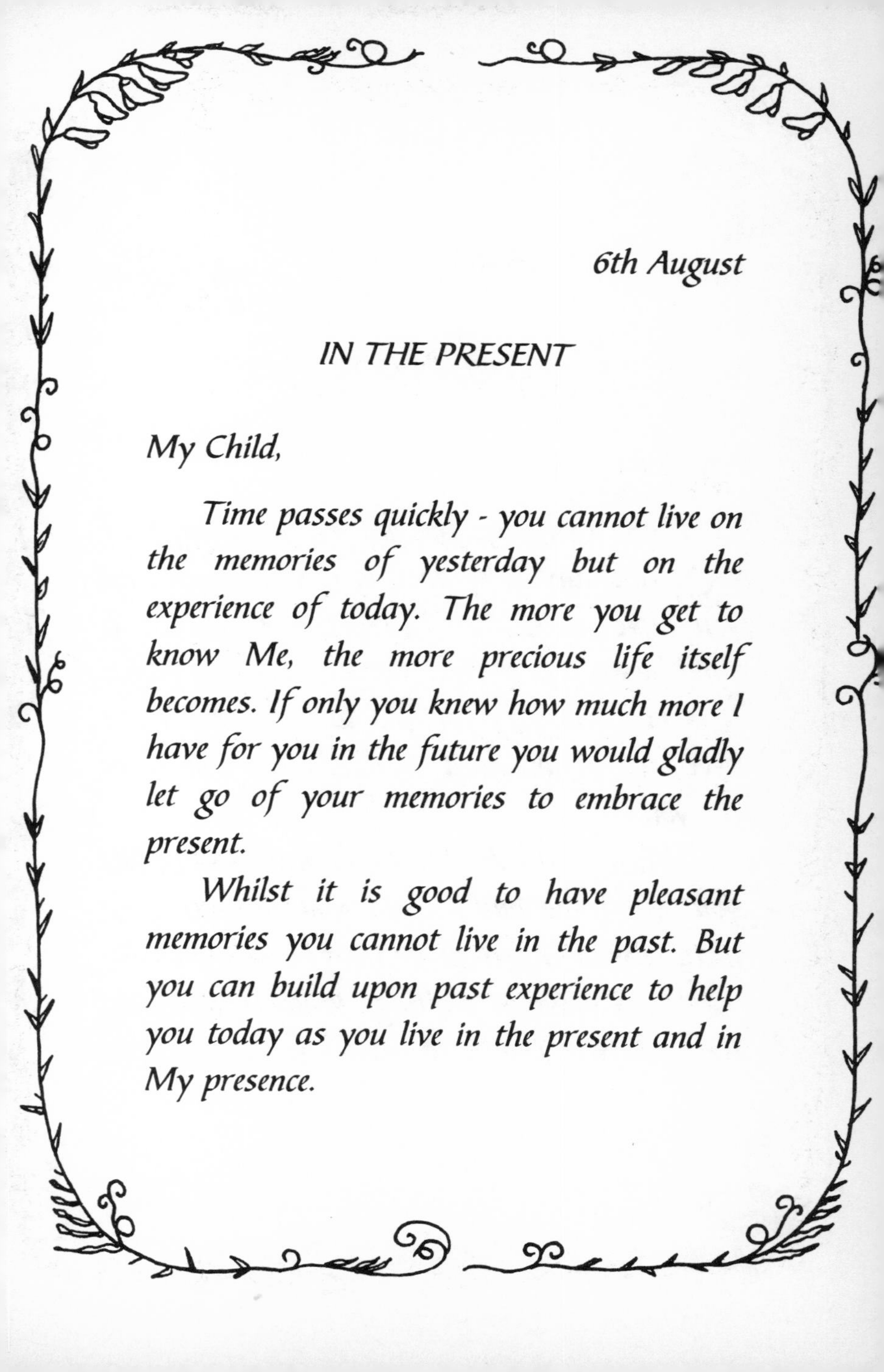

6th August

IN THE PRESENT

My Child,

Time passes quickly - you cannot live on the memories of yesterday but on the experience of today. The more you get to know Me, the more precious life itself becomes. If only you knew how much more I have for you in the future you would gladly let go of your memories to embrace the present.

Whilst it is good to have pleasant memories you cannot live in the past. But you can build upon past experience to help you today as you live in the present and in My presence.

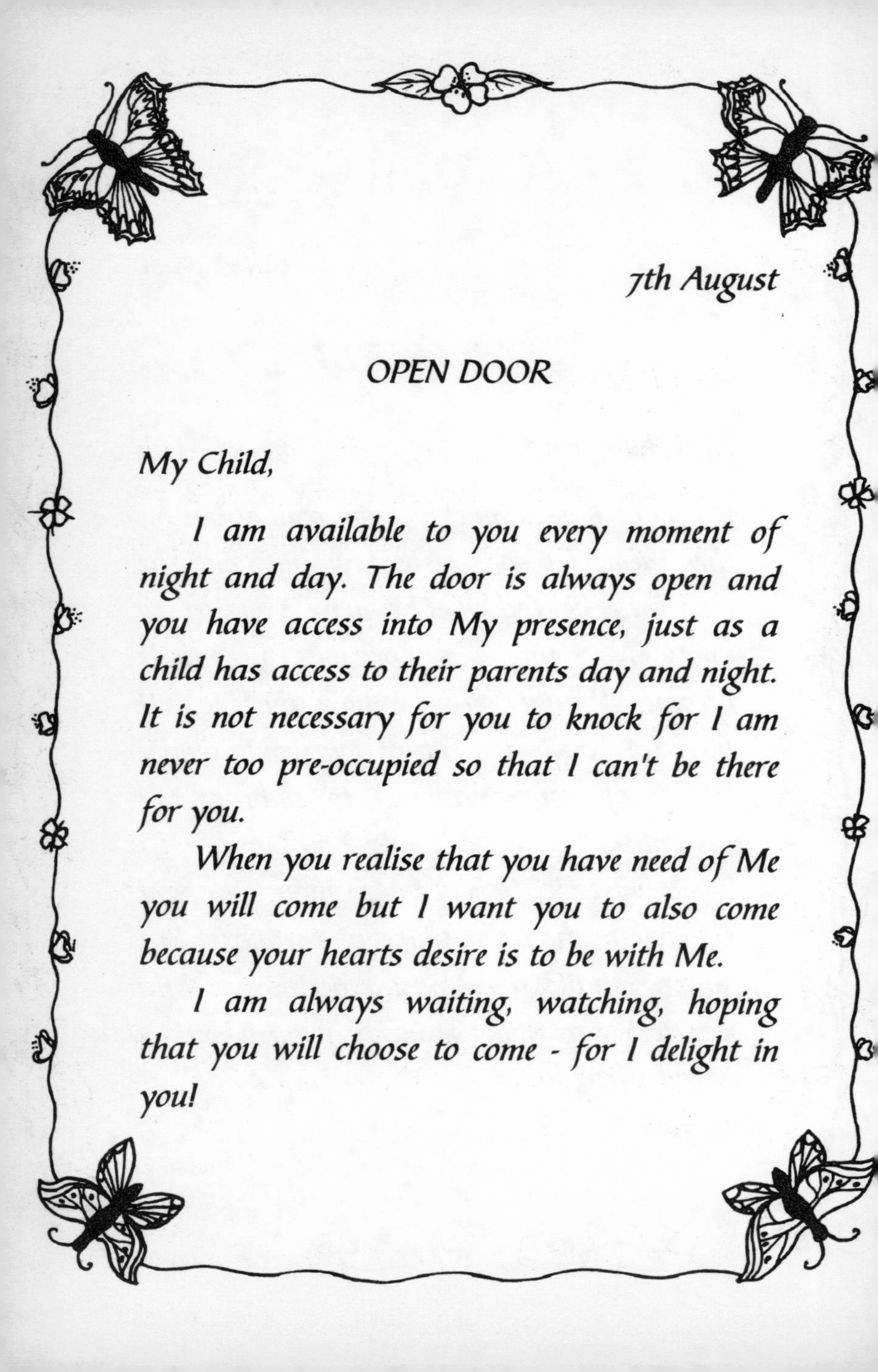

7th August

OPEN DOOR

My Child,

I am available to you every moment of night and day. The door is always open and you have access into My presence, just as a child has access to their parents day and night. It is not necessary for you to knock for I am never too pre-occupied so that I can't be there for you.

When you realise that you have need of Me you will come but I want you to also come because your hearts desire is to be with Me.

I am always waiting, watching, hoping that you will choose to come - for I delight in you!

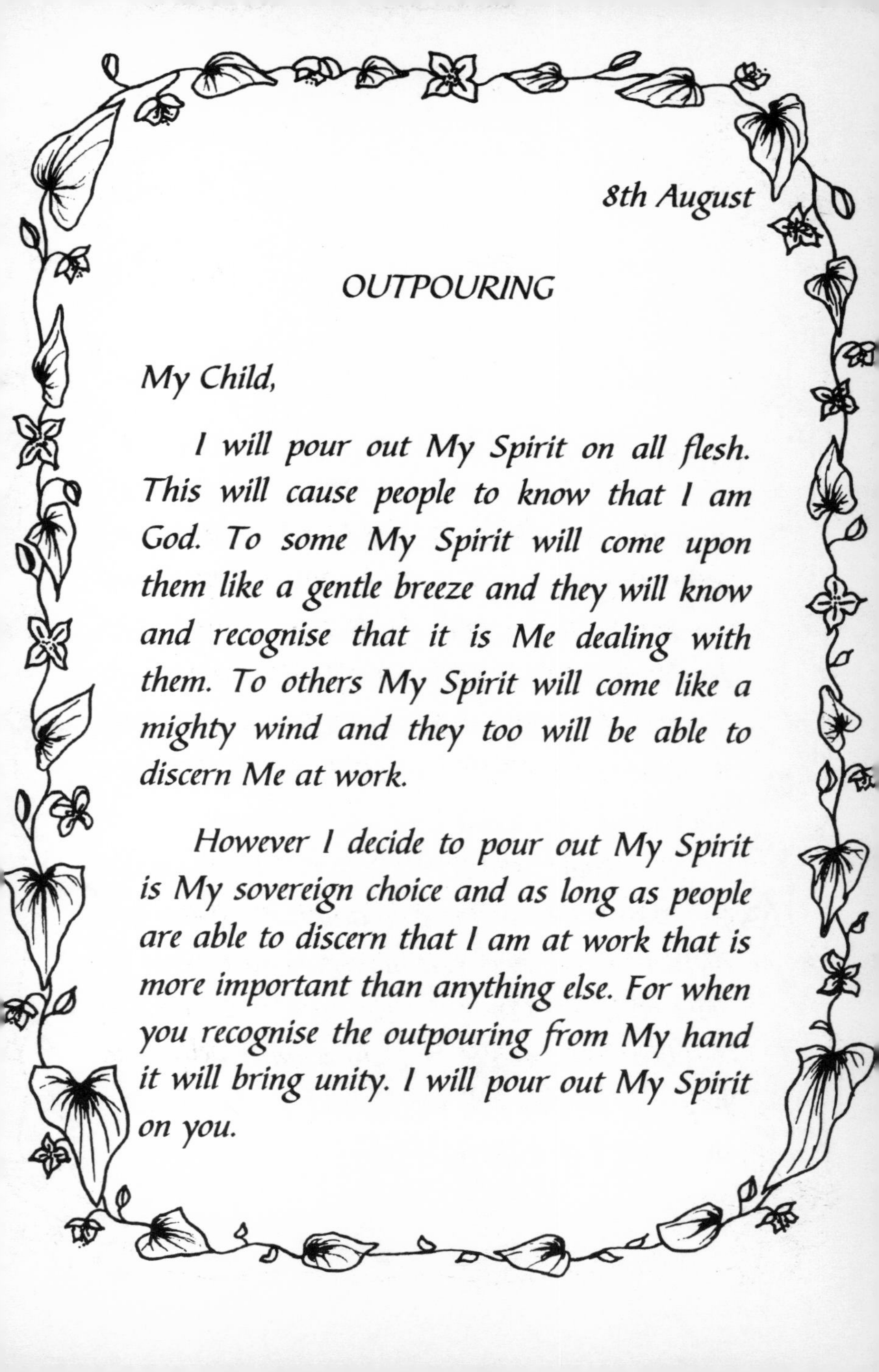

8th August

OUTPOURING

My Child,

I will pour out My Spirit on all flesh. This will cause people to know that I am God. To some My Spirit will come upon them like a gentle breeze and they will know and recognise that it is Me dealing with them. To others My Spirit will come like a mighty wind and they too will be able to discern Me at work.

However I decide to pour out My Spirit is My sovereign choice and as long as people are able to discern that I am at work that is more important than anything else. For when you recognise the outpouring from My hand it will bring unity. I will pour out My Spirit on you.

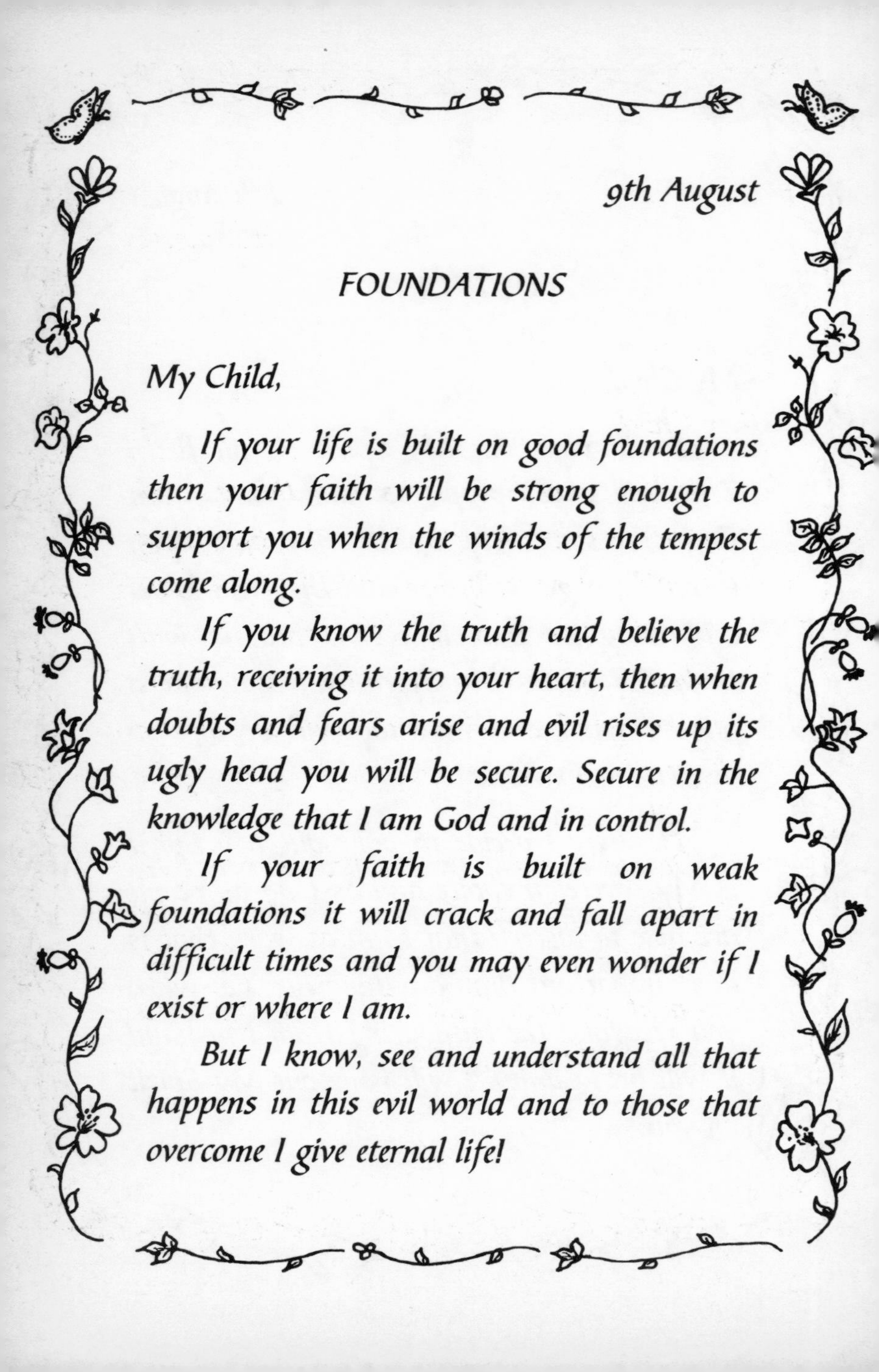

9th August

FOUNDATIONS

My Child,

If your life is built on good foundations then your faith will be strong enough to support you when the winds of the tempest come along.

If you know the truth and believe the truth, receiving it into your heart, then when doubts and fears arise and evil rises up its ugly head you will be secure. Secure in the knowledge that I am God and in control.

If your faith is built on weak foundations it will crack and fall apart in difficult times and you may even wonder if I exist or where I am.

But I know, see and understand all that happens in this evil world and to those that overcome I give eternal life!

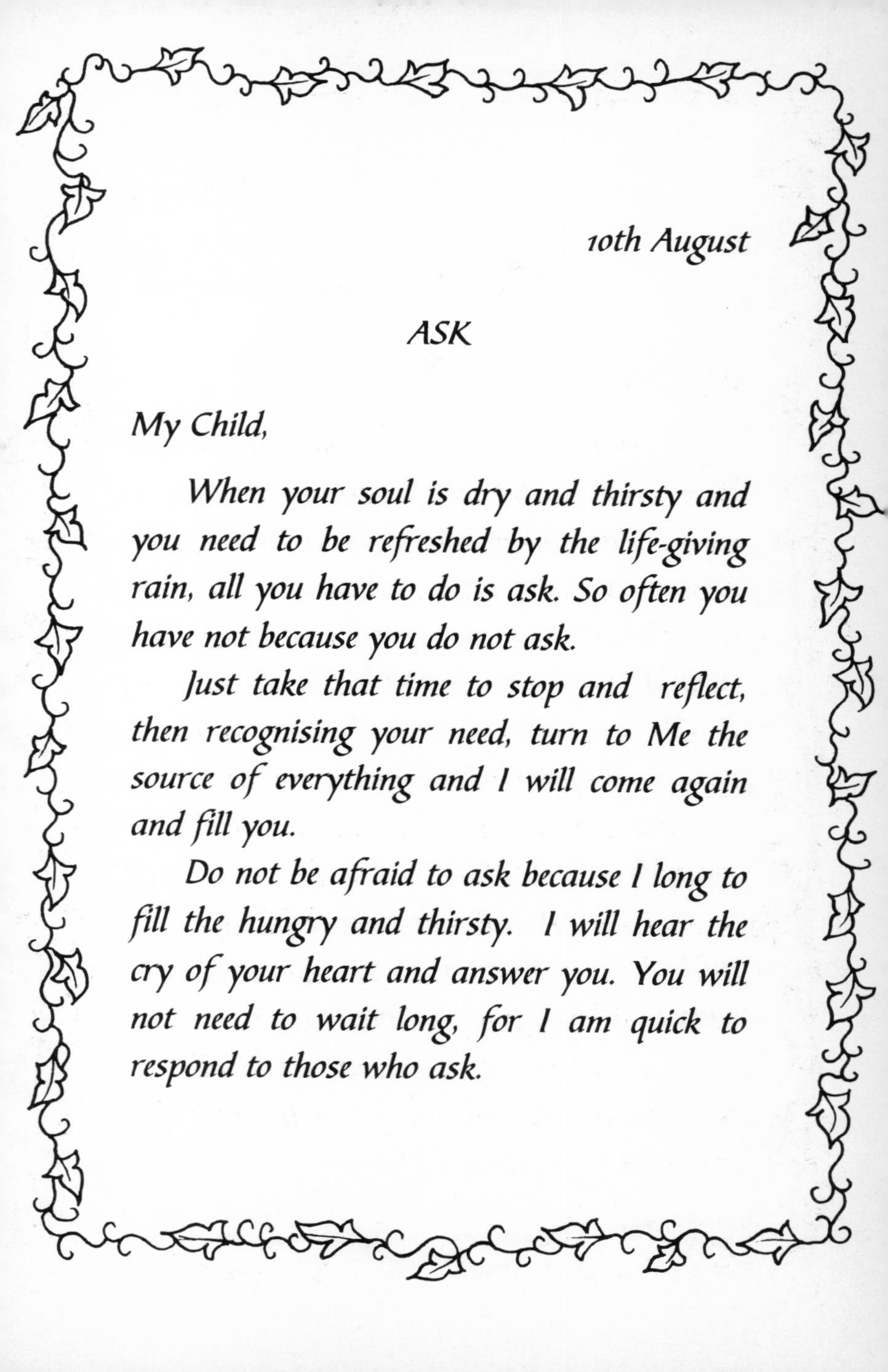

10th August

ASK

My Child,

When your soul is dry and thirsty and you need to be refreshed by the life-giving rain, all you have to do is ask. So often you have not because you do not ask.

Just take that time to stop and reflect, then recognising your need, turn to Me the source of everything and I will come again and fill you.

Do not be afraid to ask because I long to fill the hungry and thirsty. I will hear the cry of your heart and answer you. You will not need to wait long, for I am quick to respond to those who ask.

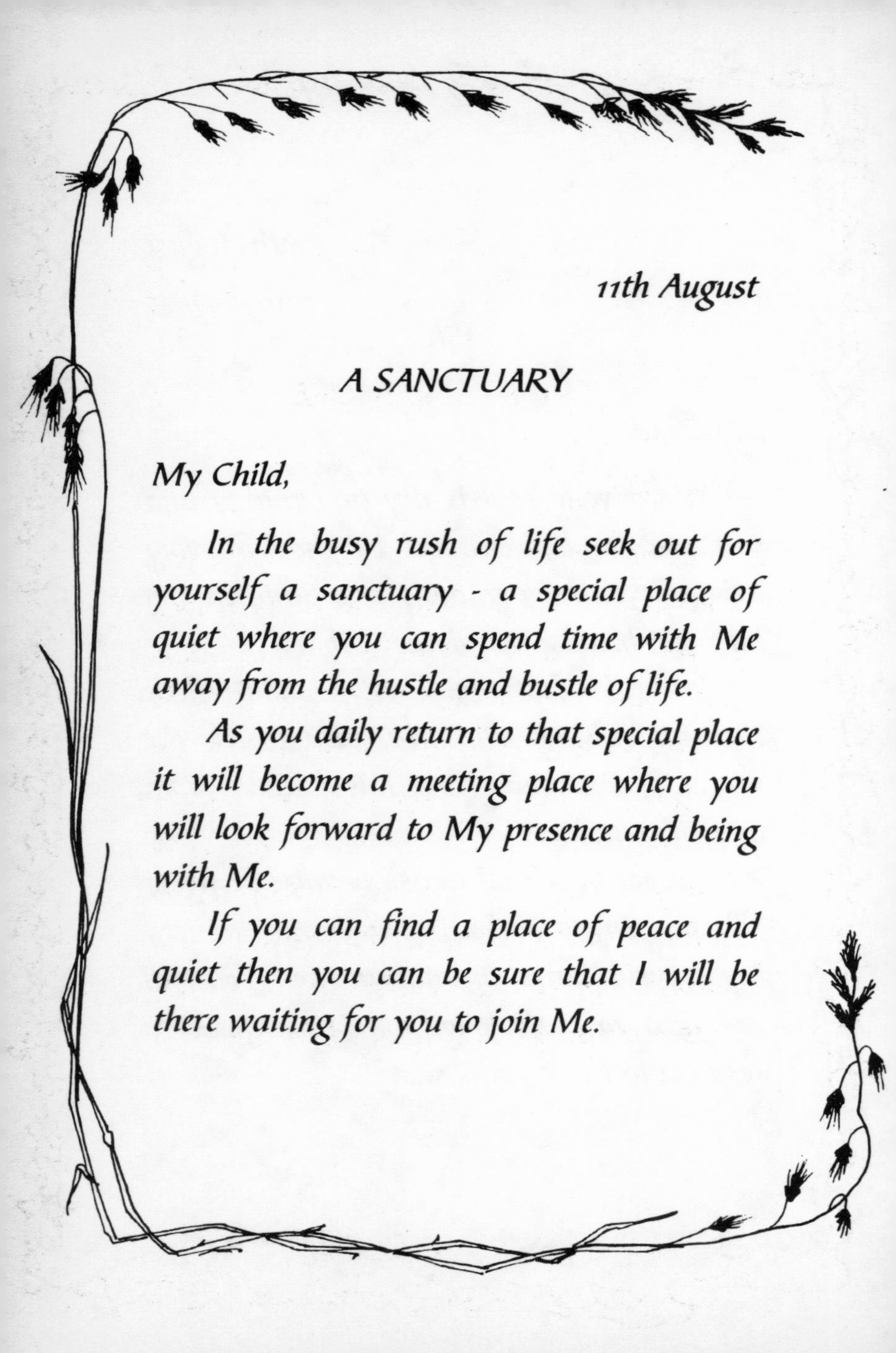

11th August

A SANCTUARY

My Child,

In the busy rush of life seek out for yourself a sanctuary - a special place of quiet where you can spend time with Me away from the hustle and bustle of life.

As you daily return to that special place it will become a meeting place where you will look forward to My presence and being with Me.

If you can find a place of peace and quiet then you can be sure that I will be there waiting for you to join Me.

12th August

CHOSEN TREASURE

My Child,

You are so precious to Me. I value you and your friendship with Me. I do not look at you with all your weaknesses and faults for I am aware that you are not yet perfect. I see the beauty in your life, the things you do and say and even think, that please Me. I see your heart and know how you long to be like Me and want you to know that I have set My love upon you unconditionally for ever. You are My chosen treasure more valued than gold.

13th August

NEW CHALLENGE

My Child,

Are you prepared to change your mind and not be set in your ways? How flexible are you to opt for something new or different?

So many people are happy in the rut that they have dug for themselves and do not want to move out of it. The deeper you get into the rut, the harder it is to crawl out of it.

I want you to be ready to respond to any new challenge I may lay before you. Not with an inflexible mind-set but a willingness of heart to embrace new things, even if you may not feel comfortable with them. If you can grasp this then a whole new world opens up to you!

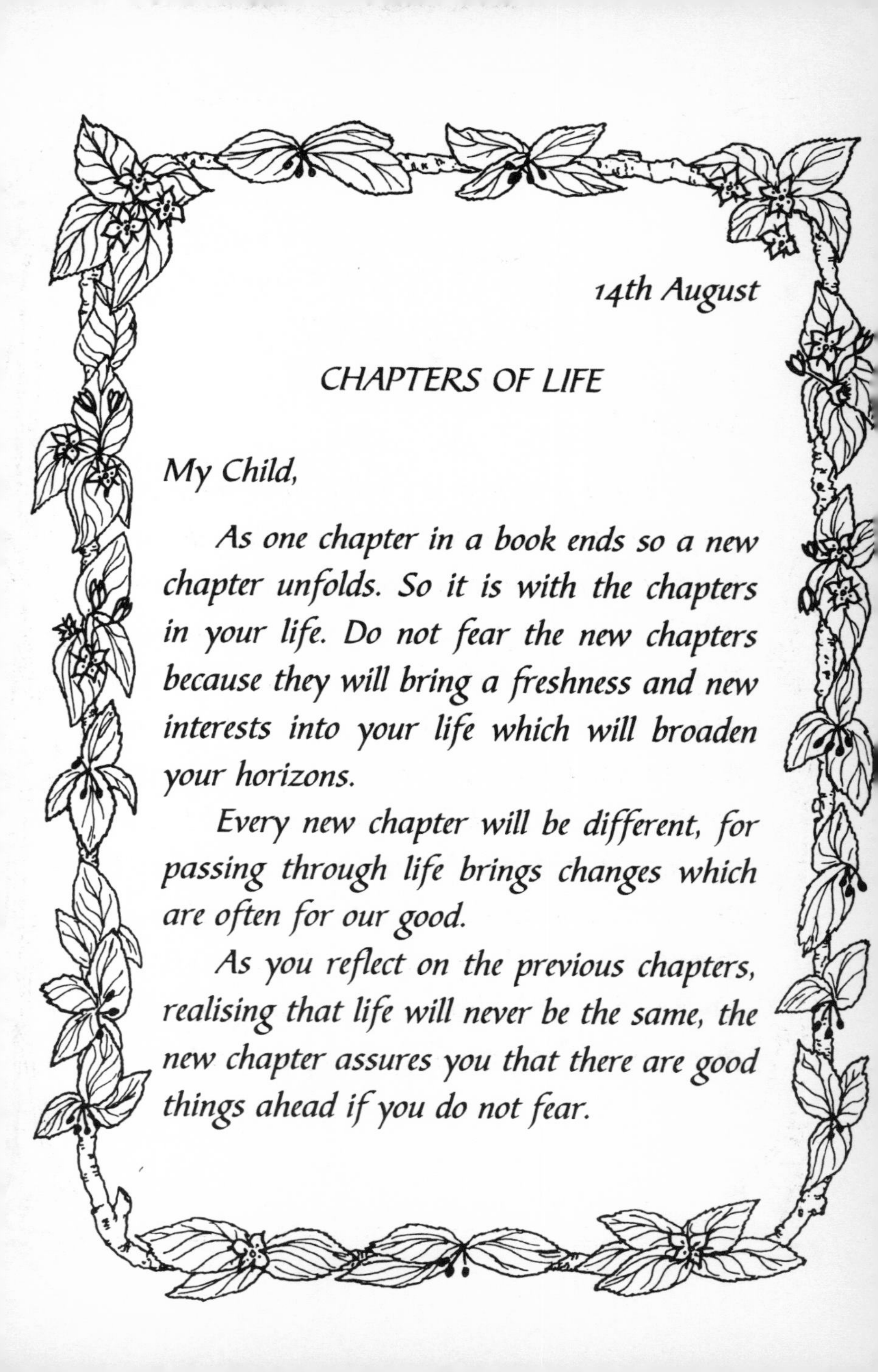

14th August

CHAPTERS OF LIFE

My Child,

As one chapter in a book ends so a new chapter unfolds. So it is with the chapters in your life. Do not fear the new chapters because they will bring a freshness and new interests into your life which will broaden your horizons.

Every new chapter will be different, for passing through life brings changes which are often for our good.

As you reflect on the previous chapters, realising that life will never be the same, the new chapter assures you that there are good things ahead if you do not fear.

15th August

RIGHT ATTITUDE

My Child,

It is so important that you always have a right attitude for this will give you peace. If you cannot be tolerant or patient, making allowances for others idiosyncrasies, then you will discover a well of frustration and unhappiness within. In the end it will be you, yourself, that suffers because of your heart attitude. When you find other people difficult, remember to look at them with My heart of compassion and eyes of love. My love is the same for each person and remember though others may find you difficult, I love you.

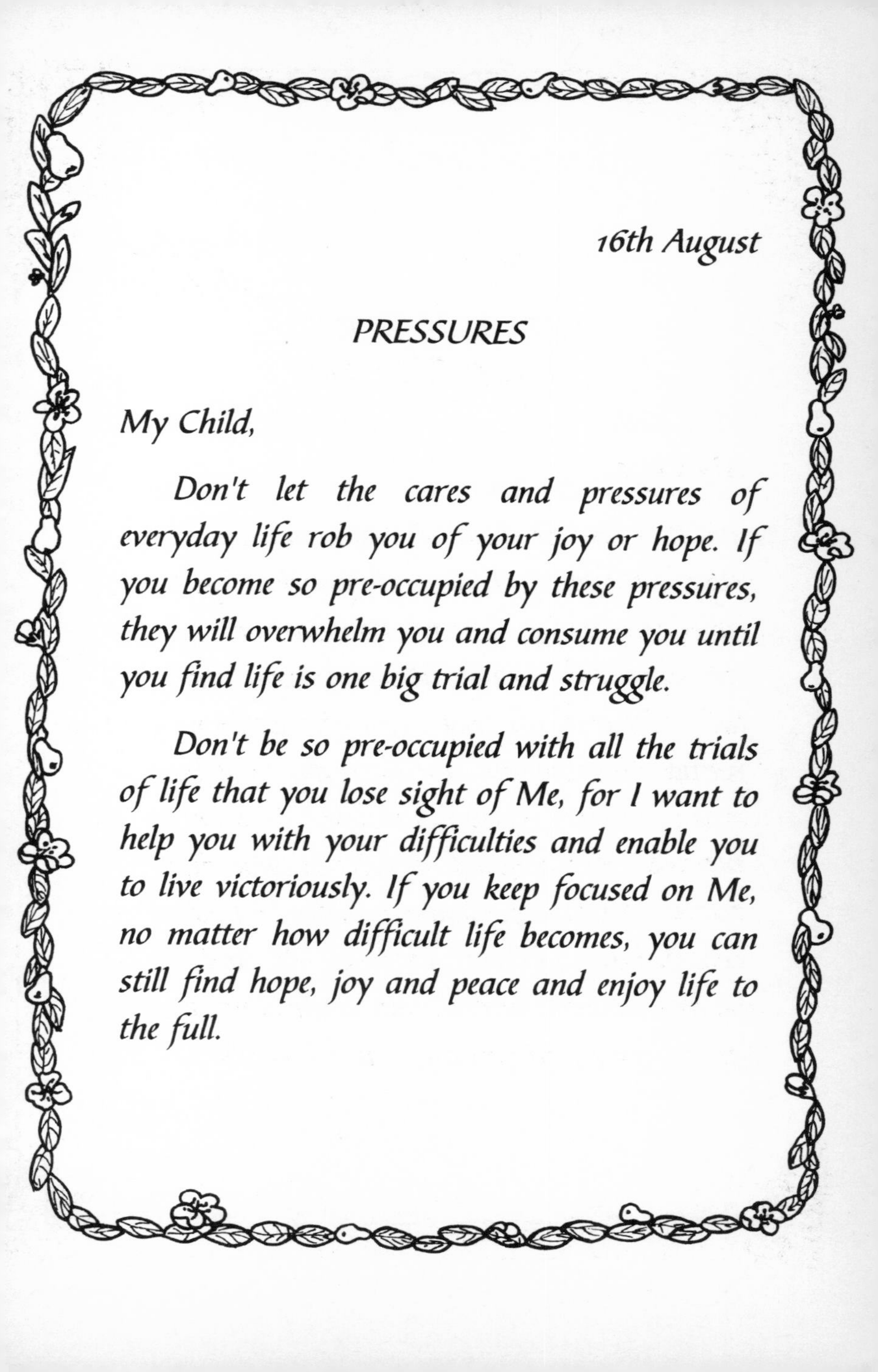

16th August

PRESSURES

My Child,

Don't let the cares and pressures of everyday life rob you of your joy or hope. If you become so pre-occupied by these pressures, they will overwhelm you and consume you until you find life is one big trial and struggle.

Don't be so pre-occupied with all the trials of life that you lose sight of Me, for I want to help you with your difficulties and enable you to live victoriously. If you keep focused on Me, no matter how difficult life becomes, you can still find hope, joy and peace and enjoy life to the full.

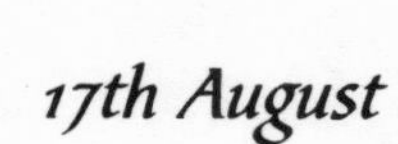

17th August

EXTRAORDINARY

My Child,

Sometimes when life seems mundane and routine it is easy to question the purpose of living. But you know that I have called you into a close relationship with Me. Knowing Me, loving Me and experiencing the fullness of life that I can give is the very purpose of living. I can turn the mundane and ordinary things of life into the extraordinary. By the power of My Holy Spirit ordinary people can become extraordinary. I have done this all through history and I can do it with you!

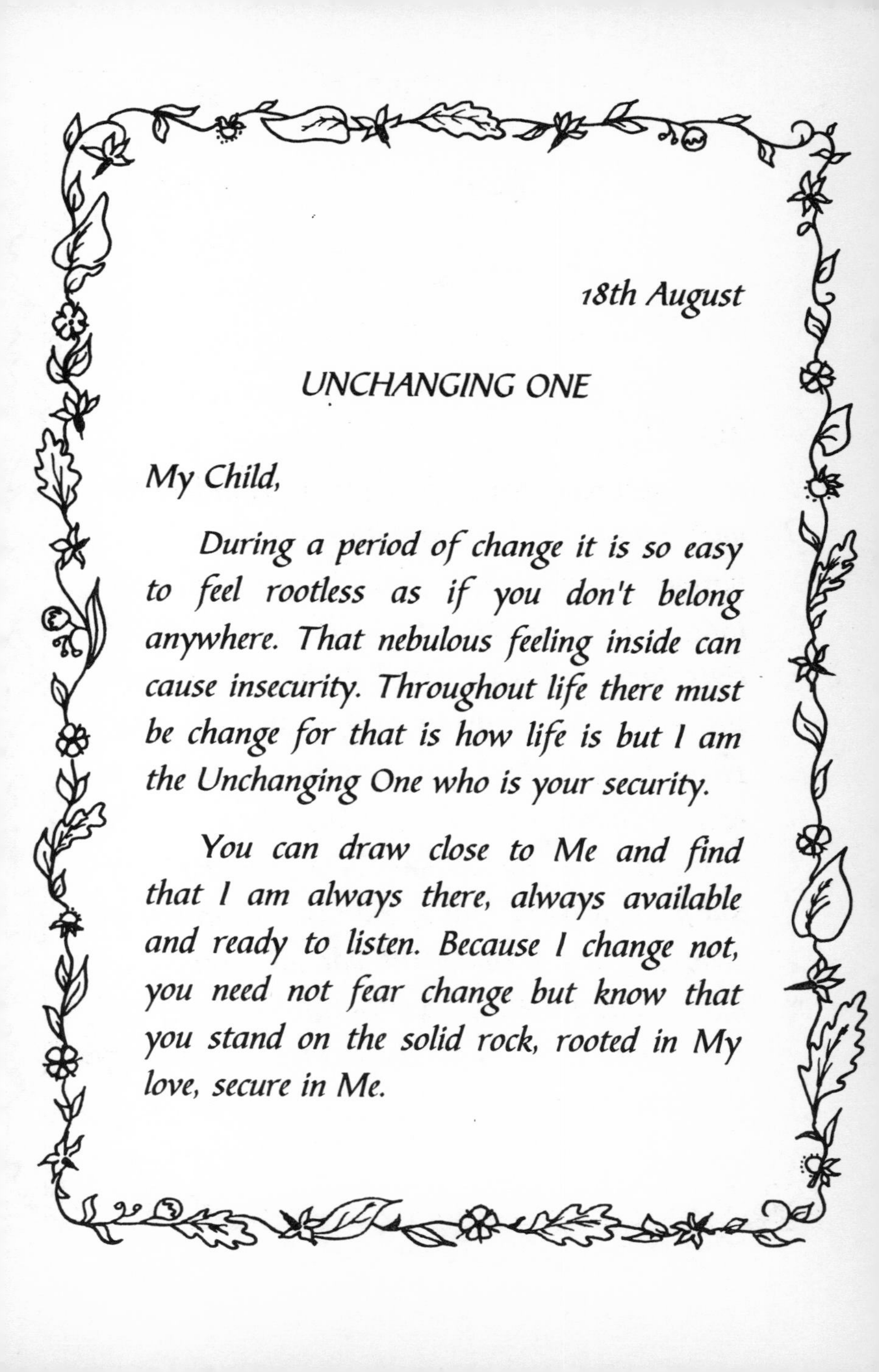

18th August

UNCHANGING ONE

My Child,

During a period of change it is so easy to feel rootless as if you don't belong anywhere. That nebulous feeling inside can cause insecurity. Throughout life there must be change for that is how life is but I am the Unchanging One who is your security.

You can draw close to Me and find that I am always there, always available and ready to listen. Because I change not, you need not fear change but know that you stand on the solid rock, rooted in My love, secure in Me.

19th August

MEETING YOUR NEEDS

My Child,

There are times when you have real need and pray for help. Often you wonder why it seems as if there is no answer, especially when you know that I have promised to hear.

Sometimes I allow you to go through that time of need in order to enable you to draw close to Me. The sooner I answer the sooner you may stop praying and I long for your fellowship. I want you to discover what a tower of strength and peace I can be to you in times of need. If I answer your prayers very quickly it will not help develop that relationship I long for you to enjoy with Me.

So persevere in prayer for I will truly meet with you which is as important as meeting your needs.

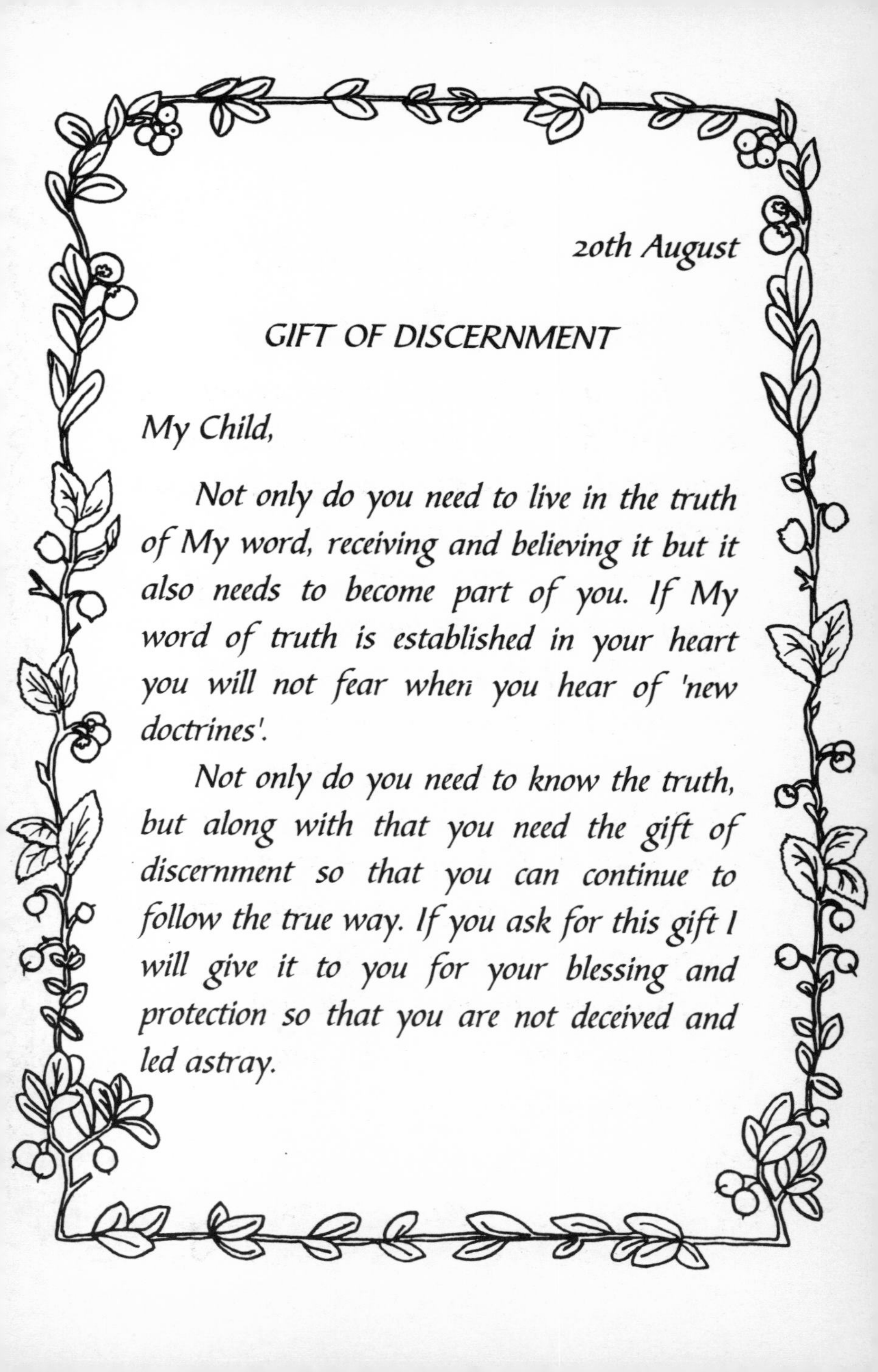

20th August

GIFT OF DISCERNMENT

My Child,

Not only do you need to live in the truth of My word, receiving and believing it but it also needs to become part of you. If My word of truth is established in your heart you will not fear when you hear of 'new doctrines'.

Not only do you need to know the truth, but along with that you need the gift of discernment so that you can continue to follow the true way. If you ask for this gift I will give it to you for your blessing and protection so that you are not deceived and led astray.

21st August

LIGHT IN THE DARKNESS

My Child,

Sometimes I allow you to go through dark and difficult times so that you will draw closer to Me. In those times, if you reach out your hand to Me, you will find Me to be all that you are needing. At the time it will seem almost too much for you to bear but afterwards you will discover the joy of a deeper intimacy as you walk with Me. You will know too just a little of what I have experienced on this earth and not only will you be able to identify with Me but with all those who need light in their darkness.

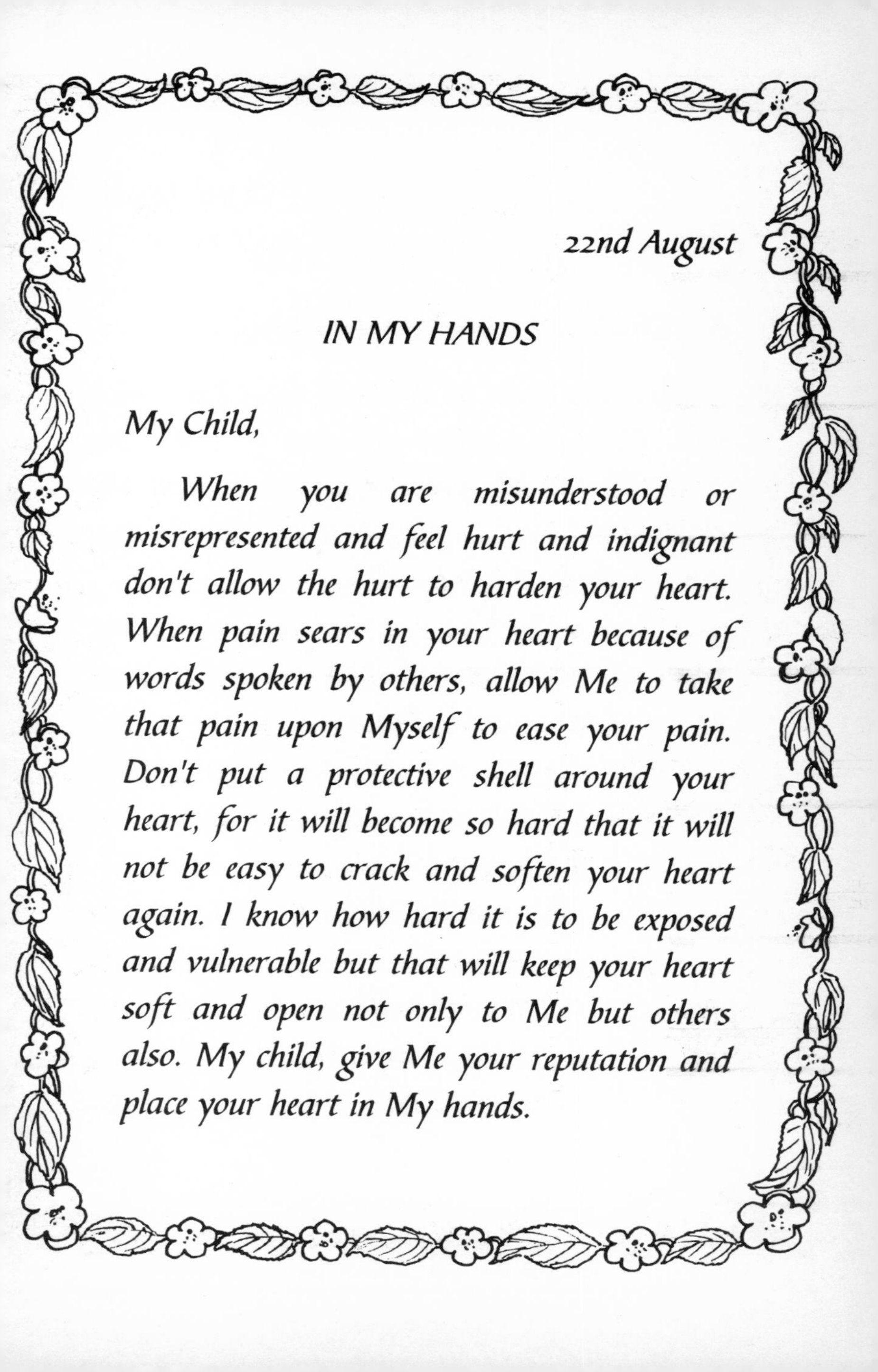

22nd August

IN MY HANDS

My Child,

When you are misunderstood or misrepresented and feel hurt and indignant don't allow the hurt to harden your heart. When pain sears in your heart because of words spoken by others, allow Me to take that pain upon Myself to ease your pain. Don't put a protective shell around your heart, for it will become so hard that it will not be easy to crack and soften your heart again. I know how hard it is to be exposed and vulnerable but that will keep your heart soft and open not only to Me but others also. My child, give Me your reputation and place your heart in My hands.

23rd August

ALWAYS WITH YOU

My Child,

Every moment of day and night I am with you. There is nowhere you can go but I am there. This is My promise to you and all My children. My eye is always upon you for you are the apple of My eye.

Never will I fail you, let you down or let you go for My hand is upon you and you are safe and secure in My hands.

Whether you are able to recognise these truths is unimportant - only that you believe the truth of My word to you.

This means that there is never a moment when you are alone - never a moment without My company. For I am always with you

and always will be.....

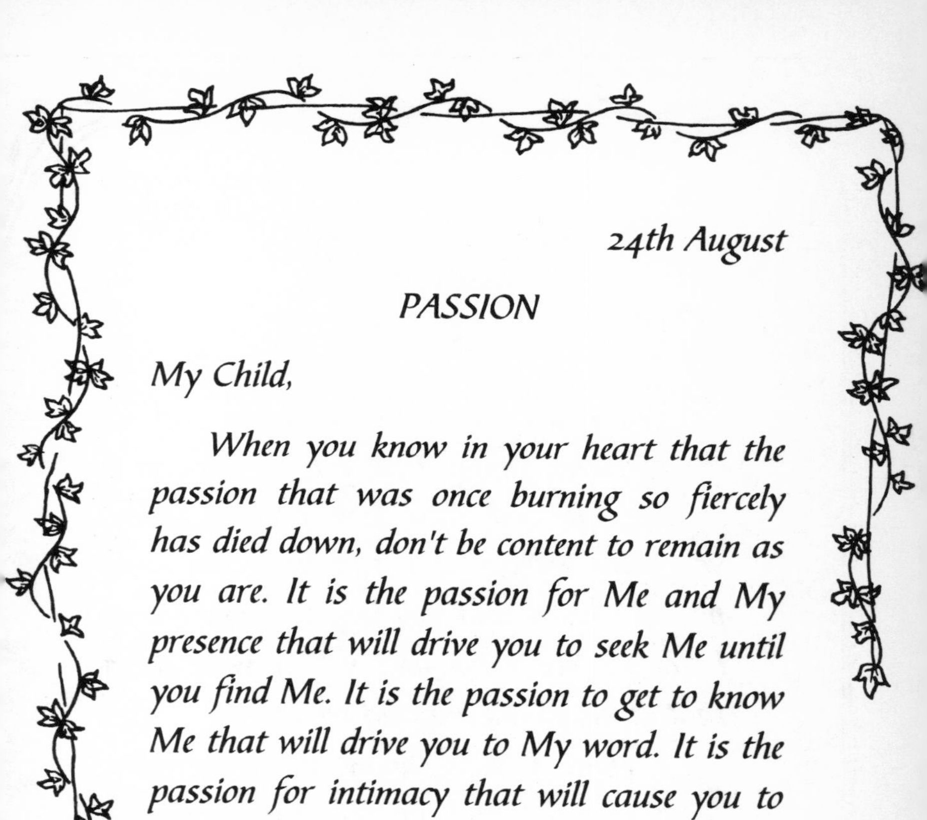

24th August

PASSION

My Child,

When you know in your heart that the passion that was once burning so fiercely has died down, don't be content to remain as you are. It is the passion for Me and My presence that will drive you to seek Me until you find Me. It is the passion to get to know Me that will drive you to My word. It is the passion for intimacy that will cause you to worship Me.

So many people are passionate about so many things but few are passionate for Me. Though it may not be fashionable to show passion - in a close intimate relationship this is quite acceptable and that is why I want to restore your passion. Will you let Me?

25th August

IMPOSSIBLE

My Child,

When you look into My word and see the awesome things that I have done in a bygone age and then look around today, you may wonder if I still have the same power. I know that you long to know Me as I am in My word and yet in your heart that seems so distant and remote.

I want you to know that yesterday, today and forever I am the same - I change not. As you see Me revealed in My word so I am today. I am looking for those who will take Me at My word, believe what I say and act upon it so you will see My power and authority displayed. If you believe this nothing will be impossible for you.

26th August

REACH OUT

My Child,

There are times when I speak to you and for many different reasons you do not respond. Not only do I keep speaking to you but I put signs along the way to attract your attention. Because I love you I will persist in speaking to you, for when I speak you can be sure that I have something important to say.

The more you ignore My voice or don't believe that it really is Me, the more I long to reach out to you. Don't lose that sensitivity to My Holy Spirit for you may miss something that not only is important but life-changing. Be ready to respond with a quickness to My voice so that you can receive My blessings.

27th August

MORE LIKE ME!

My Child,

It is because I love you so very much that I discipline you. It is because I want the very best for you and long to see you whole that I chasten you.

Though My discipline seems hard at the time, it will soften your heart. You will find that you are humbled before Me which is always good for you, even when you don't think so! Through discipline, when you have humbled yourself and your heart is soft, I can teach you to walk in My ways. Always, always I discipline you in love and this is an answer to the cry of your heart that I will make you more like ME!

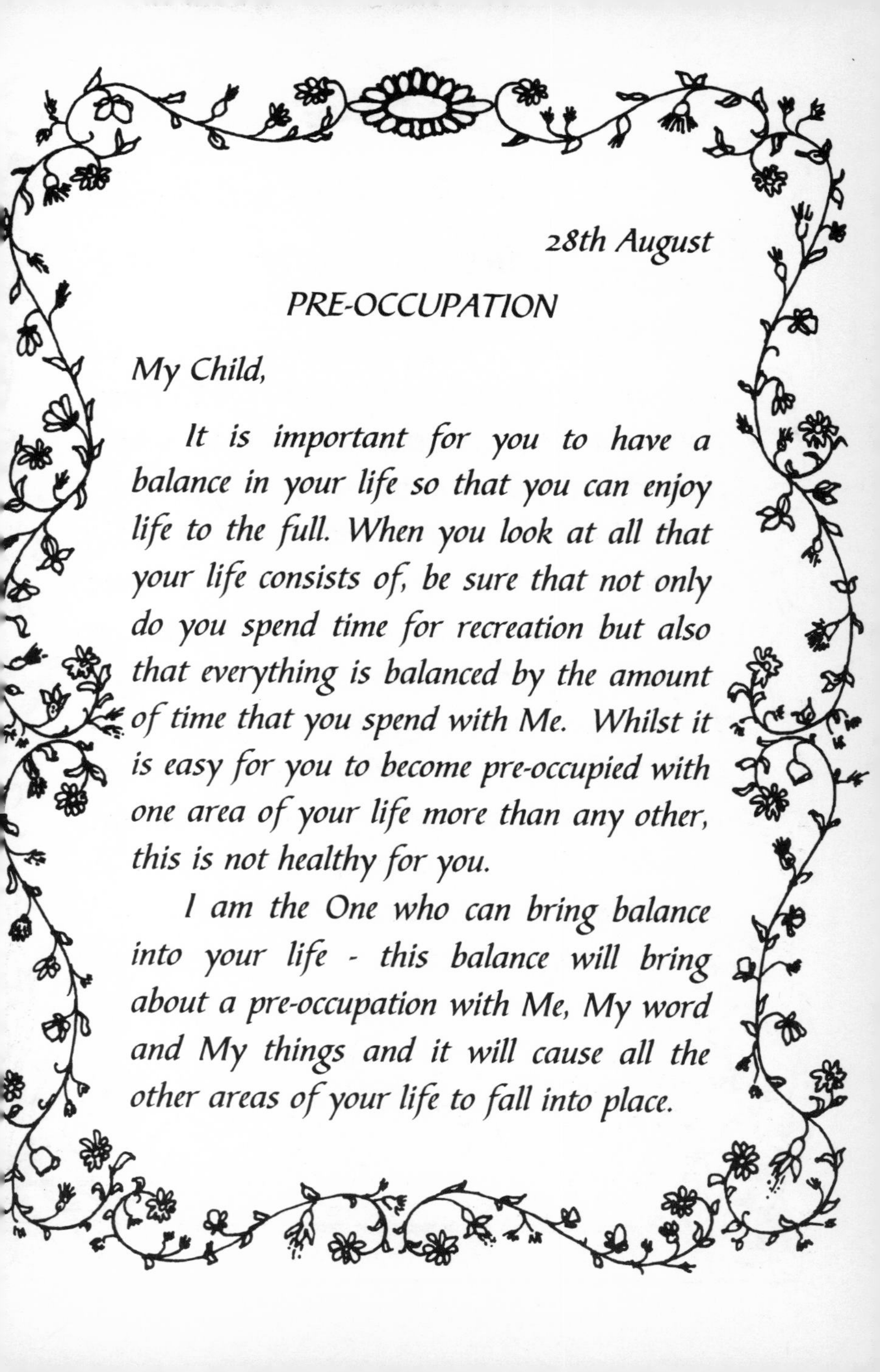

28th August

PRE-OCCUPATION

My Child,

It is important for you to have a balance in your life so that you can enjoy life to the full. When you look at all that your life consists of, be sure that not only do you spend time for recreation but also that everything is balanced by the amount of time that you spend with Me. Whilst it is easy for you to become pre-occupied with one area of your life more than any other, this is not healthy for you.

I am the One who can bring balance into your life - this balance will bring about a pre-occupation with Me, My word and My things and it will cause all the other areas of your life to fall into place.

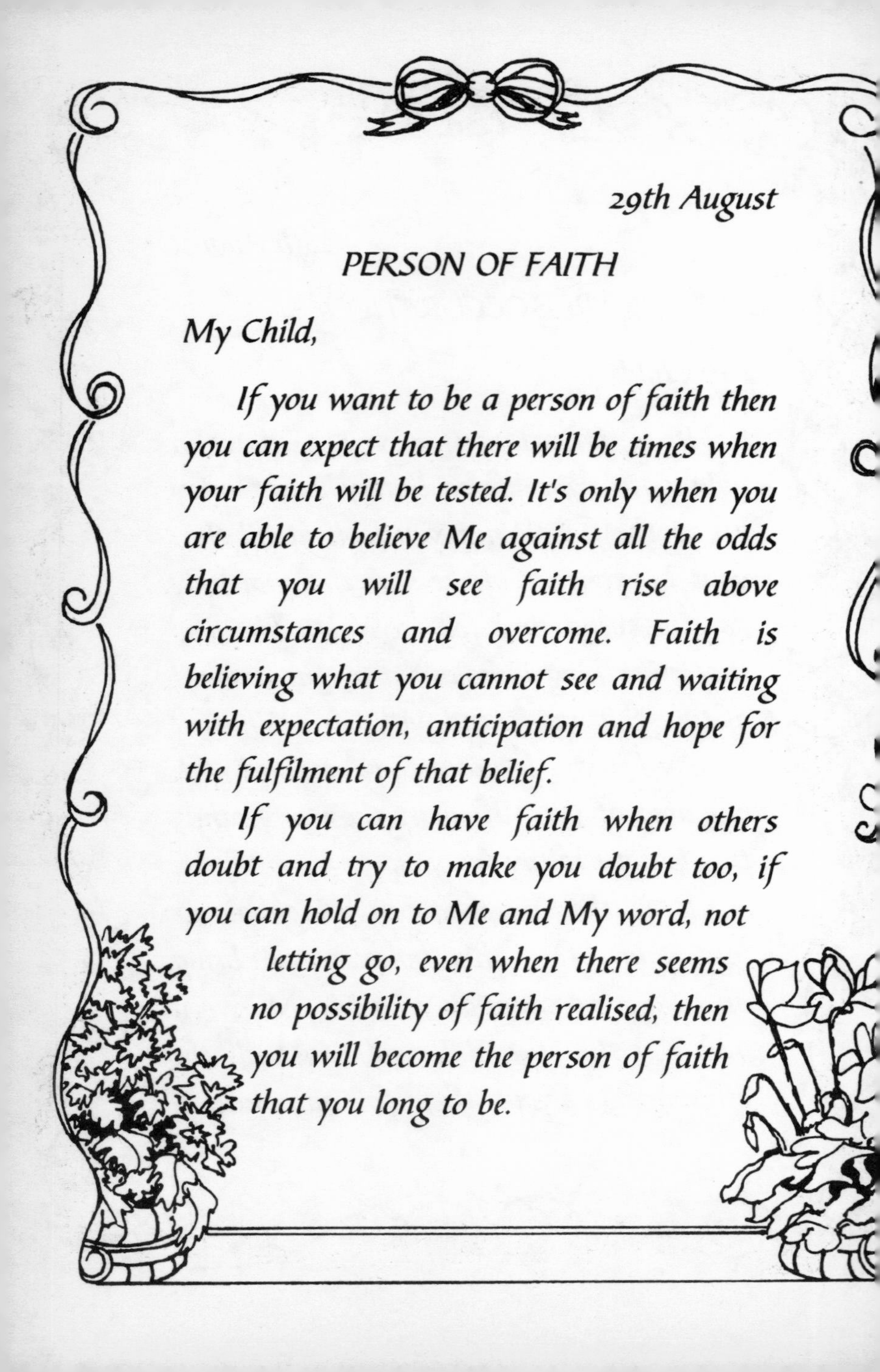

29th August

PERSON OF FAITH

My Child,

If you want to be a person of faith then you can expect that there will be times when your faith will be tested. It's only when you are able to believe Me against all the odds that you will see faith rise above circumstances and overcome. Faith is believing what you cannot see and waiting with expectation, anticipation and hope for the fulfilment of that belief.

If you can have faith when others doubt and try to make you doubt too, if you can hold on to Me and My word, not letting go, even when there seems no possibility of faith realised, then you will become the person of faith that you long to be.

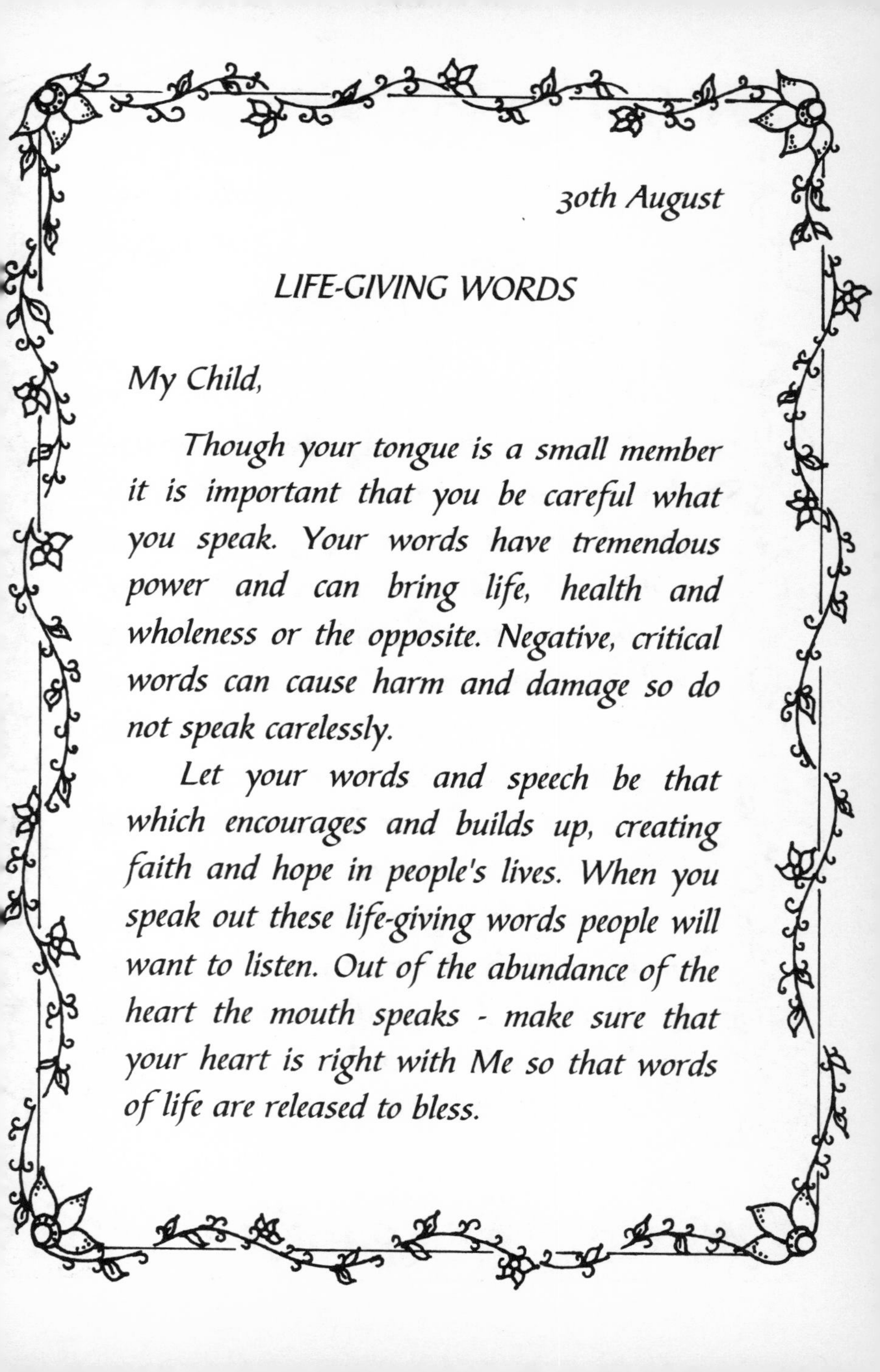

30th August

LIFE-GIVING WORDS

My Child,

Though your tongue is a small member it is important that you be careful what you speak. Your words have tremendous power and can bring life, health and wholeness or the opposite. Negative, critical words can cause harm and damage so do not speak carelessly.

Let your words and speech be that which encourages and builds up, creating faith and hope in people's lives. When you speak out these life-giving words people will want to listen. Out of the abundance of the heart the mouth speaks - make sure that your heart is right with Me so that words of life are released to bless.

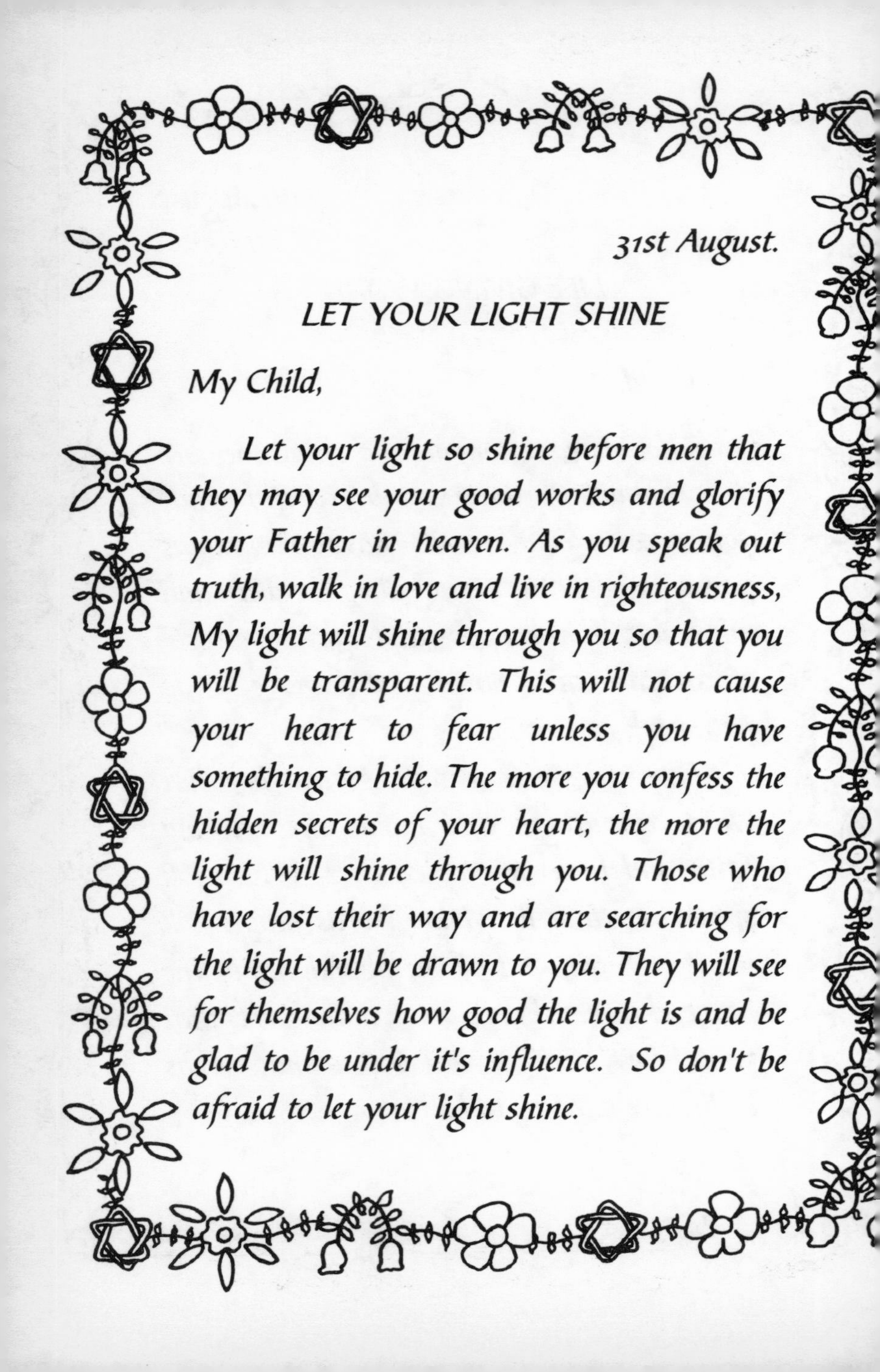

31st August.

LET YOUR LIGHT SHINE

My Child,

Let your light so shine before men that they may see your good works and glorify your Father in heaven. As you speak out truth, walk in love and live in righteousness, My light will shine through you so that you will be transparent. This will not cause your heart to fear unless you have something to hide. The more you confess the hidden secrets of your heart, the more the light will shine through you. Those who have lost their way and are searching for the light will be drawn to you. They will see for themselves how good the light is and be glad to be under it's influence. So don't be afraid to let your light shine.

1st September

ALL THE DIFFERENCE

My Child,

There will be days when you are laid aside and this will be a real frustration to you. However, if you were always able you would not appreciate the joys and blessings of health.

During times of sickness not only does it give you time to rest but also time to reflect and remember others in their suffering. So many experience much pain and suffering for many reasons and need your prayers which will make all the difference. You will find that if you can take your eyes off yourself at these times and reach out to others in prayer, you too will be supported and comforted.

2nd September

GRACE SUFFICIENT

My Child,

One of the hardest things to do is to believe that I can heal, yet accept the circumstances that you are in - unhealed. Pushing through that barrier of faith is difficult when pain and weakness is your experience. I am the Lord that heals...there is nothing too hard for Me. I am sovereign God...there is nothing I cannot do.

Can you love and trust Me in your unhealed state? Are you able to hang on believing and yet accept the limitations you have to endure? If you can do this you will know that whatever happens My grace is sufficient for you. I am concerned about your complete healing and wholeness - can you leave it with Me and trust Me?

3rd September

GRACIOUS

My Child,

No matter how people treat you learn to be gracious both in speech and deeds. Gracious words put water on the fire of angry words and calm difficult situations. It is easy to respond with words that sting and smart but that only causes pain and regret.

When you are confronted don't be quick to speak: be quick to listen and seek My help to respond in a right way. There will be many opportunities to do this as you are misunderstood or misrepresented but if you can respond in love others will know that you are different because I live in you.

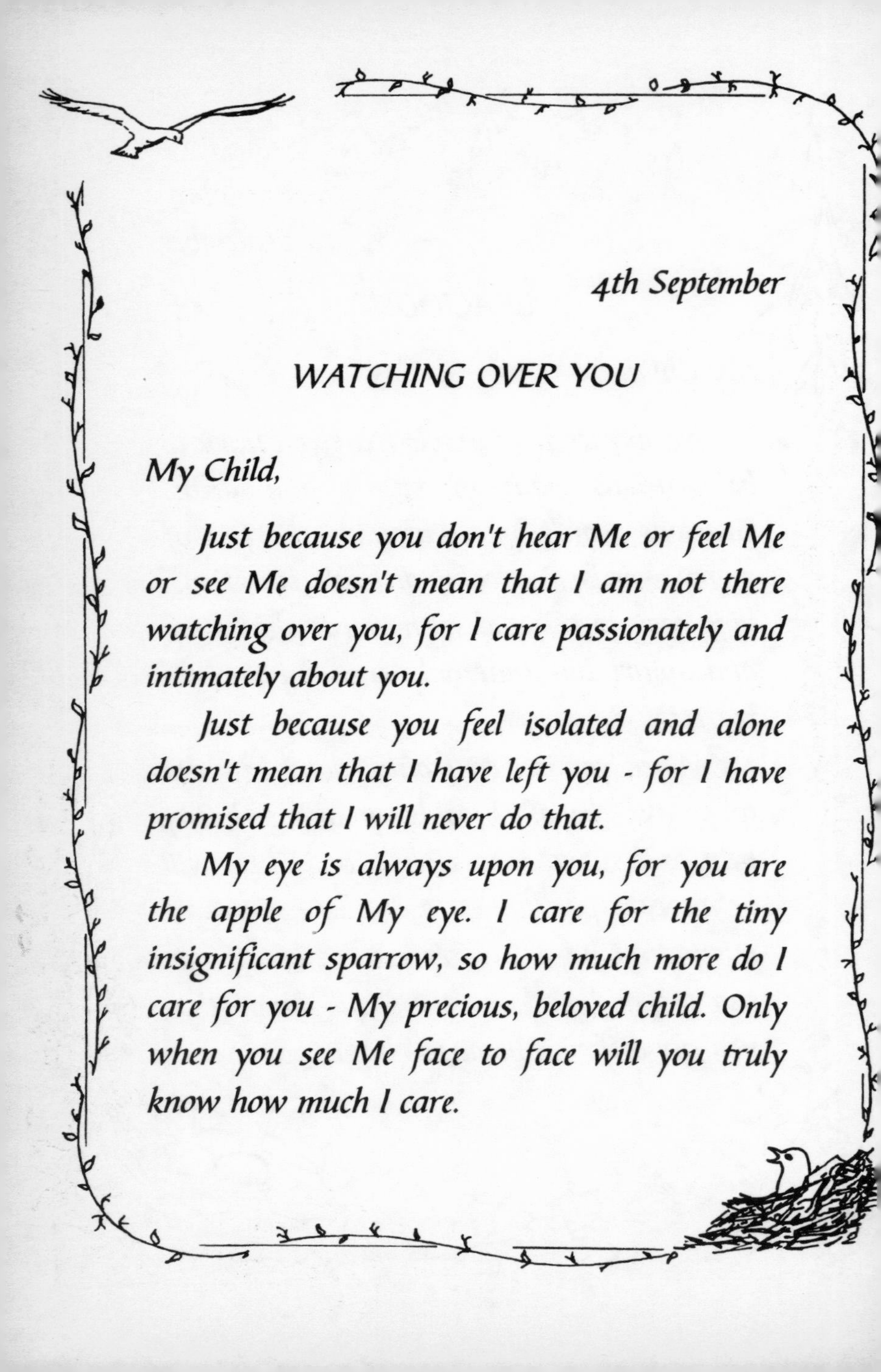

4th September

WATCHING OVER YOU

My Child,

Just because you don't hear Me or feel Me or see Me doesn't mean that I am not there watching over you, for I care passionately and intimately about you.

Just because you feel isolated and alone doesn't mean that I have left you - for I have promised that I will never do that.

My eye is always upon you, for you are the apple of My eye. I care for the tiny insignificant sparrow, so how much more do I care for you - My precious, beloved child. Only when you see Me face to face will you truly know how much I care.

5th September

YOUR VOICE

My Child,

So often evil triumphs because My people keep silent. When you see oppression, injustice and abuse with My eyes you too will be stirred to action, for you will not be able to keep quiet any longer concerning the overwhelming influence of evil. Your voice matters - it is not a lone voice and as your voice is joined to the voices of others it will make a great swell to stem the tide of evil.

It is not too late to reclaim the ground - time is running out so let your voice speak out for truth, righteousness and justice. Then you will see the floodgates open as righteousness reclaims the land.

6th September

FATHER LOVE

My Child,

There are so many who are deprived of Father love and discipline that they have no concept of a good Father. Neither do they have role models to base their lives upon.

As you know Me, the Father, and recognise My Father heart of love to all mankind, will you share My Father love with the fatherless? Only those who know and understand that I love them unconditionally and want the very best for them can do this. As you have received so much from Me will you not freely give to those who need a Father?

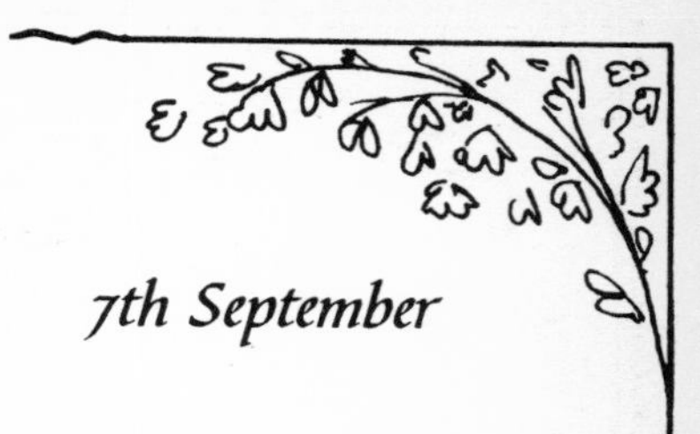

7th September

A DAY AT A TIME

My Child,

Do not fear the future for I hold the future in My hands. Your future is safe with Me because whatever happens in the future My grace, power and strength are sufficient to bring you through.

Learn to live a day at a time and do not be concerned about tomorrow's worries, for they will take care of themselves. If you can learn to live from day to day you will be able to live life to the full without fearing what may be ahead. Know that I have good plans for you - to give you hope for the future.

8th September

DROP IN THE OCEAN

My Child,

Prayer changes things. Your prayers may seem like a tiny drop in the ocean but I want you to know that every drop counts. If you can hold on to this and believe this you will realise the truth of My words to you.

Remember too that your prayers are joined with many others so that collectively they have more impact - that is why it is also good to pray with others.

It is the prayers of My children that causes Me to move and work in power, so however much you can - pray, believing to see prayer changing things.

9th September

NEW FOUND FREEDOM

My Child,

Learn to leave all your burdens at My feet so that you can learn to look into My face. When you are weighed down with burdens it is almost impossible for you to look up. If only you could look up you would see My smile of approval because you had finally let go of that which is dragging you down. Your smile would return to you for you would be able to walk in a new found freedom.

Lay down your burdens now - none of them are too big for Me but they are much too big for you.

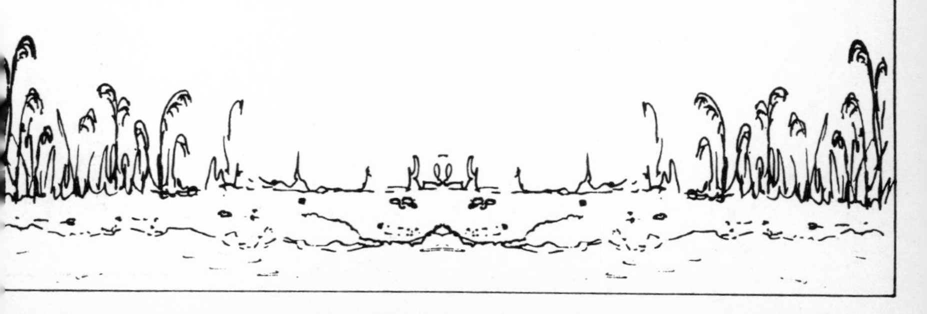

10th September

TREASURE

My Child,

There is so much treasure that I have put into your heart, yet you do not realise that it is there. Hidden treasure is no use to anyone but when it is discovered it can be put to good use.

All that is good and beautiful within you is treasure and as it is tapped so it will pour forth to bless those in need. Do not be afraid to share those things in your heart - though you may feel vulnerable, at your point of vulnerability others will identify with you and enjoy sharing your treasure, for it will encourage them!

11th September

RELEASE

My Child,

When something or someone is precious to you, it is natural that you want to hold tightly on to it. The fear of losing that which is precious to you is a very real one and can cause you to be over-protective.

If you can hold that which is precious to you lightly or even stretch out your hand and let go, giving it to Me, then whatever you release will be safe in My hands. As you let go so your hands will be open to embrace other precious things that I will want to give to you. You will find a new freedom because if you can let go, you will discover that the fear goes too and you will know My peace.

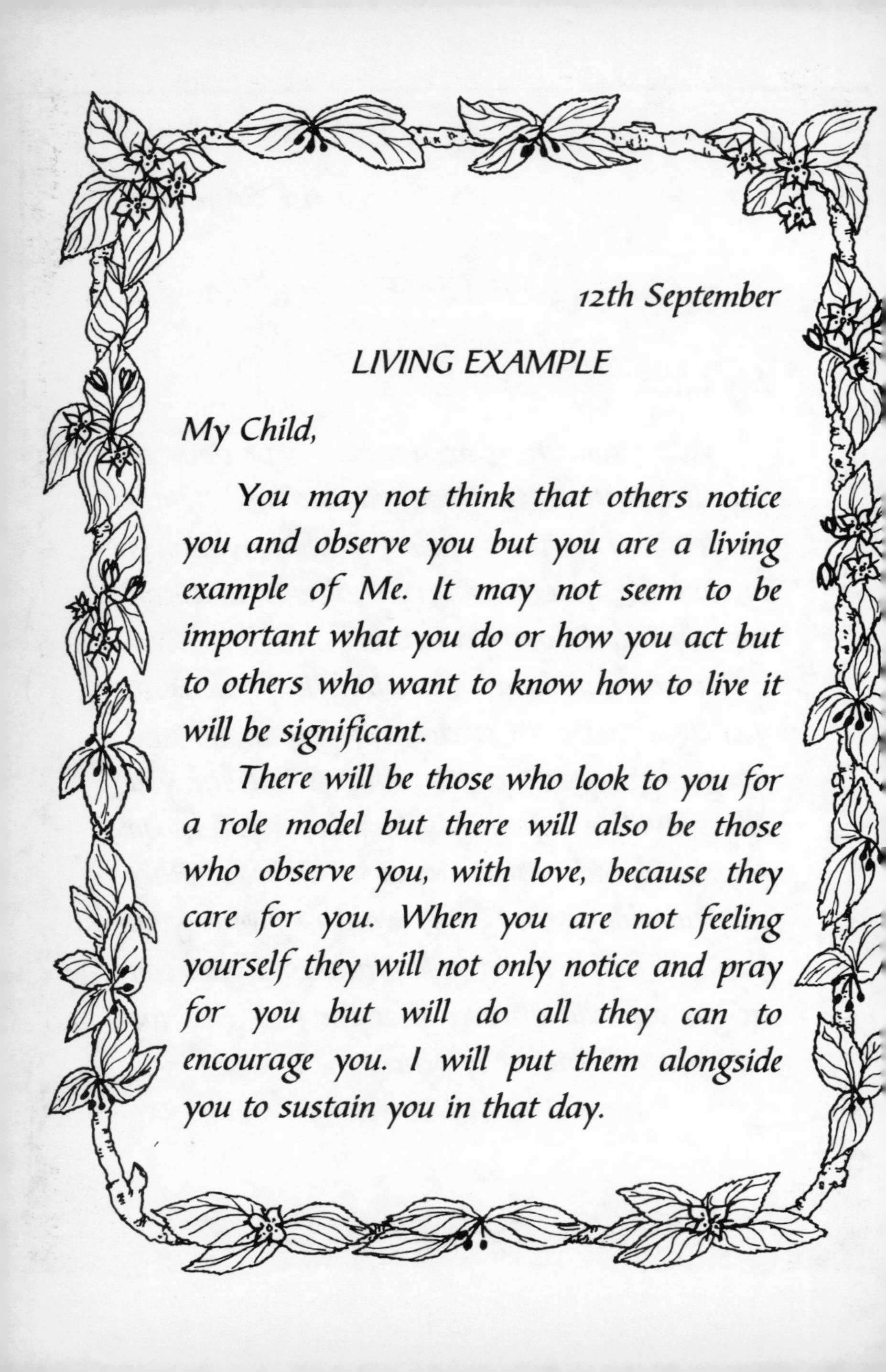

12th September

LIVING EXAMPLE

My Child,

You may not think that others notice you and observe you but you are a living example of Me. It may not seem to be important what you do or how you act but to others who want to know how to live it will be significant.

There will be those who look to you for a role model but there will also be those who observe you, with love, because they care for you. When you are not feeling yourself they will not only notice and pray for you but will do all they can to encourage you. I will put them alongside you to sustain you in that day.

13th September

FORGIVEN

My Child,

As you confess to Me those wrong things in your life, those bad attitudes, those sinful habits, I am able to forgive you and you can know My cleansing and healing. There is deep, deep joy in knowing My forgiveness for I do not remember the past, nor do I ever hold anything against you that has been confessed.

No longer do you have to bear the guilt and shame of things that you have done, for I can take all that away and cleanse you from all the effects. When you know that you are truly forgiven your happiness and relief will know no bounds... just like My forgiveness!

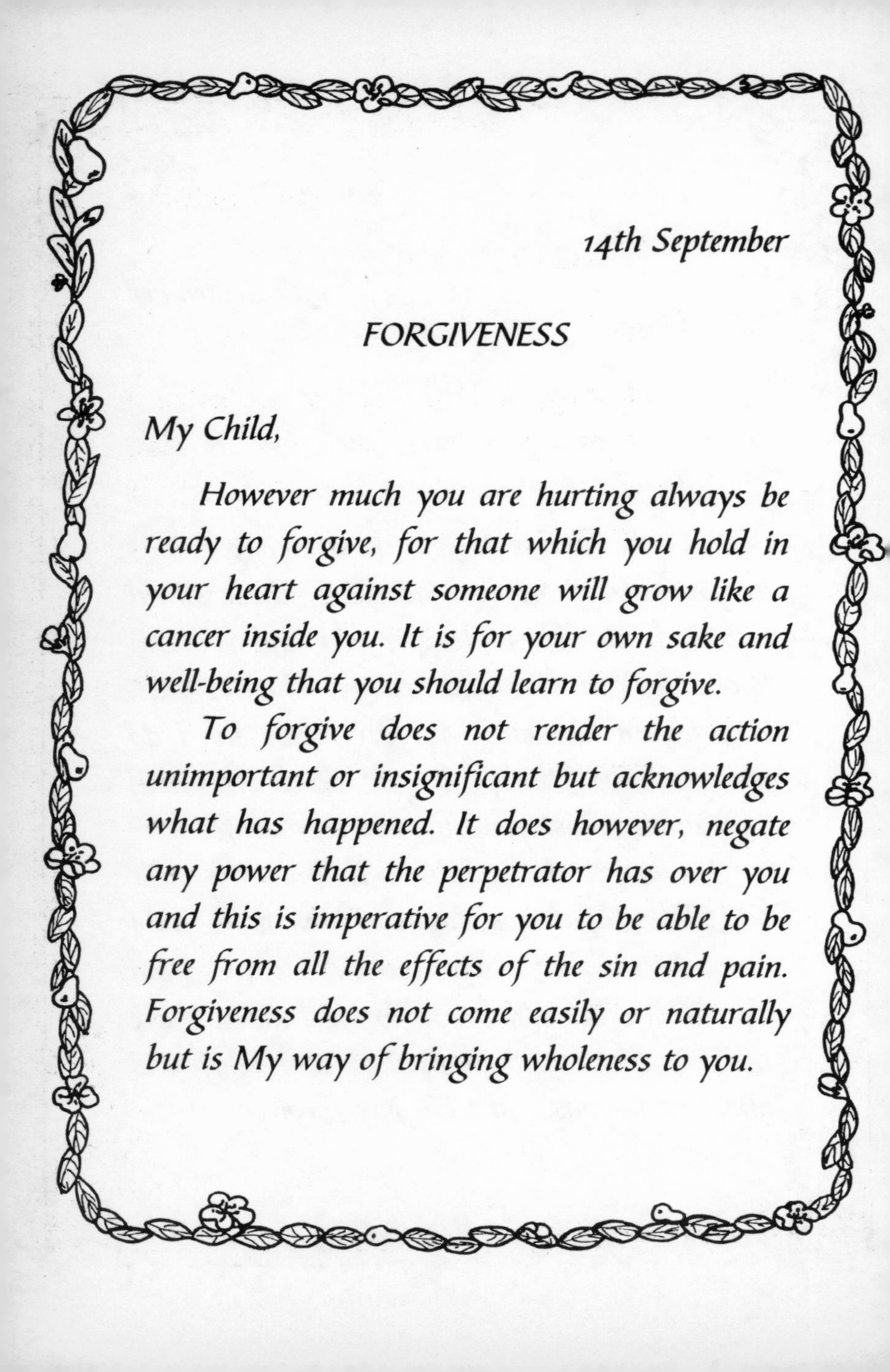

14th September

FORGIVENESS

My Child,

However much you are hurting always be ready to forgive, for that which you hold in your heart against someone will grow like a cancer inside you. It is for your own sake and well-being that you should learn to forgive.

To forgive does not render the action unimportant or insignificant but acknowledges what has happened. It does however, negate any power that the perpetrator has over you and this is imperative for you to be able to be free from all the effects of the sin and pain. Forgiveness does not come easily or naturally but is My way of bringing wholeness to you.

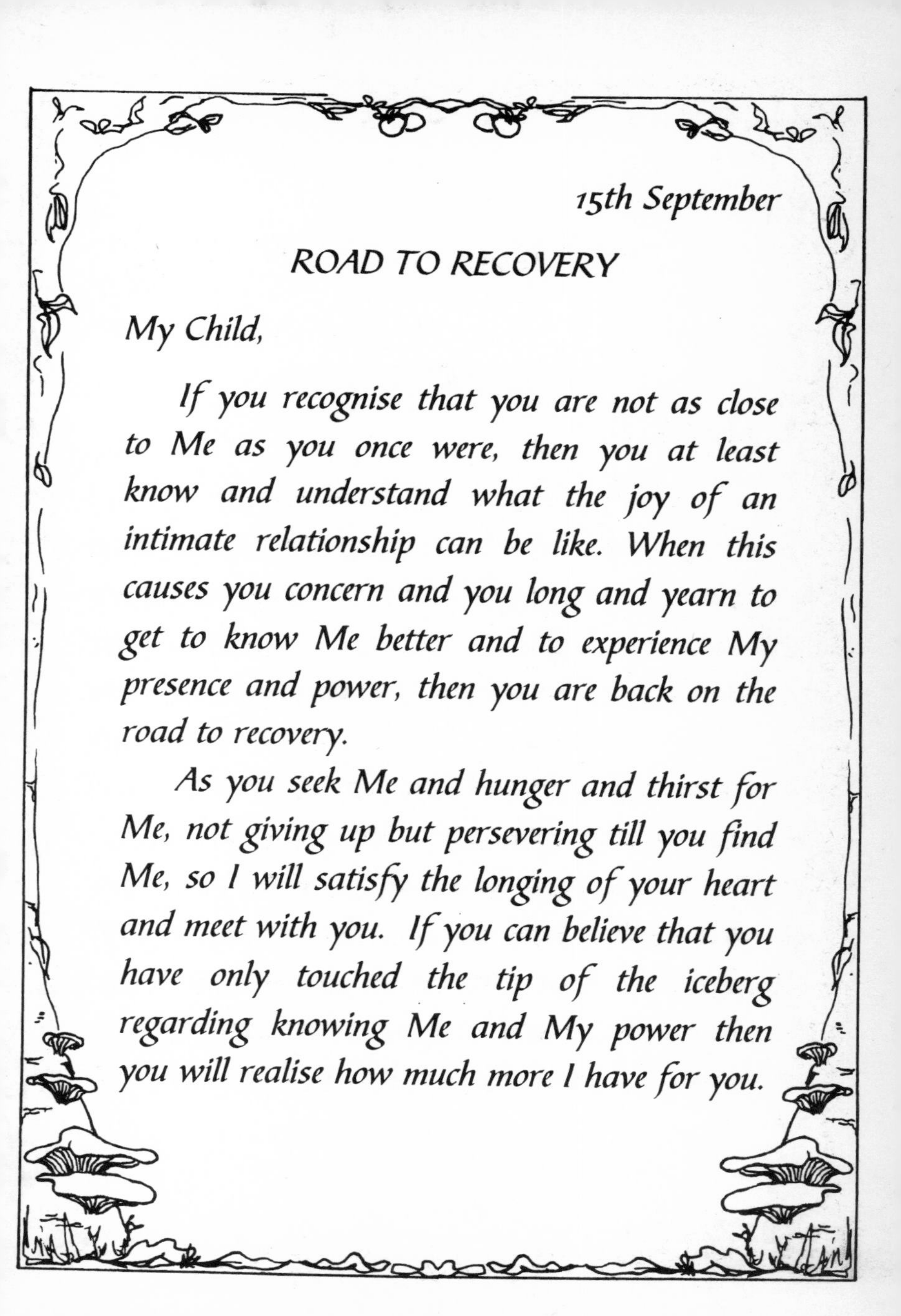

15th September

ROAD TO RECOVERY

My Child,

If you recognise that you are not as close to Me as you once were, then you at least know and understand what the joy of an intimate relationship can be like. When this causes you concern and you long and yearn to get to know Me better and to experience My presence and power, then you are back on the road to recovery.

As you seek Me and hunger and thirst for Me, not giving up but persevering till you find Me, so I will satisfy the longing of your heart and meet with you. If you can believe that you have only touched the tip of the iceberg regarding knowing Me and My power then you will realise how much more I have for you.

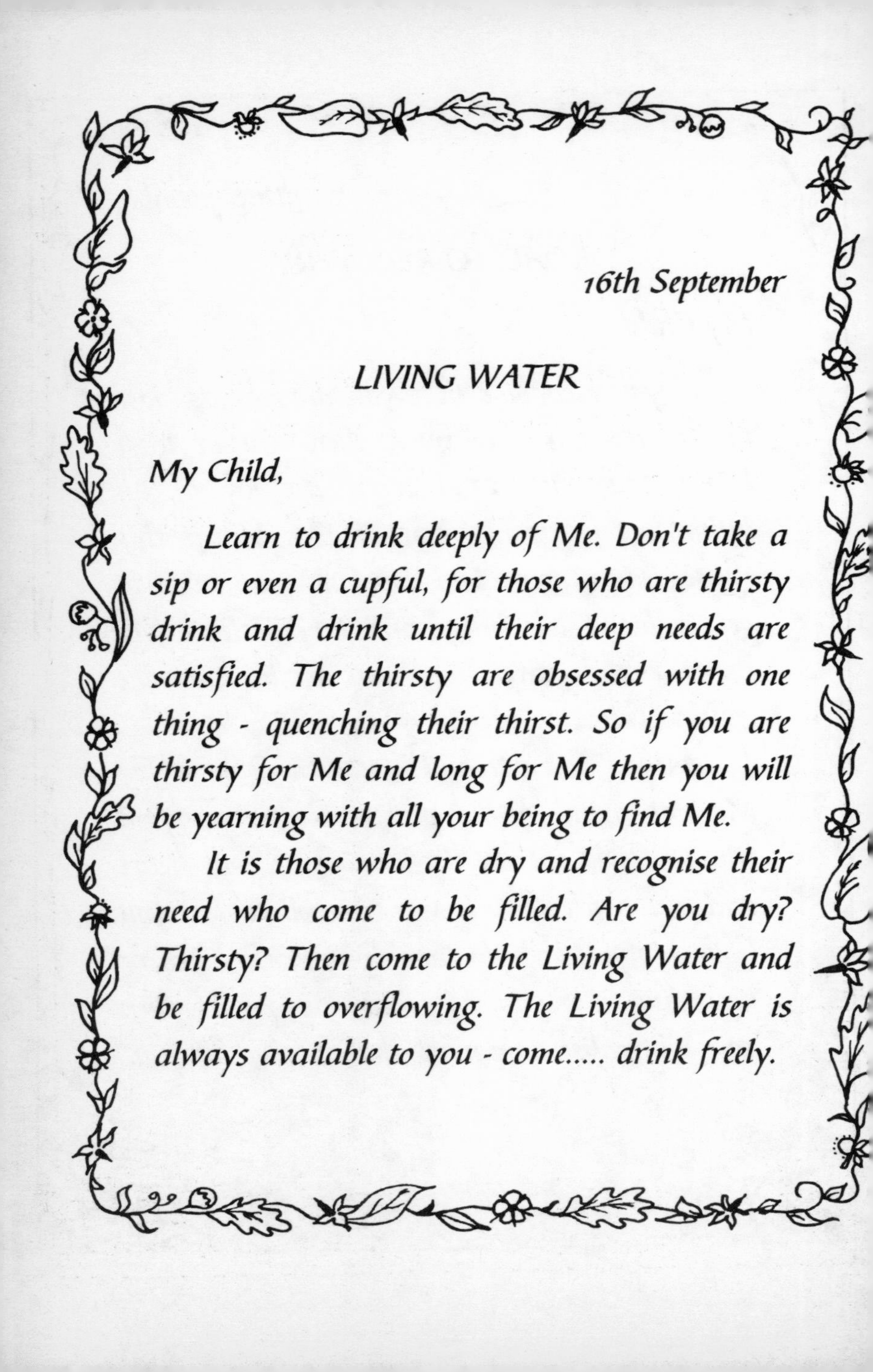

16th September

LIVING WATER

My Child,

Learn to drink deeply of Me. Don't take a sip or even a cupful, for those who are thirsty drink and drink until their deep needs are satisfied. The thirsty are obsessed with one thing - quenching their thirst. So if you are thirsty for Me and long for Me then you will be yearning with all your being to find Me.

It is those who are dry and recognise their need who come to be filled. Are you dry? Thirsty? Then come to the Living Water and be filled to overflowing. The Living Water is always available to you - come..... drink freely.

17th September

BRIDEGROOM'S RETURN

My Child,

As the Bridegroom delights over his bride so I delight over you. My bride will be radiant, passionate with love for Me, anxious to please Me and totally committed to Me.

The day of the Bridegroom's return is drawing near and I am preparing My bride - she will reflect My glory. Get ready, get ready for the Bridegroom comes - yes, I am coming for My bride. For you are part of My glorious bride and in that wonderful day I will present you to the Father, righteous, holy and spotless.

Together we shall dine at the Marriage Supper and be together forever.

18th September

YOUR HAND IN MINE

My Child,

As a child takes the hand of their Father in perfect trust so I want you to take My hand. Don't let go, thinking you know best or can go it alone, for you will surely run into trouble.

Know that as you put your hand in Mine you are safe and will be led in the right way. However difficult the way ahead is, I will reassure you and comfort you, encouraging you to keep going when everything within you wants to give up.

I will never ever slacken My hold of you or let you go because I love you too much to do that.

19th September

LAVISHED LOVE

My Child,

Before you call I will answer for even before you realise yourself what your needs are, I am already putting My plan of action into being.

I know that often your thoughts are as prayers to Me as you walk closely with Me. Sometimes it is My joy to go before you and answer those unspoken thoughts and heartfelt whispers to reassure you that your Heavenly Father is watching you and caring for you.

My response to your unspoken prayers declares My love for you, that I know exactly what you are needing and My Father heart is to care for you and provide for you. In this you will begin to understand what it means to have love lavished upon you straight from the Father's heart.

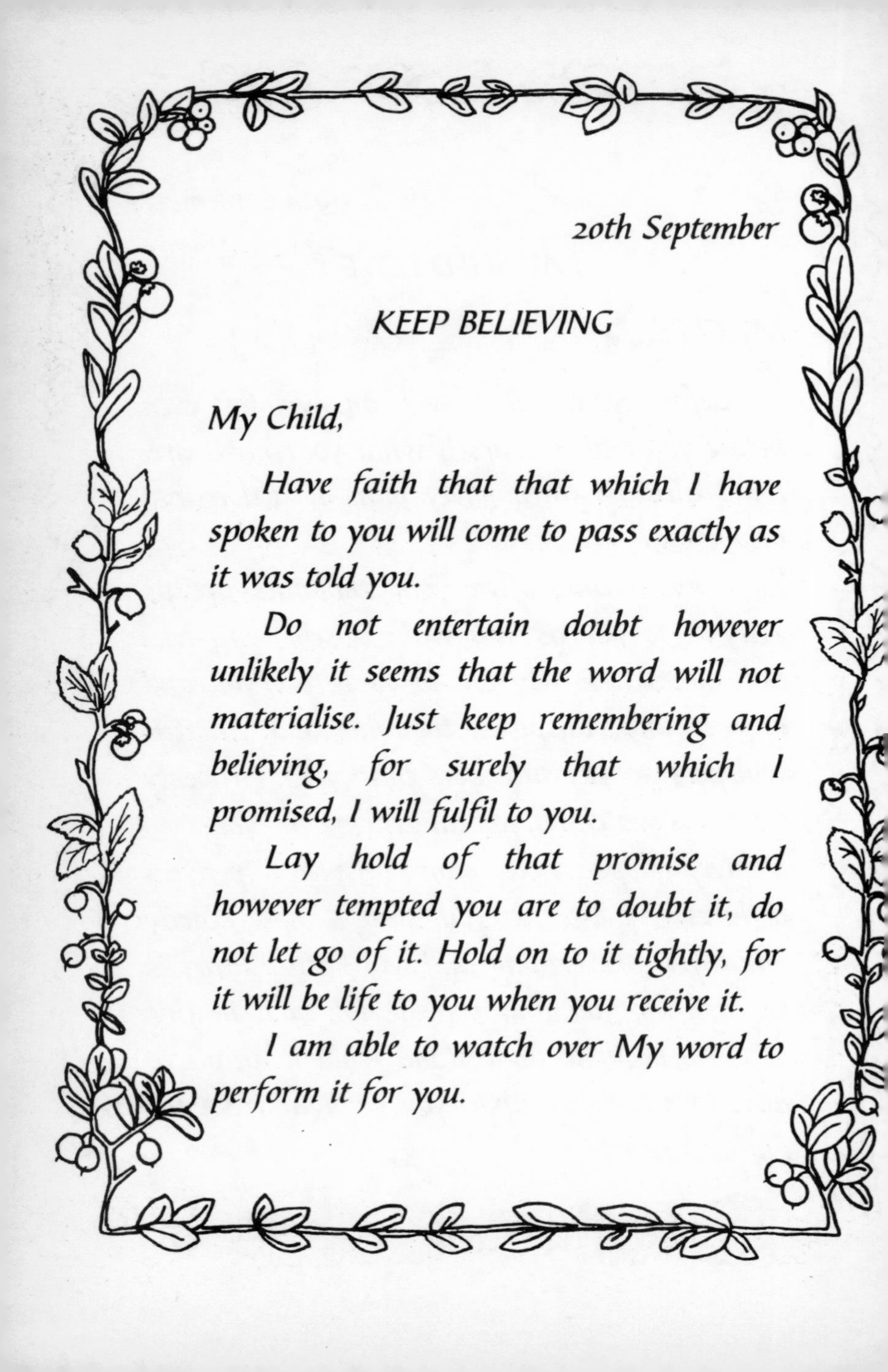

20th September

KEEP BELIEVING

My Child,

Have faith that that which I have spoken to you will come to pass exactly as it was told you.

Do not entertain doubt however unlikely it seems that the word will not materialise. Just keep remembering and believing, for surely that which I promised, I will fulfil to you.

Lay hold of that promise and however tempted you are to doubt it, do not let go of it. Hold on to it tightly, for it will be life to you when you receive it.

I am able to watch over My word to perform it for you.

21st September

RIGHTEOUS EXAMPLE

My Child,

It is not a difficult or onerous thing to be an example to others, for if you live as you should it will happen automatically without you even realising that you are such.

If you choose to walk in right ways, living the truth and obeying My word then you will be such a righteous example that others will automatically follow.

Don't be concerned about being an example - be concerned about living a righteous life and walking close to Me - surely that will be an example that others need to follow.

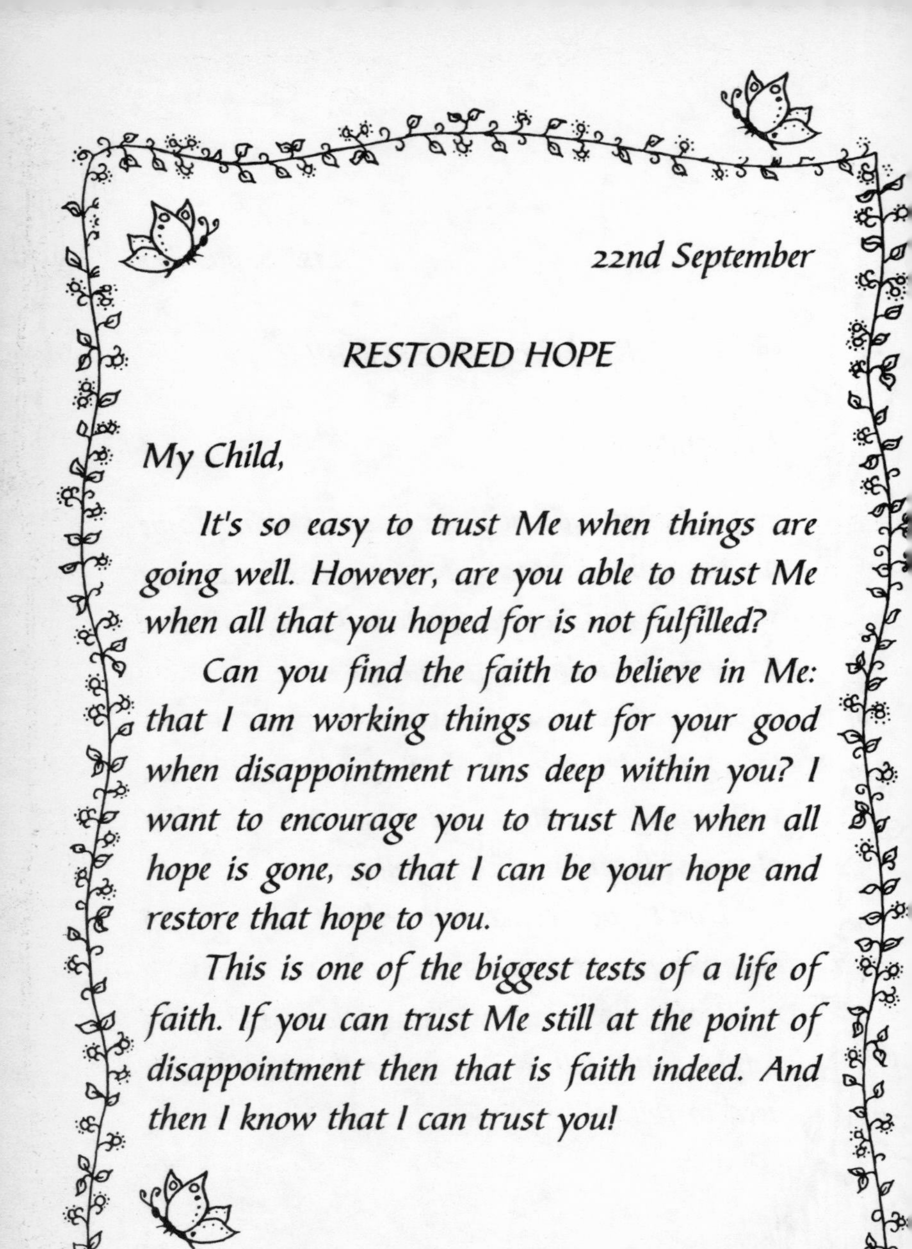

22nd September

RESTORED HOPE

My Child,

It's so easy to trust Me when things are going well. However, are you able to trust Me when all that you hoped for is not fulfilled?

Can you find the faith to believe in Me: that I am working things out for your good when disappointment runs deep within you? I want to encourage you to trust Me when all hope is gone, so that I can be your hope and restore that hope to you.

This is one of the biggest tests of a life of faith. If you can trust Me still at the point of disappointment then that is faith indeed. And then I know that I can trust you!

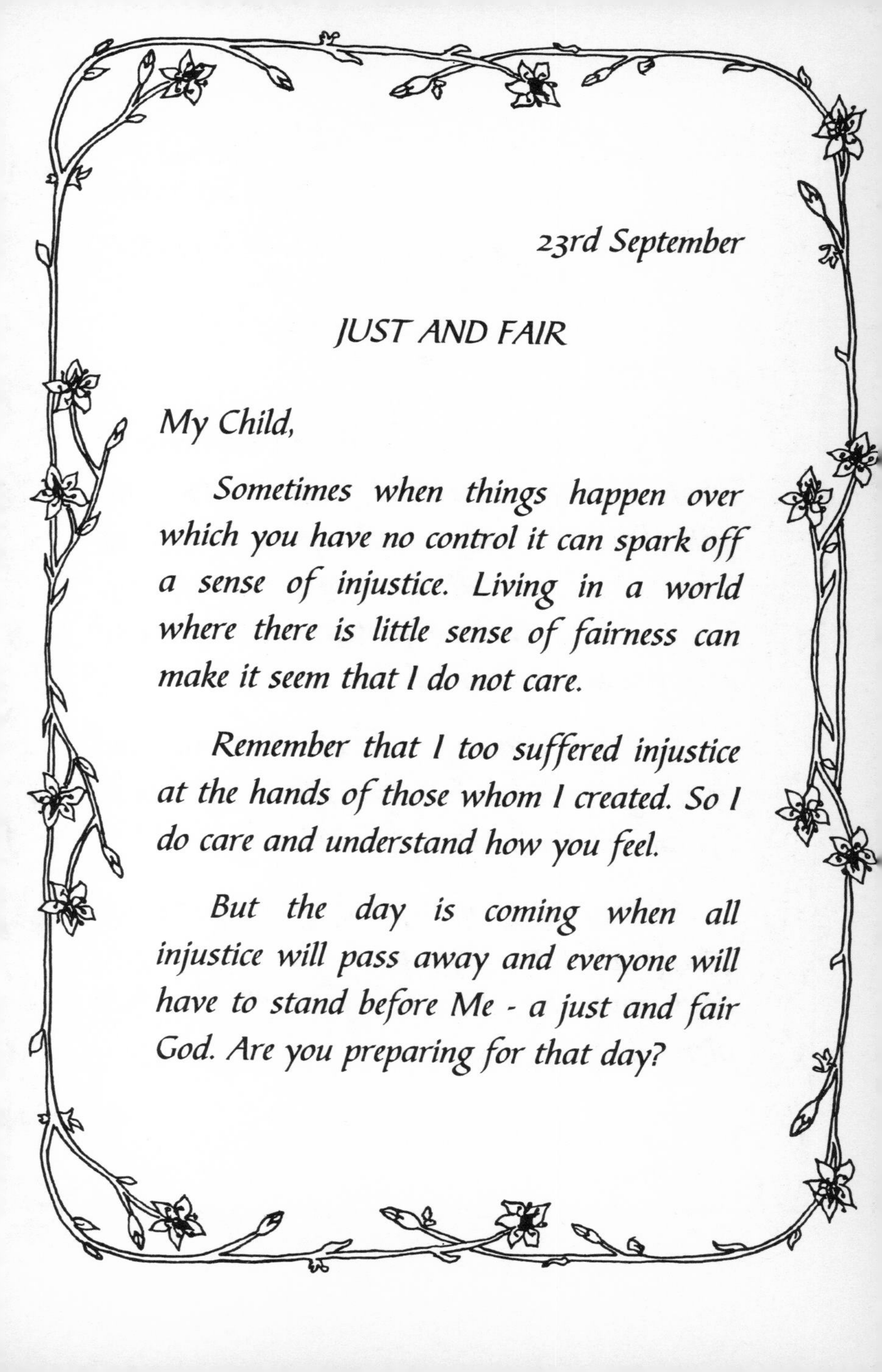

23rd September

JUST AND FAIR

My Child,

Sometimes when things happen over which you have no control it can spark off a sense of injustice. Living in a world where there is little sense of fairness can make it seem that I do not care.

Remember that I too suffered injustice at the hands of those whom I created. So I do care and understand how you feel.

But the day is coming when all injustice will pass away and everyone will have to stand before Me - a just and fair God. Are you preparing for that day?

24th September

LISTEN CAREFULLY

My Child,

If you do not listen and pay attention to what I say you could find yourself in difficulty. Not only do I speak words of comfort and love but also warning or reproof. These words will be a protection for you and keep you away from evil.

It is worth taking notice of what I say and listening to Me carefully, for My words will be life and health to you - a real blessing!

When I speak it is for a good reason and you ignore it to your peril - so determine to listen and also obey and you will find help along the way.

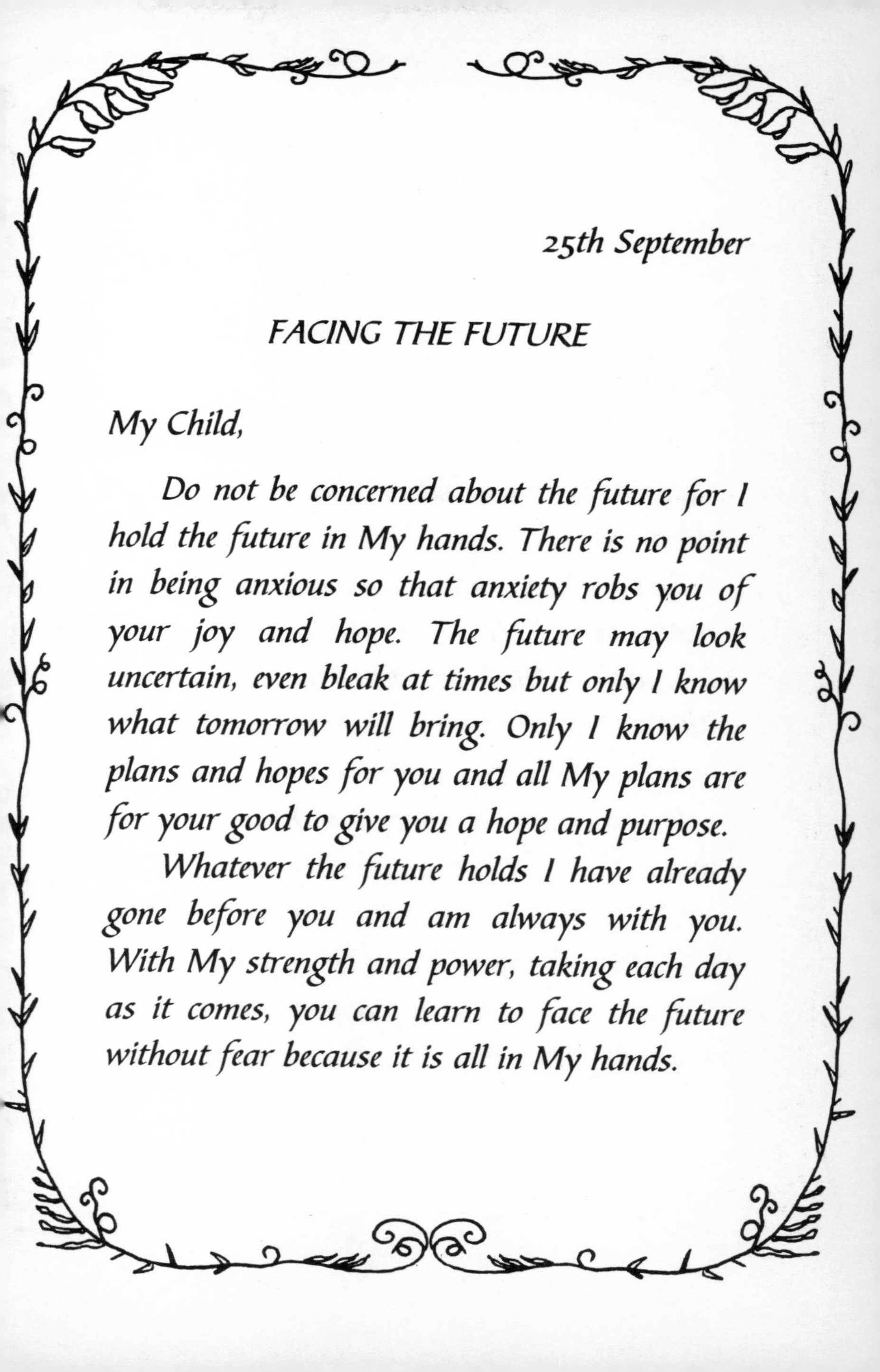

25th September

FACING THE FUTURE

My Child,

Do not be concerned about the future for I hold the future in My hands. There is no point in being anxious so that anxiety robs you of your joy and hope. The future may look uncertain, even bleak at times but only I know what tomorrow will bring. Only I know the plans and hopes for you and all My plans are for your good to give you a hope and purpose.

Whatever the future holds I have already gone before you and am always with you. With My strength and power, taking each day as it comes, you can learn to face the future without fear because it is all in My hands.

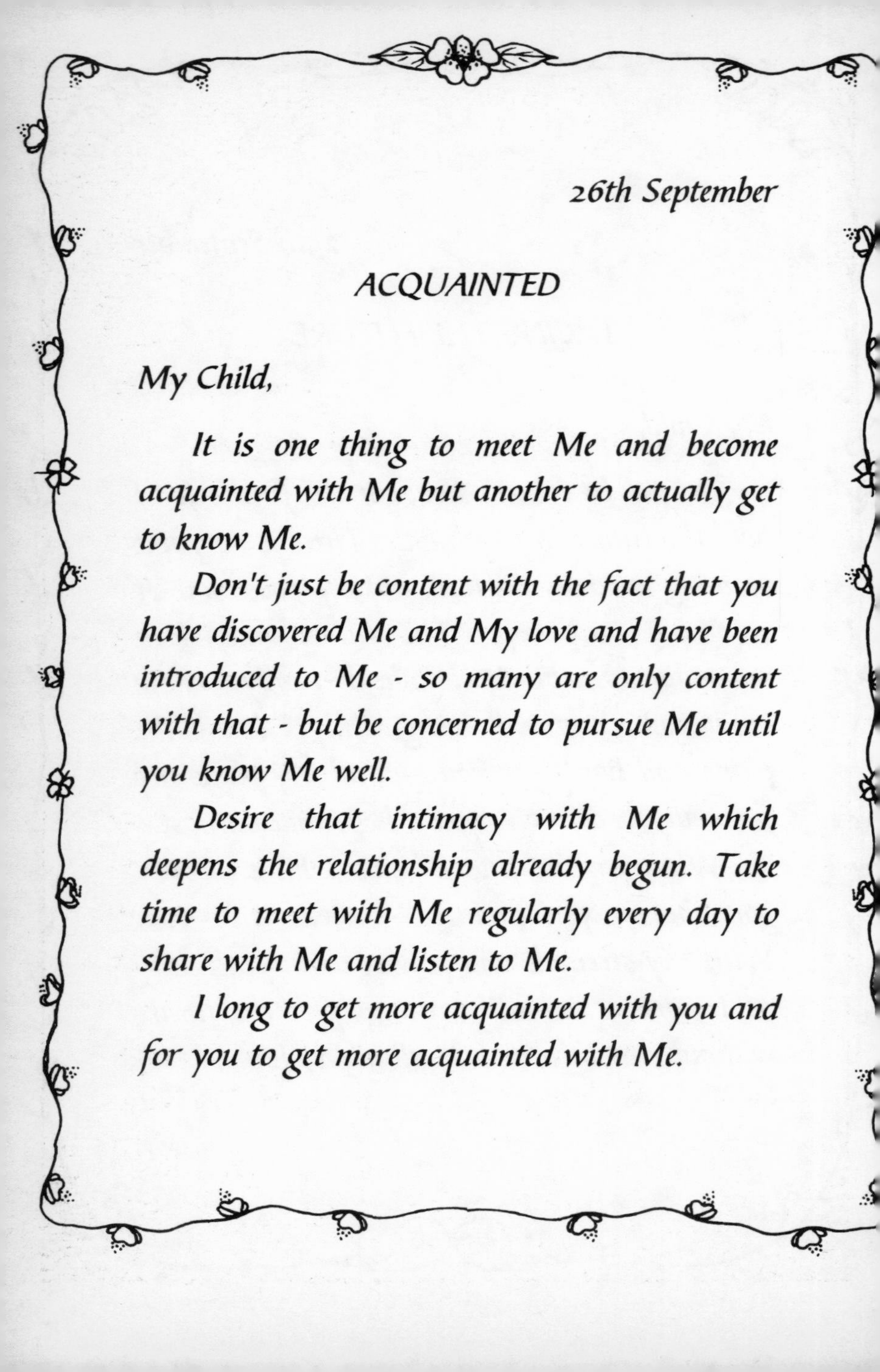

26th September

ACQUAINTED

My Child,

It is one thing to meet Me and become acquainted with Me but another to actually get to know Me.

Don't just be content with the fact that you have discovered Me and My love and have been introduced to Me - so many are only content with that - but be concerned to pursue Me until you know Me well.

Desire that intimacy with Me which deepens the relationship already begun. Take time to meet with Me regularly every day to share with Me and listen to Me.

I long to get more acquainted with you and for you to get more acquainted with Me.

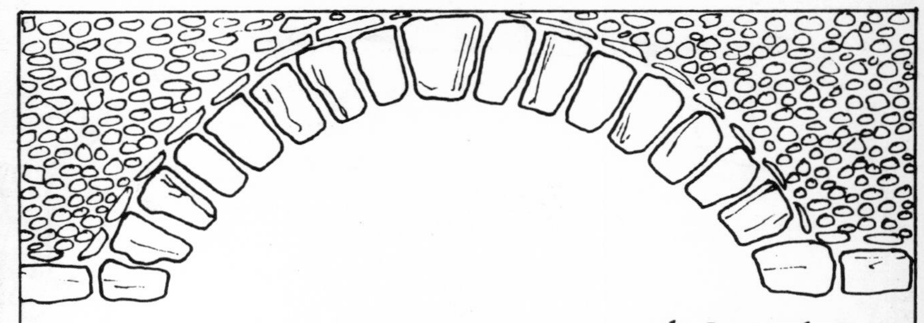

27th September

WALK THROUGH THE DOOR

My Child,

When I open a door for you and make a way for you where previously there was no way then no one can block it. My hand will keep that door open so that you can walk through unscathed into the place where I want you to be.

There is no need to be anxious that you may not see the door or may miss it for it will be so obvious to you and I will cause you to see it. There is no person or power in heaven or earth who can shut a door I have opened.

My power is omnipotent and I am sovereign Lord - walk through the door for I am The Way.

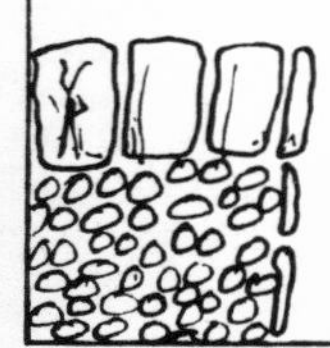

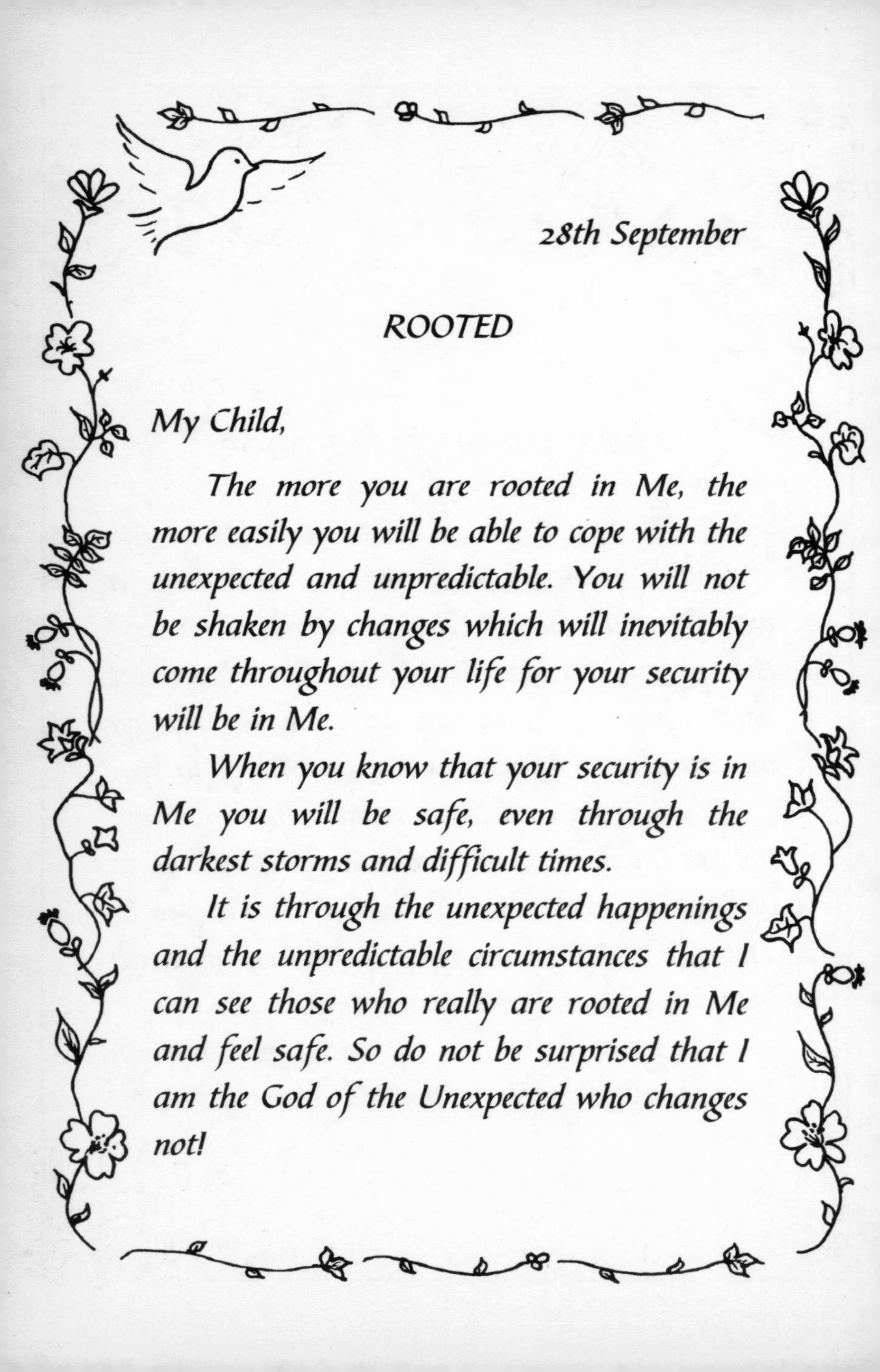

28th September

ROOTED

My Child,

The more you are rooted in Me, the more easily you will be able to cope with the unexpected and unpredictable. You will not be shaken by changes which will inevitably come throughout your life for your security will be in Me.

When you know that your security is in Me you will be safe, even through the darkest storms and difficult times.

It is through the unexpected happenings and the unpredictable circumstances that I can see those who really are rooted in Me and feel safe. So do not be surprised that I am the God of the Unexpected who changes not!

29th September

MY SHEEP

My Child,

My sheep hear My voice and follow Me. They will not follow a stranger for they do not recognise a stranger's voice.

So long as you hear My voice you do not have to worry about where I might lead you. My voice will bring reassurance to you that you are going in the right direction even if the path gets difficult.

You also have the promise of My presence wherever you go so do not fear to tread in pastures new. Wherever I lead you, all you have to do is follow and keep your eyes on Me.

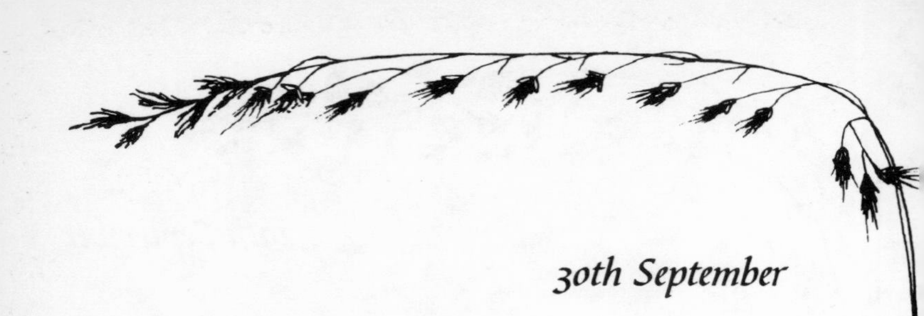

30th September

WAYS OF RIGHTEOUSNESS

My Child,

Whilst you need to be watchful and prayerful do not be overly concerned about being deceived so that you become fearful. Nothing or no one can snatch you out of My hand - for My hand is surely on your life.

So long as you desire to serve Me and follow Me I will lead you in ways of righteousness. If you keep your eyes on Me and trust Me you will not be led astray for it is impossible for Me to lead you astray.

1st October

TRANSFORMED

My Child,

Don't look over your shoulder at others and long to be like them. They too have their faults and weaknesses which hinder them.

Look up! See what I can do for you - to bring you into that place of anointing and blessing.

If you long to be like Me and to know My power then I am able to transform your life. Then you will know My purity and perfection bringing fruit into your life to My glory.

2nd October

RIVERS

My Child,

No matter how dry the ground, the rivers of My living water are not only able to penetrate it but also to go down very deep!

However dry you feel that your heart is, I am longing to pour out My living water on you. The more dry you feel you are, the more you realise your need to be filled.

As you open up your heart to Me, I will come and fill you up so that you overflow to others. Firstly acknowledge that you need My living water and then prepare yourself and expect the rivers of My living water to flow over you and in you, until you are drenched in My love.

3rd October

BEHOLD MY GLORY

My Child,

I see all the longings of your heart and I know your desire to be more like Me. This is not something that you, yourself, can do for it is the work of My Spirit. As you submit to Me and surrender to My will, walking in obedience so you will be changed to be more like Me. As you spend time in My presence, beholding My glory, so you too will reflect My glory.

Then you will display more of My likeness, My character and My nature, for you will begin to think and act in a godly way. The closer you walk with Me, the more you will become like Me, and My likeness will rest upon you.

4th October

WIN THE LOST

My Child,

When you hear the cry of My heart for the lost do not ignore that cry. Do not close your eyes and harden your heart as if it does not matter. Each person who is alive today is a soul for whom I gave My life - to purchase theirs.

As time is getting shorter so the cry of My heart is getting louder - I want My people to hear and to respond. Do you hear?

I love the lost and I want you to love them too. Feel My heart of compassion for those who do not know Me and decide in your heart to be obedient to My voice so that together we can win the lost, save the hopeless and snatch them from the jaws of eternal death.

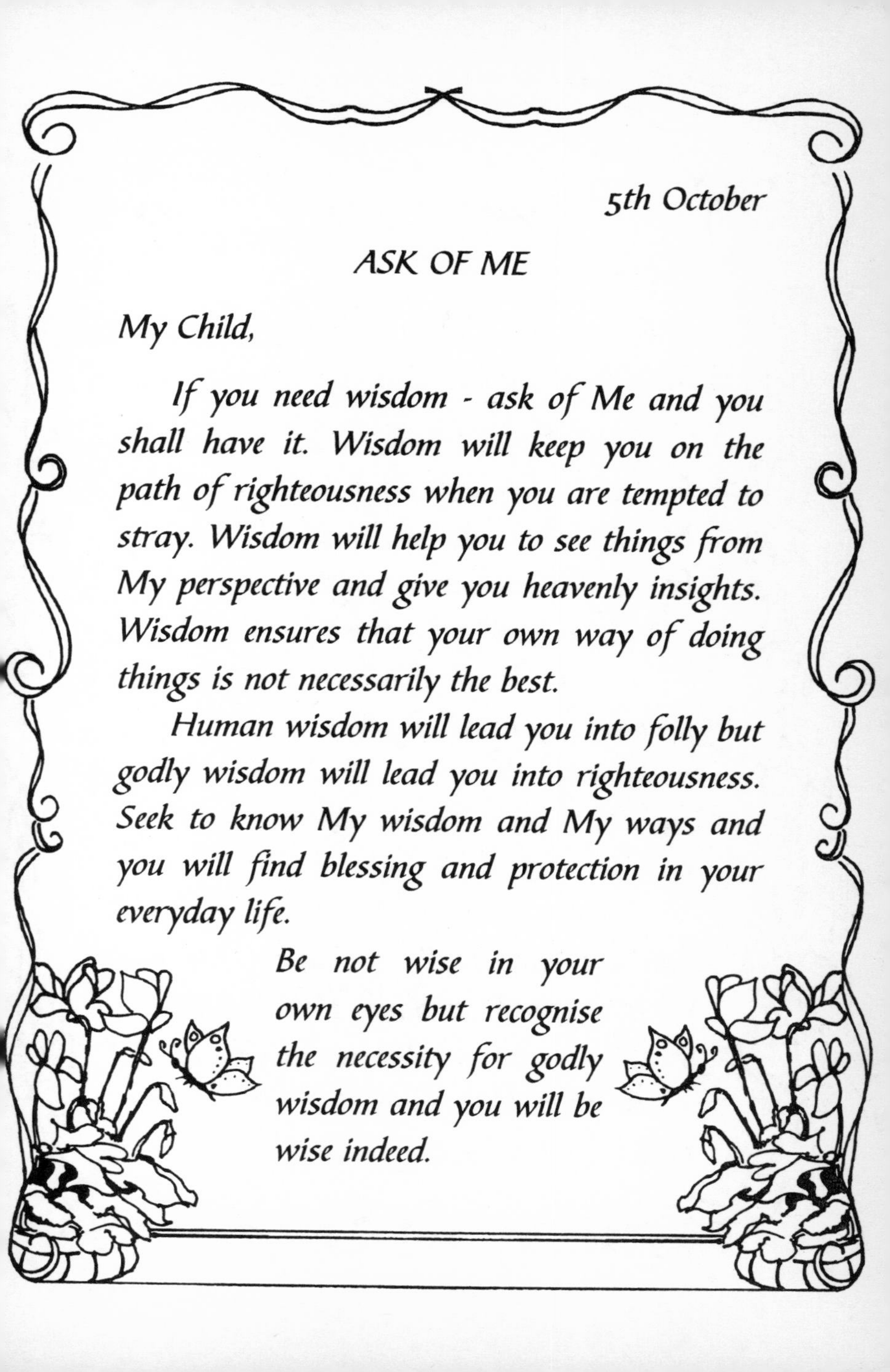

5th October

ASK OF ME

My Child,

If you need wisdom - ask of Me and you shall have it. Wisdom will keep you on the path of righteousness when you are tempted to stray. Wisdom will help you to see things from My perspective and give you heavenly insights. Wisdom ensures that your own way of doing things is not necessarily the best.

Human wisdom will lead you into folly but godly wisdom will lead you into righteousness. Seek to know My wisdom and My ways and you will find blessing and protection in your everyday life.

Be not wise in your own eyes but recognise the necessity for godly wisdom and you will be wise indeed.

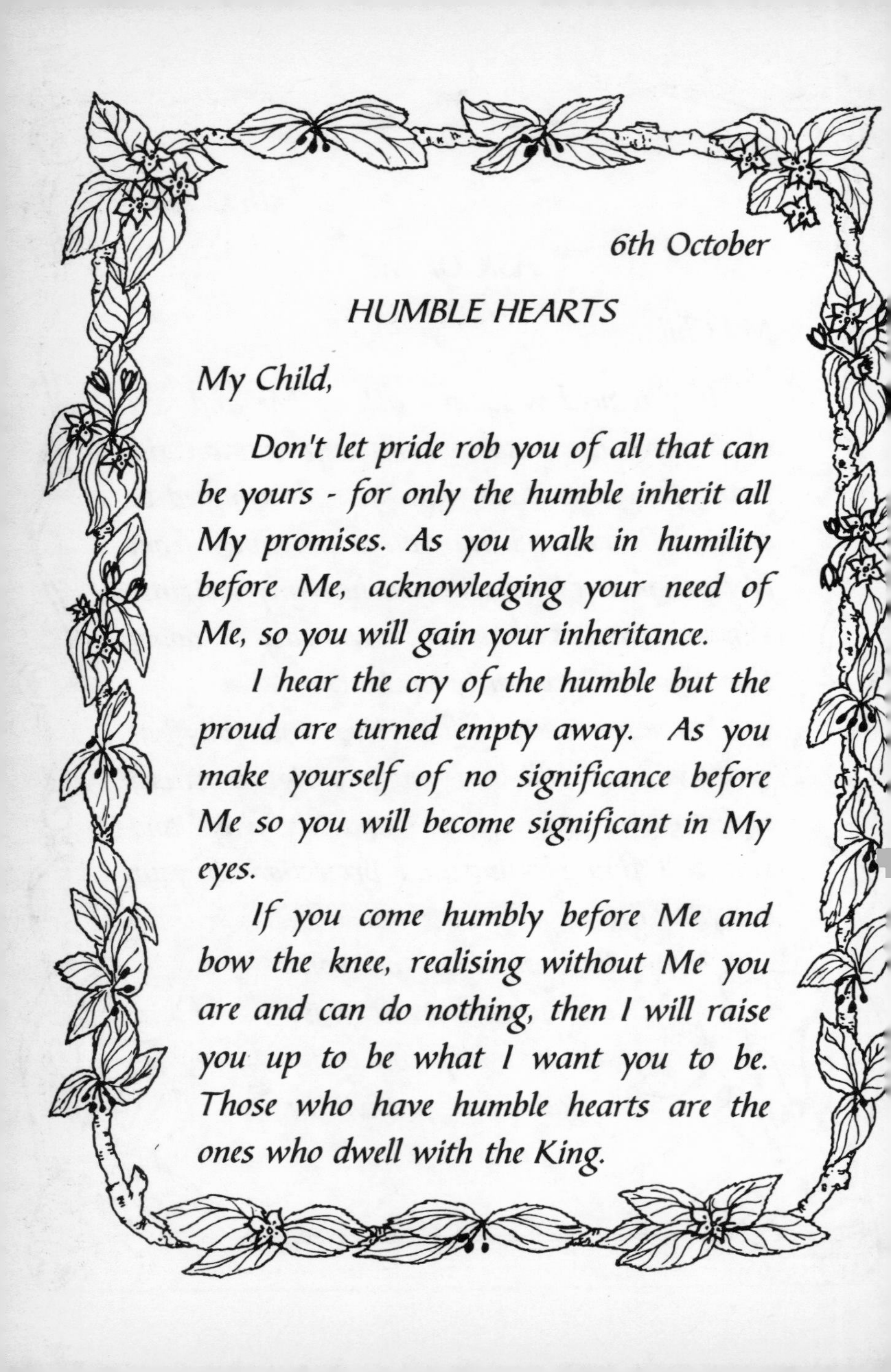

6th October

HUMBLE HEARTS

My Child,

Don't let pride rob you of all that can be yours - for only the humble inherit all My promises. As you walk in humility before Me, acknowledging your need of Me, so you will gain your inheritance.

I hear the cry of the humble but the proud are turned empty away. As you make yourself of no significance before Me so you will become significant in My eyes.

If you come humbly before Me and bow the knee, realising without Me you are and can do nothing, then I will raise you up to be what I want you to be. Those who have humble hearts are the ones who dwell with the King.

7th October

GREATEST GIFT

My Child,

Though it is a blessing to know and experience My power, the greater blessing is to know My love. Sometimes power can be a fearful thing but perfect love casts out fear. Only through the power of My love will My awesome power be revealed.

I want you to love Me more than you fear Me and to experience more of My love than power. For the power of My love is the greatest of all powers - it softens hearts and changes lives, transforming that which is ugly into something very beautiful.

If you have My love you will have the greatest power of all - if you have power without love you lack My greatest gift.

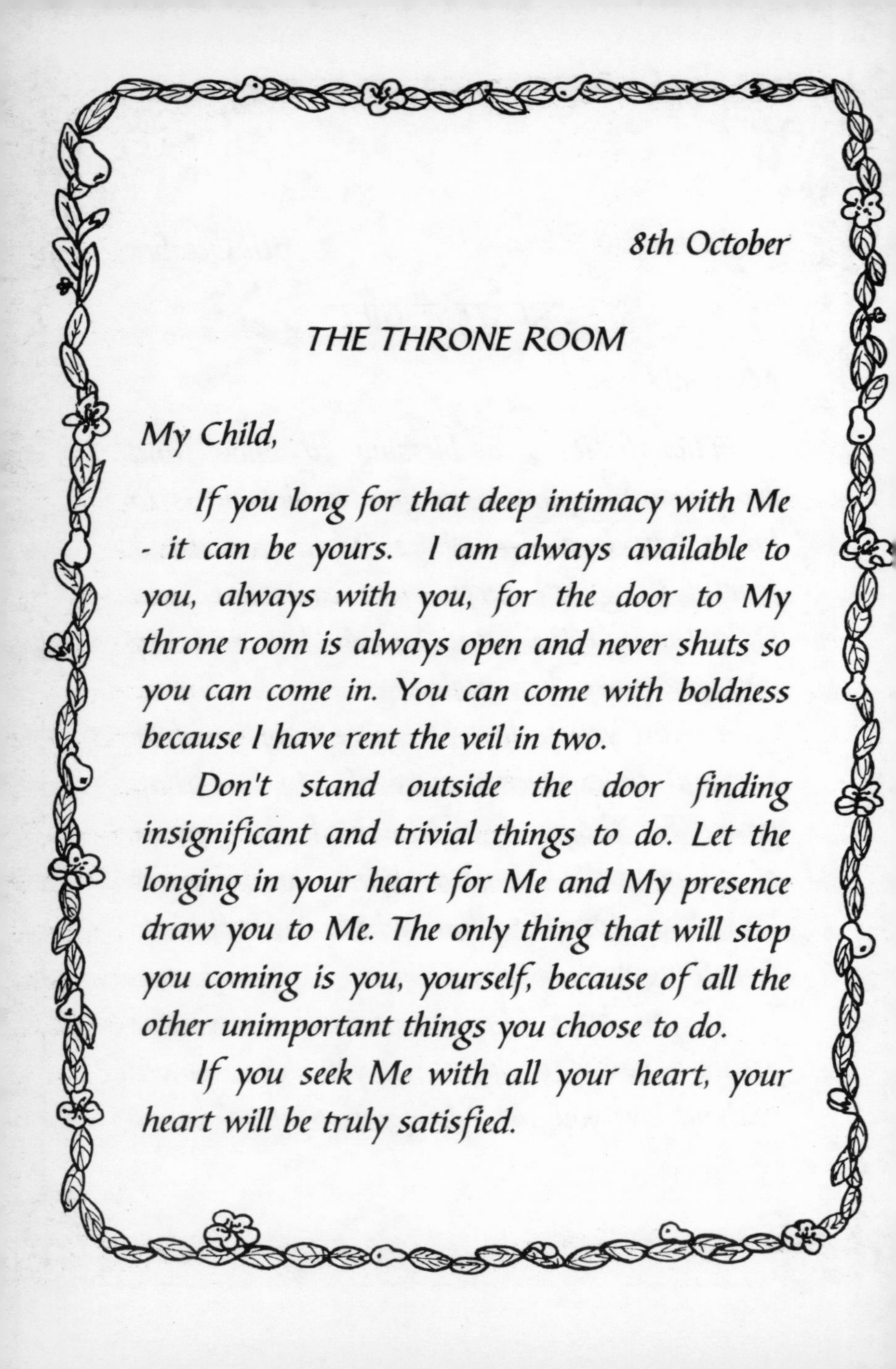

8th October

THE THRONE ROOM

My Child,

If you long for that deep intimacy with Me - it can be yours. I am always available to you, always with you, for the door to My throne room is always open and never shuts so you can come in. You can come with boldness because I have rent the veil in two.

Don't stand outside the door finding insignificant and trivial things to do. Let the longing in your heart for Me and My presence draw you to Me. The only thing that will stop you coming is you, yourself, because of all the other unimportant things you choose to do.

If you seek Me with all your heart, your heart will be truly satisfied.

9th October

HELP FOR ATTITUDES

My Child,

Watch your attitudes for how you think and feel and the way you react is so important. It is so important that you have right attitudes so that things like bitterness and resentment do not take root in your heart.

Having a right attitude often means learning to die to self and taking up your cross. No one finds this easy but I can help you do it.

Remember according to My word how blessed are they who have right attitudes for they shall reap a harvest of peace and righteousness and be a blessing to all around them.

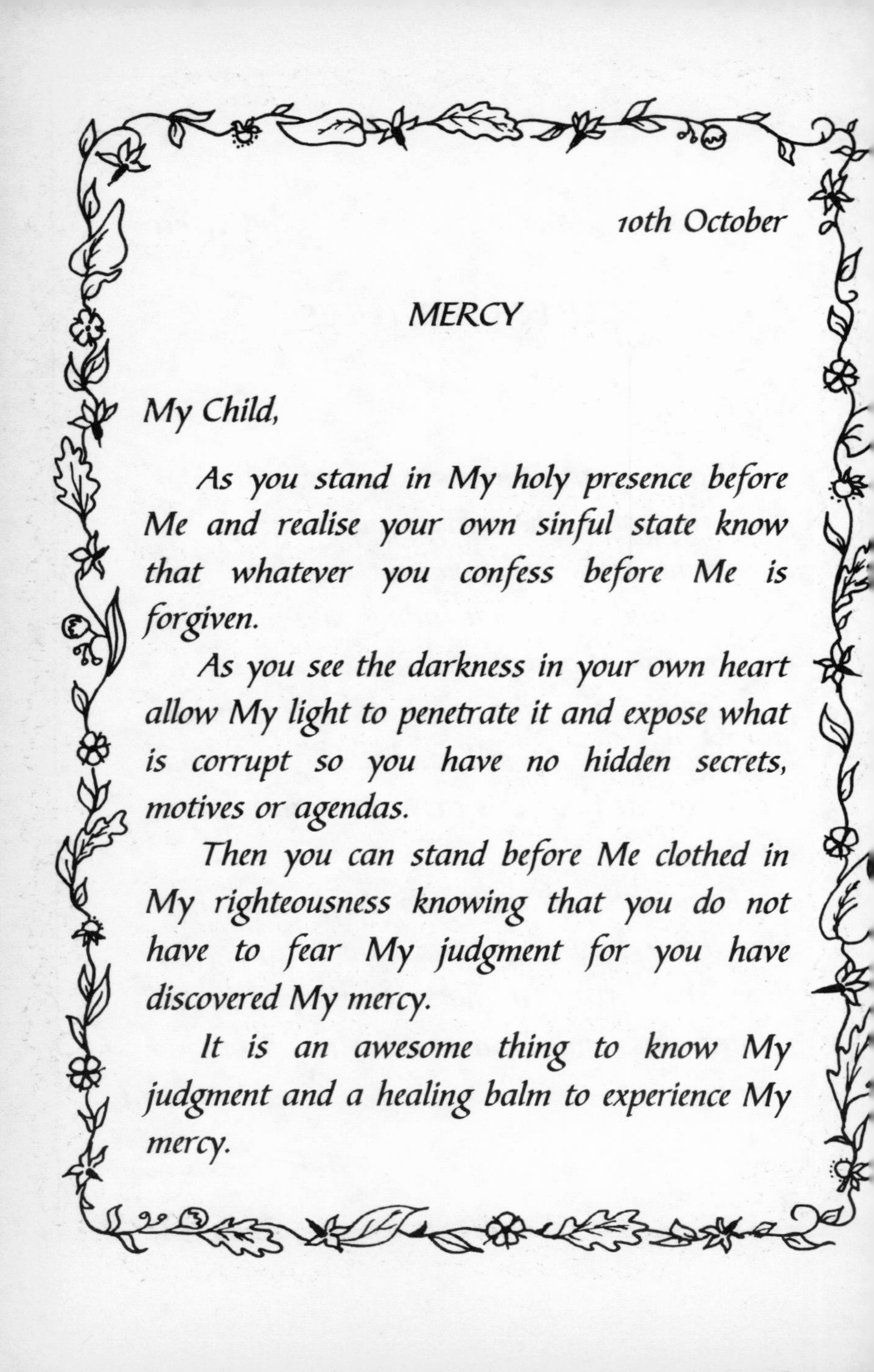

10th October

MERCY

My Child,

As you stand in My holy presence before Me and realise your own sinful state know that whatever you confess before Me is forgiven.

As you see the darkness in your own heart allow My light to penetrate it and expose what is corrupt so you have no hidden secrets, motives or agendas.

Then you can stand before Me clothed in My righteousness knowing that you do not have to fear My judgment for you have discovered My mercy.

It is an awesome thing to know My judgment and a healing balm to experience My mercy.

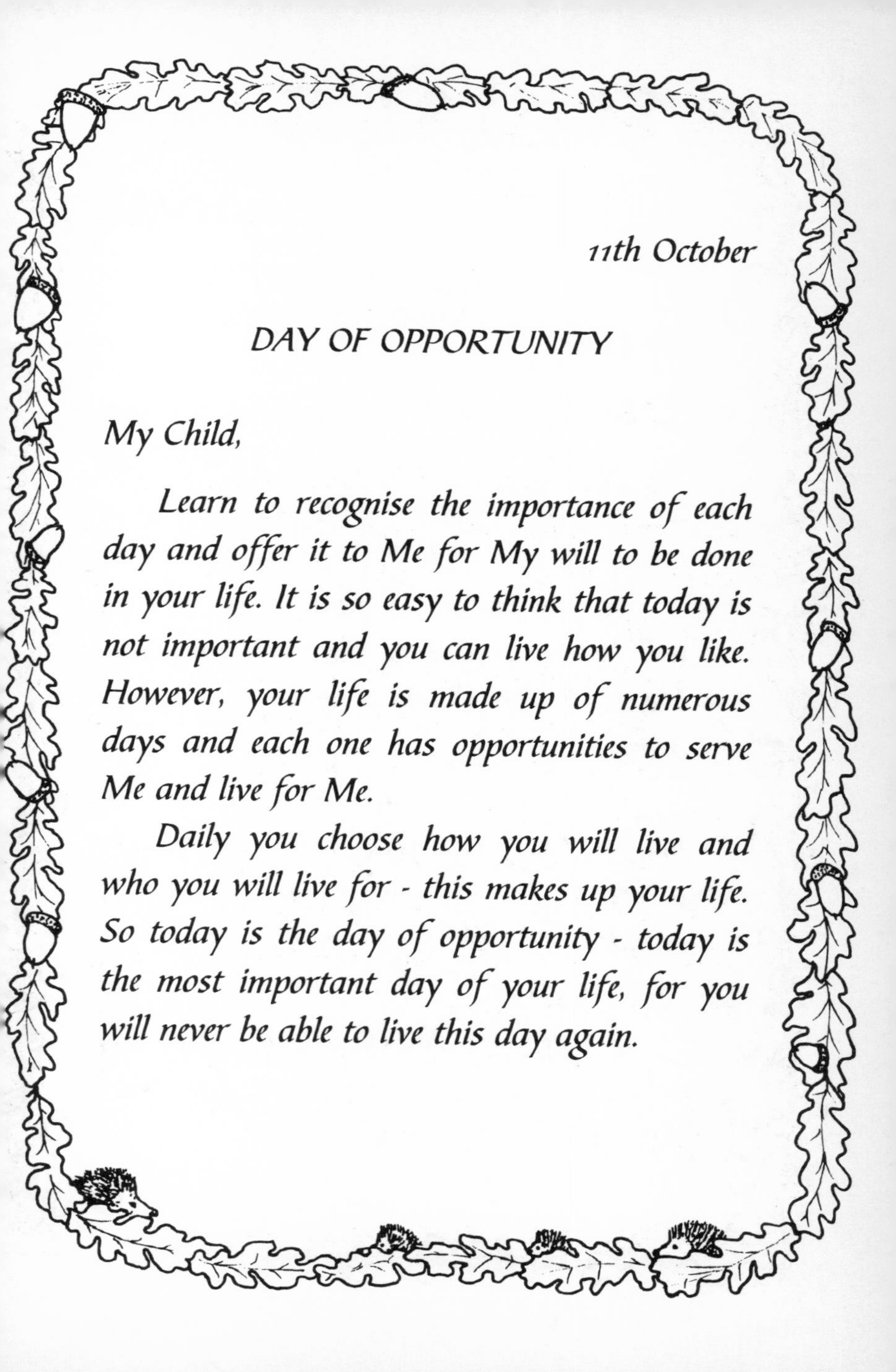

11th October

DAY OF OPPORTUNITY

My Child,

Learn to recognise the importance of each day and offer it to Me for My will to be done in your life. It is so easy to think that today is not important and you can live how you like. However, your life is made up of numerous days and each one has opportunities to serve Me and live for Me.

Daily you choose how you will live and who you will live for - this makes up your life. So today is the day of opportunity - today is the most important day of your life, for you will never be able to live this day again.

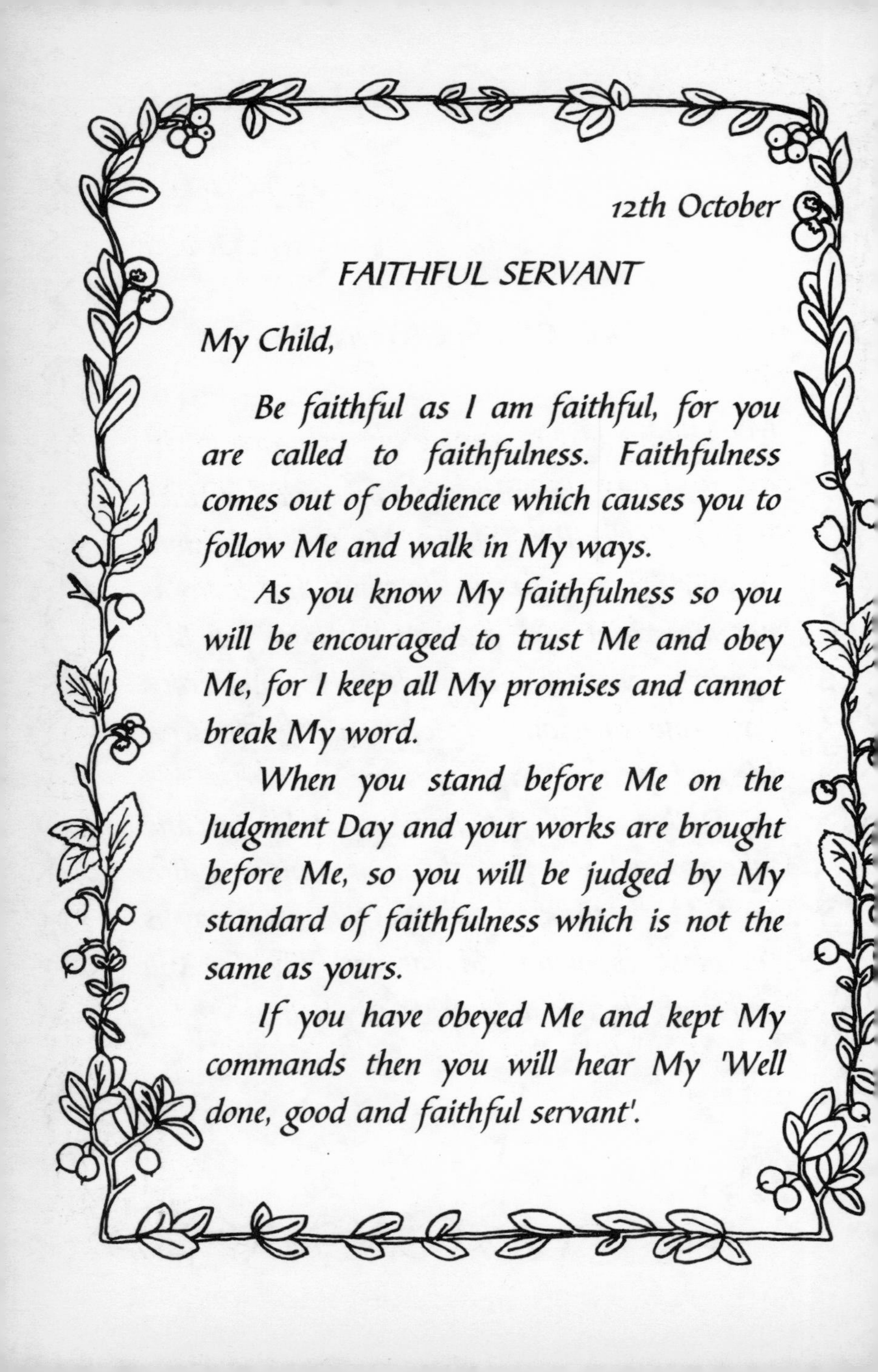

12th October

FAITHFUL SERVANT

My Child,

Be faithful as I am faithful, for you are called to faithfulness. Faithfulness comes out of obedience which causes you to follow Me and walk in My ways.

As you know My faithfulness so you will be encouraged to trust Me and obey Me, for I keep all My promises and cannot break My word.

When you stand before Me on the Judgment Day and your works are brought before Me, so you will be judged by My standard of faithfulness which is not the same as yours.

If you have obeyed Me and kept My commands then you will hear My 'Well done, good and faithful servant'.

13th October

FOR EVER

My Child,

The time of My coming draws nearer each day. As I have promised, so will I come. Every eye will see Me and instantly know who I am - The Coming King. For some it will be a day of rejoicing but not for everyone.

Make sure that each day you prepare your heart for My return. Keep awake and alert, being prayerful, for if you are not awake when I come your heart will be sad. Let Me come each day to your heart, which is open and exposed to Me, so that at My coming your eyes will see what your heart already knows - that the day of the Lord is here, for I am coming for you, to take you to be with Me for ever and ever....

14th October

SUPERNATURAL LOVE

My Child,

Do you love Me? If you can truly answer 'yes', then I ask you 'Do you love your brothers and sisters?' As you show My love to your brothers and sisters, even if you do not agree with them, so you are also declaring your love for Me.

The love you have for Me in your heart is measured by your desire to be obedient to Me. Those who truly love Me will love to do My will and to love others as themselves. Such love is not natural but a supernatural love which flows from Me to you.

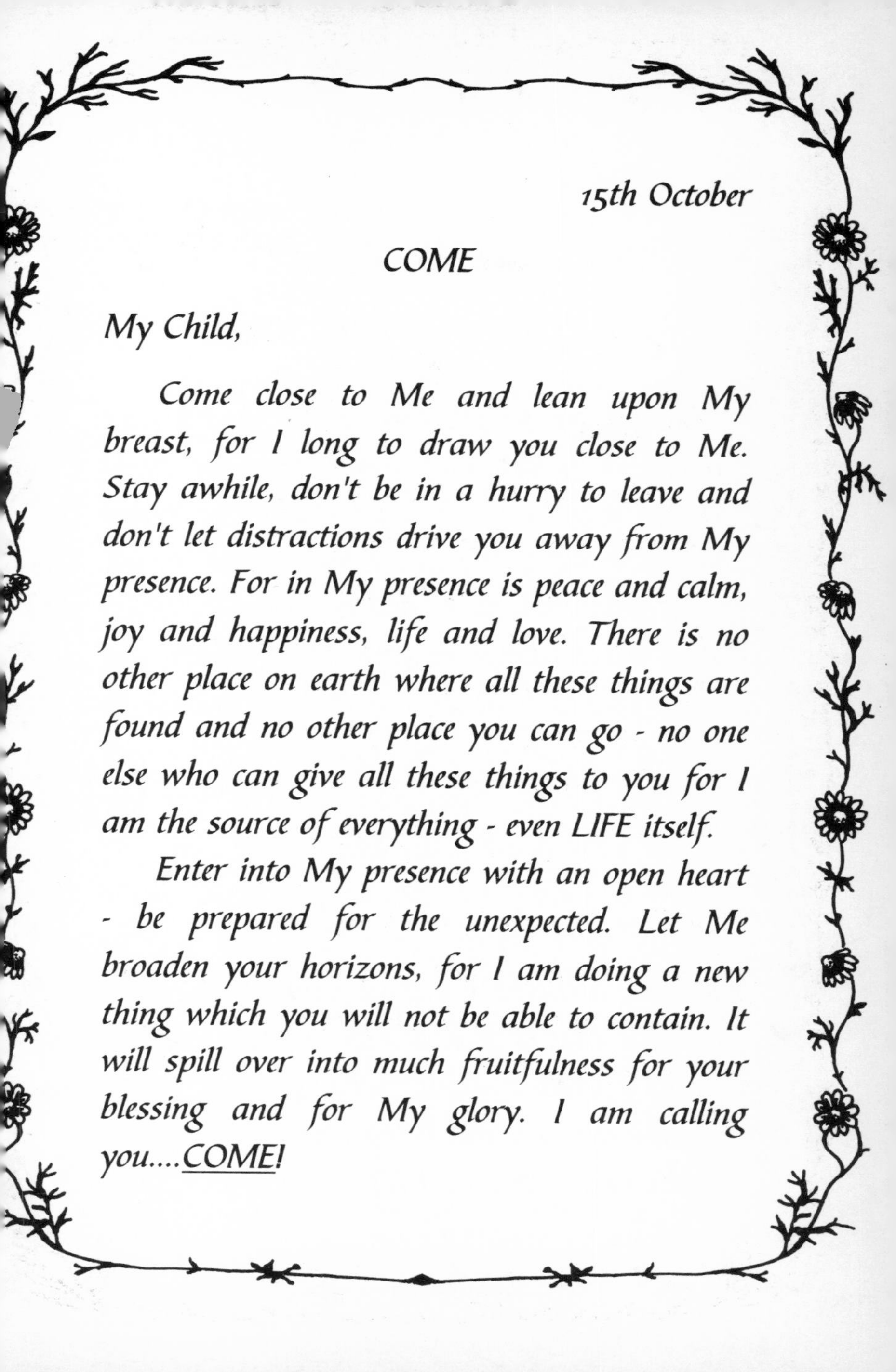

15th October

COME

My Child,

Come close to Me and lean upon My breast, for I long to draw you close to Me. Stay awhile, don't be in a hurry to leave and don't let distractions drive you away from My presence. For in My presence is peace and calm, joy and happiness, life and love. There is no other place on earth where all these things are found and no other place you can go - no one else who can give all these things to you for I am the source of everything - even LIFE itself.

Enter into My presence with an open heart - be prepared for the unexpected. Let Me broaden your horizons, for I am doing a new thing which you will not be able to contain. It will spill over into much fruitfulness for your blessing and for My glory. I am calling you....COME!

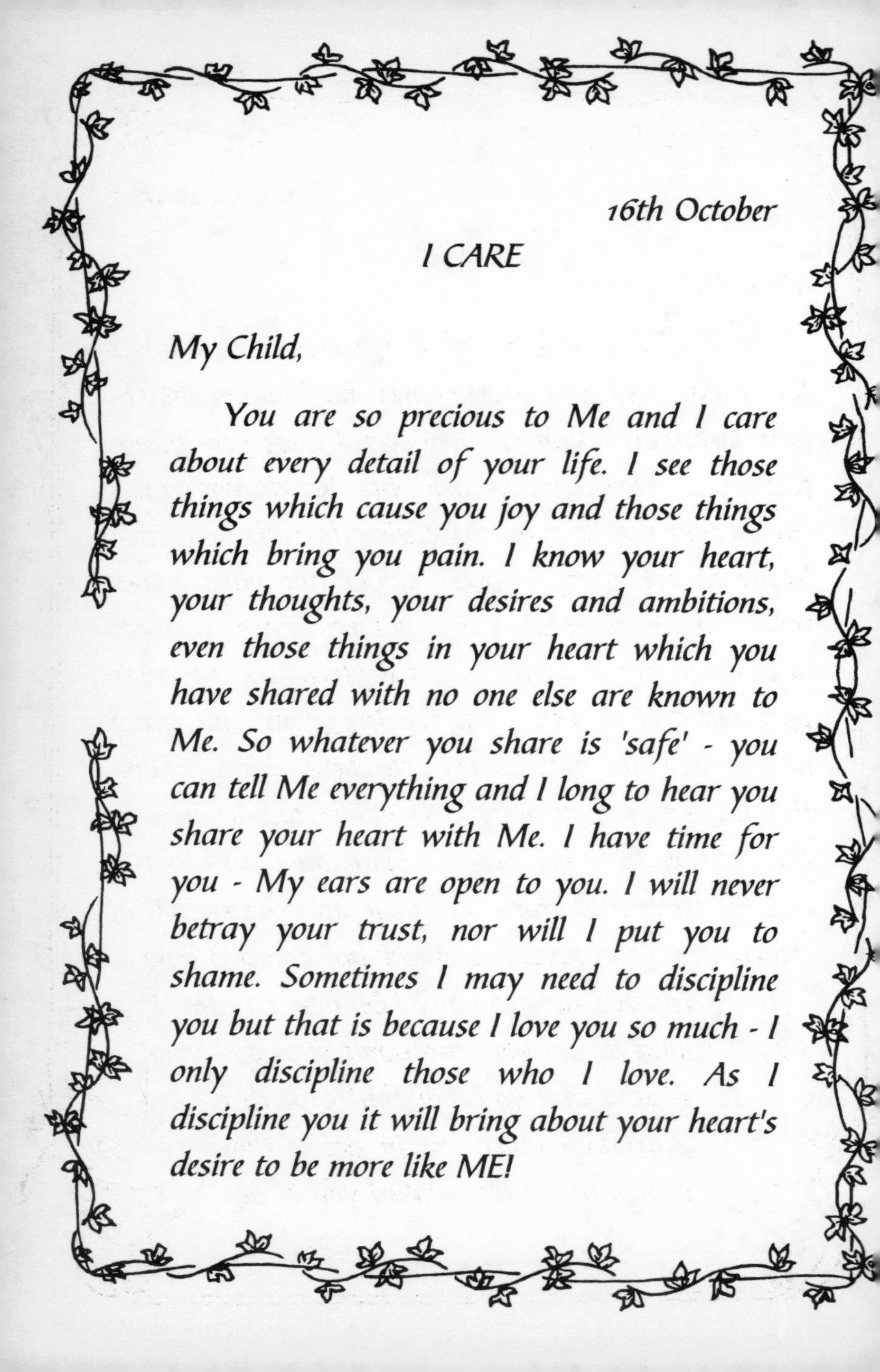

16th October

I CARE

My Child,

You are so precious to Me and I care about every detail of your life. I see those things which cause you joy and those things which bring you pain. I know your heart, your thoughts, your desires and ambitions, even those things in your heart which you have shared with no one else are known to Me. So whatever you share is 'safe' - you can tell Me everything and I long to hear you share your heart with Me. I have time for you - My ears are open to you. I will never betray your trust, nor will I put you to shame. Sometimes I may need to discipline you but that is because I love you so much - I only discipline those who I love. As I discipline you it will bring about your heart's desire to be more like ME!

17th October

LET GO

My Child,

I want you to know that I am interested in all the things that you are involved in. But now is the time to lay everything at My feet. I have new things for you... How can you fill your hands with more things when your hands are already full. You must let go of everything - lay it all on the altar - that will be a costly sacrifice and not easy to do. As you lay everything before Me I will show you what to pick up again, and what to let go so that your hands will be open to receive new things. Some things that you relinquish I will restore to you in greater measure one day - some will die forever because their usefulness has gone and the season of fruitfulness is passed. Remember how much I long for you to be close to Me, how I long to use you - so don't struggle - submit and you will find that there is a deep inner joy in doing those things that I have called you to do.

18th October

FOLLOW ME

My Child,

Have I not called you to follow Me - did I not say that daily you must take up your cross? Then why are you so surprised when taking up your cross means pain and suffering? It is dying to self and when you are able to die to self you find life in all its fullness. Do I not bring life and freedom out of death and bondage? I am LIFE! I am the very source of LIFE who enables you to enjoy life in all its fullness. The path that leads to eternity is not an easy path to follow but if you want to reign with Me you must learn to endure My sufferings. The reward is greater than the eye has seen or ear heard and is for all those who have obeyed Me because they love Me. Wait and see.

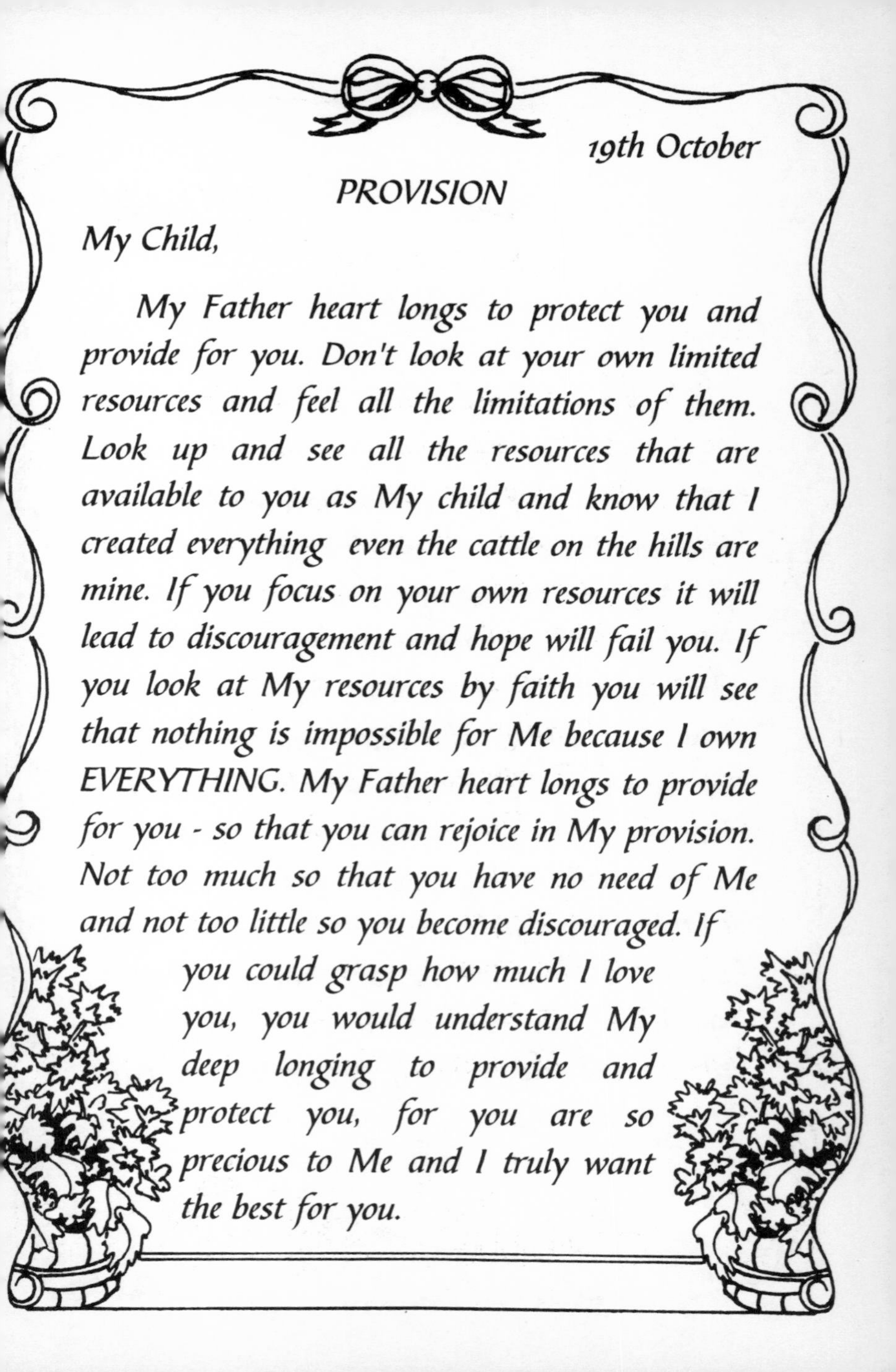

19th October

PROVISION

My Child,

My Father heart longs to protect you and provide for you. Don't look at your own limited resources and feel all the limitations of them. Look up and see all the resources that are available to you as My child and know that I created everything even the cattle on the hills are mine. If you focus on your own resources it will lead to discouragement and hope will fail you. If you look at My resources by faith you will see that nothing is impossible for Me because I own EVERYTHING. My Father heart longs to provide for you - so that you can rejoice in My provision. Not too much so that you have no need of Me and not too little so you become discouraged. If you could grasp how much I love you, you would understand My deep longing to provide and protect you, for you are so precious to Me and I truly want the best for you.

20th October

GREAT LOVE

My Child,

As you experience more of the greatness of My love in your heart, that love will flow out to others. You will see people with My eyes and feel My heart of compassion for them. Is not My heart of compassion longing for those who don't know Me as much as those who do. As My word touches your heart and changes your life so you will know those whom I want to reach and touch. You will hear Me clearly and know exactly what to say - you will not have to think about it for My words will be in your mouth and you will be surprised at what you speak. So draw close to Me, experience My love afresh and soak yourself in My word to reach those I long to touch.

21st October

HEARTBEAT

My Child,

Listen to My heartbeat it throbs with love for you. Sometimes it is so difficult for you to understand My love - pure love - because all the love you know is defiled. Every action I take on your behalf is motivated by love, enacted by love and is demonstrating My love - even the things that don't seem to make sense or add up - yes everything is done in LOVE! As a parent you only get a tiny glimpse of what it means to love your child in comparison to the way I love you as a Father. If you didn't struggle and strive sometimes, you wouldn't need the comfort of My arms of love. I am the God of all comfort who takes you aside when life gets tough and lets you experience afresh the warmth of My love for you and the comfort of My arms around you. Sometimes you just need to be still to realise how much you need Me..... and I need you!

22nd October

MY WORLD

My Child,

Feel my heart of compassion for those who do not know Me, especially those who are victims and through no fault of their own have been damaged physically, emotionally, mentally and spiritually. Don't get so caught up in your own little world that you forget those in My world who need Me. Your world is so small and Mine so vast. My world encompasses different races, so called religions, nations and peoples from every ethnic group. All these are on My heart as I see injustice, cruelty, hatred and oppression. I long to answer the cry of the oppressed but I need intercessors. Will you be one who shares My heart for all peoples in My world? Step out of your own world - I can take care of that for you and enter into My world through the door of prayer. As you pray you will see My kingdom established in My world.

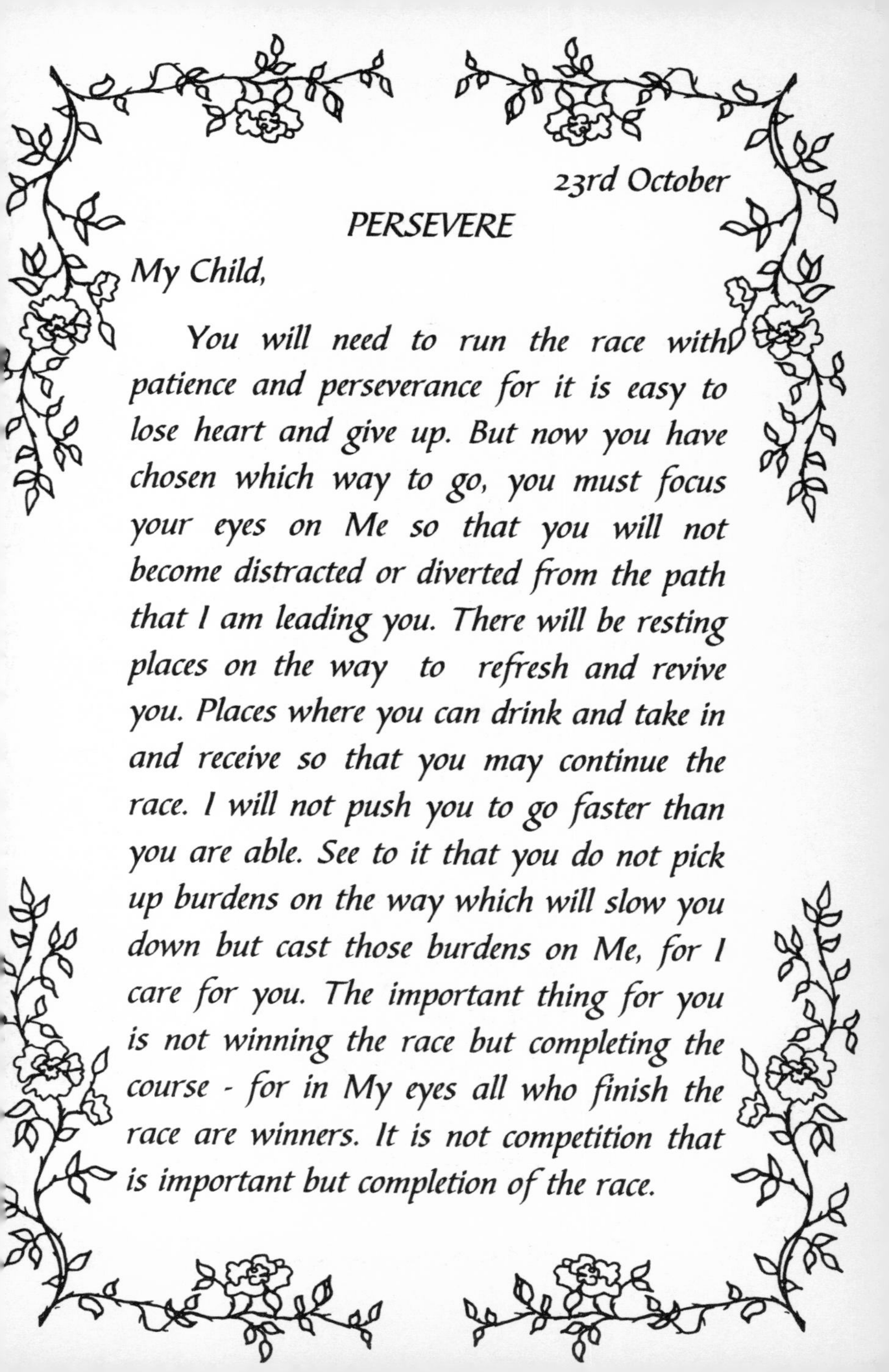

23rd October

PERSEVERE

My Child,

You will need to run the race with patience and perseverance for it is easy to lose heart and give up. But now you have chosen which way to go, you must focus your eyes on Me so that you will not become distracted or diverted from the path that I am leading you. There will be resting places on the way to refresh and revive you. Places where you can drink and take in and receive so that you may continue the race. I will not push you to go faster than you are able. See to it that you do not pick up burdens on the way which will slow you down but cast those burdens on Me, for I care for you. The important thing for you is not winning the race but completing the course - for in My eyes all who finish the race are winners. It is not competition that is important but completion of the race.

24th October

CHANGE

My Child,

Don't underestimate My power to change lives and situations. My power at work, through your prayers, can cause changes which your eyes long to see. I am working out My plans and purposes all the time - mostly unseen and unknown, waiting for the right moment to reveal exactly what I am doing and want to accomplish.

Even when situations look hopeless and may even be deteriorating I can bring about change. Even when people's hearts are ice-cold and far from Me I can warm their hearts with My love and melt those hearts. So often the changes you long to see are the desires that I have put into your heart - will I not fulfil those longings which are in My heart too. Yes I am the God who changes not but longs to bring about change. There is much I want to do, so don't give up, keep praying and remember that I also want to change you!

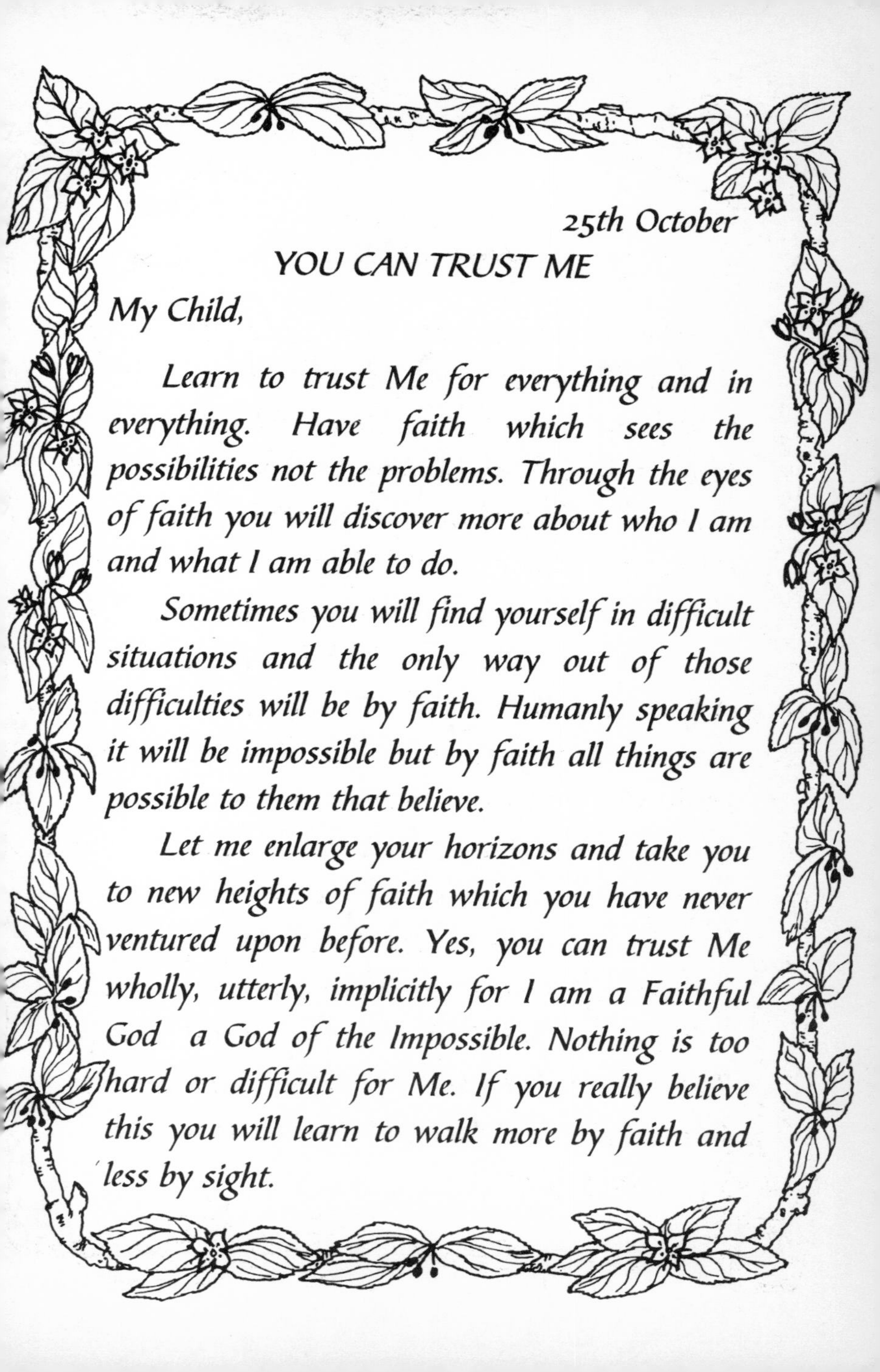

25th October

YOU CAN TRUST ME

My Child,

Learn to trust Me for everything and in everything. Have faith which sees the possibilities not the problems. Through the eyes of faith you will discover more about who I am and what I am able to do.

Sometimes you will find yourself in difficult situations and the only way out of those difficulties will be by faith. Humanly speaking it will be impossible but by faith all things are possible to them that believe.

Let me enlarge your horizons and take you to new heights of faith which you have never ventured upon before. Yes, you can trust Me wholly, utterly, implicitly for I am a Faithful God a God of the Impossible. Nothing is too hard or difficult for Me. If you really believe this you will learn to walk more by faith and less by sight.

26th October

PRAYER

My Child,

I want you to get to know Me so that prayer is your vital breath and the most natural thing to do - like breathing. Prayer is all about having a relationship with Me and drawing on that relationship in times of peace and times of stress. As you get to know Me you will become more and more certain of My will and thus be able to pray in accordance with that. As you get to know Me you will become more aware of My power and the power of prayer. This will increase your faith in prayer and cause you to want to linger in prayer and not hurry away. Indeed you will discover such joy and excitement in the secret place of prayer that you will find more and more time to pray - time will evaporate in My presence as you become caught up with Me and lay hold of Me, as Jacob, in the place of prayer.

27th October

BE PATIENT

My Child,

Be patient, don't be in a hurry. This concerns many areas of your life. Don't be in a hurry to make decisions - for the outcome may be so important. Be patient to wait till you hear My clear direction. It is so easy to miss the way and be misguided. Sometimes I know that it is so hard to wait for Me to speak or to act but I am trying to show you what to do. My timing is perfect never early and certainly never late. It may seem that at times it is too late but not in My schedule of time. Patience brings so much trust and grace into your life - if you let it - you can even know My peace as you patiently wait for Me.

I have not forgotten you nor will I ever - your patience will be rewarded.

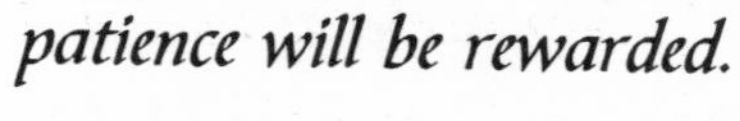

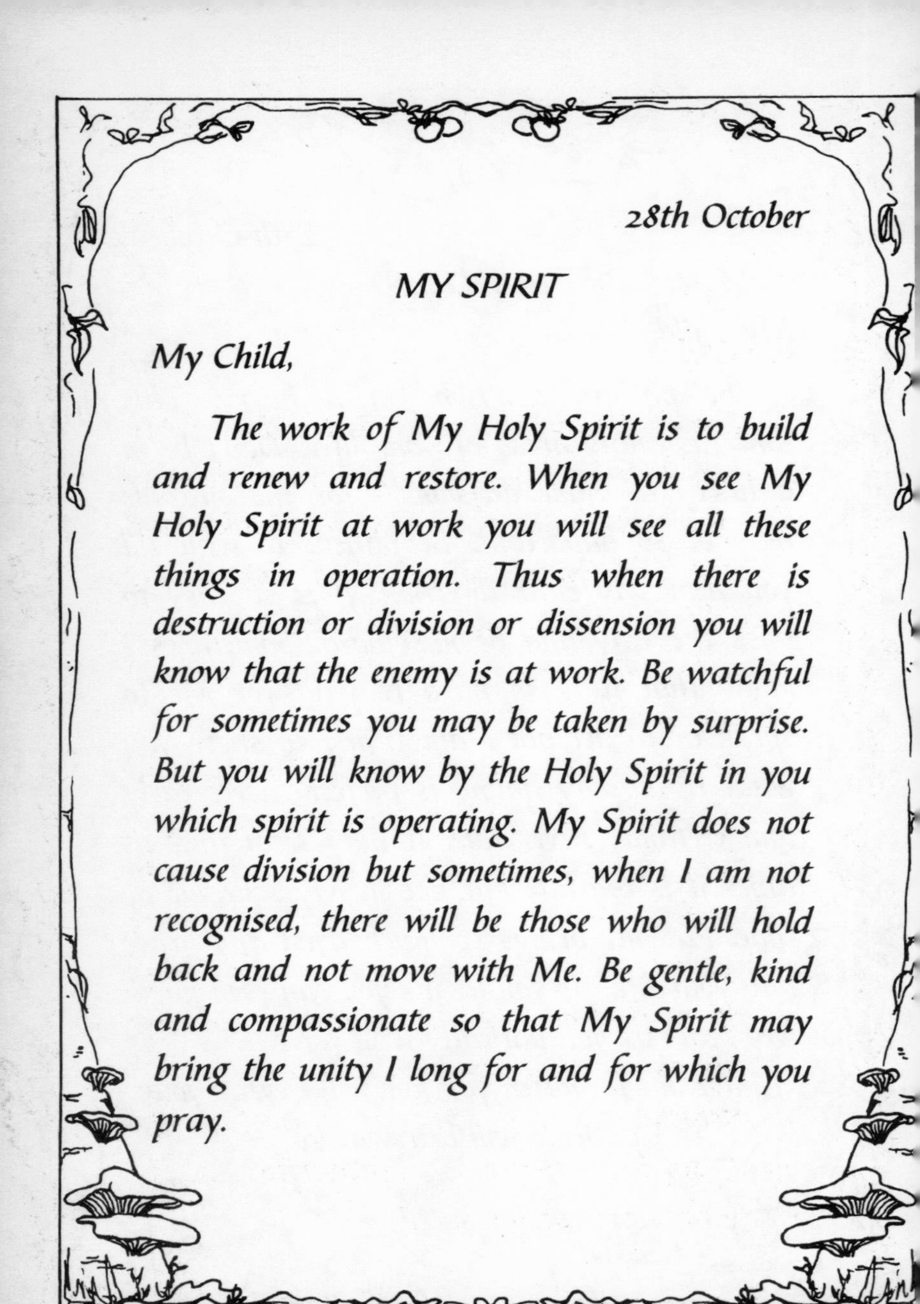

28th October

MY SPIRIT

My Child,

The work of My Holy Spirit is to build and renew and restore. When you see My Holy Spirit at work you will see all these things in operation. Thus when there is destruction or division or dissension you will know that the enemy is at work. Be watchful for sometimes you may be taken by surprise. But you will know by the Holy Spirit in you which spirit is operating. My Spirit does not cause division but sometimes, when I am not recognised, there will be those who will hold back and not move with Me. Be gentle, kind and compassionate so that My Spirit may bring the unity I long for and for which you pray.

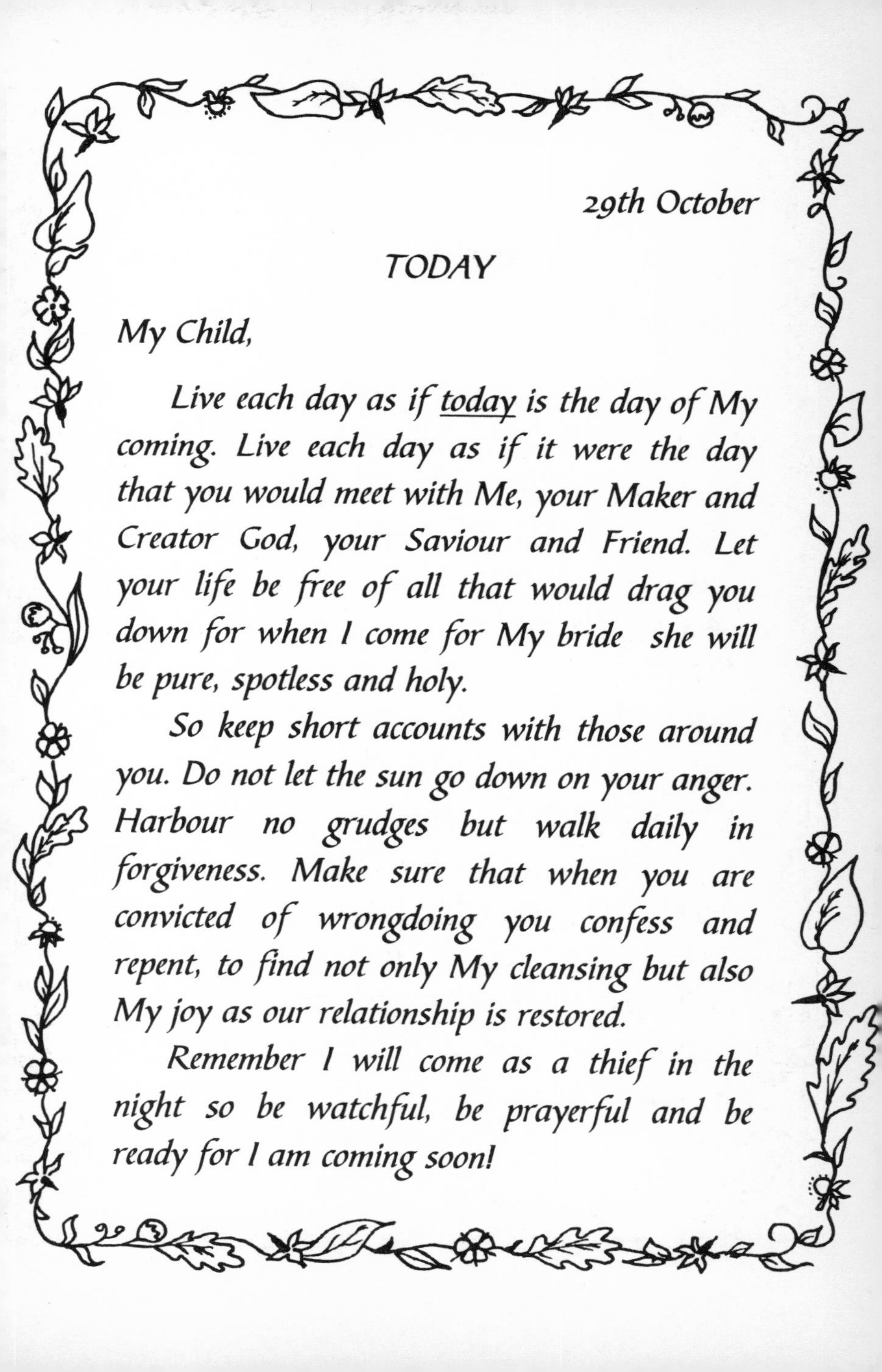

29th October

TODAY

My Child,

Live each day as if today is the day of My coming. Live each day as if it were the day that you would meet with Me, your Maker and Creator God, your Saviour and Friend. Let your life be free of all that would drag you down for when I come for My bride she will be pure, spotless and holy.

So keep short accounts with those around you. Do not let the sun go down on your anger. Harbour no grudges but walk daily in forgiveness. Make sure that when you are convicted of wrongdoing you confess and repent, to find not only My cleansing but also My joy as our relationship is restored.

Remember I will come as a thief in the night so be watchful, be prayerful and be ready for I am coming soon!

30th October

SUNSHINE

My Child,

As sure as the sun rises in the east and sets in the west so is My continued faithfulness to you. Sometimes the sun is hidden by the clouds yet it does not mean that there is no sun just because it cannot be seen. After a dull day does not the sun seem to shine more brightly than ever! It is at the moments of mist and cloud when it would seem that My presence has departed that I shine through the clouds of your circumstances and bring light. Then you will remember My faithfulness of old and know that I am tying up all the loose ends and drawing all the threads together. My faithfulness will not depart from you, neither will My love nor My presence - for I am faithful to My word.

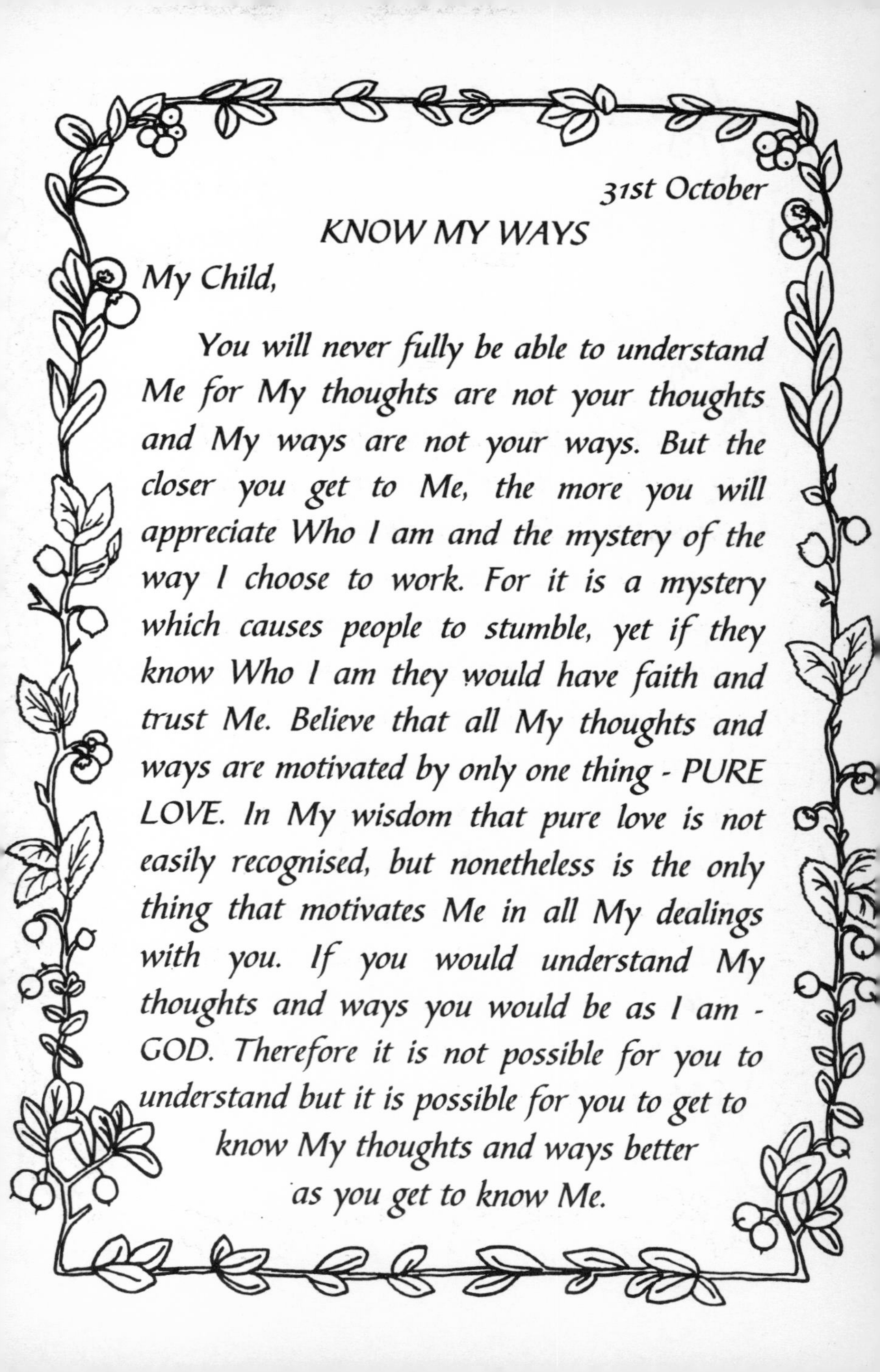

31st October

KNOW MY WAYS

My Child,

You will never fully be able to understand Me for My thoughts are not your thoughts and My ways are not your ways. But the closer you get to Me, the more you will appreciate Who I am and the mystery of the way I choose to work. For it is a mystery which causes people to stumble, yet if they know Who I am they would have faith and trust Me. Believe that all My thoughts and ways are motivated by only one thing - PURE LOVE. In My wisdom that pure love is not easily recognised, but nonetheless is the only thing that motivates Me in all My dealings with you. If you would understand My thoughts and ways you would be as I am - GOD. Therefore it is not possible for you to understand but it is possible for you to get to know My thoughts and ways better as you get to know Me.

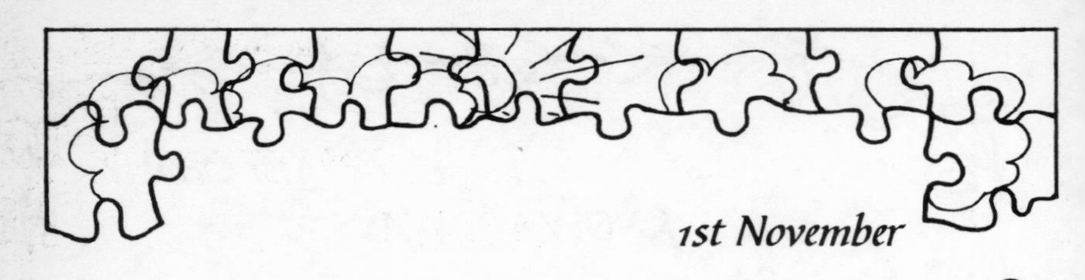

1st November

JIG-SAW

My Child,

Your life is like a jigsaw and I am putting all the pieces together to make a beautiful picture. Each piece is different and yet has a very significant part to play. Some pieces need a lot of attention and others are already in place to make the picture. You must therefore be patient because the ones that need attention will need time and space before they are ready to be put into the picture. Allow Me to work on those pieces or areas of your life that still need My gentle, loving, healing touch. Do not resist, for I am making your life into a very beautiful picture for My glory.

2nd November

BE WATCHFUL

My Child,

Be watchful, be prayerful, be ready and alert for the days in which you live are evil days. I need My people to be a holy people shining out to those around. The purity of their lives will attract those who are caught up in a net of despair and bondage and long to be free. These people who are ensnared are unable to set themselves free, so I will send My people to help them. As the darkness grows darker so the light will shine more brightly - as the light shines more brightly it will encroach upon the darkness eradicating it. So be watchful - see what I am doing: be prayerful - hear what I am doing and be ready for what I am going to do through you.

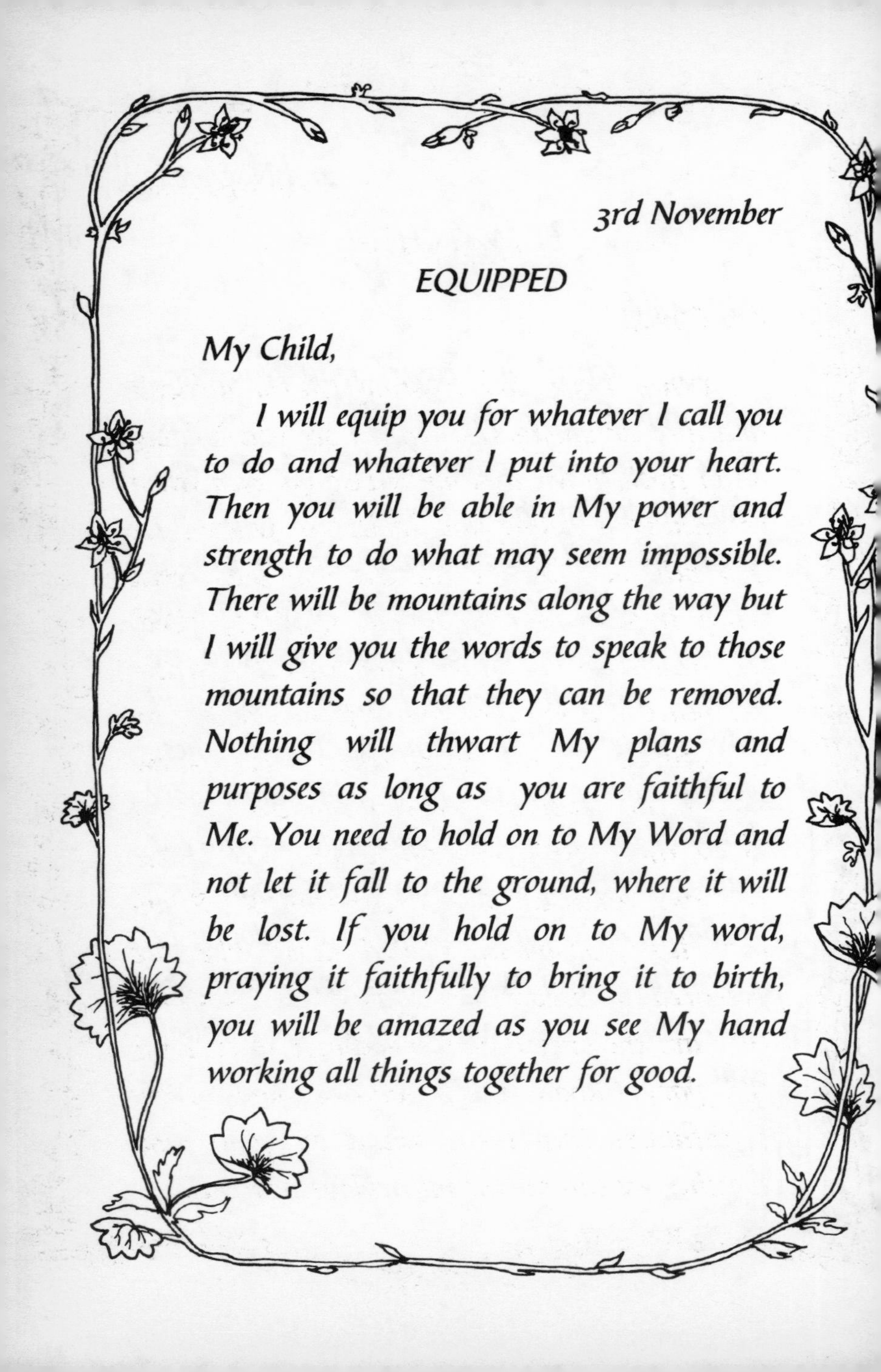

3rd November

EQUIPPED

My Child,

I will equip you for whatever I call you to do and whatever I put into your heart. Then you will be able in My power and strength to do what may seem impossible. There will be mountains along the way but I will give you the words to speak to those mountains so that they can be removed. Nothing will thwart My plans and purposes as long as you are faithful to Me. You need to hold on to My Word and not let it fall to the ground, where it will be lost. If you hold on to My word, praying it faithfully to bring it to birth, you will be amazed as you see My hand working all things together for good.

4th November

TRUST ME

My Child,

When I see you trusting Me in difficult and dire circumstances, when I see you holding on in faith to Me and not letting go, even when everything is telling you to let go, when I see you believing for the miracle you need, even when it seems so impossible, then My child, My heart rejoices, for you are truly discovering the peace and joy that comes from walking on a higher plain. My heart rejoices for I know that I can trust you if you can trust Me. I know that despite everything you will believe Me, even when all your circumstances tell you that it's foolishness. I need those who are prepared to believe Me against all odds, for they are the ones that I will choose to use for My glory. I know that if you can count on My faithfulness then I can count on yours and together we can see the miraculous achieved.

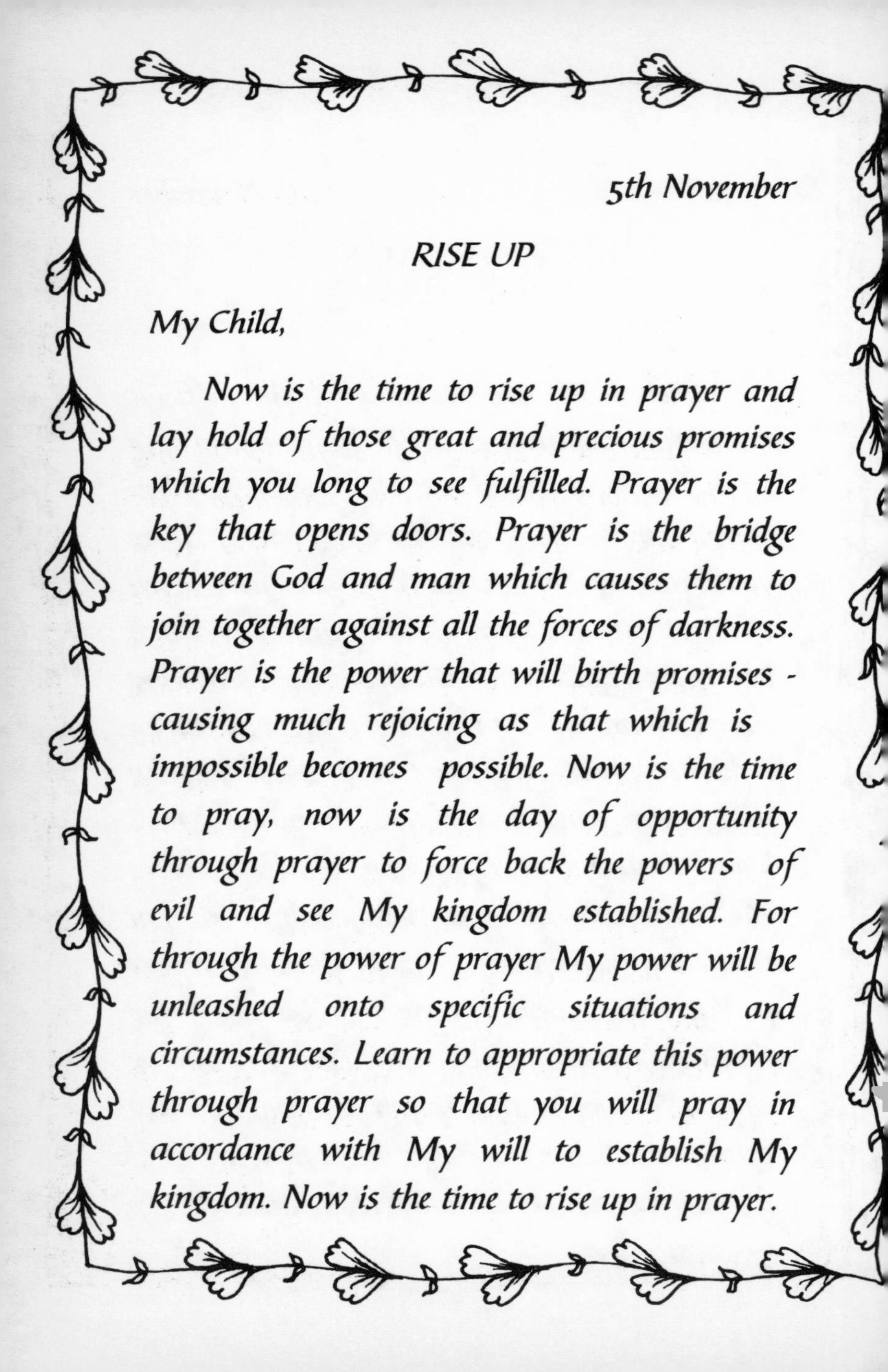

5th November

RISE UP

My Child,

Now is the time to rise up in prayer and lay hold of those great and precious promises which you long to see fulfilled. Prayer is the key that opens doors. Prayer is the bridge between God and man which causes them to join together against all the forces of darkness. Prayer is the power that will birth promises - causing much rejoicing as that which is impossible becomes possible. Now is the time to pray, now is the day of opportunity through prayer to force back the powers of evil and see My kingdom established. For through the power of prayer My power will be unleashed onto specific situations and circumstances. Learn to appropriate this power through prayer so that you will pray in accordance with My will to establish My kingdom. Now is the time to rise up in prayer.

6th November

MY VOICE

My Child,

Despite the loud clamour of the world and all the various voices that you may hear, you will be able to hear My still voice if you get to know it. You will be able to discern it from the voices of others and even your own thoughts if you learn to recognise Me saying 'This is Me'. As you get used to My voice, so you will more easily recognise it and quickly be able to dismiss other voices. You will not doubt or wonder or question, which may cause you to miss an opportunity to obey Me. You <u>will</u> know - and you will respond almost without thinking, unhesitatingly, for you will be so sure of Me. My sheep <u>know</u> My voice - learn to listen to Me - I have much to say to you.

7th November

FATHER & CHILD

My Child,

Let us walk together as Father and child knowing that as you take My hand you are safe and that I will lead you in the right direction. You need never fear as long as you hold on to Me for I am by your side. Though the way may be unknown to you it is familiar ground to Me and I know every obstacle, pitfall and problem along the way. As we walk together so we can commune one with another and be at peace in each other's presence. For like those men of old who walked on the Emmaus way so your heart will burn within you and I will teach you as we go.

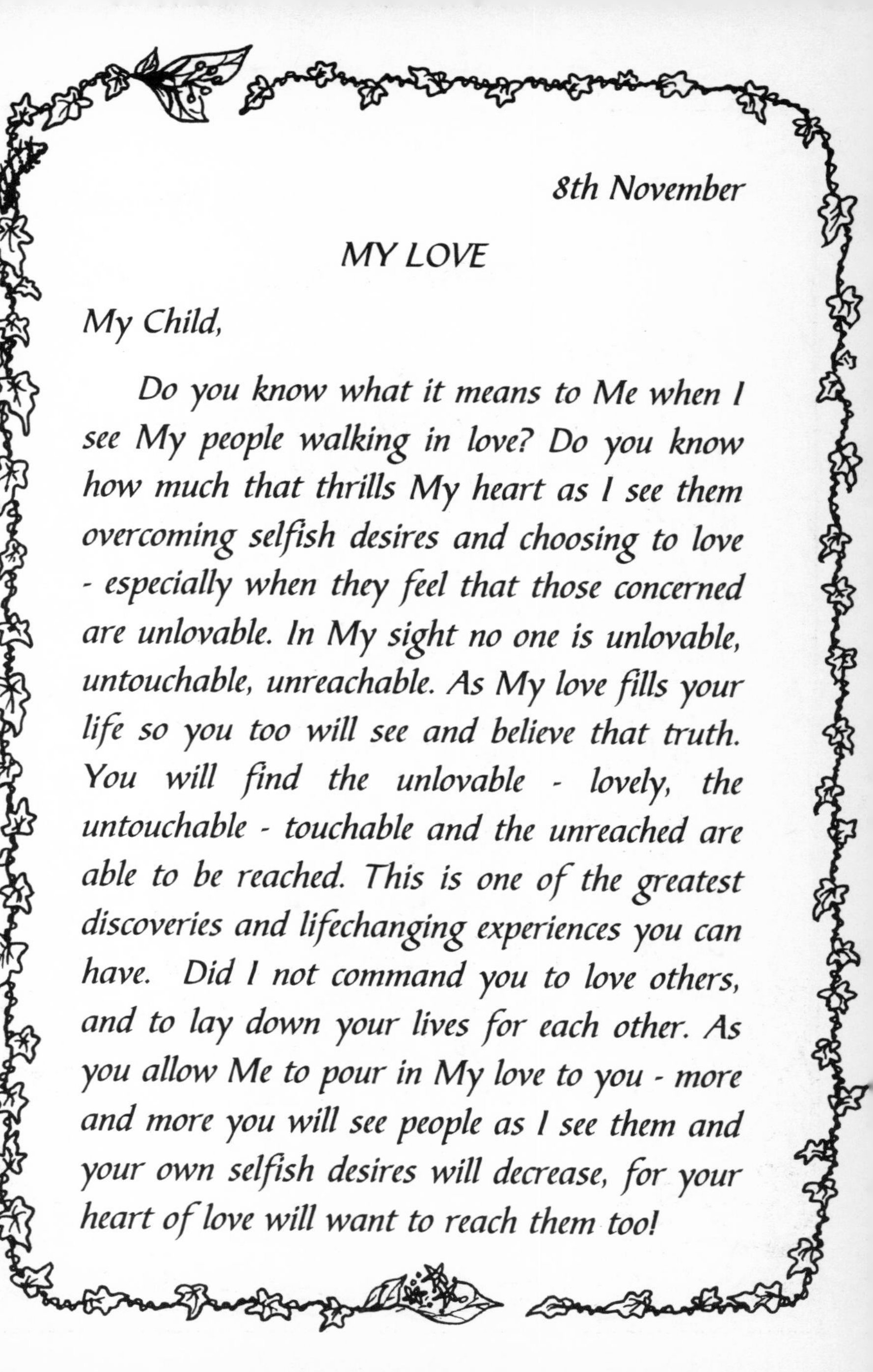

8th November

MY LOVE

My Child,

Do you know what it means to Me when I see My people walking in love? Do you know how much that thrills My heart as I see them overcoming selfish desires and choosing to love - especially when they feel that those concerned are unlovable. In My sight no one is unlovable, untouchable, unreachable. As My love fills your life so you too will see and believe that truth. You will find the unlovable - lovely, the untouchable - touchable and the unreached are able to be reached. This is one of the greatest discoveries and lifechanging experiences you can have. Did I not command you to love others, and to lay down your lives for each other. As you allow Me to pour in My love to you - more and more you will see people as I see them and your own selfish desires will decrease, for your heart of love will want to reach them too!

9th November

OPPORTUNITY

My Child,

Today is the day of opportunity. As you live each day recognise that it is a gift from Me. It is an opportunity to live for Me, to live in My presence, to live in the expectation that as we commune together we will share so much that will be a mutual blessing.

As you live with expectation in your heart it will enable you by faith to receive whatever is on My heart for you. For each day is special - every day I have work to do and you can choose to cooperate with Me to see that work accomplished. Each day I long to bless you and use you so be ready to hear each day what I have to say. As you follow My instructions it will bring you much joy and blessing - daily. So be expectant for today is the day of opportunity.

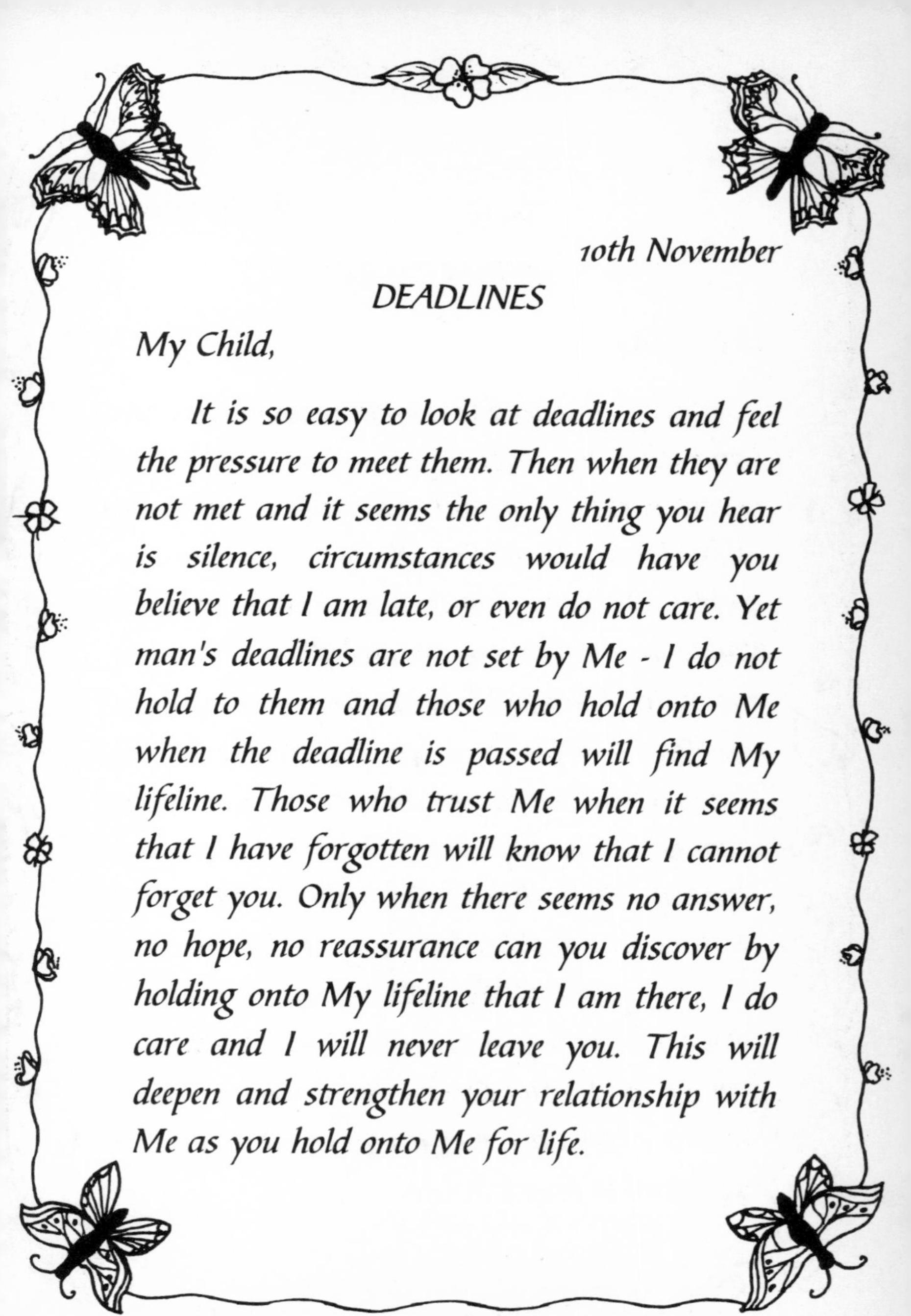

10th November

DEADLINES

My Child,

It is so easy to look at deadlines and feel the pressure to meet them. Then when they are not met and it seems the only thing you hear is silence, circumstances would have you believe that I am late, or even do not care. Yet man's deadlines are not set by Me - I do not hold to them and those who hold onto Me when the deadline is passed will find My lifeline. Those who trust Me when it seems that I have forgotten will know that I cannot forget you. Only when there seems no answer, no hope, no reassurance can you discover by holding onto My lifeline that I am there, I do care and I will never leave you. This will deepen and strengthen your relationship with Me as you hold onto Me for life.

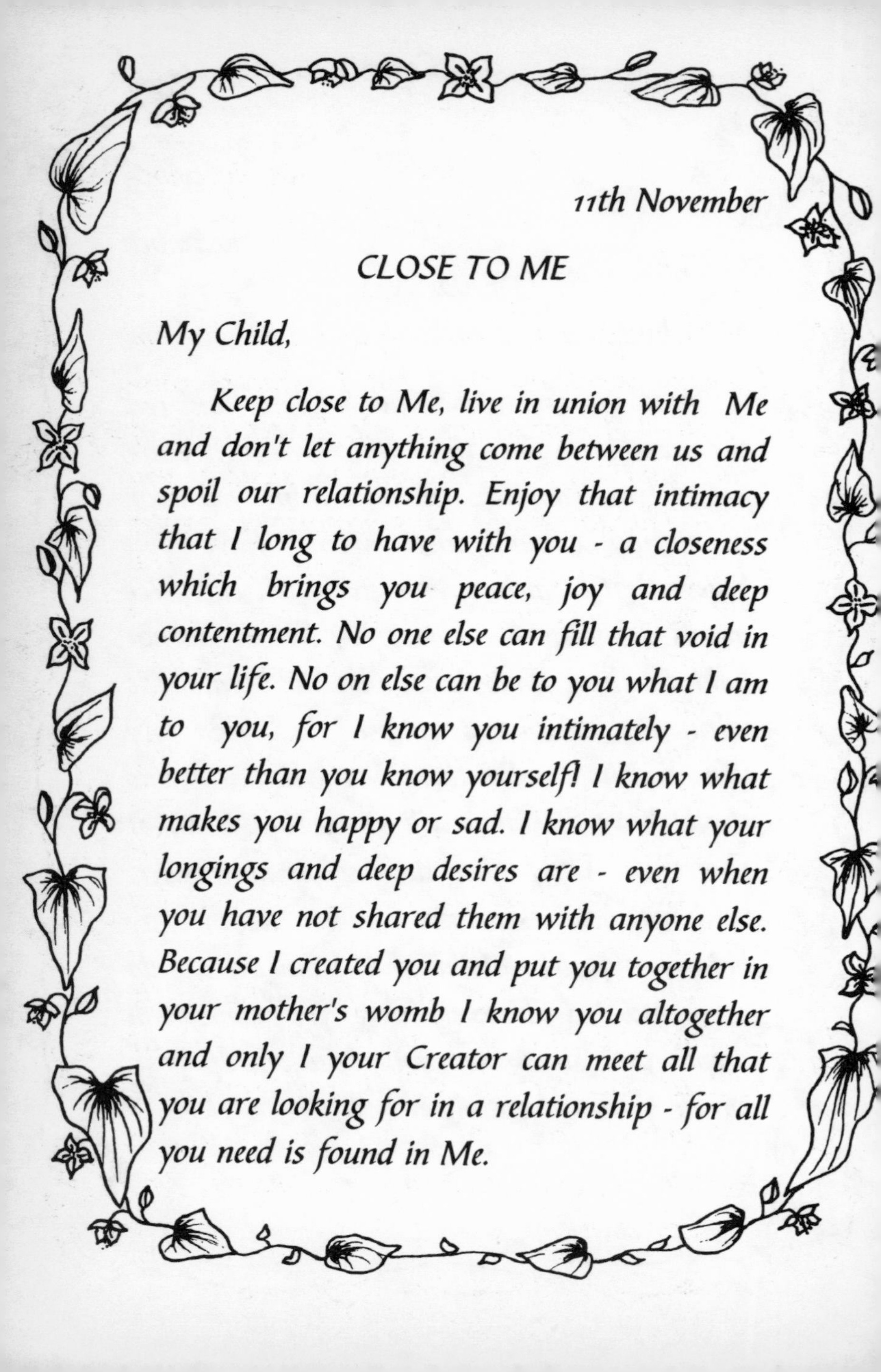

11th November

CLOSE TO ME

My Child,

Keep close to Me, live in union with Me and don't let anything come between us and spoil our relationship. Enjoy that intimacy that I long to have with you - a closeness which brings you peace, joy and deep contentment. No one else can fill that void in your life. No on else can be to you what I am to you, for I know you intimately - even better than you know yourself! I know what makes you happy or sad. I know what your longings and deep desires are - even when you have not shared them with anyone else. Because I created you and put you together in your mother's womb I know you altogether and only I your Creator can meet all that you are looking for in a relationship - for all you need is found in Me.

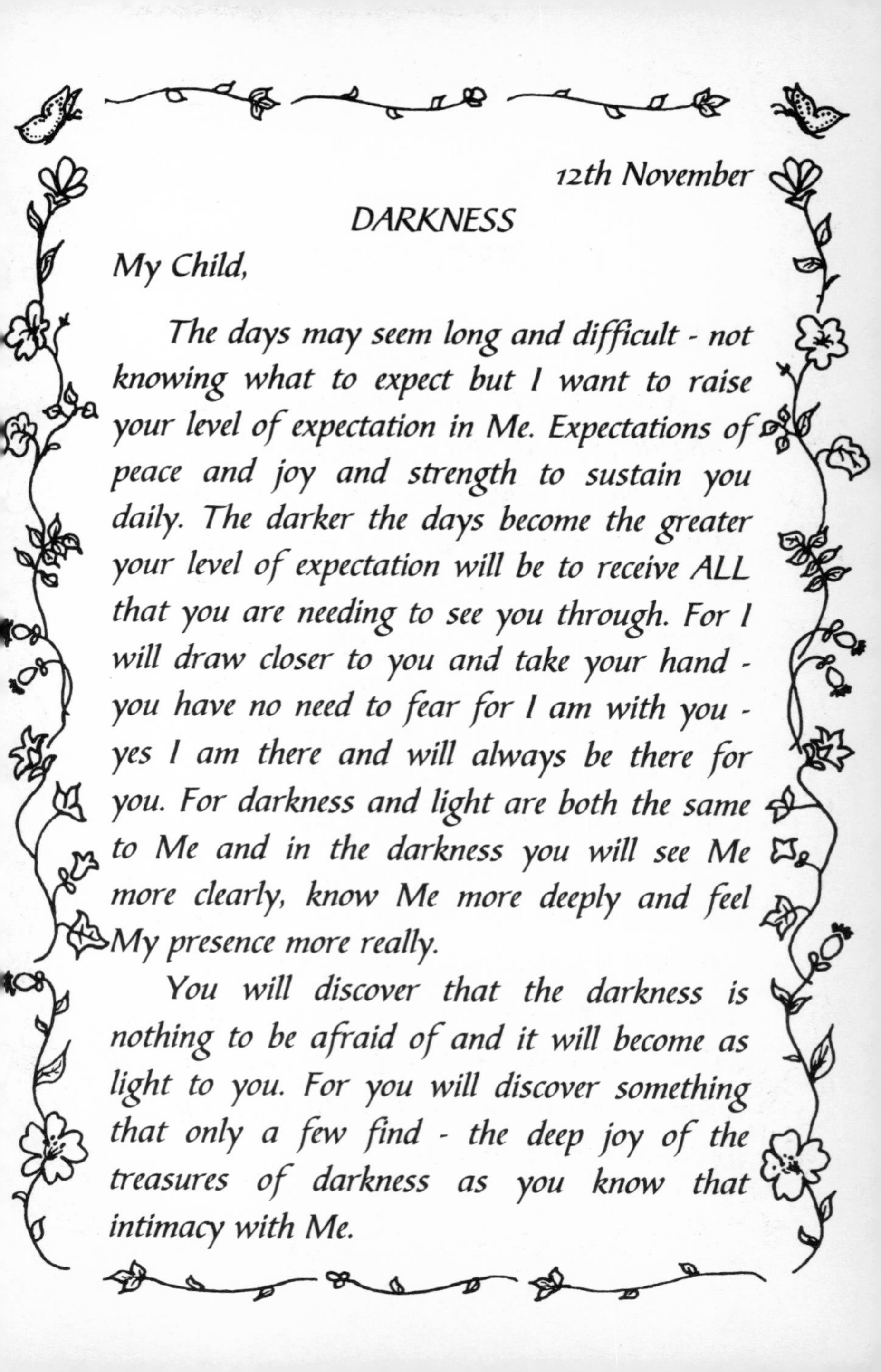

12th November

DARKNESS

My Child,

The days may seem long and difficult - not knowing what to expect but I want to raise your level of expectation in Me. Expectations of peace and joy and strength to sustain you daily. The darker the days become the greater your level of expectation will be to receive ALL that you are needing to see you through. For I will draw closer to you and take your hand - you have no need to fear for I am with you - yes I am there and will always be there for you. For darkness and light are both the same to Me and in the darkness you will see Me more clearly, know Me more deeply and feel My presence more really.

You will discover that the darkness is nothing to be afraid of and it will become as light to you. For you will discover something that only a few find - the deep joy of the treasures of darkness as you know that intimacy with Me.

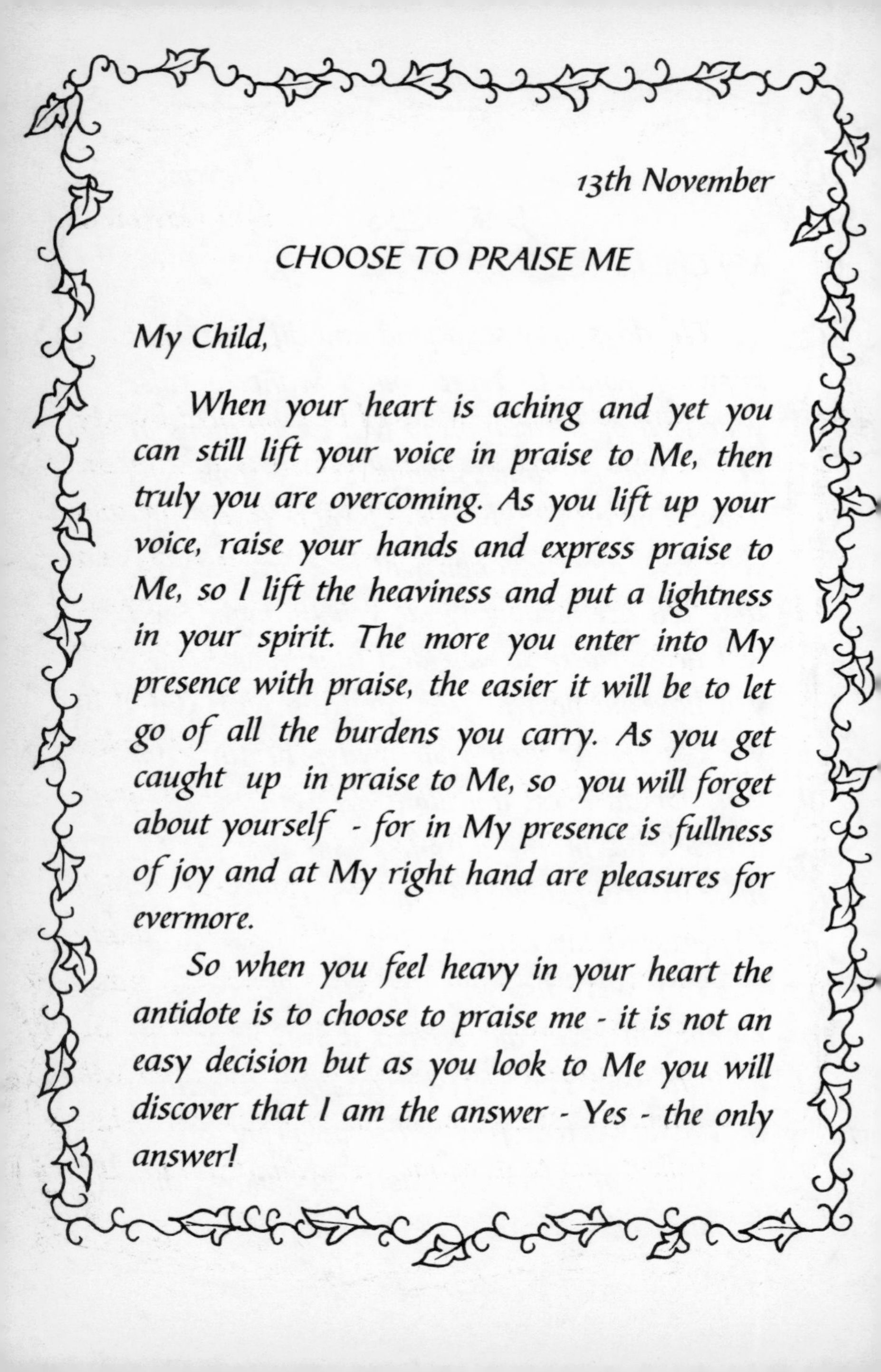

13th November

CHOOSE TO PRAISE ME

My Child,

When your heart is aching and yet you can still lift your voice in praise to Me, then truly you are overcoming. As you lift up your voice, raise your hands and express praise to Me, so I lift the heaviness and put a lightness in your spirit. The more you enter into My presence with praise, the easier it will be to let go of all the burdens you carry. As you get caught up in praise to Me, so you will forget about yourself - for in My presence is fullness of joy and at My right hand are pleasures for evermore.

So when you feel heavy in your heart the antidote is to choose to praise me - it is not an easy decision but as you look to Me you will discover that I am the answer - Yes - the only answer!

14th November

LISTEN

My Child,

Learn to listen to Me and be influenced by My Holy Spirit. There are many pressures and in the heat of the moment it is so easy to give in and succumb to that pressure, instead of resisting and standing against it. Let My Holy Spirit's power and gentleness be the force which influences you both to speak and to do. Don't be in a hurry to respond to pressure - relax, and let My Holy Spirit clear your clouded thoughts so that you will speak My words and perform My works.

There are many different influences which would seek to knock you off course, many arguments which would weigh you down, many distractions to cause you to lose your focus. So open your heart to My Holy Spirit, then you will know when to speak and what to speak and when to be silent and to do what I am telling you to do.

15th November

MY WAYS

My Child,

So many things that are in your heart will come to pass if they are of Me. For as you draw closer to Me, you will be able to identify the longings and yearnings of My heart - your spirit will leap within you as you become aware of what I want to do. The more you are in touch with Me so you will understand My ways and thoughts which are not your ways. As you hear from Me, you will sometimes be surprised as you discover things that not only you have never thought of before, but also things you would never in your wildest imagination have dreamt of.

The surprise element will witness in your spirit that this is of Me. So if you draw close to Me and discover My heart, which I want to share with you, then you can hold on in faith to all those things I have put in your heart - for they will truly come to pass.

16th November

MY PLANS

My Child,

Know that I will work out My plans and purposes in accordance with My will. Nothing will thwart what I want to do even though the enemy may try. All I ask is that you are ready and willing to do all that I ask of you. Whether you lead or follow, whether you initiate or delegate, whatever you do you need to be willing. I am building My kingdom and you must choose to build My kingdom too, for any other kingdom that is built will fall. My Kingdom will stand the test of time, for it is an eternal kingdom which will last forever and those who help to build it will enjoy it for ever with Me.

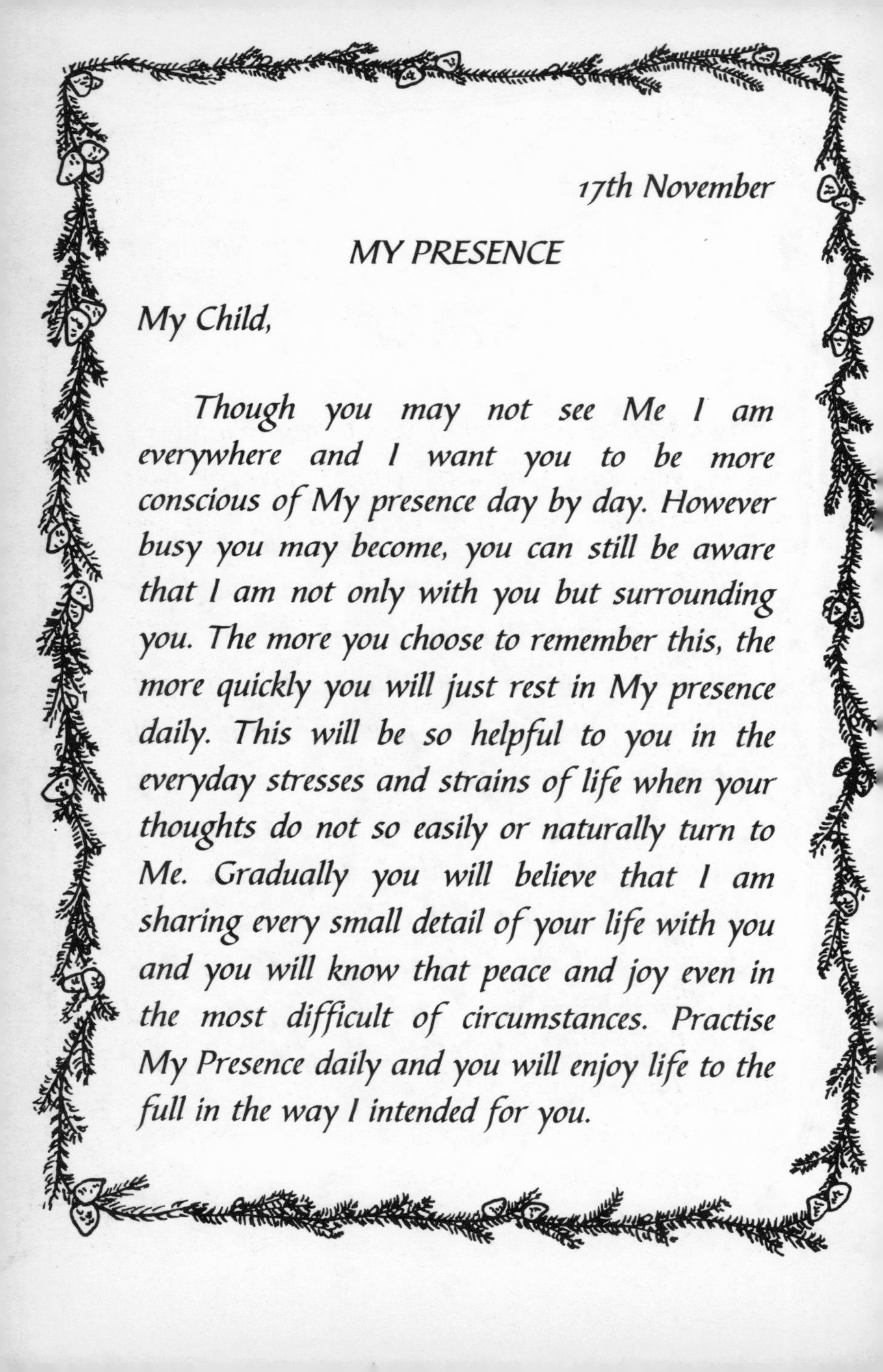

17th November

MY PRESENCE

My Child,

Though you may not see Me I am everywhere and I want you to be more conscious of My presence day by day. However busy you may become, you can still be aware that I am not only with you but surrounding you. The more you choose to remember this, the more quickly you will just rest in My presence daily. This will be so helpful to you in the everyday stresses and strains of life when your thoughts do not so easily or naturally turn to Me. Gradually you will believe that I am sharing every small detail of your life with you and you will know that peace and joy even in the most difficult of circumstances. Practise My Presence daily and you will enjoy life to the full in the way I intended for you.

18th November

MOUNTAINS

My Child,

Whatever I have called you to do, whatever I ask of you, and whatever plans I have for you will be possible, for I have equipped you and you are able. You are able not because you are strong but because in My strength and power you can do all things. If you thought that you could do it in your own strength you would have no need of Me. In your weakness, as you cry out to Me, I will hear you and thus empower you to serve Me. Don't look at some things that I ask you to do as mountains, for My power is greater than any mountain. If you speak My words to the mountain it will disappear.

Do not be anxious, but be prayerful. Do not take on tasks lightly but be prayerful.

As you obey Me you will know
My power enabling you to do
all I ask of you.

19th November

CLIMB HIGHER

My Child,

Yes, I am calling you up higher but be reassured that I am taking you. I am holding your hand. In your own strength you would not make the climb but in My strength you can do it. I will not leave you or forsake you and because I know your heart's desire to come up higher, I will encourage you by sending others along the way to help in time of need.

The climb is difficult and yes, you have to count the cost. You must be equipped and prepared so that you can journey safely. When you reach the summit you will know from the exhilaration experienced that it was worth it. It may be a slow climb and a dangerous one at times but persevere with patience and you will reach your final destination.

20th November

DO NOT FEAR

My Child,

You do not need to fear anything for I am with you and will never leave or forsake you. Counting the cost will be difficult and must be done but without fear. I want you to be real but not to be worried or anxious about taking up your cross and following Me. As a mother anticipates the birth of her baby with joy, knowing that there will be pain, so I want you to remember the joy of Jesus is available to you. A joy which overrides the pain of taking up your cross and following Me. Even though a mother knows that the painful experience of childbirth is ahead, yet she is willing to suffer that pain in order to bring life into the world. Before the birth she could not begin to imagine how deep the joy would be, but after, she knows that the pain was well worth it for the great joy that is hers. So do not fear, for great is the joy of those who take up their cross and follow Me.

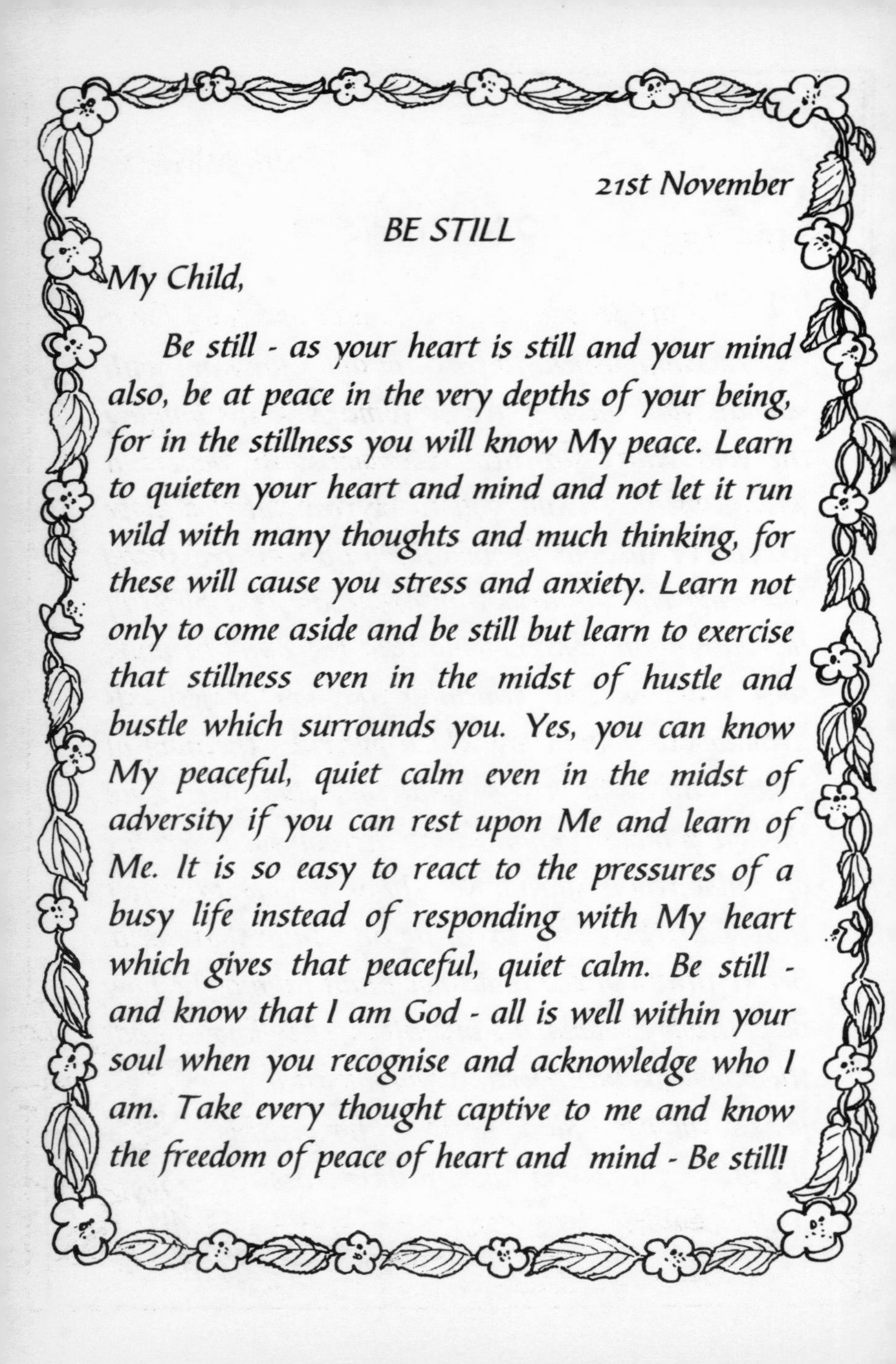

21st November

BE STILL

My Child,

Be still - as your heart is still and your mind also, be at peace in the very depths of your being, for in the stillness you will know My peace. Learn to quieten your heart and mind and not let it run wild with many thoughts and much thinking, for these will cause you stress and anxiety. Learn not only to come aside and be still but learn to exercise that stillness even in the midst of hustle and bustle which surrounds you. Yes, you can know My peaceful, quiet calm even in the midst of adversity if you can rest upon Me and learn of Me. It is so easy to react to the pressures of a busy life instead of responding with My heart which gives that peaceful, quiet calm. Be still - and know that I am God - all is well within your soul when you recognise and acknowledge who I am. Take every thought captive to me and know the freedom of peace of heart and mind - Be still!

22nd November

INTIMACY

My Child,

You are so precious to Me and as I long for a relationship with you so I am drawing you, calling you, causing you to come. Yes, the longing in your heart for that intimacy with Me, is a reflection of the longing in My heart for a close intimate relationship with you. So often I have called you and you did not heed, so often I have tried to woo you and you would not, for you could not find the time nor did you have that deep heart's desire. But now I am doing a new thing in your heart which you too perceive to be so. As I cause you to come it will get easier, for the struggle will grow less and pure joy will be yours as our relationship deepens. So you will discover as you enter into this new depth of intimacy that from the depths of repentance I will take you to the heights of My presence where there is fullness of joy.

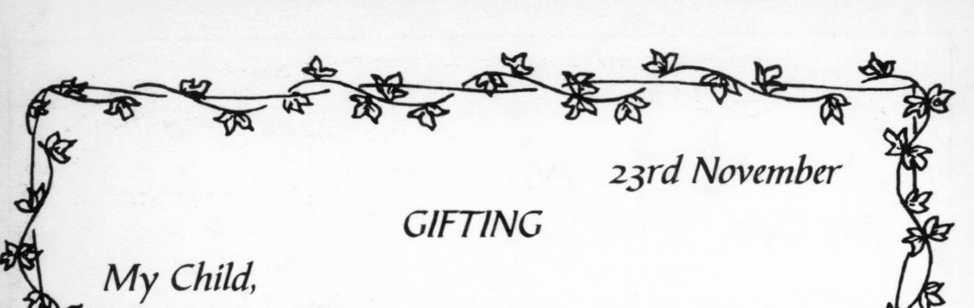

23rd November

GIFTING

My Child,

There are many resources in you which when unlocked by My Holy Spirit will bring forth much fruitfulness. You have only a little idea of the gifting I have given you and that is good, for it is My gifting to you and not something which you have earned. But as you open your life to Me and allow Me to use you, you will be surprised at what I can do in and through you. You will only see a little of the fruit - enough to encourage you and not too much so that you think you could do it without Me. There are still gifts within you that are lying dormant that I want to kindle and awaken so that you will discover more of My power and more of My purposes. As you walk humbly before Me, so you will see many opportunities for service and will be able to enter into the fullness of My blessings.

24th November

GOLD

My Child,

You are so precious to Me and I am so glad that your heart's desire is toward Me. As I am working in you during these days, know that I am refining you as pure gold. If you determine to follow Me no matter what the cost, you will surely be tested and tried but as Job discovered in days of old you will surely come forth as gold. There is a beauty and purity about gold which I want to bring about in your life. You may not be able to see it and that is not important but others will and be attracted to Me through that beauty and purity. As gold is a very precious metal, so is your preciousness to Me and even more so for you are My chosen, redeemed child of much more value than anything else in the world.

25th November

FOCUS

My Child,

The more you focus on Me and the less you focus on yourself, the more freedom you will find to be yourself in all situations and circumstances. So long as you are concerned about your own reputation and what others think of you it will cause you to be fearful, anxious and inhibit you. But when you are focused on Me and are only concerned about My reputation and share My heart, you will find such peace as you obey Me and a great freedom to speak with power that which I give unto you. You will identify with those longings in My heart and that will be your paramount concern, not how people are perceiving and receiving you. So keep your eyes on Me.

26th November

NEW HEART

My Child,

I see the longing in your heart and want you to know that I am giving you a new heart. I am exchanging your old heart for a softer one, one which is pliable in My hands and will be moulded according to My own specifications. Your new heart will be warmer, more sensitive to My Spirit which I have put within you. It will become a heart of compassion for the lost such as you have never experienced before. It will be able to feel My heart and identify with My longings and desires in a newer, deeper way. It will become a heart for intercession as you see the deep concerns of My heart for the needy lost world. You will find yourself standing in the gap pleading with Me as Abraham of old for the salvation of souls. And you will see the wonder of My salvation.

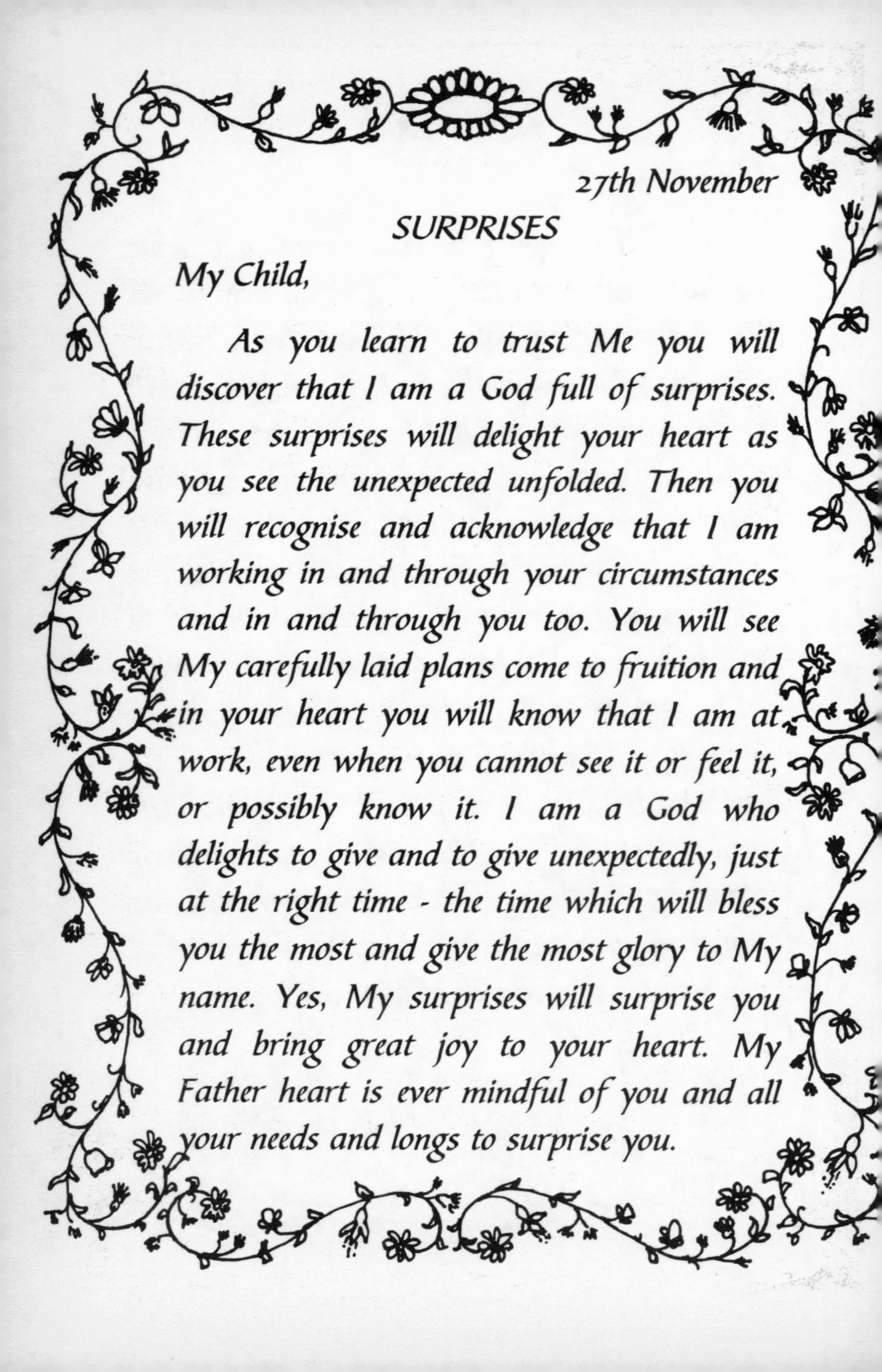

27th November

SURPRISES

My Child,

As you learn to trust Me you will discover that I am a God full of surprises. These surprises will delight your heart as you see the unexpected unfolded. Then you will recognise and acknowledge that I am working in and through your circumstances and in and through you too. You will see My carefully laid plans come to fruition and in your heart you will know that I am at work, even when you cannot see it or feel it, or possibly know it. I am a God who delights to give and to give unexpectedly, just at the right time - the time which will bless you the most and give the most glory to My name. Yes, My surprises will surprise you and bring great joy to your heart. My Father heart is ever mindful of you and all your needs and longs to surprise you.

28th November

FEAR NOT

My Child,

Don't be afraid - I am with you. You will never have to walk alone for I am with you. Though your past experiences may inhibit you to step out and follow Me, I can give you the strength to do so and put that longing in your heart which will overcome fear. Don't let fear paralyse you and take away your effectiveness as My child. I have not given you a spirit of fear but of power and love and of a sound mind.

You will have to let go of your reputation and not be concerned about it, for if you truly want to follow Me your reputation must die. Remember that I too had to walk that way so I do care and understand how you are feeling. Therefore I can help you through and give you the grace you need daily to cope. As you learn to fear Me and reverence Me, so you will be amazed at how the fear of man diminishes, for you will be more concerned about what I think than what others think of you!

29th November

BEWARE

My Child,

As you set your heart towards Me to follow Me, beware of the enemies which would seek to entice you and lead you away from that which I am calling you to do. It is so easy to be caught off guard and unaware and to be thrown into a situation where you feel pressured to act rather than to seek Me and My way. In the heat of the moment it is so easy to succumb even though in your spirit you know you shouldn't do so. When you feel that check in your spirit - beware - for that is the witness of My Spirit not to do that which you are being pressurized to do. In those moments you must be strong and firm. If you procrastinate yet know really what you should do it will cause you agony in your soul. So be watchful and prayerful and most of all beware, for the enemy seeks to devour those who have set their hearts toward Me!

30th November

APPOINTMENT

My Child,

Before you get out of bed each new day quieten your heart in My presence and lift the day ahead to Me. Having committed yourself afresh into My hands, make available the first opportunity to meet with Me in My word and in the place of prayer. If you decide to do other things first you will quickly find your time eaten up with little left for us to enjoy together. Keeping your daily appointment with Me is a habit you must nurture and protect, for it is the very core of our relationship, the very centre of your life with Me. I will never fail to keep My appointment with you, because I so look forward to meeting you each day and hearing you share your heart with Me - I love the intimacy of our relationship and have many things to share with you too.

1st December

GOOD WORKS

My Child,

There are many things in your life which need to be looked at from My perspective. It is so easy to be caught up in "much doing" of good works and in that you can find a real sense of fulfilment and purpose. Yet those very same "good works" can be the very things that take you away from what I have for you. They can even make you so busy that you have little time or desire for Me. If that happens then the good works are certainly not good for you, however much they may help other people.

I do not want to see you busy doing various kinds of good works - I want to see you and enjoy your company. As you spend time with Me you will know those good works that you are to pursue - flowing out of your relationship with Me and with My blessing and anointing. If you do good works in your own strength you will tire and lose your desire to spend time with Me.

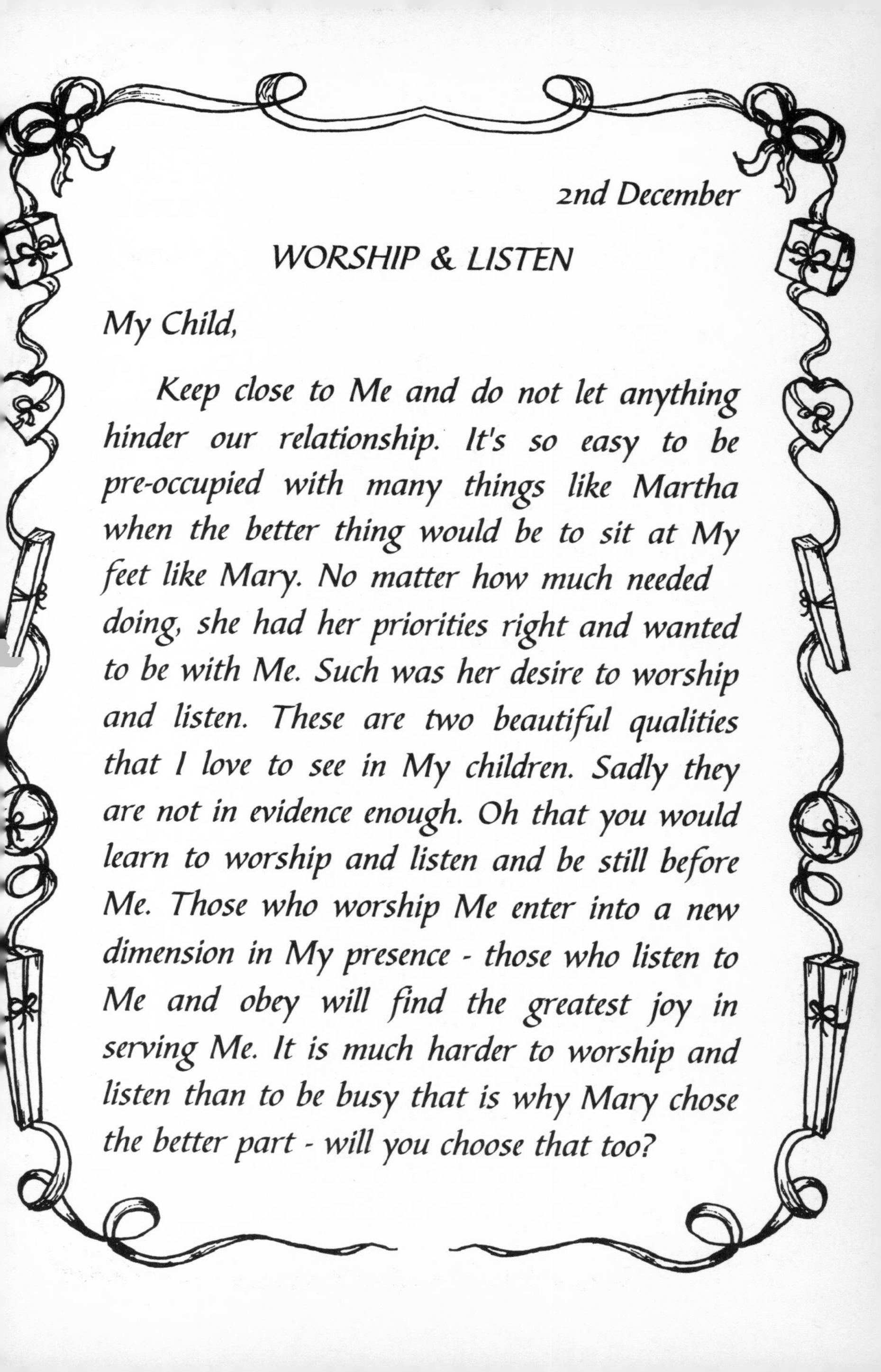

2nd December

WORSHIP & LISTEN

My Child,

Keep close to Me and do not let anything hinder our relationship. It's so easy to be pre-occupied with many things like Martha when the better thing would be to sit at My feet like Mary. No matter how much needed doing, she had her priorities right and wanted to be with Me. Such was her desire to worship and listen. These are two beautiful qualities that I love to see in My children. Sadly they are not in evidence enough. Oh that you would learn to worship and listen and be still before Me. Those who worship Me enter into a new dimension in My presence - those who listen to Me and obey will find the greatest joy in serving Me. It is much harder to worship and listen than to be busy that is why Mary chose the better part - will you choose that too?

3rd December

HOLINESS

My Child,

If you want to walk in holiness you must choose to keep short accounts with Me. You cannot live in holiness and know that there are wrong things in your life. As My Spirit convicts you of sin you must confess and repent of it immediately.

This restores our relationship and puts you back on the path of holiness from which you have strayed. Only in the dazzling light of My presence will you be able to see the awfulness of sin and how it actually destroys your life. Though you have never met anyone who is holy - you know Me and My Spirit within you is working to bring about a transformation in you to make you more like Me. This will evolve in time and needs much patience on your part to pursue Me and My Holiness so you can be holy like Me.

4th December

KNOWING ME

My Child,

I see the longing in your heart for you to get to know Me and I am calling you, drawing you to Myself. If you really want to know Me then you must learn to know My ways. For knowing Me will cause you to walk in a new way - you cannot know Me intimately and continue walking in your old ways. As you walk in the knowledge of Me and in the light of My presence you will be treading the path of holiness that you so long for. The more you get to know Me and the closer you get to Me the more established your feet will be in My ways of righteousness, truth and holiness. This will cause you great joy and much rejoicing and enable you to live in a new found freedom. For the greatest joy and freedom is found in knowing Me - there are only a few who persevere to seek Me and find Me and know Me - they are the recipients of My greatest blessings.

5th December

YOUR FATHER KNOWS

My Child,

Don't be anxious about anything. Don't let your mind be disturbed or your heart fear. Day by day I care for you in so many ways which you are totally unaware of, just like the birds of the air. Yes, daily I keep feeding the birds for I know the needs they have. I see even the tiniest sparrow fall. So don't be anxious about what you shall eat, or drink or wear for I am your Heavenly Father and your Father knows all your needs. Not only do I know all your needs but I am the only One who can do anything about it for you. If I care for the birds how much more will I care for you, for you are more precious than the birds.

So don't be anxious, keep seeking Me and My kingdom first and you will have all you need.

6th December

THE CROWD

My Child,

I know how hard it is to stand against the crowd and be different - some will love you and respect you for it whilst others will despise and hate you for those very same actions. It takes courage to stand up for your convictions and if those convictions are from Me then you can be assured of My strength to help you stand. If you are prepared to swim against the tide and not to be afraid of people's opinions then you will discover a joy and freedom and strength that others long for too. It will not be easy but despite the painful moments you will know that I have trod the path that you are treading and that you are identifying with Me. I did not come to please the crowd but to do My Father's will no matter what the cost.

7th December

AN EXAMPLE

My Child,

Don't be afraid to be an example to others for I need those who will step out and be different. Sometimes that is very difficult to do for the fear of man would grip you if you let it and paralyse you from doing what I am asking of you.

I need those who are prepared to be different and prepared to show the way so that others can follow. I will not make a spectacle of you - I will never put you to shame.

Those who are an example will have to go first - are you prepared to go first for My sake, break new ground and step out so that others may know what to do or where to go and want to follow.

Remember that this is what I had to do when I came to earth and now I am calling you to follow My example.

8th December

OTHERS

My Child,

If you look around and see what others have you will quickly become dissatisfied. It will bring disquiet into your soul and make you long for that which will bring no greater joy or happiness into your life even if you were to attain it.

If you compare yourself with others it will put you in the wrong position of judge of men and that will make you feel either superior or inferior. For in my eyes everyone is the same.

If you look to Me and see what resources I have and compare yourself with Me you will be dissatisfied. Know that I am able to give you that which will bring great contentment into your life. I am able to give lasting joy and peace and abundant life. These are the things that bring deep satisfaction so don't look at what others have or compare yourself with them -

Look to ME!

9th December

FEAR OF GOD

My Child,

If you fear Me and reverence Me you truly will be blessed, for fearing Me means that you will do only that which pleases Me. It means that you will think before you act to be sure in your heart that what you are doing is in line with My word.

When you truly know the fear of God on your life it will be a protection from evil and all its consequences, for it will cause you to walk in righteousness before Me.

The more you get to know and love Me, the more the fear of God will come upon your life. This is a right and righteous fear which will bring you much blessing and cause you to remember to be careful how you walk and live.

10th December

SURPRISED BY JOY

My Child,

As you long to bless others so I long to bless you. As you enjoy being surprised and surprising others, so do I. It is so good when others bring joy and happiness into your life especially when their very presence delights and thrills your heart. Whilst I have so many good things planned for you to bring you joy and happiness, I want you to know that your very presence and being who you are brings joy to My heart. Nothing thrills Me more than planning good things for you, nothing thrills Me more than enjoying your presence and fellowship, for I delight and rejoice in ***you****!*

11th December

BE DIFFERENT

My Child,

I know how hard it is to be different and to make a stand which is outside of convention. You may feel that difference so keenly and surely others will see it too. They may even long to step outside of convention like you. Though many will not understand you and it's hard to be misunderstood, some will admire your courage and wish they had that courage too.

I want you to know that I did not call you to be like everyone else. I have called you to be different in the way you live, for I am calling you to be like Me. You are unique - there is no one like you and as you follow Me you will become different from others but more like Me.

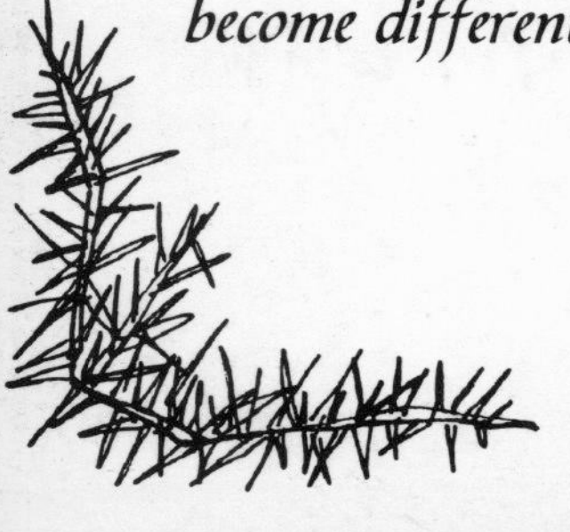

12th December

MASTER PLAN

My Child,

Don't be in a hurry - be patient and be at peace while you wait for Me. There is so much to do, so much to achieve, so many goals set yet unfulfilled. Don't look at all that needs to be done or all you want to do and feel overwhelmed by it. Instead seek Me for the master plan as to how you can achieve that which you are longing to do. If you work according to My master plan you will find that everything fits together like a jigsaw. You will discover and be amazed at the timing of My master plan and how everything runs according to a time schedule. You may be frustrated by obstacles and delays but you will be keenly aware of My hand skilfully leading and guiding and bringing all things together. So be patient for I will act and when I do, it will be glorious to behold.

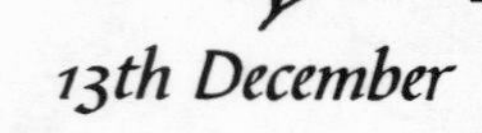

13th December

GIVING

My Child,

Sometimes it is so hard to receive when you long to be the one giving to others. It is humbling to receive and allow others to be in a position to bless you and give to you.

There are times when it is right for you to give but in doing so you must allow others the privilege of giving to you. Others too want to experience the right and privilege to give and you must not feel obligated to respond to that by reciprocal giving. For giving must be done from the heart, out of love, not out of duty. There are so many things which can be given, like love and time which do not involve financial cost but involve much sacrifice and are the greatest gifts of all to be given.

So learn to receive
as well as to give.

14th December

GIFTS

My Child,

Whatever gifts you receive they are only useful to you and sometimes to others too, as long as you choose to use them. If a gift stays boxed up it is totally useless and there is no real point in having it.

Often when you receive a gift you have no choice as to the gift but the choice is of the giver. I am the Giver who delights to give and I want you to ask for spiritual gifts you would like to have and use.

As you use the gifts I give they will not wear out but be replenished and will grow stronger and bring much fruitfulness. However, if you choose not to use them they will fade away like a muscle which is not used. The gifts must be exercised and this takes courage as well as a desire to exercise them. So allow Me to unwrap your gifts to expose and use them for the blessing of others and the glory of My name.

15th December

SUFFERING

My Child,

There are times when your heart is saddened because of the suffering of those you love. Sometimes the pain is so great that it almost overwhelms. In these moments I am there to hear all your prayers, all your heart cries and wipe away all your tears. To see others suffer and watch on helplessly is not an easy thing to do - I watched as My only Son died.

So in the suffering of loved ones and in the sadness of watching them, I do understand. I care and I am able to bring comfort because I can enter into your suffering and share it with you, helping to ease the burden you carry. Let Me ease the pain for you by sharing the burden you bear.

16th December

WILLING

My Child,

Is there a willingness in your heart to do whatever I ask of you? If your heart is willing and you really have a deep desire to be what I want you to be, and do what I want you to do, then together we can achieve the impossible.

Not only must there be a willingness but are you prepared to trust Me? Not for the things that are within your grasp but for those things which you cannot do or make happen? Can you trust me against all odds when it seems that nothing is going to happen? Are you willing to trust Me?

Can you rest in Me knowing I do know what is best and leave everything - yes, everything in My hands without snatching it back to be anxious about it again? The more you learn to trust Me, the more you will be able to rest in Me and be at peace. It is possible but are you willing?

17th December

SECURITY

My Child,

All that this world has to offer cannot give the security that is longed for in the heart. However much you long to be safe and secure in an ever changing world, there is only one place of real certainty and security and that is found in Me.

The world is an uncertain place - everything in it will one day pass away. Whatever you put your hope and trust in will be uncertain and not trustworthy, for eventually it will let you down. I am the solid, unshakeable, eternal Rock. Whatever is founded and built on Me will last for ever. When the storms come I will shelter you in the cleft of the Rock and there you will be safe and secure and find peace.

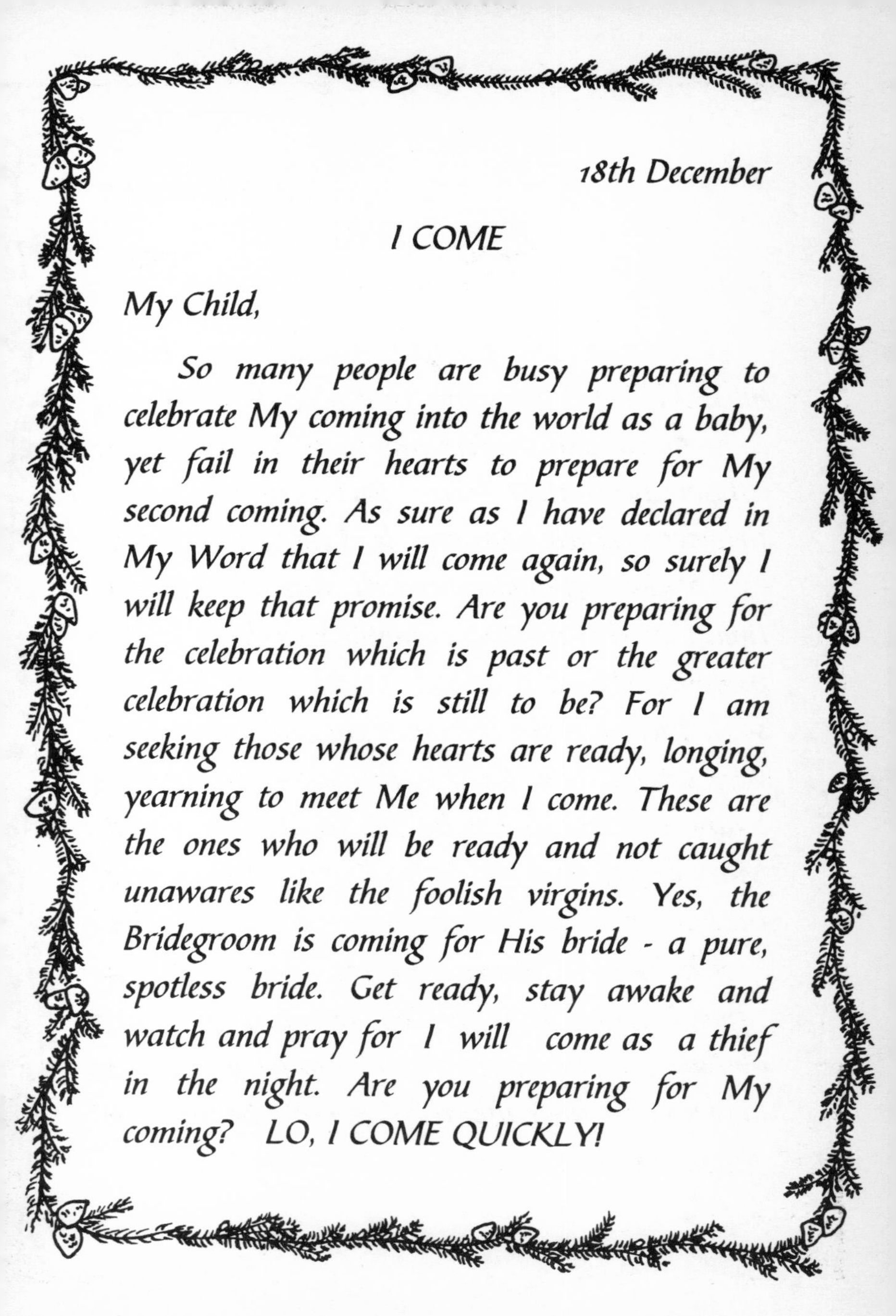

18th December

I COME

My Child,

So many people are busy preparing to celebrate My coming into the world as a baby, yet fail in their hearts to prepare for My second coming. As sure as I have declared in My Word that I will come again, so surely I will keep that promise. Are you preparing for the celebration which is past or the greater celebration which is still to be? For I am seeking those whose hearts are ready, longing, yearning to meet Me when I come. These are the ones who will be ready and not caught unawares like the foolish virgins. Yes, the Bridegroom is coming for His bride - a pure, spotless bride. Get ready, stay awake and watch and pray for I will come as a thief in the night. Are you preparing for My coming? LO, I COME QUICKLY!

19th December

INDWELLING

My Child,

Can you imagine the awesomeness Mary must have felt knowing that God Himself had come to her and dwelt within her? Yet that same awesomeness must have been overshadowed by the fact that the man who had committed his life to her did not understand. It was not an easy thing to be a virgin mother and this was prophesied that a sword would pierce her own soul. Such was the calling of the one chosen for a very special task. Such is the calling of the ones today who are chosen by Me for Myself. For as Mary experienced My indwelling by the power of the Holy Spirit so today My people can experience My indwelling them. You too can know that same awesomeness of God living in you and abiding in you - this should have an effect on how you live your life and it is not an easy calling but it is the only way to live.

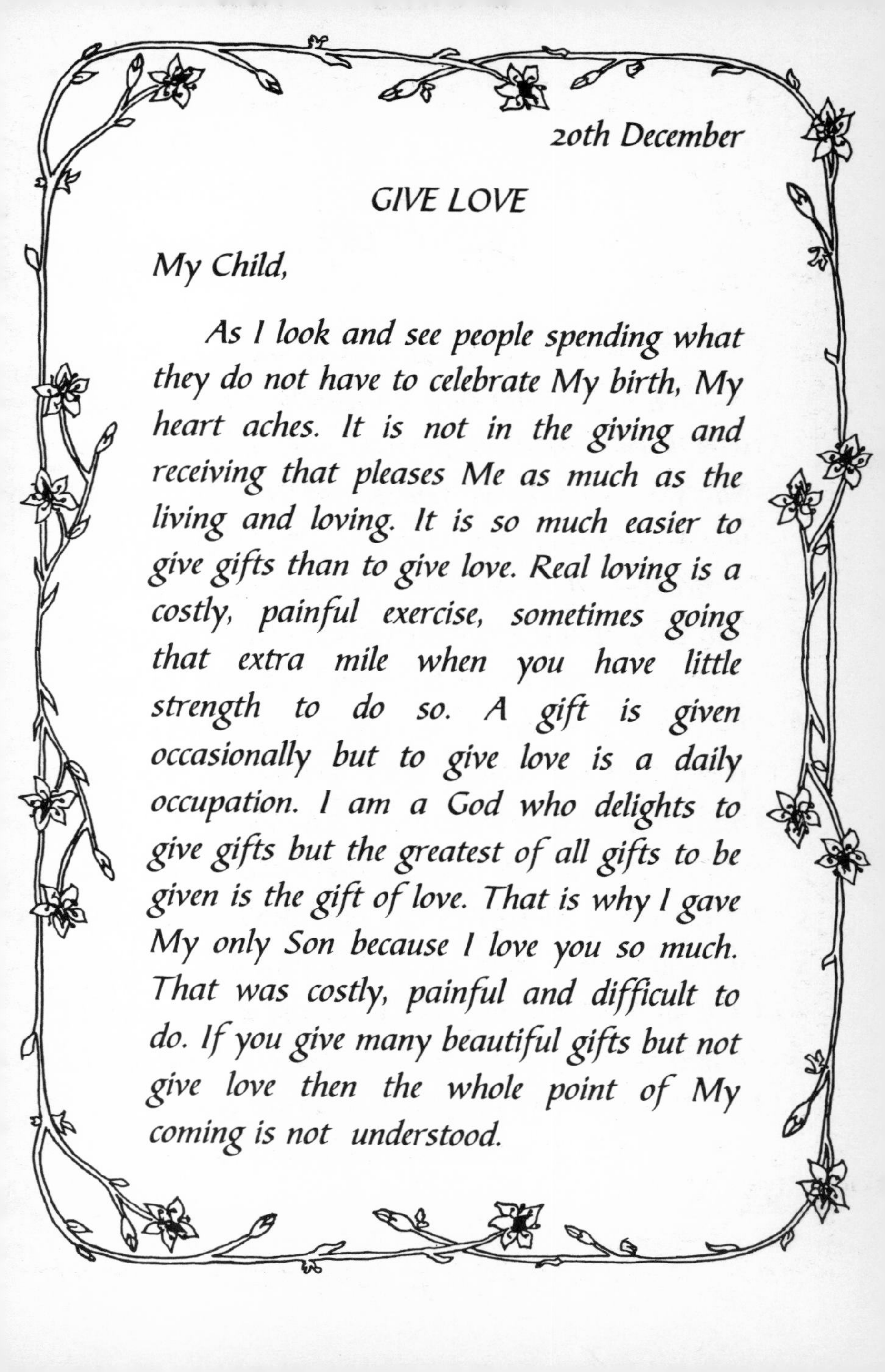

20th December

GIVE LOVE

My Child,

As I look and see people spending what they do not have to celebrate My birth, My heart aches. It is not in the giving and receiving that pleases Me as much as the living and loving. It is so much easier to give gifts than to give love. Real loving is a costly, painful exercise, sometimes going that extra mile when you have little strength to do so. A gift is given occasionally but to give love is a daily occupation. I am a God who delights to give gifts but the greatest of all gifts to be given is the gift of love. That is why I gave My only Son because I love you so much. That was costly, painful and difficult to do. If you give many beautiful gifts but not give love then the whole point of My coming is not understood.

21st December

GIFT OF LIFE

My Child,

When the wise men visited the stable where I was born in Bethlehem they gave precious gifts. But what they gave represented only a token of what they actually owned. The shepherds in contrast brought a lamb. This was their livelihood and they gave out of their poverty. It is so easy to give out of the riches one may have but so much harder to give out of poverty. It is not how much you give that shows your generosity but how much you have left after you have given.

The shepherds brought a lamb which was alive and even sacrificial. The greatest gift that you can give is your life laid down sacrificially for My sake. Remember that I became the sacrificial Lamb of God who takes away the sins of the world. I gave My life sacrificially for you.

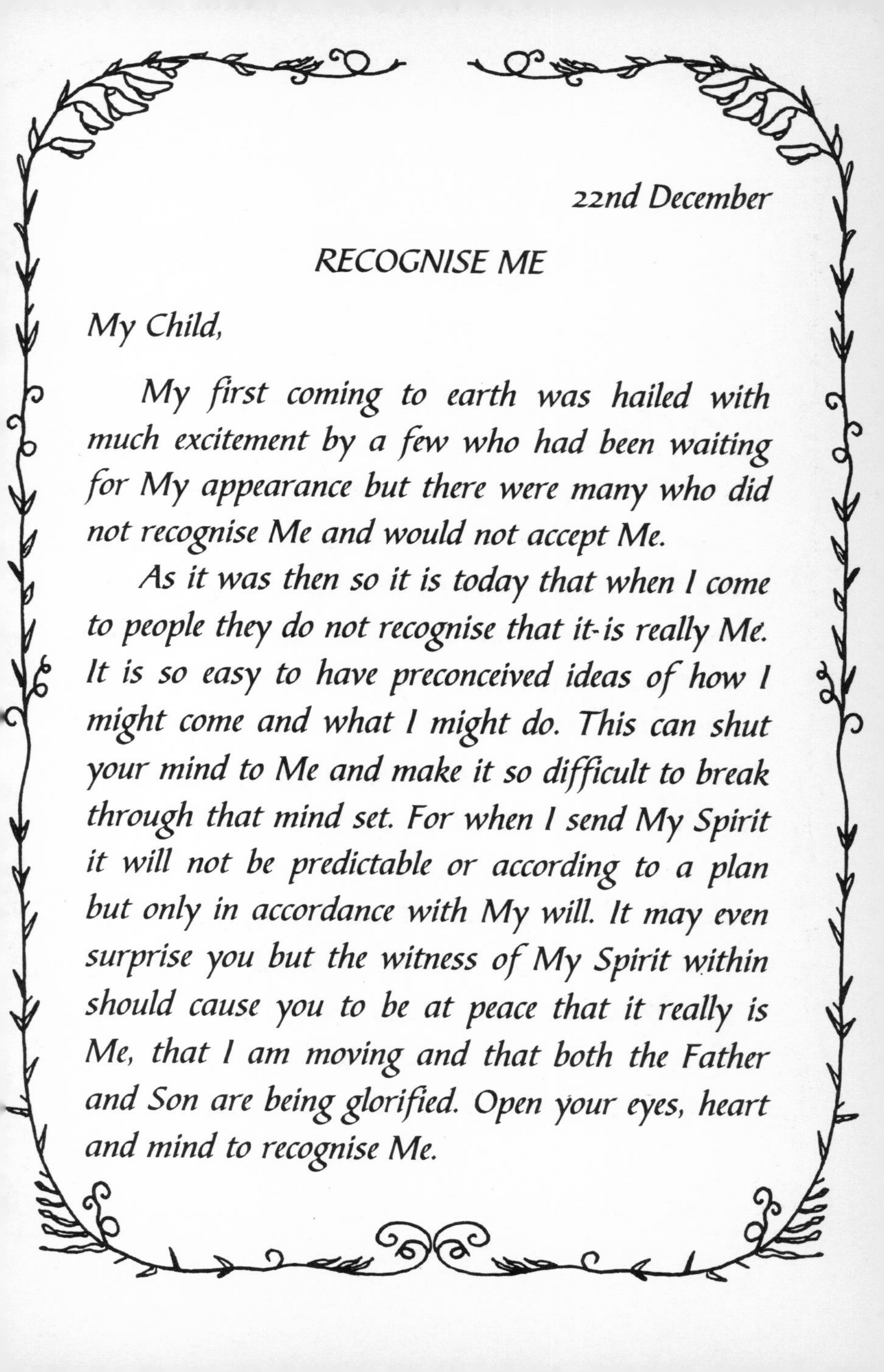

22nd December

RECOGNISE ME

My Child,

My first coming to earth was hailed with much excitement by a few who had been waiting for My appearance but there were many who did not recognise Me and would not accept Me.

As it was then so it is today that when I come to people they do not recognise that it-is really Me. It is so easy to have preconceived ideas of how I might come and what I might do. This can shut your mind to Me and make it so difficult to break through that mind set. For when I send My Spirit it will not be predictable or according to a plan but only in accordance with My will. It may even surprise you but the witness of My Spirit within should cause you to be at peace that it really is Me, that I am moving and that both the Father and Son are being glorified. Open your eyes, heart and mind to recognise Me.

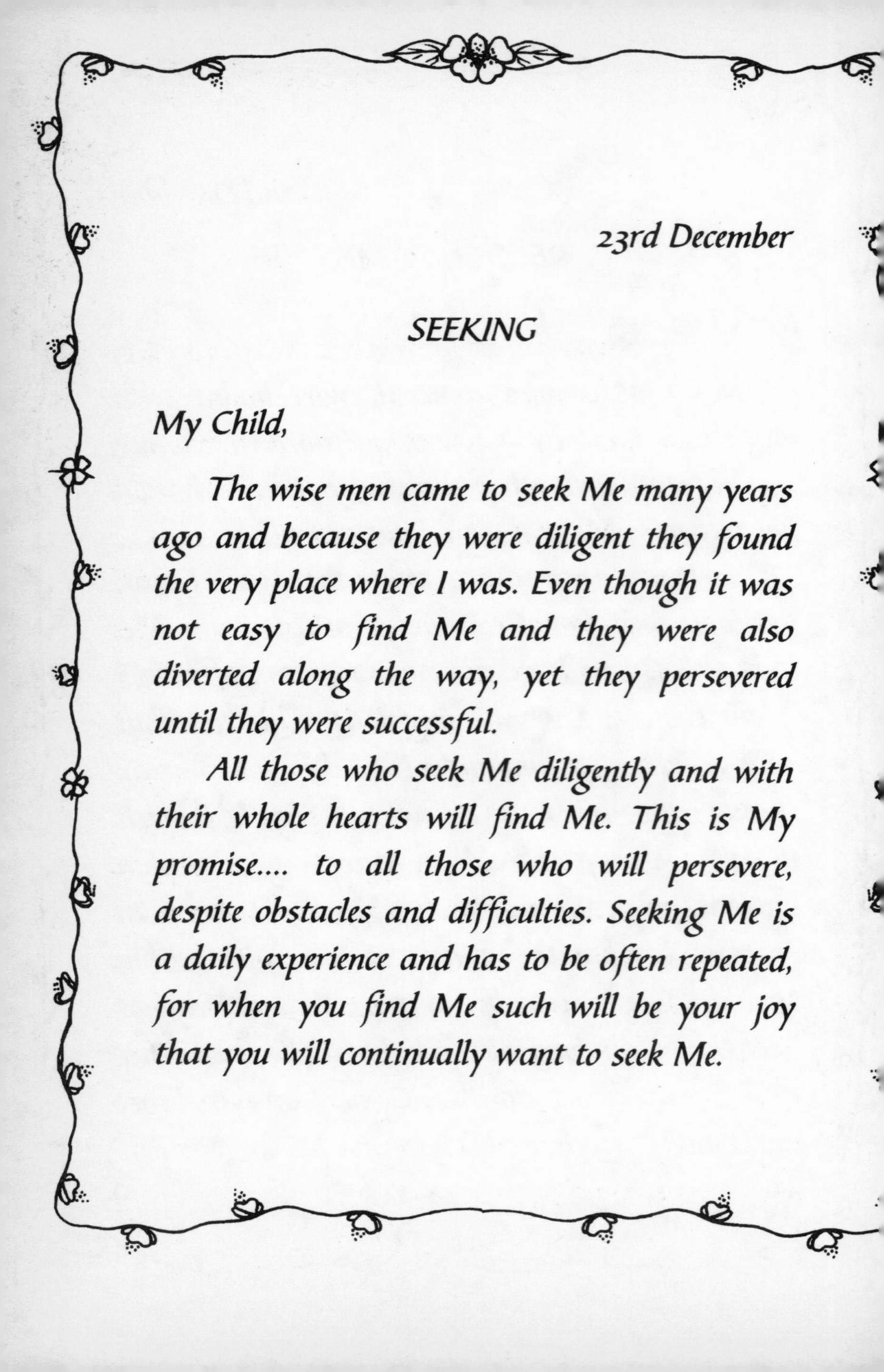

23rd December

SEEKING

My Child,

The wise men came to seek Me many years ago and because they were diligent they found the very place where I was. Even though it was not easy to find Me and they were also diverted along the way, yet they persevered until they were successful.

All those who seek Me diligently and with their whole hearts will find Me. This is My promise.... to all those who will persevere, despite obstacles and difficulties. Seeking Me is a daily experience and has to be often repeated, for when you find Me such will be your joy that you will continually want to seek Me.

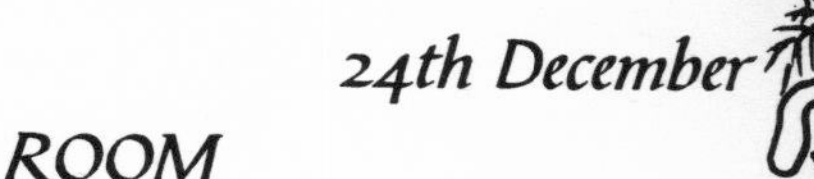

24th December

ROOM

My Child,

There was room in Mary's heart for My coming - she rejoiced at My birth despite the difficult circumstances and questions that would arise. Not only at My birth but throughout all My life many could not find it in their hearts to give Me room. My coming into Mary's life would bring many changes - this still applies today. Where there are those who open up their lives to Me it will bring about much change. Some are too comfortable to change but for those who are ready for change, the changes that I bring will be for good. As you open up your life to Me and allow Me room in your life so you will see gradual changes. This is a continual process so be sure not to shut the door of your heart, for if you do, it will shut out My blessings. How much room will you give Me in your life?

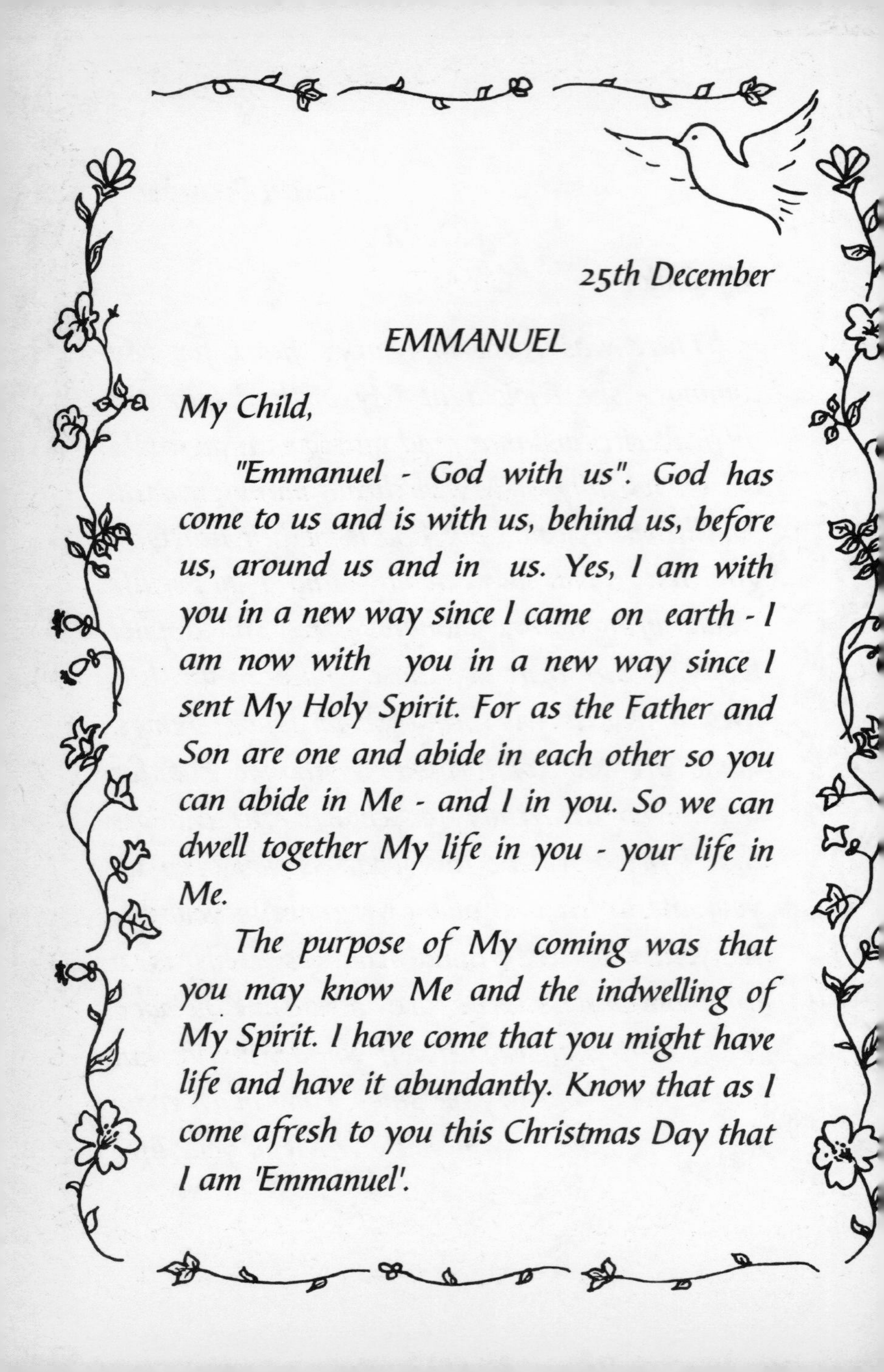

25th December

EMMANUEL

My Child,

"Emmanuel - God with us". God has come to us and is with us, behind us, before us, around us and in us. Yes, I am with you in a new way since I came on earth - I am now with you in a new way since I sent My Holy Spirit. For as the Father and Son are one and abide in each other so you can abide in Me - and I in you. So we can dwell together My life in you - your life in Me.

The purpose of My coming was that you may know Me and the indwelling of My Spirit. I have come that you might have life and have it abundantly. Know that as I come afresh to you this Christmas Day that I am 'Emmanuel'.

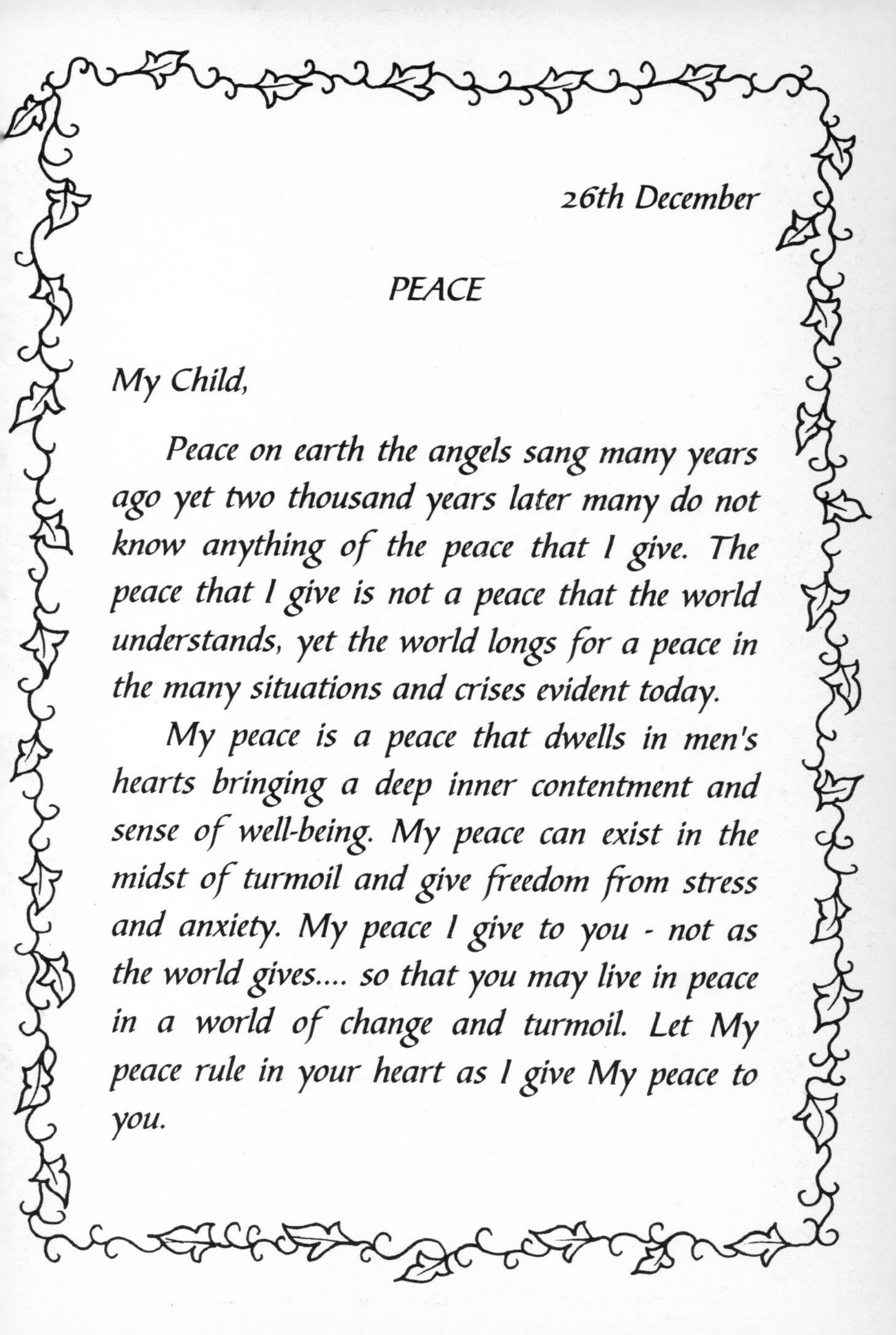

26th December

PEACE

My Child,

Peace on earth the angels sang many years ago yet two thousand years later many do not know anything of the peace that I give. The peace that I give is not a peace that the world understands, yet the world longs for a peace in the many situations and crises evident today.

My peace is a peace that dwells in men's hearts bringing a deep inner contentment and sense of well-being. My peace can exist in the midst of turmoil and give freedom from stress and anxiety. My peace I give to you - not as the world gives.... so that you may live in peace in a world of change and turmoil. Let My peace rule in your heart as I give My peace to you.

27th December

FAITH

My Child,

When your heart is full of faith and you can trust Me you will know My peace, even when it seems that things aren't coming together. So check your heart and if there is any trace of anxiety or worry, then there is more room for faith in your life.

You must learn to off-load the anxiety and get it rid from your life so that you will be able to make room for the faith that I want to put there. Faith and anxiety cannot walk hand in hand together for surely one will overwhelm and conquer the other excluding it from your life. Do you want faith or anxiety excluded from your life?

28th December

FAITH TESTED

My Child,

Don't be discouraged when you know that I have spoken to your heart and others don't have the faith to join yours. When I speak to you and show you the way or show you My will I also give you the faith to believe that that which has been spoken shall come to pass. If others do not hear for themselves or catch the vision it will be very difficult for them to exercise faith for it.

However if you can believe and do have faith then don't let words of doubt or unbelief eat that faith away and destroy it. Rather as you stand upon My word and exercise your faith, you will see others encouraged and longing to join with you in believing. As that which is impossible becomes possible, as your faith is tested and tried, so you will be able to trust Me more and I will be glorified.

29th December

THE TEACHER

My Child,

Let My Holy Spirit be your teacher. So long as you are willing to learn and have a teachable spirit I will cause your heart to be open to Me and will teach you many things.

I will help you discern that which you need to do, when to do it and how to do it. My Holy Spirit will bring to your remembrance the things that you have learnt when you need to recall them. You will be amazed at the wealth of information stored and surprised as that which you thought was forgotten is remembered.

Do not put your hope in your own ability or your own memory which may let you down but let Me be your hope as I teach you.

30th December

THOUGHTS

My Child,

What you think about reveals a lot about who you are and what's in your heart. This is very private to you - no one can possibly know all the thoughts of another. Because I created you I not only know all your thoughts, I also know every unspoken word before it is ever voiced. As you open up your thought life to Me and share your thoughts through prayer, so you will find that your thought life is intrinsically wrapped up in your relationship with Me.

*So My thoughts will be your thoughts
and those thoughts will become
prayers as we share together.
This deepens our relationship.*

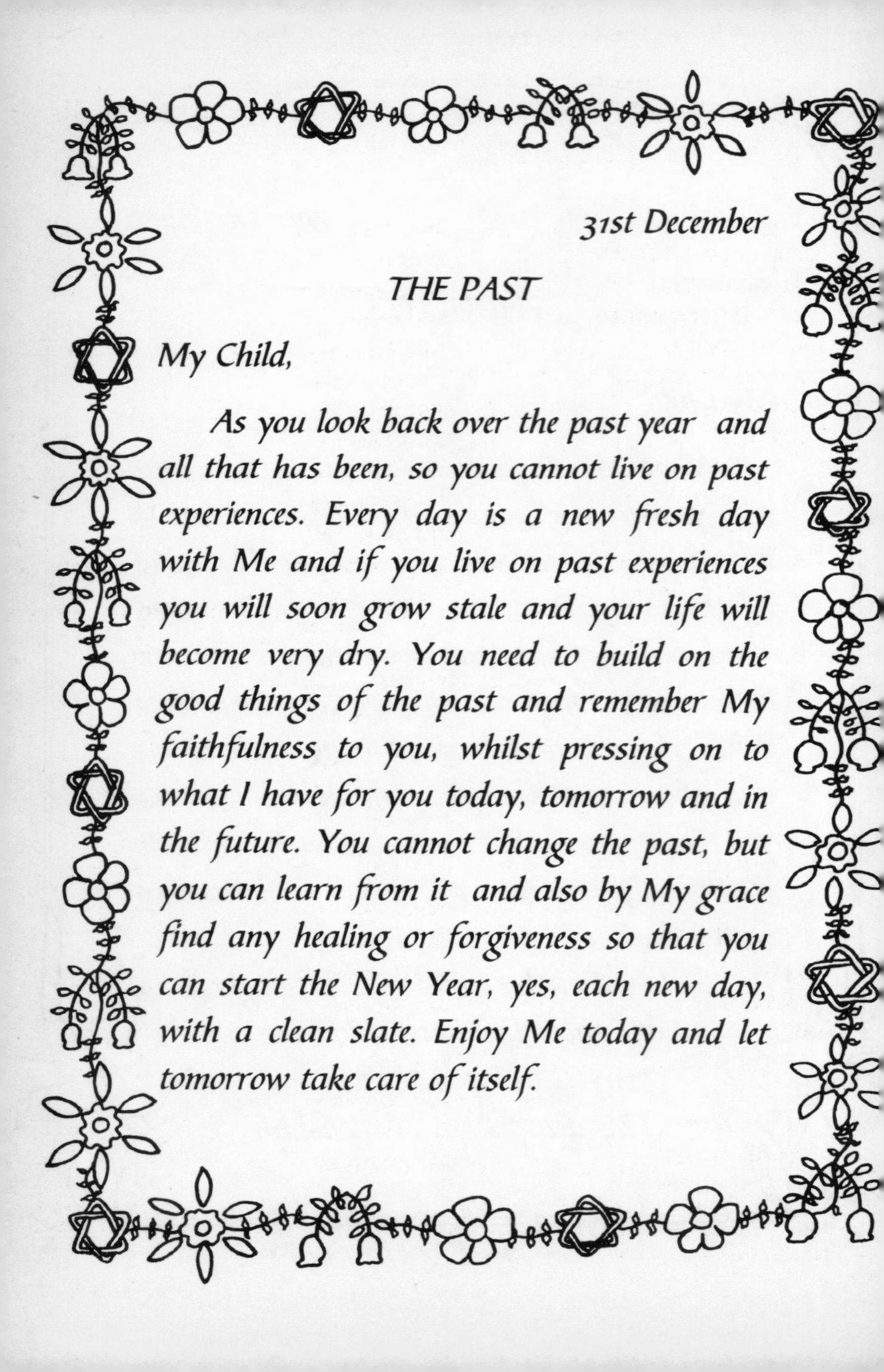

31st December

THE PAST

My Child,

As you look back over the past year and all that has been, so you cannot live on past experiences. Every day is a new fresh day with Me and if you live on past experiences you will soon grow stale and your life will become very dry. You need to build on the good things of the past and remember My faithfulness to you, whilst pressing on to what I have for you today, tomorrow and in the future. You cannot change the past, but you can learn from it and also by My grace find any healing or forgiveness so that you can start the New Year, yes, each new day, with a clean slate. Enjoy Me today and let tomorrow take care of itself.

ALPHABETICAL INDEX